D0430917

NORTH CAROLINA

SARAH BRYAN

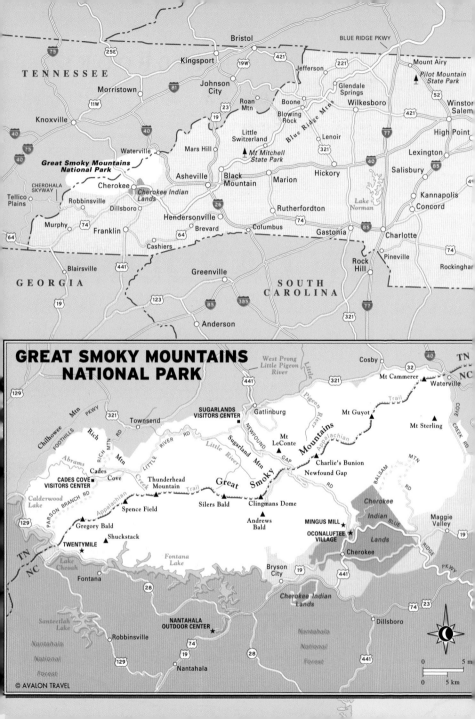

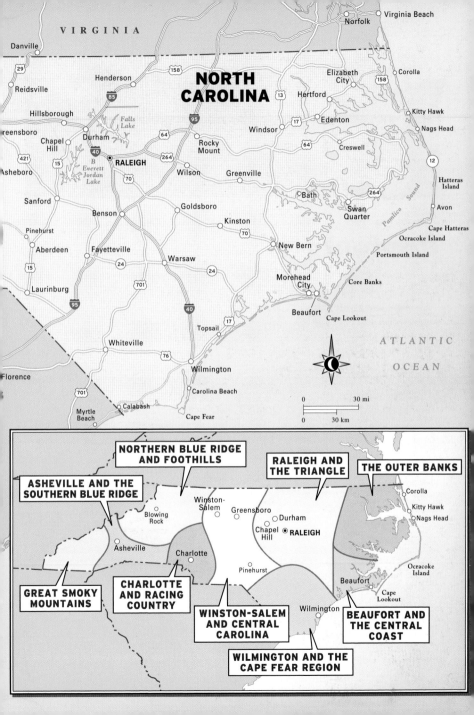

Contents

Discover
North Carolina

North Carolina gives us endless reasons to thank our lucky stars. There are seasonal milestones, like the appearance of cold-weather camellia blossoms around Christmas, and the first evening in spring when we must raise our voices outside to be heard over a thousand ringing tree frogs. There are the worlds within worlds of the natural environment. The borders of the state embrace the cottonmouth-ridden swamps and pocosins of the coastal lowlands, and the misty, lichen-covered forests of the high country. North Carolina contains the highest mountain in the eastern United States, and the most dangerous inlet on the Atlantic coast. One can set out from Raleigh in 100°F weather and arrive shivering in Asheville.

There's the gentle and graceful way that folks here have of relating to each other: a stranger on an elevator asking, "You been doing all right?" or the sheriff's deputy writing out a citation but counseling, "Don't worry, it could happen to anyone." On a normal day in North Carolina, the only open animosity you're likely to encounter is that between Duke and UNC partisans. The most refined Junior League dowager is capable of being breathtakingly catty to her son's Duke-educated wife, and if you try to merge onto the Durham Freeway with a UNC sticker on your car, better hope you're not in a hurry is all. Because we know it would reflect poorly on our schools, we here on

Tobacco Road rarely resort to internecine violence. But if tomorrow morning Tar Heel fans woke to learn that Duke basketball coach Mike Krzyzewski had been dragged off a Wilmington golf course and eaten by alligators with really bad breath, their first reaction would be delight. Then they'd get to work making sympathy casseroles. Of course, if you don't have a dog in this fight, you'll get along with everyone.

North Carolinians work in high-tech industries, teach in some of the nation's best universities, and raise strawberries, hogs, and athletes to beat the band. Classical musicians raise children who play the banjo, and there are places where one is as likely to hear Spanish or Cherokee spoken as English. The state is not so much contradictory as complex, and the complexity is what makes it an endlessly captivating place to explore.

Planning Your Trip

▶ WHERE TO GO

The Outer Banks

The scalloped edge of sand that marks where North America and the Gulf Stream part ways, the Outer Banks are a unique ecological and cultural enclave. The areas around Nags Head and the Cape Hatteras National Seashore are exciting places for windsurfing, kite flying, and surfing. History and mythology come together on Roanoke Island, where the Lost Colonists lost their way, and Ocracoke, where Blackbeard lost his head. The Banks shelter the vast Pamlico and Albemarle Sounds and the deep, still rivers along which a network of beautiful colonial towns stand sentinel. The Great Dismal Swamp is an eerie and unforgettable place for kayaking and canoeing.

Beaufort and the Central Coast

Catch an Indians game in Kinston before exploring the back roads along the swampy Neuse and Trent Rivers. Beaufort and New Bern have some of the most beautiful early architecture in the South, and Morehead City is a hot spot for seafood and scuba diving. Cape Lookout National Seashore has more than 50 miles of undeveloped shoreline, inhabited only by wild ponies and the ghosts of generations of Bankers who battled storms and the sea to make their livings here, while all along Bogue Banks are quiet, comfy family beach towns.

Wilmington and the Cape Fear Region

Wilmington, at the fringe of the Carolina Lowcountry, is a knockout year-round. The restaurants, live music, and shopping are

IF YOU HAVE . . .

- **A Weekend:** Pick one special natural area to explore: the Outer Banks, the Great Dismal Swamp, the Blue Ridge Parkway, or the Great Smoky Mountains National Park.

- **5 Days:** Add a nearby city! Charlotte, the Triangle, Asheville, Winston-Salem, Greensboro, and Wilmington are all fantastic towns.

- **A Week:** Add a festival! Check out www .visitnc.com or www.ncfestivals.com to find out what's happening during your visit.

- **10 Days:** Go camping! North Carolina's state parks preserve some spectacular natural environments, great hiking trails and boating spots, and wildlife-watching opportunities.

kayaking in the foothills of the Blue Ridge Mountains

goats grazing in the Sandhills

Winston-Salem and Central Carolina

Few visitors experience central Carolina in all its wealth. At the southeast are the Sandhills, with the golfing mecca of Southern Pines and Pinehurst, and the extraordinary Seagrove potteries. The ancient Uwharrie Mountains spring seemingly out of nowhere, sheltering deep forests and mountain lakes. The cities of Greensboro and Winston-Salem are home to great art galleries, restaurants, and colleges. Winston's Old Salem preserves the industrious village built by a band of German and Swiss religious pilgrims in the 18th century.

Charlotte and Racing Country

Charlotte is often called Banktown by those who mistakenly see its culture as one of corporate banality. But it's actually a city of stunning cultural variety, where the Old South, the New South, and the Global South are continually startling one another. Take the restaurants: One could spend a week in Charlotte just sampling taquerias, *pho* cafés, and fried chicken and soul food stands. To the north is the epicenter of our world-famous racing industry, with Lowe's Motor Speedway in Concord and dozens of museums and team shops.

Northern Blue Ridge and Foothills

There's something exciting about the ascent into the High Country—glimpses of a shadowy mountain range on the horizon; cows grazing in steep, rocky fields; hairpin turns in the road around dynamited stone faces, and the popping sound in your ears as you reach the first mountain. Friendly foothills towns like Mount Airy and Wilkesboro are rich with mountain music. Pretty old Blowing Rock retains the ambience of an elite hill station of a hundred years ago, while Boone is a progressive and eclectic college town. Here is some of the most graceful

magnets, but the old port city is best known for its antebellum homes and gardens. The region between Wilmington and the South Carolina line is the home of Venus flytraps, Calabash seafood, and great beaches. Inland, the Waccamaw and Lumber Rivers creep through dazzling blackwater swamps. Fayetteville is one of the most important U.S. stateside military hubs, as well as a fun destination for art, history, and gardens.

Raleigh and the Triangle

Raleigh, Durham, and Chapel Hill are very different, but they share a special creative verve. The many colleges here make for a progressive and intellectually stimulating climate—and volcanically exciting college sports. The live music here is some of the richest in the nation, and the area is one of the literary capitals of the South. If you have a weakness for good bookstores, you'd better come pulling a trailer. Come hungry, too, because creative inspiration is as potent in the culinary arts as in music and literature.

quirky Asheville

mountain scenery in the South, where hiking, rafting, skiing, antiquing, and gallery-hopping are favorite pursuits, but porch-setting and vista-contemplating may be the best of all.

Asheville and the Southern Blue Ridge

Few cities can boast of such artistic wealth as Asheville, from the old-time to the outré. Asheville would be a great place to visit even if it weren't in such a fabulous location, but it happens to occupy a perfect spot between the interlaced fingers of the Blue Ridge and Smokies, from which you can conveniently explore any part of the North Carolina mountains—if you can pry yourself from the city's restaurants, galleries, and quirky boutiques. Nearby natural areas like the wild Pisgah Ranger District and such scenic wonders as Chimney Rock envelop the Asheville area in lush magic.

Great Smoky Mountains

The United States' most popular national park is comprised of an enormous swath of southwestern North Carolina and eastern Tennessee, a land of endless ridges and deep wilderness full of rocky rivers and virgin forest hidden among swirling clouds. Outside the Great Smoky Mountains National Park are appealingly artsy towns like Waynesville and Sylva, the tribal seat of the Eastern Band of the Cherokee, and breathtaking rafting runs along the Nantahala, Tuckasegee, and Cheoah Rivers.

► WHEN TO GO

Spring debuts in the state's far southeast as early as late February. It creeps up to central North Carolina, and by mid-April, temperatures are pretty consistently warm (60s and 70s) in the eastern two-thirds of the state. It takes spring much longer to reach the mountains, and the highest elevations can get snow well into April.

Summer is the high season just about everywhere, and beaches are jam-packed, traffic is slow in the mountains, and throughout the state you can find festivals and outdoor music events. Beware the heat,

however, which combines with humidity and air pollution to make the hottest days quite dangerous.

Autumn comes first to the mountains, and the fall colors account for the mountains' second high season. September is roasting hot in the lowlands, but October is exquisite throughout the state. Temperatures mostly hover in the 70s and 80s in the lower elevations, and the humidity is greatly pacified, making this a great time for walking tours, canoeing, and hiking.

Winter may be milder here than in many

Cades Cove, Smoky Mountains National Park

other parts of the country, but it's winter nonetheless. In eastern and central North Carolina, daytime highs are usually in the 40s and 50s between late December and February, with frequent dips below freezing and, particularly west of I-95, one or two snowfalls. The mountains are cold in the winter, and you can expect a good snowfall now and then. You'll hear no complaints from the skiers.

▶ BEFORE YOU GO

If you're going to be spending time in the mountains, even in the summer, remember to pack for chilly weather. It really pays to layer here, for while a July afternoon may be in the 80s, the air can be downright nippy a few hours later. Similarly, it can be breezy and cool on the water during spring and summer, even if it's hot on the shore. Come prepared to protect yourself from the heat and sun in hot weather; remember to bring strong sunscreen (a year-round must) and a portable water bottle.

Cell phone signals are pretty consistent throughout central North Carolina, and certainly in the urban areas. But in many rural parts of the state, and on the Outer Banks and high in the hills, wireless signals can be scant to nonexistent, so it's a good idea to tuck a phone card in your wallet.

Explore North Carolina

▶ BEST OF NORTH CAROLINA

Not even the folks who were born and raised here can get their fill of discovering new facets of North Carolina. If you're just here to visit, you've got a lot of catching up to do. Here is a suggestion for how to spend two compressed weeks of getting to know the Tar Heel state.

Day 1

Start in Charlotte with a day of exploring museums. Visit the Levine Museum of the New South for an engaging introduction to North Carolina and Southern history, and then stop in at the Mint Museums to see their stellar collections of art and modern craft. Dine at any of Charlotte's hundreds of delicious international restaurants, and spend a night of Old South luxury at the Duke Mansion or the VanLandingham Estate.

Day 2

Explore one of Charlotte's many interesting neighborhoods—try the Plaza area, or the ethnic mosaic along South Boulevard or Central Avenue. Pick up a box of fried chicken or barbeque at lunch and hit the road. Take I-74 to the mountains (2–4 hours, depending on stops), and alight for the night at one of the bed-and-breakfasts in Tryon or Flat Rock, or at the 1920s Lake Lure Inn.

Day 3

Hop on U.S. 64 in the morning and head west. If it's the right season, you can stop and

CELEBRATING FOOD

Food is one of the things that North Carolina does best, and if you time your visit right, you can visit one of the many annual festivals that celebrate favorite local delicacies.

Up in the Smoky Mountains, as throughout much of Appalachia, ramps – a deliciously tangy kind of wild onion – are harvested from woods and creek beds just as winter creeps towards spring. Robbinsville's late-April **Smoky Mountain Romp & Ramps Festival** (www.grahamcountytravel.com) combines good mountain cooking – featuring ramps, of course – with Appalachian music and nature walks.

Charlotte is an incredible city for foodies, and one way to learn the culinary ropes here in a short time is to come to the early-June **Taste of Charlotte** (www.tasteofcharlotte.com). Dozens of area restaurants make samples of their art available, from haute European masterpieces to soul food favorites, plus plenty of international flavors from this wonderfully diverse community.

On the first Saturday in October, the historic Edwards-Franklin House in Lowgap, near Mount Airy, hosts the **Sonker Festival** (336/786-8359). Many families in this region trace their ancestry back to early German settlers, and the sonker – a deep-dish fruit or sweet potato pie – is one of the many folk traditions they carry on.

Also in early October, Morehead City's **North Carolina Seafood Festival** (www.ncseafoodfestival.org) brings many thousands of visitors to this maritime town. In addition to all sorts of seafood cooked all sorts of ways, the festival includes the annual Blessing of the Fleet, fishing tournaments, games, vendors, and live music.

cemetery angel, Hendersonville

pick apples at one of Hendersonville's pick-your-own orchards. Visit a café in Brevard or Cashiers for lunch, and then spend the afternoon exploring at the John C. Campbell Folk School in Brasstown. Spend the night in Robbinsville.

Day 4

Get an early start and hit Highway 28, winding along Fontana Lake (don't miss the dam!) into Tennessee. Spend the day touring Great Smoky Mountains National Park, making sure to see Cades Cove, Clingmans Dome, and the elk at Cataloochee. Spend the night in Bryson City (at the edge of the park), or at the Balsam Inn near Waynesville (about an hour away).

Day 5

Take U.S. 19 towards Asheville, stopping to visit the shops and cafes in Waynesville and Sylva. In the afternoon, take a walking tour of downtown Asheville before dining in style

and settling in for the night at one of the city's bed-and-breakfasts.

Day 6

Have a cup of coffee at Malaprops and hit the road. Spend a scenic and peaceful day winding your way up the Blue Ridge Parkway. Visit the craft gallery at the Moses Cone Manor at Blowing Rock and stop for a snack and shopping in Boone. Spend the night at Bluffs Lodge. Allow a full day for the trip, as the Parkway was designed for beauty rather than efficiency.

Day 7

Wake up early to see an amazing sunrise, and follow the Parkway north, almost to the Virginia line. Hop east and have your midday repast at the Snappy Lunch in Mount Airy (about an hour from the Parkway, depending on stops). In the afternoon, visit Old Salem in Winston-Salem (30 minutes from Mount Airy), or the art galleries in Winston-Salem or Greensboro (half an hour from Winston-Salem). Stay at Salem's Zevely Inn or the O. Henry in Greensboro.

Day 8

In the morning, take U.S. 64 to Asheboro (an hour or so), where you can spend the day exploring the North Carolina Zoo, or head a little farther south to Seagrove to tour area potteries. Follow U.S. 64 east to Pittsboro (about 45 minutes) and stop for supper at Pittsboro's General Store Café. Then follow U.S. 15/501 north to Chapel Hill (30 minutes), and spend a luxurious night at the Carolina Inn.

Day 9

Tour the campus of the University of North Carolina, and if you're a sports fan, visit the new Carolina Basketball Museum. Mosey the nine miles over to Durham for lunch at the Thai Café or one of the city's great taco stands.

Beaufort waterfront

Check out campuses at North Carolina Central University and Duke University. In the evening, catch a Durham Bulls game, or head back to Chapel Hill for some live music at Cat's Cradle or Local 506.

Day 10

Spend the whole day exploring the wonderful state museums of Raleigh: the North Carolina Museums of History, Natural Sciences, and Art. Pick up a hot dog for lunch at the Roast Grill—don't ask for condiments!—or have a more elegant lunch at Blue Ridge inside the Museum of Art. For supper, head over to Irregardless.

Day 11

Get a good early start, and zoom out I-40 east to Wilmington, allowing about three hours. Take an afternoon walking tour of the gorgeous historic district. At night, attend a concert at the Thalian Hall, or a show at the Soap Box Laundro-Lounge. Take your pick of beautiful bed-and-breakfasts for your night's lodging.

Day 12

If it's summertime, spend the morning hours at Wrightsville Beach—or head up U.S. 17

to New Bern for lunch, allowing at least a couple of hours for travel time. Spend the afternoon touring historic Beaufort, making sure to leave time for a visit to the Maritime Museum and the Old Burying Ground. For supper, visit a legend, Morehead City's Sanitary Fish Market.

Day 13

Explore Down East in the morning, visiting Harkers Island's Core Sound Waterfowl Museum. Wend your way up to Cedar Island, and catch the ferry to Ocracoke, a 2.5-hour voyage. Stay the night at the Captain's Landing in Ocracoke.

Day 14

Explore Ocracoke in the morning, and then, early in the day, catch the ferry to Hatteras (40 minutes on the water). From there, head up Highway 12, tracing the Outer Banks northward. Cross onto Roanoke Island, visiting the Aquarium or Fort Raleigh Historic Site, and staying at the White Doe Inn; or keep driving north to Nags Head, and spend the night at the First Colony Inn. In the evening, call your boss to say that you're so sick you couldn't possibly come back to work for another week.

▶ BEST SCENIC DRIVES

U.S. 70

U.S. 70 stretches almost the entire length of North Carolina, from Asheville to Core Sound. Its farthest-east section, a dogleg through Jones and Carteret Counties, will carry you through lovely scenery and give you a taste of life Down East. This is a great drive to take if you're staying in New Bern, because you can pick up U.S. 70 there. You'll go southeast through the Croatan National Forest before heading east to go through Seafood Central, Morehead City, and then the wonderful colonial port of Beaufort. From there, U.S. 70 follows a twisty path up along Core Sound through fishing communities and marshes full of herons and egrets. Just past the town of Stacy, you'll have a choice: You can either proceed to the Cedar Island National Wildlife Refuge at the end of the peninsula and catch the Ocracoke Ferry at Cedar Island, or backtrack on U.S. 70. They're both appealing options.

Cherohala Skyway

On the opposite end of the state, the Cherohala Skyway was built for beauty. For 36 miles, the road winds along the top of the Smoky Mountains, at elevations of well over 5,000 feet in some places, between Robbinsville and the town of Tellico Plains over the Tennessee line. The vistas are incredible, and the road is a legendary destination for motorcyclists and pleasure trippers. A few words of caution: Avoid the route in wintry weather, and fill your car's tank and your own tummy before hitting the road because there are no facilities other than bathrooms on the Cherohala Skyway. You'll feel like you're in a wilderness on top of the world.

Blue Ridge Parkway

Running more than 450 miles between the Shenandoah National Park in Virginia and

MOUNTAINS AND MUSIC

The mountains of North Carolina are as rich in traditional music and crafts as anywhere in the nation. The creative energy here draws from the arts that have been practiced here for centuries, and attracts a steady influx of newcomers who join the homegrown artists in carrying mountain traditions into the new century.

To hear great old-time and bluegrass music, you have countless choices. Here are two favorites:

MT. AIRY'S WPAQ

Among the best in the northern Blue Ridge is Mount Airy's community radio station, WPAQ. By all means tune your radio to 740 AM, but you can go one better and actually be present for the broadcast of great local music from the **Andy Griffith Theater** downtown.

ASHEVILLE'S FIDDLIN' PIG

In Asheville, check out the Fiddlin' Pig, a barbeque restaurant that hosts fantastic bluegrass bands several days a week. There's a dance floor at the Pig, and folks get up and clog between helpings of 'que.

the Great Smoky Mountains National Park in North Carolina, the Blue Ridge Parkway is the mother of all scenic roads. Covering over 200 miles in North Carolina, from Lowgap at the state line to Cherokee in the Smokies, the Parkway passes by many of the major destinations in western Carolina, including Linville Falls, Mount Mitchell, and the Biltmore House. There are great places to stay on and near the Parkway, and if you're planning on riding the length of it through North Carolina and enjoying sights along the way, you'll need at least two days because there's a great deal to see and do.

► GREEN MANSIONS: GARDEN WEEKENDS

North Carolina's natural scenery provides inspiration for artificial landscapes of almost equal beauty. Wilmington, the Triangle, and Asheville are home to great botanical gardens, and touchstones to the state's horticultural heritage.

Wilmington and Environs

It's hard to imagine anywhere more beautiful than Wilmington in the springtime. Though the old port city is a knockout at any time of year, the floral fireworks of the spring season are really something special.

Airlie Gardens is a century-old formal garden with a stunning azalea collection, a 500-year-old oak tree, and a sculpture garden dedicated to longtime gatekeeper Minnie Evans, a renowned visionary painter.

Halyburton Park encompasses almost 60 acres of native ecosystems of the southern coast, including sandhills and Carolina bays, some of this region's most distinctive features.

The gardens of Orton Plantation, down the road in Winnabow, are incredibly beautiful. The grounds of an 18th-century rice plantation hold a quintessentially scenic planter's white-columned palace surrounded by enormous live oaks, oceans of azaleas, and alligator-filled swamps. It's lush, exotic, and thoroughly gorgeous.

The Triangle

The urban Raleigh-Durham region might not be an obvious destination for garden lovers, but if you look in the right places you'll find a horticultural heaven.

First, there are the formal gardens: the Sarah P. Duke Gardens in Durham, the

GENERATIONS OF ARTISTRY

SEAGROVE POTTERY

Seagrove is an amazing place, a community of artists whose passion for their work has been going strong for more than 200 years. The **North Carolina Pottery Center** is a great starting point, where you'll learn about the roots of this local industry and the families who have made it famous for generations. Then venturing out into the town of Seagrove, and nearby communities like **Whynot** and **Westmoore,** you'll find literally dozens of working pottery studios to visit, each producing distinctive and lovely wares.

MORAVIAN ARTISANS

Up in **Winston-Salem,** the district of Old Salem preserves the history and handiwork of one of North Carolina's most interesting historic communities, that of the 18th- and 19th-century Unitas Fratrum, better known as the Moravians. These German and Swiss immigrants and their descendants were wonderful artisans, masters at creating everything from churches to chairs to cookies. At the **Museum of Early Southern Decorative Arts** in Old Salem, you can see the work of many early artisans from Salem and throughout the region.

FOLK ART IN THE MOUNTAINS

There are hundreds of artists' studios throughout the Blue Ridge and Smoky Mountains that are open to the public, and by driving down almost any major road you'll spot potters' and quilters' and carvers' shops. To browse the work of many traditional artists in one place, visit the folk art galleries on the **Blue Ridge Parkway** – the **Folk Art Center** near Asheville, and the **Moses Cone Manor** near Blowing Rock – and the **Qualla Arts and Crafts Mutual** in Cherokee, which represents many great artists of the Cherokee tribe.

Sarah P. Duke Gardens

North Carolina Botanical Gardens in Chapel Hill, and Raleigh's J. C. Raulston Arboretum.

All around the Triangle are small organic farms and dairies. Visit the Carolina Farm Stewardship Association's website (www.carolinafarmstewards.org) for a list of many such operations that welcome visitors. (If you're here on the right weekend in April, you'll love their annual Piedmont Farm Tour.)

Several fun farmers markets in the area give you a chance to sample their produce. The Carrboro Farmers' Market is small but overflowing with treasures—fruits and vegetables in season, heaps of herbs, live plants for your own garden, and fabulous cut flowers. The State Farmers Market in Raleigh is a larger affair, where farmers from throughout central North Carolina and beyond peddle a wonderful variety of seasonal produce, as well as preserves and pickles, baked goods, candies, and more Carolina treats.

Around Asheville

Asheville is the home of the North Carolina Arboretum, a garden of more than 400 acres that borders the Pisgah National Forest and the Blue Ridge Parkway. Special collections include the National Native Azalea Repository, and more than 200 bonsais. You can tour the Arboretum on foot, by Segway, and on your bike, and you can even bring your dog with you to stroll some of the trails.

At the Biltmore Estate, Frederick Law Olmstead created formal gardens of such beauty as to match the opulent mansion, and architect Richard Morris Hunt designed the conservatory where young plants are still raised for the gardens. Self-guided tours of the conservatory—and the walled, shrub, Italian, vernal, and azalea gardens—are all included in admission to the Biltmore Estate.

Asheville is also an excellent home base for excursions to other garden spots in the mountains. Don't miss the Rivercane Walk at the

John C. Campell Folk School in Brasstown, where Cherokee sculpture lines a path along Little Brasstown Creek. The Mountain Farm Museum at the edge of the Great Smoky Mountains National Park demonstrates gardening methods used on the early mountain homesteads. The Cradle of Forestry in Pisgah National Forest tells the story of how the science of modern forestry was born here in western North Carolina.

▶ HISTORIC LIGHTHOUSES

Centuries of mariners have plied the water off of North Carolina's coast, harvesting its aquatic beasts, protecting (or prowling) the shore, and skirting or foundering upon its dangerous shoals. As beautiful as North Carolina's lighthouses are, they were built not for prettiness but to perform a service of life-and-death importance. Today, the historic lights—some still in operation—are popular destinations for visitors. Some are open for "climbing" (walking to the top) and offer fantastic views; others are admired from without. The following lighthouses are some of North Carolina's favorites.

Currituck Beach Lighthouse

Built in 1875, the Currituck Beach Lighthouse is open to the public. Visitors willing and able to climb the 214 spiral steps to the top are treated to a dazzling view of Currituck Sound.

WHILE YOU'RE THERE...

Visit the Whalehead Club and the Outer Banks Center for Wildlife Education, which are both located alongside the lighthouse in Currituck Heritage Park.

Bodie Island Lighthouse

While you can't tour the inside of the Bodie

MARITIME LIFE AND LORE

Two of the state's best folklife museums are located in Carteret County within an easy drive of each other. In **Beaufort,** the **North Carolina Maritime Museum** is home to an incredible collection of artifacts that traces hundreds of years of **seafaring life** on the Carolina coast. Across the street, the museum operates the **Harvey W. Smith Watercraft Center,** a workshop where you can see traditional boats under construction and, if you're making an extended visit, even learn old-time **boatbuilding** techniques yourself.

On **Harkers Island,** the **Core Sound Waterfowl Museum** honors the heritage of the Down East region with a treasure-trove of cherished handmade objects, from nets and fish hooks to baseball uniforms and quilts. Also on Harkers Island, you can see one of coastal Carolina's most important folk arts in action at the **Core Sound Decoy Carvers Guild.**

Inland you'll find many opportunities to explore the state's folk "foodways," surely one of the most fun ways to get to know a culture. If you're around **Jamesville** during the herring run – late winter and early spring – visit the **Cypress Grill** and try the **deep-fried herring** that draws folks from hundreds of miles around. In nearby **Williamston,** the **Sunny Side Oyster Bar** is a place not only to eat great fresh oysters, but to watch expert **oyster shuckers** showing off one of the traditionally prized talents in coastal maritime communities. And of course, in just about every little town in eastern North Carolina, you'll find great barbeque; chopped whole-hog pork in a peppery vinegar sauce is the recipe famous in this part of the state.

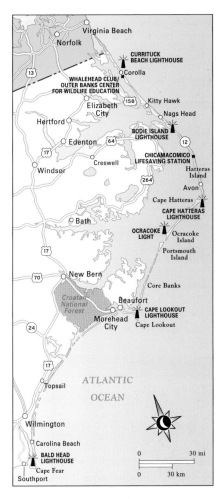

Cape Hatteras Lighthouse

learn about the history of maritime rescue on the Carolina coast.

Cape Hatteras Lighthouse

The Cape Hatteras Lighthouse, built in 1870, is the tallest brick lighthouse in the United States. For a small admission price, visitors can climb all the way to the top.

WHILE YOU'RE THERE...

Try your hand at some of the Outer Banks' favorite pastimes, like kite-flying or kite boarding, or hop the ferry over to Ocracoke.

Ocracoke Light

The Ocracoke Light was built in 1823 and originally illuminated its Fresnel lens with whale oil. Today it is the second-oldest working

Island Lighthouse, you can visit a restored keeper's house and learn about the unusual life of the lighthouse keeper. The Bodie Light has been sending its signal out to sea since 1872.

WHILE YOU'RE THERE...

Take the self-guided nature tour that starts at the lighthouse, or visit the Chicamacomico Lifesaving Station in nearby Rodanthe to

Silver Lake Harbor at Ocracoke

lighthouse in the United States. Because it's still on duty, visitors can't go inside, but there are lovely places to walk on the grounds.

WHILE YOU'RE THERE...
Stroll through the village of Ocracoke, a community with some remarkable stories to tell.

Cape Lookout Lighthouse

The Cape Lookout Lighthouse is one of the most iconic symbols of North Carolina, a black-and-white diamond-spangled tower that has stood watch since 1859. The nearby keeper's quarters give an intriguing glimpse into the isolated and meditative life of the light keeper.

WHILE YOU'RE THERE...
Enjoy Cape Lookout's 50-plus miles of unspoiled beach, where you may have a close encounter with one of the famous wild ponies of the Outer Banks.

Bald Head Lighthouse

North Carolina's oldest light is the 1818 Bald Head Lighthouse on Bald Head Island. From this strategic spot on the southern coast, the Bald Head light has seen nearly two centuries of commerce, war, and peace.

WHILE YOU'RE THERE...
Take a jaunt over to nearby Southport, a beautiful little town perfect for an afternoon's stroll.

THE OUTER BANKS

The Outer Banks are like a great seine net set along the northeastern corner of North Carolina, holding the Sounds and inner coast apart from the open ocean, yet shimmying obligingly with the forces of water and wind. The Outer Banks can be—and on many occasions have been—profoundly transformed by a single storm. A powerful hurricane can fill in a centuries-old inlet in one night, and open a new channel wherever it pleases. As recently as 2003, Hatteras Island was cut in half—by Hurricane Isabel—though the channel has since been artificially filled. This evanescent landscape poses challenges to the life that it supports, and creates adaptable and hardy plants, animals, and people.

The Sounds are often overlooked by travelers, but they are an enormously important part of the state and region. Collectively known as the Albemarle-Pamlico Estuary, North Carolina's Sounds—Albemarle, Pamlico, Core, Croatan, Roanoke, and Currituck—form the second-largest estuarine system in the country (second only to the Chesapeake Bay). They cover nearly 3,000 square miles, and drain more than 30,000. The diverse marine and terrestrial environments shelter crucial plant and animal communities, as well as estuarine systems that are essential to the environmental health of the whole region, and to the Atlantic Ocean.

Sheltered from the Atlantic, the Inner Banks are much more accommodating, ecologically speaking, than the Outer Banks. Wetlands along the Sounds invite migratory birds by the hundreds of thousands to shelter and rest,

© SARAH BRYAN

HIGHLIGHTS

Fort Raleigh National Historic Site: Here at the site of the Lost Colony, the mysterious first chapter of English settlement in the New World unfolded in the 1580s (page 33).

Ocracoke Island: On this remote island, you'll find a historic village that is the home of one of America's most unique local communities, as well as some serious water sports and walking opportunities (page 41).

The Great Dismal Swamp: This natural wonder straddling the Virginia/Carolina line is an amazing place for canoeing or kayaking, bird-watching, and sightseeing (page 44).

Somerset Place Historic Site: The graceful architecture and exotic setting of this early plantation contrast with the tragic history of its slavery days (page 48).

Pettigrew State Park: Lake Phelps, the centerpiece of Pettigrew State Park, is an attractive enigma, a body of shallow water and deep history (page 48).

Mattamuskeet National Wildlife Refuge: The landmark lodge on Lake Mattamuskeet towers over a dramatic waterscape that attracts migratory birds by the tens of thousands (page 50).

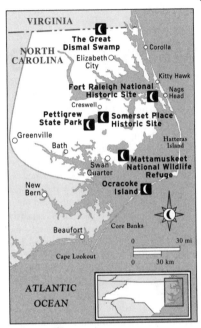

LOOK FOR ◖ TO FIND RECOMMENDED SIGHTS, ACTIVITIES, DINING, AND LODGING.

while pocosins (a special kind of bog found in the region) and maritime forests have nurtured a great multitude of life for eons. Here is where North Carolina's oldest towns—Bath, New Bern, and Edenton—set down roots, from which the rest of the state grew and bloomed. In Washington County, 4,000-year-old canoes pulled out of Lake Phelps testify to the region's unplumbed depths of history.

PLANNING YOUR TIME

The reasons for visiting the coast in spring and summer are obvious: the beach, the restaurants and attractions that are only open in-season, and the warm-weather festivals. But coastal North Carolina is beautiful four seasons of the year, and for many people fall and winter are favorite times to visit.

Around the time that the beach-bound traffic starts to thin out a little, towards the end of summer, eastern North Carolina's other busy season begins. Slow-moving trucks carry loads of loose tobacco leaves, bound from the field to the barn for curing. Stray yellow-green, wilted leaves litter the roadsides, blown off the trucks. On Saturdays in the early autumn, the air is heavy in pockets with the smoke of yard fires, as folks clear out their summer gardens and the hot-weather overgrowth on their properties, and prepare for the cool-weather planting season. Collard patches are put in, often right alongside houses. At their sweetest after

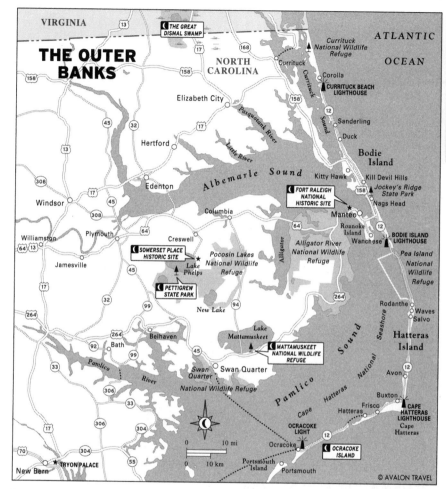

being touched by frost, collards are a favorite among fanciers of greens who prefer that musty mildness to the acrid twang of mustard greens. Cotton comes ripe late in the year. As the bolls begin to ripen, farm workers strip off the plants' leaves, until only the flowering bolls remain atop the stalks. The stark beauty of a field of ripe cotton is a mesmerizing sight.

Fall and winter are wonderful times for canoeing and kayaking on eastern North Carolina's rivers, creeks, and swamps. The weather is often more than mild enough for comfort, and the landscape and wildlife are not so obscured by tropical verdancy as they are in the spring and summer. A word of caution: Don't assume that you won't encounter alligators or snakes in the winter. They're never far away, and even a brief warm spell can have them out of their dens and looking for trouble. Wear snake boots if you have them, don't wade or swim in fresh water, and keep a lookout for gators' snouts along the surface of the water. Oftentimes all that's visible of

PRONUNCIATION PRIMER

North Carolina is full of oddly pronounced place names, and this farthest northeast corner is a good place to pause for our first lesson in talking like a native. The Outer Banks are a garland of peculiar names, as well as names that look straightforward but are in fact pronounced in unexpectedly quirky ways. If you make reference publicly to the town of Corolla, and pronounce it like the Toyota model, you'll be recognized right away as someone "from off." It's pronounced "Ker-AH-luh." Similarly, Bodie Island, site of the stripy lighthouse, is pronounced "Body," as in one's earthly shell. That same pattern of pronouncing Os as Ahs, as in "stick out your tongue and say 'ah,'" is repeated farther down the coast at Chicamacomico, which comes out "Chick-uh-muh-CAH-muh-co." But just to keep you on your toes, the rule doesn't apply to Ocracoke, which is pronounced like the Southern vegetable and Southern drink: "Okra-coke."

Farther south along the banks is the town of Rodanthe, which has an elongated last syllable, "Ro-DANTH-ee." On Roanoke Island, Manteo calls out for a Spanish emphasis, but is in fact front-loaded, like so many Carolina words and names. It's pronounced "MAN-tee-oh," or "MANNY-oh." Next door is the town of Wanchese. This sounds like a pallid dairy product, "WAN-cheese." Inland, the Cashie River is pronounced "Cuh-SHY," Bertie County is "Ber-TEE," and Chowan County is "Chuh-WON." Think the names around here are singular? Just wait 'til you get to the mountains.

an alligator are his nostrils and the little bony ridges of his brow. Spend enough time around gators, and you'll become accustomed to scanning the water before putting in.

Autumn, of course, is peak hurricane season. Dazzlingly beautiful in their ferocity, hurricanes are an unforgettable experience for anyone who has lived through one. For all the thrill, though, one should go to great pains to avoid them. Evacuation orders must always be obeyed, because hurricanes really are deadly, and highly unpredictable.

INFORMATION AND SERVICES

The **Aycock Brown Welcome Center** at Kitty Hawk (U.S. 158, MP 1.5, 252/261-464, www.outerbanks.org, 9 A.M.–5 P.M. daily Dec.–Feb., 9 A.M.–5:30 P.M. daily Mar.–May and Sept.–Nov., 9 A.M.–6 P.M. daily June–Aug.), Outer Banks Welcome Center at Manteo, and Cape Hatteras National Seashore Visitors Center on Ocracoke, are all clearinghouses for regional travel information. The **Outer Banks Visitors Bureau** (www.outerbanks.org) can be reached directly at 877/629-4386.

Major **hospitals** are located in Nags Head,

Windsor, Washington, Edenton, Ahoskie, and Elizabeth City. On Ocracoke, only accessible by air or water, non-emergency medical situations can be addressed by **Ocracoke Health Center** (305 Back Rd., 252/928-1511, after hours 252/928-7425). (Note that 911 works on Ocracoke, as everywhere else.)

GETTING THERE AND AROUND

The closest major airport to this region is the **Norfolk International Airport** (2200 Norview Ave., 757/857-3351, www.norfolk airport.com), approximately an hour from the northern Outer Banks. **Raleigh-Durham International Airport** (2600 W. Terminal Blvd., 919/840-2123, www.rdu.com) is 3–5 hours from most Outer Banks destinations.

Only two bridges exist between the mainland and the northern Outer Banks. U.S. 64/264 crosses over Roanoke Island to Whalebone, just south of Nags Head. Not too far north of there, Highway 158 crosses from Point Harbor to Southern Shores. Highway 12 is the main road all along the northern Outer Banks.

If you look at a map, Highway 12 is shown

crossing from Ocracoke to Cedar Island, as if there's an impossibly long bridge over Pamlico Sound. In fact, that stretch of Highway 12 is a ferry route. The **Cedar Island-Ocracoke Ferry** (800/856-0343, www.ncdot.org/transit/ferry), which is a 2.25-hour ride, costs $15 per regular-sized vehicle, one-way. The other ferries (all with information at www.ncdot.org/transit/ferry), from north to south, are: **Currituck-Knotts Island** (877/287-7488, free, 45 min.); **Hatteras-Ocracoke** (800/368-8949, free, 40 min.); and **Ocracoke-Swan Quarter** (800/345-1665, $15/regular-sized vehicle, one-way, 2.5 hours). There is also an inland ferry between **Bayview and Aurora** (252/964-4521, free, 30 min.).

Nags Head and Vicinity

The Outer Banks of North Carolina, unlike many barrier islands elsewhere in the world, are not attached to anchoring coral reefs. Instead, the Banks are a long sandbar, constantly eroding and amassing, slip-sliding into new configurations with every storm. The wind is the invisible player in this process, the man behind the curtain giving orders to the water and the sand. The enormous dune known as Jockey's Ridge was a landmark to early mariners, visible from miles out to sea.

According to legend, Nags Head was a place of sinister peril to those seafaring men. Islanders, it's said, would walk a nag or mule, carrying a lantern around its neck, slowly back and forth along the beach, trying to lure ships into the shallows where they might founder or wreck, making their cargo easy pickings for the land pirates.

It was the relentless wind at Kill Devil Hill that attracted the Wright brothers to North Carolina. It also brought the Rogallos, pioneer hang-glider inventors. Today, it brings thousands of enthusiasts every year, hang-gliders and parasailers, kite-boarders and kite-flyers. Add to these pursuits sailing, surfing, kayaking, hiking, birding, and, of course, beach-going, and the northern Outer Banks are perhaps North Carolina's most promising region for outdoor adventurers. Several reserves encompass large swaths of the unique ecological environments of the Banks, though increasingly the shifting sands are given over to the gamble of human development.

NAGS HEAD
IN 1849

My first impressions of Nag's Head were very favorable...when we hove in sight of the harbor, in the gray of the morning, and saw the sun rise over Nag's Head, making still more than the usual contrast between the white sand-hills and the dark, beautiful green of its clusters of oak, when we discerned the neat white cottages among the trees, the smoke curling lazily from the low chimneys, the fishing-boats and other small craft darting to and fro, the carts plying between the shore and the dwellings, the loiterers who were eager to know who and how many had arrived...

Gregory Seaworthy, *Nags Head, or, Two Months Among "the Bankers"*
(1849)

SIGHTS
Wright Brothers National Memorial

Though they are remembered for a 12-second flight on a December morning in 1903, Wilbur and Orville Wright actually spent more than three years coming and going between their home in Dayton, Ohio, and Kitty Hawk, North Carolina. As they tested their gliders on Kill Devil Hill, the tallest sand dune on the Outer Banks, the Wright brothers were assisted by many Bankers. The locals fed and housed them, built hangars, and assisted with countless practicalities that helped make the brothers' experiment a success. On the morning of December 17, 1903, several local men were present to help that famous first powered flight get off the ground. John Daniels, a lifesaver from a nearby station, took the iconic photograph of the airplane lifting off. It was the first and only photograph he ever made. He was later quoted in a newspaper as saying of the flight, "I didn't think it amounted to much." But it did, and that flight is honored at the Wright Brothers National Memorial (Milepost 7.5 of Hwy. 158, Kill Devil Hills, 252/473-2111, www.nps.gov/wrbr, park open daily year-round, visitors center 9 A.M.–6 P.M. daily June–Aug., 9 A.M.–5 P.M. daily Sept.–May). At the visitors center, replica gliders are on display, along with artifacts from the original gliders and changing displays sponsored by NASA. You can also tour the reconstructed living quarters and flight hangar, and, of course, climb Kill Devil Hill to get a glimpse of what that first aviator saw.

Jockey's Ridge State Park

Jockey's Ridge State Park (Carolista Dr. off Milepost 12 of Hwy. 158, Nags Head, 252/441-7132, www.jockeysridge statepark.com, 8 A.M.–6 P.M. daily Nov.–Feb., 8 A.M.–7 P.M. daily Mar. and Oct., 8 A.M.–8 P.M. daily Apr., May, and Sept., 8 A.M.–9 P.M. daily June–Aug.) contains 420 acres of a strange and amazing environment, the largest active sand dune system in the eastern United States. Ever-changing, this oceanside desert is maintained by the constant action of the northeast and southwest winds. Visitors can walk on and among the dunes. It's a famously great place to fly kites, go sand-boarding, and hang-glide. (Hang-gliding requires a valid USHGA rating and a permit supplied by the park office.)

Nags Head Woods Ecological Preserve

Bordering Jockey's Ridge is another unique natural area, the Nature Conservancy's Nags Head Woods Ecological Preserve (701 W. Ocean Acres Dr., about 1 mile from Milepost 9.5 of Hwy. 158, 252/441-2525, dawn–dusk daily year-round). Nags Head Woods is over 1,000 acres of deciduous maritime forest, dunes, wetlands, and inter-dune ponds. More than 50 species of birds nest here in season, including ruby-throated hummingbirds, green

© JOHN RICHBURG

Nags Head wilderness

herons, and red-shouldered hawks, and it is also home to a host of other animals and unusual plants. Maps to the public trails are available at the visitors center.

Kitty Hawk Woods

Slightly smaller but no less important is the Nature Conservancy's Kitty Hawk Woods (south of Hwy. 158 at Kitty Hawk, trail access from Woods Rd. and Birch Ln., off Treasure St., 252/261-8891, dawn–dusk daily year-round). These maritime forests harbor the unusual species of flora and fauna of the maritime swale ecosystem, a swampy forest sheltered between coastal ridges. Kitty Hawk Woods is open to the public for hiking and birding, and can be explored from the water as well. A canoe and kayak put-in is next to the parking lot of **Kitty Hawk Kayaks** (6150 N. Croatan Rd./Hwy. 158, 252/261-0145, www.khkss.com).

Currituck Heritage Park

The shore of Currituck Sound is an unexpected place to find the art deco home of a 1920s industrial magnate. The **Whalehead Club** (1100 Club Rd., off of Milepost 11 from Route 12, www.whaleheadclub.com, visitors center open 11 A.M.–5 P.M. daily, standard tours 9 A.M.–4 P.M. daily, specialty tours require 24 hours advance notice, $5–15) was built as a summer cottage by Edward Collings Knight, Jr., an industrialist whose fortune was in railroads and sugar. This beautifully simple yellow house—only a "cottage" by the standards of someone like Knight—sits on a peaceful spit of land that catches the breeze off the sound. It's the centerpiece of Currituck Heritage Park, where visitors can picnic, wade, or launch from the boat ramp, in addition to touring the house.

Next to the Whalehead Club is the **Outer Banks Center for Wildlife Education** (Currituck Heritage Park, Corolla, 252/453-0221, www.ncwildlife.org, 9 A.M.–5 P.M. daily, free). With exhibits focusing on the native birds, fish, and other creatures of Currituck Sound, the Center also has a huge collection of antique decoys—an important folk tradition of the Carolina coast—and offers many special nature and art programs

---

INNOCENCE EXCEPTED

In 1728, William Byrd of Westover, a Virginia planter and man of letters, took part in an expedition to mark the dividing line between his home state and North Carolina. In his *Histories of the Dividing Line,* he detailed his adventures in the marshy wilds of Carolina, including a March 1728 encounter with a pair of castaways at Currituck Inlet.

> While we continued here, we were told that on the south shore, not far from the inlet, dwelt a marooner, that modestly called himself a hermit, though he forfeited that name by suffering a wanton female to cohabit with him.

> His habitation was a bower, covered with bark after the Indian fashion, which in that mild situation protected him throughout the year. (Check the website for a program calendar.)

pretty well from the weather. Like the ravens, he neither plowed nor sowed, but subsisted chiefly upon oysters, which his handmaid made a shift to gather from the adjacent rocks. Sometimes, too, for change of diet, he sent her to drive up the neighbor's cows, to moisten their mouths with a little milk. But as for raiment, he depended mostly upon his length of beard, and she upon her length of hair, part of which she brought decently forward, and the rest dangled behind quite down to her rump, like one of Herodotus's East Indian pygmies.

> Thus did these wretches live in a dirty state of nature, and were mere Adamites, innocence only excepted.

---

throughout the year. (Check the website for a program calendar.)

The 1875 **Currituck Beach Lighthouse** (Currituck Heritage Park, 252/453-4939, 10 A.M.–6 P.M. daily Easter–October, 10 A.M.–5 P.M. daily in November, closed December–Easter, closed in very rough weather, $7, children under 7 free) stands on the other side of the Center for Wildlife Education. It is one of the few historic lighthouses that visitors can climb. The 214-step spiral staircase leads to the huge Fresnel lens, and a panoramic view of Currituck Sound.

Corolla Wild Horse Museum

In the town of Corolla, the circa-1900 Corolla Schoolhouse has been transformed into a museum honoring the wild horses of the Outer Banks. The Corolla Wild Horse Museum (1126 Schoolhouse Ln., Corolla, 252/453-8002, 10 A.M.–4 P.M. Mon.–Sat. in the summer, off-season hours vary, free) tells of the history of the herd, which once roamed all over Corolla, but now live in a preserve north of the town.

ENTERTAINMENT AND EVENTS

Chip's Wine and Beer Market (Milepost 6, Croatan Hwy./Route 158, Kill Devil Hills, 252/449-8229, www.chipswinemarket.com) is, in addition to what the name suggests, the home of **Outer Banks Wine University.** In at least two classes a week, Chip himself and other instructors host wine and beer tastings with an educational as well as gustatory bent.

Nightlife

The **Outer Banks Brewing Station** (Milepost 8.5, Croatan Hwy./Hwy. 158, Kill Devil Hills, 252/449-2739, www.obbrewing.com) was founded in the early 1990s by a group of friends who met in the Peace Corps. The brewery/restaurant they built here was designed and constructed by Outer Bankers, modeled on the design of the old life-saving stations so important in the region's history. The pub serves several very gourmet homebrews at $4.50 for a pint, and $6 for four five-ounce samplers. They've also got a nice lunch and supper menu,

THE OUTER BANKS

COURTESY OF ONCLE BERNARD ON FLICKR.COM

Currituck Heritage Park

with elaborate entrées as well as the requisite pub fare.

Bacu Grill (Outer Banks Mall, Milepost 14 on Hwy. 158, Nags Head, 252/480-1892), a Cuban-fusion restaurant, features live jazz and blues music, and serves good beer, wine, and snacks into the wee hours of the morning. **Kelly's Outer Banks Restaurant and Tavern** (Milepost 10.5 on Hwy. 158, Nags Head, 252/441-4116, www.kellysrestaurant.com, 4:30 P.M.–midnight Sun.–Thurs., 4:30 P.M.–2 A.M. Fri.–Sat.) is also a good bet for live music, and has a long wine list with some lovely vintages. **Lucky 12 Tavern** (3308 S. Virginia Dare Tr., Nags Head, 252/255-5825, www.lucky12tavern.com, 11:30 A.M.–2 A.M. daily) is a traditional sports bar with TVs, foosball, and New York–style pizza.

SPORTS AND RECREATION
Hiking and Touring

The **Currituck Banks National Estuarine Preserve** (Hwy. 12, 252/261-8891, www.nc-nerr.org) protects nearly 1,000 acres of woods and water extending into Currituck Sound. A third-of-a-mile boardwalk runs from the parking lot to the sound, and a primitive trail runs from the parking lot 1.5 miles through the maritime forest.

Back Country Outfitters and Guides (107-C Corolla Light Town Center, Corolla, 252/453-0877, http://outerbankstours.com) leads a variety of tours in the Corolla region, including Segway beach tours, wild horse–watching trips, kayaking, and other off-road tours.

Surfing

The North Carolina coast has a strong surfing culture—not to mention strong waves—making this a top destination for experienced surfers and those who would like to learn.

Island Revolution Surf Co. and Skate (252/453-9484, www.islandrevolution.com, group lessons $60/person, private $75, must be older than 8 and a good swimmer) offers private and one-on-one surfing lessons as well as board rentals. So do **Ocean Atlantic Rentals** (Corolla Light Town Center, 252/453-2440, www.oar-nc.com, $50/person group lessons, $75 private, $120 couples, must know how

© JIMMY MCDONALD

windsurfers

to swim, locations also in Duck, Nags Head, and Avon), and **Corolla Surf Shop** (several locations, 252/453-9283, www.corollasurf shop.com, 9 years old and up).

Online resources for Outer Banks surfing include the website of the Outer Banks District of the Eastern Surfing Association (http://outerbanks.surfesa.org), www.wright coastsurf.com, www.obxsurfinfo.com, and www.surfkdh.com.

Kayaking

The Outer Banks combines two very different possible kayaking experiences—the challenge of ocean kayaking, and the leisurely drifting zones of the salt marshes and back creeks. **Kitty Hawk Sports** (798 Sunset Blvd., 252/453-6900, www.kittyhawksports.com) is an old and established outdoors outfitter that leads kayaking and other expeditions. Another good bet is **Kitty Hawk Kayaks** (6150 N. Croatan Hwy., Kitty Hawk, 866/702-5061, www.khkss.com), which teaches kayaking and canoeing, rents equipment for paddling and surfing, and leads tours (including overnight expeditions) through gorgeous waterways in pristine habitats, in cooperation with the Nature Conservancy.

Kitty Hawk Kites (877/359-8447, www .kittyhawk.com), which *National Geographic Adventure* magazine calls one of the "Best Adventure Travel Companies on Earth," has locations throughout the Outer Banks, including at Corolla. They too teach and lead hanggliding, parasailing, Jet Skiing, kiteboarding, kayaking, and lots more ways to ride the wind and water.

ACCOMMODATIONS

The **(First Colony Inn** (6720 Virginia Dare Trail, Nags Head, 800-368/9390, www.first colonyinn.com, $69–299/night depending on season) is a wonderful 1932 beachfront hotel. This regional landmark has won historic preservation and landscaping awards for its 1988 renovation, which involved moving the entire building, in three pieces, three miles south of its original location. The pretty and luxurious rooms are surprisingly affordable.

The **Sanderling Resort and Spa** (1461

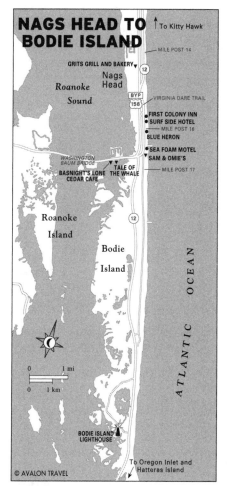

NAGS HEAD TO BODIE ISLAND

To Kitty Hawk

MILE POST 14

GRITS GRILL AND BAKERY

Nags Head

Roanoke Sound

VIRGINIA DARE TRAIL

FIRST COLONY INN
SURF SIDE HOTEL
MILE POST 16
BLUE HERON

SEA FOAM MOTEL
SAM & OMIE'S

WASHINGTON BAUM BRIDGE
TALE OF THE WHALE
BASNIGHT'S LONE CEDAR CAFE
MILE POST 17

Roanoke Island

Bodie Island

ATLANTIC OCEAN

0   1 mi
0   1 km

BODIE ISLAND LIGHTHOUSE

To Oregon Inlet and Hatteras Island

© AVALON TRAVEL

Elijah Baum Rd., Kitty Hawk, 252/255-2829, www.baldview.com, $125–200, no children or pets) is a modern residence located on a beautiful property along the sound, with four nicely appointed guestrooms and a carriage house. The three guest rooms at the **Duck Inn** (1158 Duck Rd., Duck, 252/261-2300, www.the duckinnbnb.com, $125–250/night, depending on season) are also on the sound, with a nice dock and gazebo for guests to use. The **Colington Creek Inn** (1293 Colington Rd., Kill Devil Hills, 252/449-4124, www.colingtoncreekinn.com, $198/night year-round, no children or pets) is a large outfit with a great view of the sound and the creek it's named for.

The **Cypress House Inn** (Milepost 8, Beach Rd., Kill Devil Hills 800/554-2764, www.cypresshouseinn.com, $89–189, depending on season) is a very traditional coastal Carolina-style house, built in the 1940s, with an easy walk to the beach. Its hurricane shutters and cypress-paneled rooms will give you a taste of Outer Banks life in the days before the motels and resorts.

In Kitty Hawk and Nags Head, you'll find an abundance of motels, from chains to classic 1950s mom-and-pops. The **Surf Side Hotel** (6701 Virginia Dare Tr., Nags Head, 800/552-7873, from $55 out of season, from $165 in-season) is a favorite for simple and comfortable accommodations, with standard rooms and efficiencies in a location right on the dunes. All rooms at the **Blue Heron** (6811 Virginia Dare Tr., Nags Head, 252/441-7447, from $50 out of season, from $130 in-season) face the ocean. The Blue Heron has a heated indoor pool as a consolation on rainy days. Super-affordable is the **Sea Foam Motel** (7111 Virginia Dare Tr., Nags Head, 252/441-7320, from $62 out of season, from $110 in-season), an old-timer with a lot of retro appeal. Other good choices in the area include the **Colony IV By The Sea** (405 S. Virginia Tr., Kill Devil Hills, 252/441-5581, from $70 out of season, from $85 in-season) and **Beach Haven Motel** (Ocean Rd. Milepost 4, Kitty Hawk, 252/261-4785, from $65 out of season, from $105 in-season).

Duck Rd., near Duck, 877/650-4812, www.thesanderling.com, $130–450) is a full-sized, conventional resort, with three lodges, a spa, three restaurants (on- and off-site) including the **Lifesaving Station,** housed in an 1899 maritime rescue station, and various sports and recreational rental options.

Bed-and-breakfasts include the sound-front **Cypress Moon Inn** (1206 Harbor Ct., Kitty Hawk, 877/905-5060, www.cypressmoon inn.com, no guests under 18), with three pretty guest rooms. The **Baldview B&B** (3805

FOOD

Sam & Omie's (7728 S. Virginia Dare Trail, Nags Head, 252/441-7366, www.samandomies.net, 7 A.M.–10 P.M. March–mid-Dec.) was opened during the summer of 1937, a place for charter fishing customers and guides to catch a spot of breakfast before setting sail. It still serves breakfast, with lots of options in the eggs and hotcakes department, including a few specialties like crab and eggs Benedict. It also has a dinner menu starring seasonal steamed and fried oyster, Delmonico steaks, and barbecue.

Tale of the Whale (7575 S. Virginia Dare Tr., Nags Head, 252/441-7332, www.taleofthewhalenagshead.com, dinner entrées $15–50) sits at a beautiful location, at the very edge of the water with a pier jutting into Roanoke Sound. There's outdoor music from a pier-side gazebo and a dining room with such a great view of the water that it feels like the inside of a ship—but the real draw is the incredibly extensive menu of seafood, steak, and pasta specials. They also have an imaginative cocktail menu.

Grits Grill and Bakery (5000 S. Croatan Hwy., Nags Head, 252/449-2888, 6 A.M.–3 P.M.) is a favorite for breakfast, famous for its biscuits, Krispy Kreme donuts, eggs, and, of course, grits.

The **Blue Point** (1240 Duck Rd., Duck, 252/261-8090, www.goodfoodgoodwine.com, $20–35) has a nouveau Southern menu, with staples like catfish and trout done up in the most creative ways. Among the specialties, fresh Carolina shrimp is presented on "barley risotto," with broccolini, wine-soaked raisins, and lemon arugula pesto. Try the key lime pie with raspberry sauce, Kentucky bourbon pecan pie, or seasonal fruit cobblers. After-dinner drinks (among them espresso martinis and special dessert wines) complement an amazing wine list, which is, if anything, even more impressive than the menu. There are at least a dozen vintages in almost every category (prices ranging from $7/glass to $250/bottle), and several top-notch single-malts and small-batch bourbons. The Blue Point also occupies an amazing building, a custom-built waterside home with diner-style seating, an open kitchen with a counter and bar stools running its length, checkered floors, and a big screen porch. Reservations can be made online as well as by phone up to a month in advance, and are very necessary: Peak hours in season are booked two and three weeks in advance, while even winter weekends are usually booked solid several days before.

Owens' Restaurant (Milepost 16.5 on Beach Rd., Nags Head, 252/441-7309, www.owensrestaurant.com) has been in operation at Nags Head for more than 60 years, and in addition to their good seafood menu, visitors enjoy looking over the owners' collection of historical artifacts from Outer Banks maritime life.

Tortuga's Lie (Milepost 11.5 on Hwy. 158 on Beach Rd., 252/441-7299, www.tortugaslie.com) has a good and varied menu specializing in seafood (some of it local) cooked in Caribbean-inspired dishes, with some good vegetarian options.

For casual and on-the-go chow options at Nags Head, try **Maxximuss Pizza** (5205 S. Croatan Hwy., Nags Head, 252/441-2377), which specializes in calzones, subs, and panini, in addition to pizza; **Yellow Submarine** (Milepost 14, Hwy. 158 Bypass, Nags Head, 252/441-3511), a super-casual subs and pizza shop; **Majik Beanz** (4104 S. Virginia Dare Tr., Nags Head, 252/255-2700) for coffee and shakes; or **New York Bagels** (Milepost 14 on Hwy. 158, 252/480-0106).

Roanoke Island

Roanoke Island was the site of the Lost Colony, one of the strangest mysteries in all of American history. Its sheltered location—nestled between the Albemarle, Roanoke, and Croatan Sounds, and protected from the ocean by Bodie Island—made Roanoke Island a welcoming spot for that party of ocean-weary Englishmen in the 1580s. Unhappily, they lacked the foresight to use one of the bed-and-breakfast inns in Manteo or Wanchese as their home base, so that after a hard day of fort-building they could relax with a hot bath and free Wi-Fi. Instead they cast their lots in the wilderness, and what befell them may never be known.

At the northern end of Roanoke Island is the town of Manteo and the Fort Raleigh National Historic Site. This is where most of the tourist attractions and visitor services are concentrated. At the southern end is Wanchese, where some of Dare County's oldest families carry on their ancestral trades of fishing and boatbuilding.

◖ FORT RALEIGH NATIONAL HISTORIC SITE

Fort Raleigh National Historic Site (1401 National Park Dr., Manteo, 252/473-5772, www.nps.gov/fora, park open sunup–sundown daily year-round except Christmas Day, visitors center 9 A.M.–5 P.M. daily Sept.–May, 9 A.M.–6 P.M. daily June–Aug., admission to park free, admission charged to Elizabethan Gardens and "The Lost Colony") comprises much of the original site of this first English settlement in the New World. Some of the earthworks associated with the original 1580s fort remain and have been preserved. The visitors center displays some of the artifacts discovered during this restoration effort. Two nature trails in the park explore the island's natural landscape and the location of a Civil War battle.

Within the National Historic Site, two of Manteo's most famous attractions operate autonomously. About 60 years ago, Manteo's

© MARK PILLSBURY

sea turtle at North Carolina Aquarium on Roanoke Island

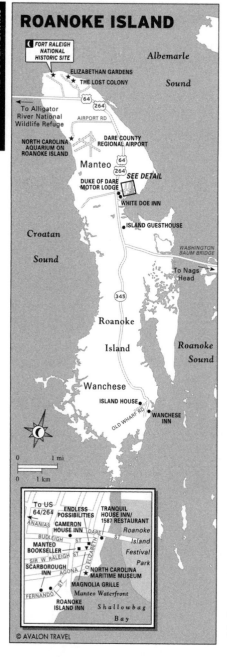

Elizabethan Gardens (Fort Raleigh National Historic Site, 252/473-3234, www.elizabeth angardens.org, hours vary by season and day of the week, $8 adult, $5 ages 5–17) was conceived by the Garden Club of North Carolina as a memorial to the settlers of Roanoke Island. Much of the beautifully landscaped park recreates the horticulture of the colonists' native England in the 16th century. Many special nooks throughout the gardens hold treasures, such as: an ancient live oak believed to have been standing in the colonists' time; a Shakespearean herb garden; and a 19th-century statue of Virginia Dare that lay underwater off the coast of Spain for two years, was salvaged from a fire in Massachusetts, and upon her arrival in North Carolina in the 1920s was considered so racy that for decades she was tossed back and forth like a hot potato all across the state.

Also within the park boundaries is the Waterside Theater. North Carolina has a long history of outdoor drama celebrating regional heritage, and the best known of the many productions across the state is Roanoke Island's **"The Lost Colony"** (Fort Raleigh National Historic Site, Roanoke, 252/473-3414, www.the lostcolony.org, $16 adults, $15 seniors, $8 children 11 and under, $20 "producer's circle" seats). Chapel Hill playwright Paul Green was commissioned to write the drama in 1937, to celebrate the 350th anniversary of Virginia Dare's birth. What was expected to be a single-season production has returned almost every year for more than 70 years, interrupted only occasionally for emergencies such as prowling German U-boats.

SIGHTS

The wonderful **North Carolina Maritime Museum,** whose mother ship is located in Beaufort, operates a branch here on Roanoke Island (104 Fernando St., Manteo, 252/475-1750, 9 A.M.–5 P.M. Tues.–Sat., free). In addition to the many traditional Outer Banks working watercraft on display, the museum holds boat-building and -handling courses at its George Washington Creef Boathouse. Visitors not enrolled in classes can still come

THE LOST COLONY

On July 4, 1584, an expedition of Englishmen commissioned by Sir Walter Raleigh dropped anchor near Hatteras Island. Within a couple of days, local Native Americans were coming and going from the English ships, scoping out trade goods and making proffers of Southern hospitality. They got on famously, and when the Englishmen crossed the ocean again to bring tidings of the land they had found to Raleigh and the Queen, two Indian men, Manteo and Wanchese, came along as guests. It seems that Wanchese was somewhat taciturn and found London to be no great shakes, but Manteo got a kick out of everything he saw, and decided that Englishmen were all right.

In 1585, a new expedition set out for Roanoke, this time intending to settle in earnest. When they reached the Pamlico Sound, their bad luck began. Most of their store of food was soaked and ruined when seawater breached the ship, so from the moment they arrived on shore they were dependent on the mercy of the Indians. Manteo and Wanchese went to Roanoke chief Wingina to discuss the Englishmen's plight. Wanchese, who was, it would turn out, a man of superior insight, tried to convince Wingina to withhold help. But Manteo pled the colonists' case convincingly, and the Englishmen were made welcome. Winter rolled around, and the colonists, having grown fat and happy on the Indians' food, and were doing precious little to attain self-sufficiency. Then a silver cup disappeared from the Englishmen's compound. It was posited that the thief came from a nearby village, which was promptly burned to the ground. Worried about his own people, Wingina shuttered the soup kitchen, hoping the English would either starve or go away. Instead, they killed him. Three weeks later, an English supply ship arrived with reinforcements of men and materiel, but they found the colony deserted.

Yet another attempt was made, this time with whole families rather than gangs of rowdy single men. A young couple named Eleanor and Ananais Dare were expecting a child when they landed at Roanoke, and soon Virginia Dare was born, the first English child born in America. The Native American situation grew worse, though, and the Roanoke tribe, now under the leadership of Wanchese, were unwilling to aid a new wave of colonists. Manteo, still a friend, tried to enlist the help of his kinfolks, but they were facing lean times as well. John White, leader of the expedition and grandfather of Virginia Dare, lit out on what he planned would be a fast voyage back to England for supplies and food. Through no fault of his own, it was three years before he was able to come back. When he did, he found no sign of the settlers, except "CRO" carved on a tree, and "CROATOAN" on a rail.

Thus began 400 years of wonderment and speculation that will probably never be resolved. Some believe that the English were killed, some that they were captured and sold into slavery among tribes farther inland. Several communities in the South of uncertain or mixed racial heritage believe themselves to be descendants of the lost colonists (and some evidence suggests that this might in fact be possible). The answers may never be found, and for the foreseeable future the mystery will still hang heavily over Roanoke Island and its two towns: Manteo and Wanchese.

---

in and watch traditional boat builders at work in the shop.

The **North Carolina Aquarium on Roanoke Island** (374 Airport Rd., 3 miles north of Manteo, 866-332-3475, www.ncaquariums.com/ri/riindex.htm, 9 A.M.–5 P.M. daily, $8 adults, $7 seniors, $6 ages 6–17, under 5 free) is one of three state aquariums here on the North Carolina coast. It's a great place to visit and see all sorts of marine fauna: sharks and other, less ferocious, fish, crustaceans, octopuses, turtles, and more. Like its sister aquariums, it's also a research station where marine biologists track and work to conserve the native creatures of the coast.

Roanoke Island Festival Park (1 Festival

Park, Manteo, 252/475-1500, www.roanoke island.com, 9 A.M.–5 P.M. daily Feb. 19–Apr. 1, 9 A.M.–6 P.M. daily Apr. 1–Nov. 1, 9 A.M.–5 P.M. daily Nov. 1–Dec. 31, closed Jan. 1–Feb. 19, $8 adults, $5 ages 6–17, under 5 free) is a state-operated living history site. The highlight is the *Elizabeth II,* a reconstruction of a 16th-century ship like the ones that brought Sir Walter Raleigh's men to the New World. There are also a museum, a reconstructed settlement site, and several other places where costumed interpreters will tell you about daily life in the Roanoke colony.

ENTERTAINMENT AND EVENTS

Outer Banks Epicurean Tours (252/305-0952, www.outerbanksepicurean.com) are a wonderful way to dine royally, while learning about the rich culinary traditions of this region and how the Banks' natural history creates this unique cuisine. The four-hour tours, which start at $95/person (not including the price of any alcohol you wish to order), give a teeth-on introduction to the native fish and shellfish of the area and the heritage of the people who harvest them, to bees and beekeeping, local wineries and microbreweries, coastal barbecue, indigenous and colonial cuisines, and many other topics.

SHOPPING

Manteo Booksellers (105 Sir Walter Raleigh St., 252/473-1221, www.manteobooksellers .com, 10 A.M.–6 P.M. daily) is a great independent bookstore, specializing in Outer Banks history and nature, but with a wide selection for all tastes.

Endless Possibilities (105 Budleigh St., 252/475-1575, www.ragweavers.com, 10 A.M.–5 P.M. Mon.–Sat.) is an unusual sort of a shop. Here you can buy cool purses, boas, rugs, and other adornments of home and body, made from recycled second-hand clothes. All the profits go to support the Outer Banks Hotline Crisis Intervention and Prevention Center, a regional help line for victims of rape and domestic violence, and an HIV/AIDS

information center. And if you happen to be in Manteo for long enough, you can even take lessons here to learn how to weave.

ACCOMMODATIONS

The ◖ **White Doe Inn** (319 Sir Walter Raleigh St., 800/473-6091, www.whitedoeinn.com, from $175 out of season, from approx. $350 in-season) is one of North Carolina's premier inns. The 1910 Queen Anne is the largest house on the island, and is on the National Register of Historic Places. Rooms are exquisitely furnished in turn-of-the-century finery. Guests enjoy a four-course breakfast, evening sherry, espresso and cappuccino any time, and a 24-hour wine cellar. Spa services are available on-site, and you need only step out to the lawn to play croquet or bocce.

The **Roanoke Island Inn** (305 Fernando St., 877/473-5511, www.roanokeislandinn.com, $150–200) has been in the present owner's family since the 1860s. It's a beautiful old place, with a big porch that overlooks the marsh. They also rent a single cottage on a private island, five minutes away by boat, and a nice cypress-shingled bungalow in town. Another top hotel in Manteo is the **Tranquil House Inn** (405 Queen Elizabeth Ave., 800/458-7069, www.1587.com, $99–229). It's in a beautiful location (hard not to be, on this island), and downstairs is one of the best restaurants in town, 1587. The **Scarborough Inn** (524 Hwy. 64, 252/473-3979, from $45 out of season, from $85 in-season) is a small hotel with 12 rooms and great rates. It's the sort of old-time hotel that's hard to find these days.

The **Cameron House Inn** (300 Budleigh St., Manteo, 800/279-8178, http://cameron houseinn.com, $120–205) is a cozy 1919 Arts and Crafts–style bungalow. All of the indoor rooms are furnished in a lovely and understated Craftsman style, but the nicest room in the house is the porch, which has an outdoor fireplace, fans, and flowery trellises.

The **Island Guesthouse** (706 Hwy. 64, 252/473-2434, www.theislandmotel.com, rooms from $60 out of season, from $85 in-season, cottages from $125 out of season, from $200 in-season, pets welcome with fee) offers simple and comfortable accommodations in its guest house, with two double beds, air conditioning, and cable TV in each room. They also rent out three tiny, cute cottages. Another affordable option is the **Duke of Dare Motor Lodge** (100 S. US 64, 252/473-2175, www.ego.net, from $42 in-season). It's a 1960s motel, not at all fancy, but a fine choice when you need an inexpensive place to lay your head.

Over in Wanchese, the **Wanchese Inn** (85 Jovers Ln., Wanchese, 252/475-1166, www.roanokeisland.net/wancheseinn, from $69 out of season, from $129 in-season) is a simple and inexpensive bed-and-breakfast. It's a nice Victorian house (with modern rooms), and there is a boat slip and available on-site parking for a boat and trailer. The **Island House** (104 Old Wharf Rd., 252/473-5619, www.islandhouse-bb.com, $85–175) was built in the early 1900s for a local Coast Guardsman, with wood cut from the property and nails forged on-site. It's very comfortable and quiet, and a big country breakfast is served every day.

FOOD

⟨ Basnight's Lone Cedar Cafe (Nags Head–Manteo Causeway, 252/441-5405, www.lonecedarcafe.com, 5 P.M.–closing Mon.–Wed., 11:30 A.M.–3 P.M. and 5 P.M.– closing Thurs.–Sat., 11 A.M.–closing Sun., closed in winter, lunch entrées $6–18, dinner entrées $18–31) is a water-view bistro that specializes in local food—oysters from Hyde and Dare Counties, fresh-caught local fish, and North Carolina chicken, pork, and vegetables. It's one of the most popular restaurants on the Outer Banks, and they don't take reservations, so be sure to arrive early. The full bar is open until midnight.

The **Full Moon Cafe** (208 Queen Elizabeth St., 252/473-6666, www.thefullmooncafe.com, 11:30 A.M.–9 P.M. daily in season, call for off-season hours, $10–30) is simple and affordable, specializing in quesadillas and enchiladas, wraps, sandwiches, a variety of seafood and chicken bakes, and quiches. Despite the seemingly conventional selection, the food here is so good that the Full Moon has received glowing reviews from the *Washington Post* and the *New York Post*—quite a feat for a little café in Manteo.

The **Magnolia Grille** (408 Queen Elizabeth St., 252/475-9877, www.roanokeisland.net/magnoliagrille, 7 A.M.–4 P.M. Sun. and Mon., 7 A.M.–8 P.M. Tues.–Sat.) is a super-inexpensive place for all three meals of the day, and snacks in between. They've got a great selection of breakfast omelets, burgers, salads, soups, and deli sandwiches, with nothing costing more than $7.

Cape Hatteras National Seashore

To many Americans, Cape Hatteras is probably familiar as a name often repeated during hurricane season. Hatteras protrudes farther to the southeast than any part of North America, a landmark to centuries of mariners, and a prime target for storms.

Cape Hatteras, the "Graveyard of the Atlantic," lies near Diamond Shoals, a treacherous zone of shifting sandbars that lies between the beach and the Gulf Stream. Two channels, Diamond Slough and Hatteras Slough, cross the shoals in deep enough water for a ship to navigate safely, but countless ships have missed their mark and gone down off of Cape Hatteras. The 1837 wreck of the steamboat *Home* on the Shoals, which killed 90 passengers, led Congress to pass the Steamboat Act, which established the requirement of one life vest per passenger in all vessels.

Hurricane Isabel in 2003 inflicted tremendous damage, and even opened a new channel right across Hatteras Island, a 2,000-foot-wide swash that was called Isabel Inlet. It separated the towns of Hatteras and Frisco, washing out a large portion of the highway that links the Outer Banks. For some weeks afterwards, Hatteras residents had to live as their forebears had, riding ferries to school and to the mainland. The inlet has since been filled in and Highway 12 reconnected, but Isabel Inlet's brief reign of terror and inconvenience highlighted the vulnerability of life on the Outer Banks.

BODIE ISLAND

The 156-foot **Bodie Island Lighthouse** (6 mi. south of Whalebone Junction), whose huge Fresnel lens first beamed in 1872, was the third to guard this stretch of coast. The first light was built in the 1830s, but leaned like the Tower of Pisa. The next stood straight, but promised to be such a tempting target for the Yankee Navy during the Civil War that

© MARK PILLSBURY

Bodie Island Lighthouse

COURTESY OF ONCLE BERNARD ON FLICKR.COM

Cape Hatteras Lighthouse

the Confederates blew it up themselves. (An unfortunate flock of geese nearly put the third lighthouse out of commission soon after its first lighting, when they collided with and damaged the lens.) The lighthouse is not open to the public, but the keeper's house has been converted into a visitors center (252/441-5711, call for seasonal hours). This is also the starting point for self-guided nature trails to Roanoke Sound through the beautiful marshy landscape of Bodie Island.

The **Oregon Inlet Campground** (Hwy. 12, 877/444-6777, $20/night), operated by the National Park Service, offers camping behind the sand dunes, with cold showers, potable water, and restrooms.

HATTERAS ISLAND

Cape Hatteras makes a dramatic arch along the North Carolina coast, sheltering the Pamlico Sound from the ocean as if in a giant cradling arm. The cape itself is the point of the elbow, a totally exposed, vulnerable spit of land that's irresistible to hurricanes because it juts so far to

the southeast. Along the Cape Hatteras National Seashore, Hatteras Island is just barely wide enough to support a series of small towns—Rodanthe, Waves, Salvo, Avon, Buxton, Frisco, and the village of Hatteras—and a great deal of dramatic scenery on all sides.

Sights

Lifesaving operations are an important part of North Carolina's maritime heritage. Corps of brave men occupied remote stations along the coast, ready at a moment's notice to risk—and sometimes to give—their lives to save foundering sailors in the relentlessly dangerous waters off the Outer Banks. In Rodanthe, the **Chicamacomico Life Saving Station** (Milepost 39.5 on Hwy. 12, Rodanthe, 252/987-1552, www.chicamacomico.net, noon–5 P.M. Mon.–Fri. mid-Apr.–Nov., $6, $5 under 17 and over 62 years old) preserves the original station building, a handsome, gray-shingled 1874 building, the 1911 building that replaced it—and which now houses a museum of fascinating artifacts from maritime rescue operations—and a complex of other buildings and exhibits depicting the lives of lifesavers and their families.

Cape Hatteras Lighthouse (near Buxton, 252/473-2111, www.nps.gov/caha/planyour visit, $7, $3.50 children and seniors, children smaller than 3'5" not permitted), at 208 feet tall, is the tallest brick lighthouse in the United States. It was built in 1870 to protect ships at sea from coming upon the Shoals unaware. It still stands on the cape, and it is open for climbing during the warm months. If you have a healthy heart, lungs, and knees, and are not claustrophobic, get your ticket and start climbing. The lighthouse is open daily from the third Friday in April–Columbus Day: 9 A.M.–4:30 P.M. in the spring and fall; 9 A.M.–5:30 P.M. early June–Labor Day. Tickets are required and are sold on the premises beginning at 8:15 A.M. Climbing tours run every ten minutes starting at 9 A.M.

Sports and Recreation
Pea Island National Wildlife Refuge (Hwy.

12, 10 mi. south of Nags Head, 252/473-1131, www.fws.gov/peaisland) occupies the northern reach of Hatteras Island. Much of the island is covered by ponds, making this an exceptional place for watching migratory waterfowl. Two nature trails link some of the best bird-watching spots, and one, the half-mile North Pond Wildlife Trail, is fully wheelchair-accessible. Viewing and photography blinds are scattered along the trails for extended observation.

The Outer Banks owe their existence to the volatile action of the tides. The same forces that created this habitable sandbar also make this an incredible place for water sports. **Canadian Hole,** a spot in the sound between Avon and Buxton, is one of the most famous windsurfing and sail-boarding places in the world. (It goes without saying that it's also perfect for kite-flying.) The island is extraordinarily narrow here, so it's easy to tote your board from the sound side over to the ocean for a change of scene.

As with any sport, it's important to know your own skill level and choose activities accordingly. Beginners and experts alike, though, can benefit from the guidance of serious water sports instructors. **Real Kiteboarding** (Cape Hatteras, 866-732-5548) is the largest kiteboarding school in the world. They offer kiteboarding camps and classes in many aspects of the sport for all levels. **Outer Banks Kiting** (Avon, 252/305-6838, www.outerbankskiting.com) also teaches lessons and two-day camps, and carries boarders out on charter excursions to find the best spots.

There are all manner of exotic ways to tour Hatteras. **Equine Adventures** (252/995-4897, www.equineadventures.com) leads two-hour horseback tours through the maritime forests and along the beaches of Cape Hatteras. With **Hatteras Parasail** (Hatteras, 252/986-2627, www.hatterasparasail.com, $60 parasail ride, $35 kayak tour) you can ride 400 feet in the air over the coast, or even higher with **Burrus Flightseeing Tours** (Frisco, 252/986-2679, www.hatterasislandflightseeing.com, $35–62.50/person depending on flight and number of riders in party).

Accommodations

Among the lodging choices on Hatteras Island is the very fine **Inn on Pamlico Sound** (49684 Hwy. 12, Buxton, 252/995-7030, www.innonpamlicosound.com, $120–295 depending on season). The inn is right on the sound, with a private dock and easy waterfront access. The dozen suites are sumptuous and relaxing, many with their own decks or private porches. Another good choice is the **Cape Hatteras Bed and Breakfast** (46223 Old Lighthouse Rd./Cape Point Way, Buxton, 800/252-3316, $79–139), which is only a few hundred feet from the ocean. Guests rave about the breakfasts.

Simpler motel accommodations include the clean, comfortable, and pet-friendly **Cape Pines Motel** (47497 Hwy. 12, Buxton, 866/456-9983, $49–139 depending on season, $20/pet); the **Outer Banks Motel** (47000 Hwy. 12, Buxton, 252/995-5601, www.outerbanksmotel.com, $49–300 depending on season and style of accommodation), with both motel rooms and cottages; and the **Avon Motel** (Avon, 252/995-5774, www.avonmotel.com, $43–131 depending on season and style of accommodation, $10/pet), a pet-friendly motel that has been in business for more than 50 years.

CAMPING
Rodanthe Watersports and Campground (24170 Hwy. 12, 252/987-1431, www.watersportsandcampground.com) has a sound-front campground for tents and RVs under 25 feet, with water and electrical hookups and hot-water showers. Rates are $19.25 per night for two people, $4.75 for each additional adult, $3 for children and dogs, and an extra $4.75 per night for electrical hookup.

The Park Service operates two campgrounds in this stretch of the National Seashore. The **Frisco Campground** opens in early April, and **Cape Point Campground** at Buxton opens in late May (46700 Lighthouse Rd., Buxton, and 53415 Billy Mitchell Rd., Frisco, 877/444-6777, $20/night). At Frisco, one actually camps in the dunes, whereas at

Cape Point, like the other NPS campgrounds here, the campsites are level and located behind the dunes. All have cold showers, bathrooms, and potable water. **Frisco Woods Campground** (Hwy. 12, Frisco, 800/948-3942, www.outer-banks.com/friscowoods, $30–90/night depending on accommodations and season) has a full spectrum of camping options, from no-utilities tent sites and RV sites with partial or full hookup to one- and two-bedroom cabins. The campground has wireless Internet access, hot showers, and a coin laundry.

Food

Though the **Restaurant at the Inn on Pamlico Sound** (Hwy. 12, Buxton, 252/995-7030, www.innonpamlicosound.com) is primarily for guests of the inn, if you call in advance you might be able to get a reservation for dinner even if you're staying elsewhere. The chef likes to use fresh-caught seafood,

sometimes caught by the guests themselves earlier in the day. Vegetarian dishes and other special requests are gladly served.

For breakfast, try the **Gingerbread House** (52715 Hwy. 12, Frisco, 252/995-5204), which serves great baked goods made on the premises.

◖ OCRACOKE ISLAND

Sixteen miles long, Ocracoke Island comprises the southernmost reach of the Cape Hatteras National Seashore. The history of Ocracoke Island is, frankly, a little bit eerie. There's the remoteness, first of all. One of the most geographically isolated places in North Carolina, it's only accessible today by water and air. Regular ferry service didn't start until 1960, and it was only three years before that that Ocrakokers had their first paved highway. In 1585, it was one of the first places in North America seen by Europeans, when the future Lost Colonists ran aground here. It may have been during the time they were waylaid at

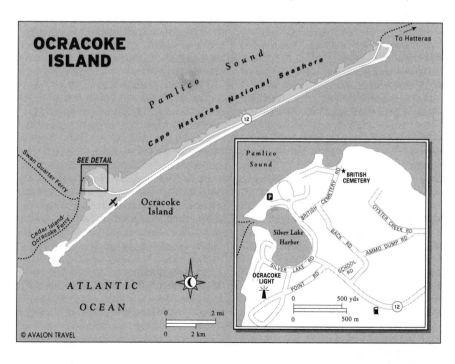

Ocracoke ("Wococon," they called it) that the ancestors of today's wild ponies first set hoof on the Outer Banks. Theirs was not the last shipwreck at Ocracoke, and in fact, flotsam and goods that would wash up from offshore wrecks was one of the sources of sustenance for generations of Ocracokers.

In the early 18th century, Ocracoke was a favorite haunt of Edward Teach, better known as the pirate Blackbeard. He lived here at times, married his 14th wife here, and died here. Teach's Hole, a spot just off the island, is where a force hired by Virginia's Governor Spottswood finally cornered and killed him, dumping his decapitated body overboard (it's said to have swum around the ship seven times before going under), and sailing away with the trophy of his head on the bowsprit.

All of **Ocracoke Village,** near the southern end of the island, is on the National Register of Historic Places. While the historical sites of the island are highly distinctive, the most unique thing about the island and its people is the culture that has developed here over the centuries. Ocracokers have a "brogue" all their own, similar to those of other Outer Banks communities, but so distinctive that, in the unlikely event that there were two native Ocracokers who didn't know each other already, and they happened to cross paths somewhere out in the world, they would recognize each other right away as neighbors (and probably cousins) by the cadences of their speech.

Ocracoke Lighthouse

A lighthouse has stood on Ocracoke since at least 1798, but due to constantly shifting sands, the inlet that it protected kept sneaking away. Barely 20 years after that first tower was built, almost a mile stretched between it and the water. The current Ocracoke Light (village of Ocracoke, 888/493-3826) was built in 1823, originally burning whale oil to power the beam. It is still in operation—the oldest operating light in North Carolina, and the second oldest in the nation. Because it's on active duty, the public is not able to tour the inside, but a boardwalk nearby gives nice views.

British Cemetery

The British Cemetery (British Cemetery Rd.) is not, as one might suppose, a colonial burial, but rather a vestige of World War II. During the war, the Carolina coast was lousy with German U-boats. Many old-timers today remember catching a glimpse of a furtive German sub casing the beach. Defending the Outer Banks became a pressing concern, and on May 11, 1942, the HMS *Bedfordshire,* a British trawler sent to aid the U.S. Navy, was torpedoed by a German U-558. The *Bedfordshire* sank, and all 37 men aboard died. Over the course of the next week, four bodies washed up on Ocracoke—those of Lieutenant Thomas Cunningham, Ordinary Telegraphist Stanley Craig, and two unidentified men. An island family donated a burial plot, and there the four men lie today, memorialized with a plaque that bears a lovely verse by Rupert Brooke, the young poet of World War I and member of the British Navy, who died of disease on his way to the battle of Gallipoli.

Sports and Recreation

Ride the Wind Surf Shop gives individual and group surfing lessons, for adults and children, covering ocean safety and surfing etiquette in addition to board handling. A three-day surf camp for kids ages 9–17 ($200, or $75/day) gives an even more in-depth tutorial. Ride the Wind also leads sunrise, sunset, and full-moon kayak tours around the marshes of Ocracoke ($35).

The **Schooner Windfall** (departs from Community Store Dock, Ocracoke, 252/928-7245, www.schoonerwindfall.com), a beautiful 57-foot, old fashioned–looking schooner, sails on three one-hour tours a day around Pamlico Sound. Passengers are allowed, and even encouraged, to try their hand at the wheel or trimming the sails.

Accommodations

The **Captain's Landing** (324 Hwy. 12, 252/928-1999, www.thecaptainslanding.com, from $200 in-season, from $100 out of season), with a perch right on Silver Lake (the harbor) looking towards the lighthouse, is a modern hotel owned by a descendant of Ocracoke's oldest families. Suites have 1.5 baths, full kitchens, comfortable sleeper sofas for extra guests, and decks with beautiful views. They also have a bright, airy penthouse with two bedrooms, an office, a gourmet kitchen, and even a laundry room. The Captain's Cottage is a private two-bedroom house, also smack on the water, with great decks and its own courtyard.

The **Pony Island Motel and Cottages** (785 Irvin Garrish Hwy., 866/928-4411, www.pony islandmotel.com, from $100 in-season, from $60 out of season) has been in operation since the late 1950s, and run by the same family for more than 40 years. It has regular and efficiency motel rooms, and four cottages on the grounds. Clean rooms, a good location, and year-round good prices make this a top choice on the island.

Edwards of Ocracoke (800/254-1359, www.edwardsofocracoke.com, from $53 spring and fall, from $100 summer) has several cozy bungalows typical of coastal Carolina, referred to here as "vintage accommodations." The mid-20th century vacation ambiance is very pleasant, the cabins are very clean and well kept, and the prices are great.

The **Island Inn** (25 Lighthouse Rd., 252/928-4351, www.ocracokeislandinn.com, from $60 out of season, from $100 in-season, no children) is on the National Register of Historic Places, and bills itself as the oldest operating business on the Outer Banks. It was built in 1901, first used as an Odd Fellows Hall, later as a barracks during World War II. The building is made of salvaged shipwreck wood, which everyone knows brings strange juju; add that fact to the 1950s murder of a caretaker, and the discovery of colonial bones under the lobby, and it's a given that the place is haunted. The resident wraith is believed to be a lady ghost, because she seems to enjoy checking out female guests' cosmetics and clothes, which will sometimes turn up in the morning in places other than where they were left the night before. No one's ever seen her, but her footsteps are sometimes heard in empty

© MARK PILLSBURY

shells and starfish on an Outer Banks beach

rooms, and she causes odd things to happen—most notably, unraveling an entire roll of toilet paper in the presence of a terrified guest. Like many hotel ghosts, she is most active during the inn's less crowded seasons.

CAMPING

At **Ocracoke Campground** (4352 Irvin Garrish Hwy., Ocracoke, 877/444-6777, $23/night), campsites are right by the beach, behind the dunes. Remember to bring extra-long stakes to anchor your tent in the sand.

Food

Ocracoke's **Café Atlantic** (1129 Irvin Garris Hwy., 252/928-4681, $14–21) has a large and eclectic menu, with tastes venturing into Italian, Nuevo Latino, and local fare. Lunch and dinner choices can be as simple as a BLT or a crab cake (with Pamlico Sound crabmeat), to *caciucco,* an Italian seafood stew. While many restaurants will accommodate vegetarians with a single pasta dish at the end of the entrée list, Café Atlantic has tons of non-meat-or-seafood options. They've also got an extensive wine list.

Across the Sounds

Referred to historically as the Albemarle, and sometimes today as the Inner Banks, the mainland portion of northeastern North Carolina is the hearth of the state's colonial history, the site of its first European towns and earliest plantation and maritime economies.

The Great Dismal Swamp is here, a region thought of by early Carolinians and Virginians as a diseased and haunted wasteland, the sooner drained the better. They succeeded to some extent in beating back the swamp waters and vapors, but left enough for modern generations to recognize as one of the state's crown jewels, a natural feature as valuable to humans as to the bears and wolves who hide within.

Early cities like Edenton and Bath were influential centers of government and commerce, and today preserve some of the best colonial and early federal architecture in the Southeast. The vast network of rivers and creeks include some of the state's best canoeing and kayaking waters, and along the Albemarle Regional Canoe/Kayak Trail, there are a growing number of camping platforms on which to spend an unforgettable night listening to owls hoot and otters splash. Country kitchens are found throughout the small towns here, and there are even a few old-fashioned fish shacks in which to sample the inland seafood traditions. Water is the soul of this region, with the Sounds and the

rivers and swamps guiding life on the land as surely as if it were touched by the ocean.

◖ THE GREAT DISMAL SWAMP

Viewed for centuries as an impediment to progress, the Great Dismal Swamp is now recognized for the national treasure that it is, and tens of thousands of acres are protected. There are several points from which to gain access to the interior of the Dismal Swamp. A few miles south of the Carolina/Virginia line, on Highway 17, is the **Dismal Swamp Welcome Center** (2356 Hwy. 17 N., South Mills, 877/771-8333, www.dismalswamp.com, 9 A.M.–5 P.M. daily Memorial Day–Halloween, 9 A.M.–5 P.M. Tues.–Sat. the rest of the year). Should you be arriving by water, you'll find the Welcome Center at Mile 28 on the Intracoastal Waterway. You can tie up to the dock here and spend the night, if you wish, or wait for one of the four daily lock openings (8:30 A.M., 11 A.M., 1:30 P.M., and 3:30 P.M.) to proceed. There are also picnic tables and grills here, and restrooms open day and night.

Another area of the swamp to explore is the **Great Dismal Swamp National Wildlife Refuge** (Suffolk, VA, 757/986-3705, www.albemarle-nc.com/gates/gdsnwr, open daylight hours), which straddles the state line. Two main entrances are outside of Suffolk,

water tupelo at Merchants Millpond near the Great Dismal Swamp

Virginia, off of the White Marsh Road/Route 642. These entrances, Washington Ditch and Jericho Lane, are open 6:30 A.M.–8 P.M. daily between April 1–September 30, and 6:30 A.M.–5 P.M. October 1–March 31. In the middle of the refuge is Lake Drummond, an eerie 3,100-acre natural lake that's a wonderful place for canoeing. (Contact Refuge headquarters for directions on navigating the feeder ditch that lets out into Lake Drummond.) You may see all sorts of wildlife in the swamp—including poisonous cottonmouths, canebrake rattlers, and copperheads, and possibly even black bears. One more word of caution: Controlled hunting is permitted on certain days in October, November, and December, so if visiting in the fall, wear bright clothing, and contact refuge staff in advance of your visit to find out about closures.

ELIZABETH CITY

The **Museum of the Albemarle** (501 S. Water St., 252/335-1453, www.museumofthe albemarle.com, 9 A.M.–5 P.M. Tues.–Sat.,

2–5 P.M. Sun.) is a relatively new, and growing, museum. It explores the four centuries of history in northeastern North Carolina since the first English settlers arrived at Roanoke. Come here to learn about the Lost Colonists, the pirates who swarmed in this region, the folkways of the Sound country, and more.

EDENTON

Incorporated in 1722 but inhabited long before that, Edenton was one of North Carolina's most important colonial towns, and remains one of its most beautiful.

Historic District

The whole town is lined with historic buildings, and several especially important sites are clustered within a few blocks of each other near the waterfront. The easiest starting point for a walking tour (guided or on your own) is the headquarters of the **Edenton State Historic Site** (108 Broad St., 252/482-2637, www.edenton.nchistoricsites.org, 9 A.M.–5 P.M. Mon.–Sat. and 1–5 P.M. Sun. Apr.–Oct., 10 A.M.–4 P.M. Mon.–Sat. and 1–4 P.M. Sun. Nov.–Mar.), also referred to as the Edenton Visitors Center. The 1782 **Barker House** (505 S. Broad St., 252/482-7800, www.edenton historicalcommission.org, 10 A.M.–4 P.M. Mon.–Sat., 1–4 P.M. Sun.), a stunning Lowcountry palazzo, was the home of Penelope Barker, an early revolutionary and organizer of the Edenton Tea Party. It's now the headquarters of the Edenton Historical Commission, and the location of their bookstore. The 1758 **Cupola House** (408 Broad St., 252/482-2637, www.cupolahouse.org, 9 A.M.–4:30 P.M. daily, tickets available at Edenton Visitors Center) is a National Historical Landmark, a home of great architectural significance. Although much of the original interior woodwork was removed in 1918 and sold to the Brooklyn Museum, where it remains, the Cupola House has been restored meticulously inside and out, and its colonial gardens re-created. Also a designated National Historical Landmark is the **Chowan County Courthouse** (111 E. King St., 252/482-2637, www.edenton.nchistoricsites.org, hours vary by season), a superb 1767 brick building in the Georgian style. It's the best-preserved colonial courthouse in the United States.

Accommodations and Food

The **Lords Proprietors' Inn** (300 N. Broad St., 888/394-6622, www.edentoninn .com, from $170) occupies not one but four exceptional historic buildings: the 1901 main White-Bond House, the 1801 Satterfield House, a 1915 tobacco storage barn remodeled with beautiful guestrooms, and the 1870 Tillie Bond House cottage. Each one of these is artfully restored, with soft and restful furnishings. Breakfast cook Janie Granby prepares wonderful specialties like lemon soufflé pancakes, and North Carolina native and star chef Kevin Yokley prepares four-course dinners that are dazzling. Entrées include grilled swordfish with artichoke vinaigrette, lamb porterhouse chops with dried cherry sauce, and breast of Muscovy duck with red currant sauce. The other courses are no less impressive.

The **Granville Queen Inn** (108 S. Granville St., 866/482-8534, www.granvillequeen.com, $95–140) is a rather splendid early-1900s mansion decorated in a variety of early 20th-century styles. Breakfasts are as ornate and elegant as the house itself, featuring poached pears, potato tortillas, crepes, and much more.

Holladay's Island Camping Platforms (315 Cannon's Ferry Rd., Tyner, 252/482-8595, www.visitedenton.com, price varies depending on number of campers, $20/night one person, privy at campsite) are part of the Albemarle Regional Canoe/Kayak Paddling Trail. The five 16- by 24-foot raised platforms sit in the middle of the Chowan River about 20 miles from Edenton, and about one mile from the nearest boat ramp. (To find out about more camping platforms in the region, visit www .roanokeriver-partners.org.)

WINDSOR

A small, historic town on the Cashie River, Windsor is the county seat of Bertie County. Historic architecture, good food, and wetlands exploration are equally compelling reasons to

visit this lesser-known treasure of the Albemarle region. Pronunciation is a little perverse here: The county name is pronounced "Ber-TEE," and the river is the "Cuh-SHY."

Sights

Hope Plantation (132 Hope House Rd., 252/794-3140, www.hopeplantation.org, 10 A.M.–5 P.M. Mon.–Sat. and 2–5 P.M. Sun. Apr.–Oct., 10 A.M.–4 P.M. Mon.–Sat. and 2–5 P.M. Sun. Nov.–Mar., $8, $7 seniors, $3 under 18) was built in 1803 for the former Governor David Stone. Stone did not live to see his 50th birthday, but by the time of his death he had been the governor of North Carolina, a U.S. senator and congressman, a state senator, a Superior Court judge, and a seven-times-elected member of the State House. He graduated from Princeton and passed the bar when he was 20; he was the father of 11 children, and one of the founders of the University of North Carolina. High among his most impressive accomplishments was the construction of this wonderful house. Characterized by a mixture of Georgian and Federal styles with significant twists of regional and individual aesthetics, Hope House is on the National Register of Historic Places. Also on the National Register, and now on the grounds of the plantation, is the brick-end, gambrel roof King-Bazemore House. The King-Bazemore House was built in 1763, and is also a highly significant example of its form.

The **Roanoke-Cashie River Center** (112 W. Water St., Windsor, 252/794-2001, www.partnershipforthesounds.org/Roanoke CashieRiverCenter.aspx, 10 A.M.–4 P.M. Tues.– Sat., $2, $1 children) has interpretive exhibits about this region's history and ecology. There is a canoe ramp outside where you can get out into the Cashie River, and canoe rentals are available ($10/hour, $25 for a half-day, and $35 for a whole day).

Southeast of Windsor on the Cashie River, the **San Souci Ferry** (Woodard and San Souci Rds., 252/794-4277, 6:30 A.M.–6 P.M. Mar. 16–Sept. 16, 6:45 A.M.–5 P.M. Sept. 17–March 15) operates, as it has for generations, by a cable and a honk of the horn. To cross the river, pull up to the bank, honk your horn, and wait. Directly the ferryman will emerge and pull you across.

Food

Bunn's Bar-B-Q (127 King St., 252/794-2274, from $5) is a barbeque and Brunswick stew joint of renown, an early gas station converted in 1938 to its present state. Super-finely chopped barbeque is the specialty, with coleslaw, cornbread, and plenty of sauce from those little red bottles you see on every surface.

WILLIAMSTON AND VICINITY

Williamston is at the junction of U.S. 17 and U.S. 64. If you're passing through town, Williamston is a great place to stop for barbecue or a fresh seafood meal.

Sights

A little ways west of Williamston on U.S. 13/64 Alt., you'll find the town of Robersonville and the **St. James Place Museum** (U.S. 64 Alt. and Outerbridge Rd., open year-round by appointment, call Robersonville Public Library at 252/795-3591). A Primitive Baptist church built in 1910 and restored by a local preservationist and folk art enthusiast, St. James Place is an unusual little museum that fans of Southern craft will not want to miss. A serious collection of traditional quilts is the main feature of the museum. Of the 100 on display, nearly half are African American quilts—examples of which are much less likely to survive and find their way into museum collections than are their counterpane counterparts made by white quilters. Getting a glimpse of the two traditions side by side is an education in these parallel Southern aesthetics.

On the same highway is **East Carolina Motor Speedway** (4918 U.S. 64 Alt., 252/795-3968, www.ecmsracing.com, pits open at 3 P.M., grandstands at 5 P.M., usually Apr.–Oct.), a 0.4-mile hard-surface track featuring several divisions, including late-model street stock, modified street-stock, super stock four-cylinder, and four-cylinder kids' class.

Food

Come to Williamston on an empty stomach. It has an assortment of old and very traditional eateries. The **Sunny Side Oyster Bar** (1102 Washington St., 252/792-3416, open from 5:30 P.M. Mon.–Sat. and from 5 P.M. Sun., Sept.–Apr., www.sunnysideoysterbarnc.com) is the best known, a seasonal oyster joint open in the months with the letter R—that is, oyster season. It's been in business since 1935, and is a historic as well as gastronomic landmark. Oysters are steamed behind the restaurant, and then hauled inside and shucked at the bar. Visit the restaurant's website to acquaint yourselves with the shuckers. In eastern North Carolina, a good oyster shucker is regarded as highly as a good artist or athlete, and rightly so. The Sunny Side doesn't take reservations, but it fills to capacity in no time flat, so come early.

Down the road a piece, **Martin Supply** (118 Washington St., 252/792-2123), an old general store, is a good place to buy local produce and preserves, honey, molasses, and hoop cheese. Also on Washington Street is the **R&C Restaurant** (211 Washington St., 252/792-3161), a country kitchen with a special aptitude for collard greens and crispy cornbread. **Griffin's Quick Lunch** (204 Washington St., 252/792-2873) is a popular old diner with good barbecue. Back on U.S. 64, **Shaw's Barbecue** (U.S. 64 Alt., 252/792-5339) serves eastern Carolina-style barbecue, as well as good greasy breakfasts.

East of Williamston at the intersection of U.S. 64 and Highway 171, the small Roanoke River town of Jamesville is home to a most unusual restaurant that draws attention from all over the country (it's even been featured in the *New York Times*). The **Cypress Grill** (1520 Stewart St. off U.S. 64, 252/792-4175) is an unprepossessing wooden shack right-smack on the river, a survivor of the days when Jamesville made its living in the herring industry, dragging the fish out of the water with horse-drawn seine nets. Herring—breaded and seriously deep-fried, not pickled or sweet—is the main dish here, though they also dress the herring up in other outfits, and serve bass, flounder, perch, oyster, catfish, and other fish too. The Cypress Grill is open for the three and a half months of the year (from the second Thurs. in Jan. through the end of Apr.), when the herrings run, and you could hardly have a more intensely authentic, small-town dining experience anywhere else.

EAST ON U.S. 64

The eastern stretch of U.S. 64 runs along the Albemarle Sound between Williamston and the Outer Banks, passing through the towns of Plymouth, Creswell, and Columbia before it crosses over to Roanoke Island. Here you'll encounter evidence of North Carolina's ancient past, old-growth forests; recent past, a plantation with a long and complex history of slavery; and the present, art galleries and abundant wildlife-watching and recreational opportunities.

Somerset Place Historic Site

Somerset Place Historic Site (2572 Lake Shore Rd., Creswell, 252/797-4560, www.ah.dcr .state.nc.us/Sections/hs/somerset/somerset .htm, 9 A.M.–5 P.M. Mon.–Sat. and 1–5 P.M. Apr.–Oct., 10 A.M.–4 P.M. Tues.–Sat and 1–4 P.M. Sun. Nov.–Mar., free) was one of North Carolina's largest and most profitable plantations for the 80 years leading up to the Civil War. In the late 18th century and early 19th centuries, 80 Africa-born men, women, and children were brought to Somerset to labor in the fields. The grief and spiritual disorientation they experienced, and the subsequent trials of the slave community that grew to include more than 300 people, are told by the historian Dorothy Spruill Redford in the amazing book *Somerset Homecoming*. Somerset is a significant place from many historical standpoints, but the story of its African American community makes it one of this state's most important historic sites.

Somerset Place is an eerily lovely place to visit. The restored grounds and buildings, including the Collins family's house, slave quarters, and many dependencies, are deafeningly quiet, and the huge cypress trees growing right up to the quarters and the mansion make the place feel almost prehistoric. Visitors are permitted to walk around the estate at their leisure. A small bookshop on the grounds is a good source for books about North Carolina history in general, and African American history in particular.

Pettigrew State Park

On the banks of Lake Phelps, Pettigrew State Park (2252 Lakeshore Rd., Creswell, 252/797-4475, www.ncparks.gov/visit/parks /pett/main.php) preserves a weird ancient waterscape that's unlike anywhere else in the state. Archaeology reveals that there was a human presence here a staggering 10,000 years ago. The lake, which is five miles across, has yielded more than 30 ancient dugout canoes, some as much as 4,000 years old and measuring more than 30 feet. The natural surroundings are ancient too, encompassing some of eastern North Carolina's only remaining old-growth forests. Pungo Lake, a smaller body of water within the park, is visited by 50,000 migrating snow geese over the course of the year, an unforgettable sight for wildlife watchers.

Visitors to Pettigrew State Park can camp at the family campground ($15/day), which has drive-to sites and access to restrooms and hot showers, or at primitive group campsites (starting at $9/day).

Art Galleries

Pocosin Arts (corner of Main and Water Sts., Columbia, 252/796-2787, www.pocosin arts.org, 10 A.M.–5 P.M. Tues.–Sat.) has helped spur a renaissance of craft in eastern North Carolina, teaching community classes in ceramics, fiber arts, sculpture, jewelry making, metalwork, and many other arts. At the sales gallery, beautiful handmade items are available for purchase, and the main gallery displays many kinds of folk art from eastern North Carolina.

Sports and Recreation

Palmetto-Peartree Preserve (entrance is east of Columbia on Pot Licker Rd./Loop Rd./SR 1220, 252/796-0723, www.palmetto peartree.org) is a 10,000-acre natural area, wrapped in 14 miles of shoreline along the Albemarle Sound and Little Alligator Creek. Originally established as a sanctuary for the red cockaded woodpecker, this is a great location for bird-watching and spotting other wildlife (which include, in addition to the birds, alligators, wolves, bears, and bobcats); hiking, biking, and horseback riding along the old logging trails through the forest; and canoeing and kayaking. The preserve's excellent paddle trail passes by Hidden Lake, a wonderfully secluded cypress-swamp blackwater lake. There is an overnight camping platform at the lake, which can be used in the daytime without a permit for bird-watching and picnicking. To stay overnight, arrange for a permit through the Roanoke River Partners (252/792-3790, www.roanokeriverpartners.org).

Once the southern edge of the Great Dismal Swamp, **Pocosin Lakes National Wildlife Refuge** (headquarters at Walter B. Jones, Sr., Center for the Sounds, U.S. 64, six miles south of Columbia, 252/796-3004, www.fws.gov /pocosinlakes) is an important haven for many species of animals, including migratory waterfowl, and re-introduced red wolves. Five important bodies of water lie within the Refuge: Pungo Lake, New Lake, the 16,600-acre Lake Phelps, and stretches of the Scuppernong and Alligator Rivers. All of these areas are good spots for observing migratory waterfowl, but Pungo Lake is particularly special in the fall and winter, when snow geese and tundra swans visit in massive numbers—approaching 100,000—on their round-trip Arctic journeys.

The landscape here was drastically altered by a tremendous wildfire that burned for days in the summer of 2008, blanketing towns as far away as Raleigh with thick smoke. Wildfire is an important part of the natural cycle here, however, and now is a unique opportunity to watch the regeneration of an ecosystem.

WASHINGTON, BATH, AND BELHAVEN

On the north side of the Pamlico River, as you head towards Mattamuskeet National Wildlife Refuge and the Outer Banks, the towns of Washington, Bath, and Belhaven offer short diversions into the nature and history of this region.

North Carolina Estuarium

The North Carolina Estuarium (223 E. Water St., Washington, 252/948-0000, www.partnership forthesounds.org/NorthCarolinaEstuarium .aspx, 10 A.M.–4 P.M. Tues.–Sat., $3, $2 children) is a museum about both the natural and cultural history of the Tar-Pamlico River basin. In addition to the exhibits, which include live native animals, historic artifacts, and much more, the Estuarium operates pontoon boat tours on the Pamlico River. River roving is free, but reservations are required.

Turnage Theater

Washington has a great performing arts facility in the restored early 20th-century Turnage Theater (150 W. Main St., Washington, 252/975-1711, www.turnagetheater.com). All sorts of performances take place at the Turnage throughout the year, including by prominent artists from around the country. There are concerts of all kinds of music, productions by touring dance troupes and regional theater companies, and screenings of classic movies.

Historic Bath

North Carolina's oldest town, Bath was chartered in 1705. The town is so little changed that even today it is mostly contained within the original boundaries laid out by the explorer John Lawson. For its first 70 or so years, Bath enjoyed the spotlight as one of North Carolina's most important centers of trade and politics—home of governors, refuge from Indian wars, frequent host to and victim of Blackbeard. Much as Brunswick Town, to the south, was made redundant by the growth of Wilmington, Bath faded into obscurity as the town of Washington grew in the years after the Revolution. Today almost all of Bath is designated as Historic Bath (252/923-3971, www.bath.nchistoricsites.org, visitors center and tours 9 A.M.–5 P.M. Mon.–Sat. and 1–5 P.M. Sun. Apr.–Oct., 10 A.M.–4 P.M. Tues.–Sat. and

© TOBY HILTON

snow geese at Lake Mattamuskeet

1–4 P.M. Sun. Nov.–Mar., admission charged for the Palmer-Marsh and Bonner Houses). Important sites on the tour of the village are the 1734 St. Thomas Church, the 1751 Palmer-Marsh House, 1790 Van Der Veer House, 1830 Bonner House, and, from time immemorial, a set of indelible hoofprints said to have been made by the devil's own horse.

Belhaven Memorial Museum

The name of Belhaven Memorial Museum (210 E. Main St., Belhaven, 252/943-6197, www.beaufort-county.com/belhavenmuseum, 1–5 P.M. Thurs.–Tues.) gives no hint as to what a very strange little institution this is. The museum houses the collection of Miss Eva—Eva Blount Way, who died in 1962 at the age of 92—surely one of the most accomplished collectors of oddities ever. The local paper wrote of her in 1951 that, "housewife, snake killer, curator, trapper, dramatic actress, philosopher, and preserver of all the riches of mankind, inadequately describes the most fascinating person you can imagine." Miss Eva kept among her earthly treasures

a collection of pickled tumors (one weighs 10 pounds), a pickled one-eyed pig, a pickled two-headed kitten, cataracts (pickled), and—deep breath—three pickled human babies. There's also a dress that belonged to a 700-pound woman, a flea couple dressed in wedding togs, 30,000 buttons, and assorted snakes that Miss Eva felt needed killing. It must haven taken a very long time to carry everything over here, but Miss Eva's collection is now on public display, the core of the Belhaven Memorial Museum's collection.

◀ MATTAMUSKEET NATIONAL WILDLIFE REFUGE

Near the tiny town of Swan Quarter, the Mattamuskeet National Wildlife Refuge (Hwy. 94, between Swan Quarter and Englehard, 252/926-4021, www.fws.gov/mattamuskeet) preserves one of North Carolina's most remarkable natural features, as well as one of its most famous buildings. Lake Mattamuskeet, 18 miles long by 6 miles wide, is the state's largest natural lake, and being an average of a foot and half deep—five feet at its deepest point—it is a most unusual environment. The hundreds of thousands of waterfowl who rest here on their seasonal rounds make this a world-famous location for bird-watching and wildlife photography.

Old-timers in the area have fond memories of dancing at the **Lodge at Lake Mattamuskeet,** one of eastern North Carolina's best known buildings. The huge old building was constructed in 1915, and was at the time the world's largest pumping station, moving over one million gallons of water per minute. In 1934, it was bought by the federal government along with the wildlife sanctuary, and the Civilian Conservation Corps transformed it into the lodge that was a favorite gathering place for the next 40 years. The lodge is closed at the time of this writing, but is undergoing restoration for future public use.

Hiking and biking trails thread through the refuge, but camping is not permitted. In season, beware of hunters and keep an eye out as well for copperheads, cottonmouths, two kinds of rattlesnakes, and alligators. Bears and red wolves abound as well. Within the administration of the Mattamuskeet Refuge is the **Swan Quarter National Wildlife Refuge** (252/926-4021, www.fws.gov/swanquarter), located along the north shore of the Pamlico Sound, and mostly accessible only by water. This too is a gorgeous waterscape full of wildlife.

BEAUFORT AND THE CENTRAL COAST

Coming east from Raleigh towards the beaches and sounds of Carteret County, you'll start to feel the ocean when you're still many miles away from its shore. Somewhere between Kinston and New Bern, a good hour's drive from the Atlantic, the sky begins to expand in a way that suggests reflected expanses of water, like a mirage felt rather than seen. Getting closer to the coast, the pine forests on either side of the highway are peppered with mistletoe bundles. New Bern and Beaufort, centers of colonial commerce, connected North Carolina to the greater Atlantic world. Both towns are wonderfully preserved, ideal places for self-guided strolls with lots of window-shopping.

Below the crooked elbow of the Neuse River, the Croatan National Forest surrounds hidden lakes and tiny towns. To the northeast,

Cedar Island National Wildlife Refuge is a vast plain of marshes, gradually dropping off into Pamlico Sound. Cape Lookout National Seashore shelters the mainland from the ocean, a chain of barrier islands where a remote port, once one of the busiest maritime towns in North Carolina, and a whaling village, nearly washed away by a series of storms, now stand empty but for seagulls and ghosts.

You may hear folks in North Carolina refer to any point on the coast, be it Wilmington or Nags Head, as "Down East." In the most authentic, local usage of the term, Down East really refers to northeastern Carteret County, to the islands and marsh towns in a highly confined region along the banks of Core Sound, north of Beaufort. Like seemingly every scenic spot in North Carolina, Down East communities are

© SARAH BRYAN

HIGHLIGHTS

◖ **Tryon Palace:** The splendid and, in its day, controversial seat of colonial government in North Carolina is reconstructed in New Bern's historic district, a significant destination worthy of a whole day's leisurely exploration (page 57).

◖ **Kinston:** Few small towns can boast of such architectural wealth as Kinston. From the variety of old-time storefronts along Queen Street to the Victorian wedding cakes and shotgun houses in the residential neighborhoods, Kinston is a living museum of Southern popular architecture (page 62).

◖ **North Carolina Maritime Museum:** North Carolina's seafaring heritage, in living traditions as well as history, is represented in fascinating exhibits and activities at this great museum (page 67).

◖ **Beaufort's Old Burying Ground:** Even if it weren't the final resting place of the "Little Girl Buried in a Bottle of Rum," this little churchyard would still be one of the prettiest and most interesting cemeteries in the South (page 68).

◖ **Core Sound Waterfowl Museum:** Actually a museum about people rather than ducks, the Waterfowl Museum eloquently tells of the everyday lives of past generations of Down Easterners, while bringing their descendants together to re-forge community bonds (page 72).

◖ **Cape Lookout National Seashore:** The more than 50 miles of coastline along Core and Shackleford Banks, now home to only wild horses and turtle nests, were once also the home of Bankers who made their livings in the fishing, whaling, and shipping trades (page 74).

◖ **North Carolina Aquarium:** Sharks and jellyfish and their aquatic kindred show their true beauty in underwater habitats at the aquarium, and trails and boat tours lead to the watery world outdoors (page 76).

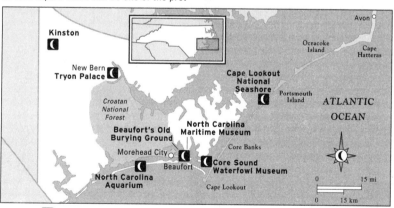

LOOK FOR ◖ TO FIND RECOMMENDED SIGHTS, ACTIVITIES, DINING, AND LODGING.

BEAUFORT

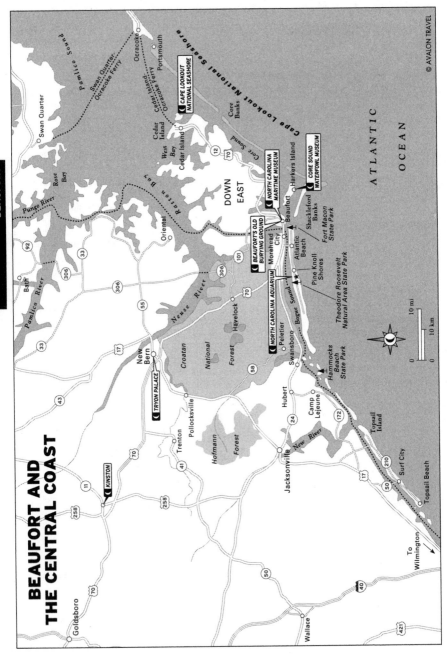

BEAUFORT AND THE CENTRAL COAST

Pamlico Sound

Swan Quarter

Swan Quarter–Ocracoke Ferry

Ocracoke

Portsmouth

Cedar Island–Ocracoke Ferry

Cedar Island Ferry

West Bay

Cedar Island

🏛 CAPE LOOKOUT NATIONAL SEASHORE

Core Banks

Pamlico River

Rose Bay

Pungo River

Bath

92

33

306

306

Oriental

101

55

Neuse River

306

70

Havelock

Pamlico River

33

17

New Bern

🏛 TRYON PALACE

43

70

258

258

11

🏛 KINSTON

Goldsboro

70

Pollocksville

Trenton

41

Croatan

National

Forest

Hofmann

Forest

Camp Lejeune

24

Hubert

172

Jacksonville

New River

17

50

210

Surf City

Topsail Island

Topsail Beach

To Wilmington

40

50

421

Wallace

58

Peletier

Swansboro

Hammocks Beach State Park

Bogue Sound

🏛 NORTH CAROLINA AQUARIUM

Morehead City

🏛 BEAUFORT'S OLD BURYING GROUND

Atlantic Beach

Pine Knoll Shores

Theodore Roosevelt Natural Area State Park

Fort Macon State Park

Shackleford Banks

Beaufort

🏛 NORTH CAROLINA MARITIME MUSEUM

Harkers Island

🏛 CORE SOUND WATERFOWL MUSEUM

Core Sound

12

70

Bay River

Bay Sound

DOWN EAST

Cape Lookout National Seashore

ATLANTIC OCEAN

© AVALON TRAVEL

10 mi

10 km

0

0

undergoing seismic cultural shifts as people "from off" move into the area, as young people leave home to make their lives and livings elsewhere, and as forces like global trade and environmental changes make the traditional maritime occupations of the region increasingly untenable. Nevertheless, Down Easterners fight to preserve the core treasures of Core Sound. Conservation and historic preservation efforts are underway, and they've already netted some victories. The best place to witness Down Easterners' passionate dedication to preserving their heritage is at the Core Sound Waterfowl Museum on Harkers Island. Members of the little communities along the sound have brought precious family objects to be displayed at the museum, and the quilts, family photos, baseball uniforms, oyster knives, net hooks, and other treasures eloquently tell of their love of the water, the land, and each other.

PLANNING YOUR TIME

The standard beach-season rules apply to the coastal areas covered in this chapter. Lodging prices go up dramatically between Memorial Day and Labor Day, and though you might score a rock-bottom price if you visit on a mild weekend out of season, you might also find that some of the destinations you'd like to visit are closed.

North Carolina Sea Grant (www.ncseagrant .org) provides wallet cards listing the seasons for different seafood caught and served in Carteret County. The cards can be ordered by mail, or downloaded and printed from the website.

Late summer and early autumn are hurricane season all through the Southeast. Hurricane paths are unpredictable, so if you're planning a week on the beach, and know that a hurricane is hovering over Cuba, it won't necessarily hit North Carolina, though the central Carolina coast is always an odds-on favorite for landfall. Chances are you'll have pretty fair warning if a storm is coming—you won't wake up one morning to find your motel room windows covered with plywood, and everybody else in town gone—but it's always a good idea to familiarize yourself with evacuation routes, and not take chances. A storm that's too far

offshore to cause any weather problems can still mess up beach conditions, making waves and currents that are exciting for surfing but way too dangerous for swimming. (These caveats are relevant to the whole North Carolina coast, not just this region.)

Barring storms, the fall is a really beautiful time on the beaches here. The coastal weather is sometimes warm right into November, and though the water may be too chilly for swimming then, there's hardly a nicer time for walking tours of the old towns—except, of course, azalea season in the spring.

INFORMATION AND SERVICES

Hospitals in the area include **Carteret General Hospital** (3500 Arendell St., 252/808-6000, www.ccgh.org) in Morehead City (where the author was born), **Craven Regional Medical Center** (2000 Neuse Blvd., 252/633-8111, www.uhseast.com) in New Bern, **Duplin General Hospital** (401 North Main Street, 910/296-0941, www.uhs east.com) in Kenansville, **Lenoir Memorial Hospital** (100 Airport Rd., 252/522-7000, www.lenoirmemorial.org) in Kinston, and **Wayne Memorial Hospital** (2700 Wayne Memorial Dr., 919/736-1110, www.wayne health.org) in Goldsboro.

Extensive travel information is available from the **Crystal Coast Tourism Authority** (3409 Arendell St., 877/206-0929, www.crys-talcoastnc.org).

GETTING THERE AND AROUND
By Car

One of the state's main east–west routes, U.S. 70, gives easy access to almost all of the destinations in this chapter. From Raleigh to Beaufort is a distance of a little over 150 miles, but keep in mind that large stretches of the highway are in commercial areas with plenty of traffic and red lights. U.S. 70 continues past Beaufort, snaking up along Core Sound through little Down East towns like Otway and Davis, finally petering out in the town of Atlantic. At Sea Level, Highway 13 branches to the north, across the Cedar Island Wildlife Refuge and ending at the Cedar Island–Ocracoke Ferry.

Down south, to reach the Bogue Banks (Atlantic Beach, Emerald Isle, and neighboring beaches) by road, bridges cross Bogue Sound on Highway 58 at both Morehead City and Cedar Point (not to be confused with Cedar Island).

By Ferry

Except for the visitors center at Harkers Island, Cape Lookout National Seashore can only be reached by ferry. Most ferries operate between April and November, with some exceptions. Portsmouth, at the northern end of the park, is a short ferry ride from Ocracoke, but Ocracoke is a very long ferry ride from Cedar Island. The **Cedar Island-Ocracoke Ferry** (800/856-0343) is part of the state ferry system, and costs $15 one-way for regular-sized vehicles (pets allowed). It takes 2.25 hours to cross Pamlico Sound, but the ride is fun, and embarking from Cedar Island feels like sailing off the edge of the earth. The **Ocracoke-Portsmouth ferry** is a passenger-only commercial route, licensed to Captain Rudy Austin. Call 252/928-4361 to ensure a seat. There's also a vehicle and passenger ferry, Morris Marina Kabin Kamps and Ferry Service (877/956-6568), **from Atlantic to Long Point** on the North Core Banks, leashed or in-vehicle pets are allowed.

Commercial ferries cross every day **from mainland Carteret County** to the southern parts of the National Seashore. There is generally a ferry route between Davis and Great Island, but service can be variable; check the Cape Lookout National Seashore website (www.nps.gov/calo) for updates.

From Harkers Island, passenger ferries to Cape Lookout Lighthouse and Shackleford Banks include Calico Jacks (252/728-3575), Harkers Island Fishing Center (252/728-3907), Local Yokel (252/728-2759), and Island Ferry Adventures at Barbour's Marina (252/728-6181).

From Beaufort, passenger ferries include Outer Banks Ferry Service (252/728-4129), which goes to both Shackleford Banks and to Cape Lookout Lighthouse; Island Ferry Adventures (252/728-7555) and Mystery Tours (252/728-7827) run to Shackleford Banks. Morehead City's passenger-only Waterfront Ferry Service (252/726-7678) goes to Shackleford Banks as well. On-leash pets are generally allowed, but call ahead to confirm for Local Yokel, Island Ferry Adventures, and Waterfront Ferry Service.

Back on the mainland, a 20-minute free passenger ferry **crosses the Neuse River** between Cherry Branch (near Cherry Point) and Minesott Beach in Pamlico County every half-hour (vehicles and passengers, pets allowed, 800/339-9156).

New Bern

New Bern's history is understandably a great draw, and that, coupled with its beautiful natural setting at the confluence of the Neuse and Trent Rivers, makes it one of North Carolina's prime spots for tourism and retirement living. Despite the considerable traffic it draws, it is still a small and enormously pleasant city.

One all-important note: how to say it. It's your choice of "NYEW-bern" or "NOO-bern"—and in some folks' accents it sounds almost like "Neighbor"—but never "New-BERN."

HISTORY

New Bern's early days were marked by tragedy. It was settled in 1710 by a community of Swiss and German colonists under the leadership of English surveyor John Lawson (author of the wonderful 1709 *A New Voyage to Carolina,* available today in reprint from the University of North Carolina Press), and Swiss entrepreneur Christoph von Graffenried (from Bern, of course). More than half of the settlers died en route to America, and those who made it across alive suffered tremendous hardship

in their first months and years. Lawson and Graffenried were both captured in 1711 by the Tuscarora tribe, in one of the opening sallies of the Tuscarora War. Graffenried was released—according to some accounts, because he wore such fancy clothes that the Tuscarora feared killing the governor. Lawson was burned at the stake, the first casualty of the Tuscarora War.

Despite early disaster, New Bern was on its feet again by the mid-18th century, at which time it was home to the colony's first newspaper, and its first chartered academy. It also became North Carolina's capital, an era symbolized by the splendor of Tryon Palace, one of the most recognizable architectural landmarks in North Carolina.

During the Civil War, New Bern was captured early by Ambrose Burnside's forces, and despite multiple Confederate attempts to retake the city, it remained a Union stronghold for the balance of the war. It became a center for African American resistance and political organization through the Reconstruction years, a story grippingly told in historian David Cecelski's *The Waterman's Song* (also UNC Press).

SIGHTS
◖ Tryon Palace

Tryon Palace (610 Pollock St., 252/514-4956, www.tryonpalace.org, 9 A.M.–5 P.M. Mon.–Sat., 1–5 P.M. Sun., last guided tour begins at 4 P.M., gardens open in the summer until 7 P.M., museum shop 9:30 A.M.–5:30 P.M. Mon.–Sat.,

Confederate monument, New Bern

1 P.M.–5:30 P.M. Sun.; $15 adults admission to all buildings and gardens, $6 grades 1–12; $8 adults admission just to gardens, kitchen office, blacksmith shop, and stables, $3 grades 1–12) is a rather remarkable feat of historic re-creation, a from-the-ground-up reconstruction of the 1770 colonial capitol and governor's mansion. Tryon Palace was a magnificent project the first time around too. Governor William Tryon bucked the preferences of Piedmont Carolinians, and had his and the colonial government's new home built here in the coastal plain. He hired English architect John Hawks to design the complex, what would become a Georgian house upon an estate laid out in the Palladian style. The Palace's first incarnation was a fairly short one. It stood for a scant quarter-century before burning in 1798, and as the by-now state of North Carolina had relocated its governmental operations to Raleigh, there was no need to rebuild the New Bern estate.

It continued, however, to live on in Carolinians' imaginations for a century. In the early 20th century, a movement was afoot to rebuild Tryon Palace. By the 1950s, both the funds and, incredibly, John Hawks' original drawings and plans had been secured, and over a period of seven years the Palace was rebuilt. Today it's once again one of the most striking and recognizable buildings in North Carolina.

Tryon Palace is open for tours year-round, and it hosts many lectures and living history events throughout the year. One of the best times to visit is during the Christmas season, when not only is the estate decorated beautifully for the season, but they celebrate **Jonkonnu,** a colonial African American celebration that was once found throughout the Caribbean and Southeastern United States. For many generations it was celebrated in eastern North Carolina, and here at Tryon Palace the tradition is recreated. At Jonkonnu—also called Junkanoo, John Canoe, and several other variations—African and African American slaves would put on a Mardi Gras–like frolic with deep African roots, parading through the plantation to music and wearing outlandish costumes, some representing folk characters associated with the celebration. It was a sort of upside-down day, when the social order was momentarily inverted, and the slaves could boldly walk right up onto the master's porch and demand gifts or money. Some whites got into the spirit of the celebration, and played along with this remarkable pantomime. It was a tradition fraught with both joy and sorrow, tapping into deeply volatile issues. Tryon Palace puts on a great recreation of Jonkonnu, one that's both lively and enlightening.

When you visit Tryon Palace, allow yourself plenty of time—a whole afternoon or even a full day. There are several buildings on the property where tours and activities are going on, the gardens are well worth seeing, and the surrounding neighborhood contains some wonderful old houses.

In the year 2010, in honor of New Bern's 300th anniversary, Tryon Palace plans to open the doors of its North Carolina History Education Center, an enormous new complex along the Trent River, next to the Tryon Palace gardens, with galleries, a performance hall, outdoor interpretive areas, and a great deal more.

New Bern Firemen's Museum

The New Bern Firemen's Museum (408 Hancock St., 252/636-4087, www.newbern museums.com, 10 A.M.–4 P.M. Mon.–Sat., $5 adults, $2.50 children) is a fun little museum—an idyll for the gearhead with an antiquarian bent. The museum houses a collection of 19th- and early 20th-century fire wagons and trucks, and chronicles the lively and contentious history of firefighting in New Bern. The city was the first in North Carolina, and one of the first in the country, to charter a fire department. After the Civil War, three fire companies operated here, one of which was founded before the War, and one founded during the Yankee occupation. (The third was a boys' bucket brigade, a sort of training program for junior firefighters.) During Reconstruction, every fire was occasion for a competition, as residents would gather around to see which company got to a blaze first—the good old boys or the carpetbaggers.

Attmore-Oliver House

The beautiful 1790 Attmore-Oliver House (510 Pollock St., 252/638-8558, www.newbern historical.org, hours and tour schedule vary, call for specifics, $4 adults, free for students) is a nice historic house museum, with exhibits about New Bern's very significant Civil War history. It's also the headquarters of the New Bern Historical Society.

Birthplace of Pepsi

We often think of Coca-Cola as the quintessential Southern drink, but it was here in New Bern that Caleb Bradham, a drugstore owner, put together what he called Brad's Drink—later Pepsi-Cola. Pepsi-Cola Bottling Company operates a soda fountain and gift shop at the location of Bradham's pharmacy, called the Birthplace of Pepsi (256 Middle St., 252/636-5898, www.pepsistore.com).

ENTERTAINMENT AND EVENTS

New Bern's historic Harvey Mansion has a cozy old-fashioned pub in its cellar, the **1797**
Steamer Bar (221 S. Front St., 252/635-3232). As one would gather from its name, the pub serves steamed seafood and other light fare. **Captain Ratty's Seafood Restaurant** (202–206 Middle St., 800/633-5292, www .captanrattys.com) also has a bar that's a popular gathering spot for locals and tourists alike.

SHOPPING

New Bern is a great place for antique shopping. The majority of the shops are within the 220–240 blocks of Middle Street. There are also periodic antique shows (and even a salvaged antique architectural hardware show) at the New Bern Convention Center. See www.visitnewbern.com for details.

Tryon Palace is a fun shopping spot for history buffs and home-and-garden fanciers. The historical site's **Museum Shop** (Jones House at Eden and Pollock Sts., 252/514-4932, 9:30 A.M.–5:30 P.M. Mon.–Sat., 1–5:30 P.M. Sun.) has a nice variety of books about history and architecture, as well as handcrafts and children's toy and games. The **Garden Shop** (610 Pollock St., 252/514-4932, 10 A.M.–5 P.M. Mon.–Sat., 1–5 P.M. Sun.) sells special bulbs and plants, when in season, grown in Tryon Palace's own greenhouse. Out of season you can still find a nice variety of gardening tools and accessories. A Shop Pass is available at the Museum Shop; this allows you to visit the shops at Tryon Palace without paying the entrance fee.

SPORTS AND RECREATION

At New Bern's Sheraton Marina, **Barnacle Bob's Boat and Jet Ski Rentals** (100 Middle St., Dock F, 252/634-4100, www.boatand-jetskinewbern.com, 9 A.M.–7 P.M. daily) rents one- and two-person Jet Skis ($65/hour, $45/half-hour) and 6–8-person pontoon boats ($65/hour, $220/4 hours, $420/8 hours).

ACCOMMODATIONS

The **Aerie Bed and Breakfast** (509 Pollock St., 800/849-5553, www.aerieinn.com, $119–169) is the current incarnation of the 1880s Street-Ward residence. Its seven luxurious guest rooms are done up in Victorian furniture and earth-tone fabrics reflecting the house's earliest era. There is a lovely courtyard for guests to enjoy, and the inn is only one short block from Tryon Palace.

Also on Pollock Street, a few blocks away, are the **Harmony House Inn** (215 Pollock St., 800/636-3113, www.harmonyhouseinn.com, $99–175), the **Howard House Bed and Breakfast** (207 Pollock St., 252/514-6709, www.howardhousebnb.com, $89–149), and the **Meadows Inn** (212 Pollock St., 877/551-1776, www.meadowsinn-nc.com, $106–166). All three are appealing 19th-century houses decorated in the classic bed-and-breakfast style, and easy walking distance to Tryon Palace and to downtown.

There are plenty of weekend/vacation rental houses in eastern North Carolina, but New Bern's **Sparrow House** (220 E. Front St., 252/349-2441, www.thesparrowhouse.com) is one of a kind. It's a four-story antebellum brick city house, built in 1843 by a shipbuilder. The Sparrow House sleeps up to 12 people in its four bedrooms, and at $395/night on weekends ($289/weeknight), it's actually a very reasonable way to spend vacation bucks for families likely to rent two or more hotel rooms.

Camping

New Bern's **KOA Campground** (1565 B St., 800/562-3341, www.newbernkoa.com) is just on the other side of the Neuse River from town, located right on the riverbank. Choices include 20-, 30-, 40-amp RV sites, "kamping kabins and lodges," and tent sites. Pets are allowed, and there is a dog park on-site. The campground is set up with free wireless access, so you can check your email from a rental paddleboat, if you've a mind to. Stop by the New Bern Convention Center's tourist information center before checking in, and pick up a KOA brochure for some major coupons.

FOOD

The Italian restaurant [C] **Nikola's** (1503-A S. Glenburnie Rd., 252/638-6061, www.nikolas-restaurant.com, $15–25) is both very small and very popular, so reservations are recommended.

Specialties include flounder stuffed with crabmeat, scallops, and shrimp, and Flounder Nikola's, filleted and laced with ham in white sauce; veal or chicken Romani sautéed in wine with mushrooms and artichoke hearts; and veal or chicken Fiorentina, with meat sauce, creamed spinach, and mozzarella served over pasta. Vegetarian entrées are all in the pasta category, but offer plenty of great options.

Down-home food choices include the **Country Biscuit Restaurant** (809 Broad St., 252/638-5151), which is open for breakfast, and is popular for, not surprisingly, its biscuits. **Moore's Olde Tyme Barbeque** (3711 Hwy. 17 S./Martin Luther King, Jr., Blvd., 252/638-3937) is a family business, in operation (at a series of different locations) since 1945. They roast and smoke their own barbeque in a pit on-site, burning wood that you'll see piled up by the shop. The menu is short and simple—featuring pork barbeque, chicken, shrimp, fish, hush puppies, fries, and slaw—and their prices are lower than many fast-food joints.

There are lots of good snack stops in New Bern, places to grab a bite or a cup of coffee before a day of touring on foot or on the water. The **Trent River Coffee Company** (208 Craven St., 252/514-2030, www.trentrivercoffee.com) is a casual coffee shop in a cool old downtown storefront, and the coffee is good. It's sometimes patronized by well-behaved local dogs, who lie under the tables patiently while their owners read the newspaper. This is a nice meeting place, and a dark oasis in the summer heat. **Port City Java** (323 Middle St., 252/633-7900, www.portcityjava.com) is an international chain, but it started in Wilmington, and has many locations on the North Carolina coast. The punch packed by Port City coffee is reliably good. One often stumbles upon cafés in communities where you wouldn't expect to be able to buy strong coffee, and it's at those times that a cup of espresso or a coffee shake is most appreciated. The **Cow Café** (319 Middle St., 252/672-9269) is a pleasant downtown creamery and snack shop with some homemade ice cream flavors you can't find anywhere else.

Croatan National Forest and Vicinity

A huge swath of swampy wilderness, the Croatan National Forest covers all the ground between the Neuse, Trent, and White Oak Rivers, and Bogue Sound, from New Bern to Morehead City and almost all the way to Jacksonville. Despite its size, Croatan is one of the lesser-known and less developed federal preserves in the state. The nearby towns (all three of them) of Jones County, population just over 10,000, enjoy a similar atmosphere of otherworldly sequestration, where barely traveled roads lead to dark expanses of forest and swamp, and old, narrow village streets.

CROATAN NATIONAL FOREST

Headquartered just off U.S. 70, south of New Bern, the Croatan National Forest (141 E. Fisher Ave., New Bern, 252/638-5628,

BEAUFORT

JOHN LAWSON ON ALLIGATORS

Explorer John Lawson, in his *A New Voyage to Carolina*, describes a 1709 encounter with an alligator on the Neuse River.

The Allegator is the same, as the Crocodile, and differs only in Name. They frequent the sides of Rivers, in the Banks of which they make their Dwellings a great way under Ground...Here it is, that this amphibious Monster dwells all the Winter, sleeping away his time till the Spring appears, when he comes from his Cave, and daily swims up and down the Streams...This Animal, in these Parts, sometimes exceeds seventeen Foot long. It is impossible to kill them with a Gun, unless you chance to hit them about the Eyes, which is a much softer Place, than the rest of their impenetrable Armour. They roar, and make a hideous Noise against bad Weather, and before they come out of their Dens in the Spring. I was pretty much frightened with one of these once, which happened thus: I had built a House about half a Mile from an Indian Town, on the Fork of the Neus-River, where I dwelt by my self, excepting a young Indian Fellow, and a Bull-Dog, that I had along with me. I had not then been so long a Sojourner in America, as to be thoroughly acquainted with this Creature. One of them had got his Nest directly under my House, which stood on pretty high Land, and by a Creek-side, in whose Banks his Entring-place was, his Den reaching the Ground directly on which my House stood. I was sitting alone by the Fire-side (about nine a Clock at Night, some time in March) the Indian Fellow being gone to Town, to see his Relations; so that there was no body in the House but my self and my Dog; when, all of a sudden, this ill-favour'd Neighbour of mine, set up such a Roaring, that he made the House shake about my Ears, and so continued, like a Bittern (but a hundred times louder, if possible), for four or five times. The Dog stared, as if he was frightened out of his Senses; nor indeed, could I imagine what it was, having never heard one of them before. Immediately I had another Lesson; and so a third. Being at that time amongst none but Savages, I began to suspect, that they were working some Piece of Conjuration under my House, to get away with my Goods...At last, my Man came in, to whom when I had told the Story, he laugh'd at me, and presently undeceiv'd me, by telling me what it was that made that Noise.

www.cs.unca.edu/nfsnc) has few established amenities for visitors, but plenty of land and water trails to explore.

Hiking

The main hiking route is the **Neusiok Trail,** which begins at the Newport River Parking area and ends at the Pinecliff Recreation Area on the Neuse, crossing 20 miles of beach, salt marsh, swamp, pocosin, and pinewoods. The 1.4-mile **Cedar Point Tideland Trail** covers estuary marshes and woods, starting at the Cedar Point boat ramp near Cape Carteret. The half-mile **Island Creek Forest Walk** passes through virgin hardwood forests and marl (compacted shell) outcroppings.

Boating

The park has designated the spectacular **Saltwater Adventure Trail.** This water route (roughly 100 miles in length) starts at Brice's Creek south of New Bern, winds along north to the Neuse River, then follows the Neuse all the way to the crook at Harlowe, where it threads through the Harlowe Canal. The route then heads down to Beaufort and all the way through Bogue Sound, turning back inland on the White Oak River, and ending at Haywood Landing north of Swansboro. If you're up for the challenge, it's an incredible trip. For boat rentals, try **Brice's Creek Canoe Trails** (141 East Fisher Ave., New Bern, 252/636-6606).

Camping

Three campsites in the Croatan Forest are developed. **Neuse River** (also called Flanners Beach, $10–15) has 25 sites with showers and flush toilets. **Cedar Point** ($15), has 40 campsites with electricity, showers, and flush toilets. **Fisher's Landing** (free) has nine sites, but no facilities other than vault toilets. Primitive camping areas are at Great Lake, Catfish Lake, and Long Point.

TRENTON

A little ways outside of the Croatan National Forest is the impossibly pretty village of

© SARAH BRYAN

Trent River at Pollocksville

Trenton. The Jones County seat's tiny, historic business district is an appropriate focal point for this bucolic area. A Revolutionary-era millpond, presided over by a large wooden mill, is a good picnic spot. It also makes for a nice destination for a short stroll after a meal at **Pop Tucci's** (141 W. Jones St., 252/448-1101) or the **Old Plant Diner** (346 W. Jones St., 252/448-1600). The 1880s board-and-batten Grace Episcopal Church sits next to a cemetery full of Victorian stones showing earthly chains rent asunder and heavenward-pointing hands.

◖ KINSTON

The town of Kinston does not appear on many tourist maps, but those who overlook it are missing out. It's been through some rough years recently, especially due to the economic vacuum left by the vanishing tobacco industry, which for generations made Kinston quite a prosperous place. The town is very much alive,

KINSTON'S MUSIC LEGACY

Music has always been a big deal here, and African American Kinstonians have made immeasurable contributions to American music, from jazz to R&B to gospel. James Brown discovered what Kinston had to offer when, in Greensboro in 1964, he met and hired a talented young drummer and college student named Melvin Parker, a native of Kinston. Melvin accepted the job on the condition that Brown also hire his little brother – a saxophonist named Maceo. Melvin and Maceo Parker were not the only Kinstonians to tour with Brown's band. Band leader Nat Jones, trombonist Levi Raspberry, trumpeter Dick Knight, and quite a few other young men from this area made names for themselves and helped create the groundbreaking sound of funk. Plans are in the works to celebrate Kinston's African American musical history (and future). To find out if an event is planned for when you'll be in town, contact the **Kinston Community Council for the Arts** (400 N. Queen St., 252/527-2517, www.kinstoncca.com).

though, and interesting things are happening here, particularly in the arts and in historic preservation.

Sights

Like a lot of towns that were prosperous for many years and suddenly experienced a drying-up of funds, Kinston is an architectural time capsule. Driving (or better yet, walking) the several downtown blocks of **Queen Street,** the town's main artery, is an education in early 20th-century commercial architecture. The Hotel Kinston is the town's tallest building, an 11-story hotel with a ground level that's a crazy blend of Art Deco and Moorish motifs. The 1914 post office is a big, heavy beaux arts beauty, and the Queen Street Methodist Church is turreted within an inch of its life. The People's Bank building

testifies to the heyday of early 20th-century African American commerce. With its many strange and daring experiments in building styles, Queen Street looks like a crazy quilt, but the buildings are beautifully complementary in their diversity. In the Herritage Street neighborhood, near the bend of the river, block upon block of grand old houses stand in threadbare glory, and on the other side of town, shotgun houses, that icon of Southern folk housing, line the alleys of the old working-class neighborhood.

The remains of the Confederate ironclad gunboat **CSS *Neuse*** are on display in Kinston, near the spot where she was scuttled in 1865 to keep her out of the hands of the advancing Union Army. All that remains is the core of the 158-foot-by-34-foot hull, but even in such deteriorated condition the *Neuse* is a striking feat of boatbuilding.

Entertainment and Events

Kinston is blessed with a great local arts engine, the **Kinston Community Council for the Arts** (400 N. Queen St., 252/527-2517, www.kinstoncca.com, 10 A.M.–6 P.M. Tues.–Fri., 10 A.M.–2 P.M. Sat.), which has the kind of energy and artistic vision one would expect to find in a much larger city. It occupies an old storefront on Queen Street, remodeled into a gorgeous gallery and studio space. In addition to the many community events that are hosted here, KCCA has consistently innovative exhibits in the main gallery. From avant-garde photography and collage to a recent exhibition of dozens of custom motorcycles, the Kinston Arts Council is a significant and provocative art space.

Sports and Recreation

The **Kinston Indians,** an old baseball team who are nowadays a Class-A affiliate of the Cleveland Indians, play their home games at historic **Grainger Stadium.** Grainger is a homey 1949 field, the second-oldest in the Carolina League. There's nothing like a baseball game in a small town that really, really cares, and baseball ranks nearly as high

BEAUFORT

BEAUFORT

EARLY MENTAL INSTITUTIONS

Two of the state's most remarkable museums, both tiny and little-known, are located in Goldsboro and Kinston, about half an hour apart and an easy drive from Raleigh. They both display artifacts from the history of early mental institutions, from Cherry Hospital – formerly the state Asylum for the Colored Insane – in Goldsboro, and the Caswell Center, a residential home for the developmentally disabled in Kinston. These museums are not for the faint of heart; amid lists of accomplishments and milestones of medicine are hints and intimations of a tragic past, of suffering on an overwhelming scale and misguided early-20th-century attempts at progressive mental healthcare. Emblematic of these institutions' shared past is the fact that each museum has on display a cage, an early solution for controlling unruly patients.

Cherry Hospital is still a state-operated inpatient psychiatric hospital, located on the same grim, industrial-looking campus where the first patient was admitted in 1880. It was a segregated hospital, housing only African American patients, until 1965. The strikingly unselfconscious **Cherry Museum** focuses mainly on the history of the staff and the evolution of medical treatment at the facility, but among the displays one catches fleeting glimpses of what life may have been like here for the early patients. A framed page in one display case lists "Some Supposed Causes of Insanity in the Early Years," and among them are "religion," "jealousy," "hard study," "business trouble," "love affair," "pregnancy,"

"masturbation," "la grippe," "blow on head," and, most curious, simply "trouble." In a day when the definition of insanity was so all-encompassing, and, compounding the terror, African Americans had little or no legal recourse to protect themselves from false charges or incarceration, one can only imagine how many of the "insane" here were in fact healthy, lucid people who fallen on hard times or committed some infraction of racial etiquette. In the earliest days, "therapy" consisted of work – picking crops in the fields, laboring in the laundry, or making bricks by the ton in the brickyard (which were then sold by the state for a profit). Clearly, such horrors as these are long behind us. They weren't confined to Cherry Hospital at the time, and certainly don't occur here today (or any time in recent generations), but the grief of the tens of thousands of people who lived here in the early 1900s hangs heavy in the air.

To visit Cherry Museum, you must enter the campus of Cherry Hospital (201 Stevens Mill Rd., Goldsboro, 919/731-3417, www.cherry-hospital.org), on Highway 581, near I-70 and U.S. 117, outside of Goldsboro. (You'll see a sign on I-70.) Once on campus, follow the signs to the museum. Once there, you must ring the doorbell and wait to be admitted. The public is admitted 8 A.M.-5 P.M. Monday-Friday.

Down the road in Kinston, about half an hour east, you'll find the **Caswell Center Museum and Visitors Center.** The Caswell Center admitted its first patients in 1914 as the Caswell School for the Feeble Minded.

as music on the list of Kinstonians' favorite things. At a memorable weekday afternoon Indians game in the 2007 season, the opening pitch was delayed when the stadium's PA system malfunctioned and failed to play the recording of the national anthem. After a few impatient moments, a loud-voiced man in the crowd began singing. The rest of the crowd joined him at " . . .can you see . . ." and sang the anthem all the way through (staying on pitch right through the high note—this is a musical town). When the singing was over, the players turned their backs to the flag just long enough to applaud the crowd, before they took the field and played ball.

Accommodations and Food

Several chain motels are located just outside of the downtown area. The **Hampton Inn** (1382 U.S. 258 S., 252/523-1400, www.hampton inn.com, around $85) is convenient and comfortable, and the staff are especially nice.

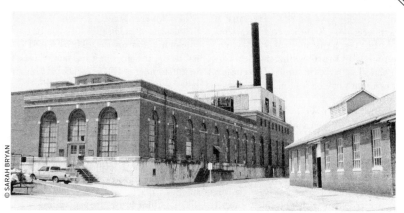

© SARAH BRYAN

BEAUFORT

Cherry Hospital

Like Cherry Hospital, the Caswell Center is still an active inpatient facility, and also like Cherry Hospital, it is nothing like the bleak place documented in the museum's displays about the first years here. But this too is an eye-opening education in early attitudes towards mental healthcare. The Caswell Center's museum is more blunt in its presentation than the delicate Cherry Museum, confronting directly the sad facts of its history by exhibiting objects like the combination straight-jacket-rompers that the earliest patients had to wear, and addressing the Depression-era overcrowding and lack of food. Though the Caswell Center's patients were all white until the era of integration, they were like the residents of the Asylum for the Colored Insane in that among their ranks were mentally healthy people – unwed mothers, people with physical handicaps, juvenile delinquents – who were crowded into dormitories with the patients who did suffer from retardation. An articulate love letter written from one patient, clearly not retarded, to another hints at the bizarre contradictions of life in an early mental institution.

The Caswell Center Museum and Visitors Center (2415 W. Vernon Ave., Kinston, 252/208-3780, www.caswellcenter.org) is open 8 A.M.-5 P.M. Monday-Friday and other times by appointment.

Both museums are free, but please make a donation to help ensure that their amazing stories will continue to be told.

There are quite a few good places to eat in Kinston. The best bet for a quick and tasty sandwich is the **Peach House** (412 W. Vernon Ave., 252/522-2526). For Carolina barbecue, **King's BBQ** (405 E. New Bern Rd., 800/332-6465, www.kingsbbq.com) has been a local favorite for more than 60 years. You'll see billboards throughout the area for their "Famous Pig in a Puppy," pork barbecue baked into a hush puppy sandwich. They also hit the nail on the head with their Brunswick stew, fried chicken, fried sea trout, and "banana pudding in an edible waffle bowl." King's also does a mail-order business in hand-chopped pork barbecue for $8 a pound.

Beaufort and Vicinity

It's an oft-cited case of the perversity of Southern speech that Beaufort, North Carolina, receives the French treatment of "eau"—so it's pronounced "BO-furt"—whereas Beaufort, South Carolina, a rather similar Lowcountry port town south of Charleston, is pronounced "Byew-furt."

The third-oldest town in North Carolina, Beaufort holds its own with its elders, Bath and New Bern, in the pretty department. The little port was once North Carolina's window on the world, a rather cosmopolitan place that sometimes received news from London or Barbados sooner than from Raleigh. The streets are crowded with extremely beautiful old houses, many built in a double-porch, steep-roofed style that shows off the early citizenry's cultural ties to the wider Caribbean and Atlantic world.

In the late 1990s, a shipwreck was found in Beaufort Inlet that is believed to be that of the *Queen Anne's Revenge,* a French slaver captured by the pirate Blackbeard in 1717 to be the flagship of his unsavory fleet. He increased its arsenal to 40 cannons, but it was nevertheless sunk in the summer of 1718. Blackbeard himself was killed at Ocracoke Inlet a few months later, and it took five musketballs and 40 sword wounds to finish him off. His body was dumped overboard, but his head carried on its master's infamous career a little longer, scaring folks from atop a pike in Virginia. Incredibly cool artifacts from the *QAR* keep emerging from the waters of the inlet. Beaufort had been a favorite haunt of Blackbeard's, and you can find out all about him at the North Carolina Maritime Museum.

From the Maritime Museum, it's just a few steps to Beaufort's cafés, antique shops, and docks, clustered along Front Street. From the docks you can see Carrot Island, with its herd of wild horses, one of the last in eastern North

winter cornfield on the central coast

© SARAH BRYAN

BLACKBEARD AND BONNET: THE BOYS OF 1718

In the 18th century, the Carolina coast was positively verminous with pirates. For the most part they hung out around Charleston Harbor, like a bunch of rowdies on a frat house balcony, causing headaches for passers-by. Some liked to venture up the coast, however, into the inlets and sounds of North Carolina. Our most famous pirate guests were Blackbeard, whose real name was Edward Teach, and Stede Bonnet. They did most of their misbehaving in our waters during the year 1718.

Blackbeard is said never to have killed a man except in self-defense, but clearly he was so bad he didn't need to kill to make his badness known. He was a huge man with a beard that covered most of his face, and his hair is usually depicted twisted up into ferocious dreadlocks. He wore a bright red coat and festooned himself with every weapon small enough to carry; and as if all that didn't make him scary enough, he liked to wear burning cannon fuses tucked under the brim of his hat. He caused trouble from the Bahamas to Virginia, taking ships, treasure, and child brides as fancy led him.

Poor Stede Bonnet. With a name like that, he should have known better than to try to make a living intimidating people. He is said to have been something of a fancy-pants, a man with wealth, education, and a nagging wife. To get away from his better half, he bought a ship, hired a crew, and set sail for a life of crime. Though never quite as tough as Blackbeard, with whom he was briefly partners, Bonnet caused enough trouble along the Southern coast that the gentlemen of Charleston saw to it that he was captured and hanged. Meanwhile, the Virginia nabobs had also had it with Blackbeard's interference in coastal commerce, and Governor Spottswood dispatched his men to kill him. This they did at Ocracoke, but it wasn't easy; even after they shot, stabbed, and beheaded Blackbeard, his body taunted them by swimming laps around the ship before finally giving up the ghost.

Blackbeard has in effect surfaced again. In 1996, a ship was found off the North Carolina coast that was identified as Blackbeard's flagship, the *Queen Anne's Revenge*. All manner of intriguing artifacts have been brought up from the ocean floor: cannons and blunderbuss parts, early hand grenades, even a penis syringe supposed to have been used by the syphilitic pirates to inject themselves with mercury. (During one standoff in Charleston Harbor, Blackbeard and his men took hostages to ransom for medical supplies. Perhaps this explains why they were so desperate.) To view artifacts and learn more about Blackbeard, Stede Bonnet, and their lowdown ways, visit the North Carolina Maritime Museum in Beaufort and in Southport, as well as the websites of the *Queen Anne's Revenge* (www.qaronline.com) and the Office of State Archaeology (www.arch.dcr.state.nc.us).

Carolina, and you can catch a ride on a ferry or tour boat to cross the sound to the Cape Lookout National Seashore, or get a close-up glimpse of wildlife in the surrounding salt marshes.

SIGHTS
◀ North Carolina Maritime Museum

The North Carolina Maritime Museum (315 Front St., 252/728-7317, www.ah.dcr.state .nc.us/sections/maritime/, 9 A.M.–5 P.M. Mon.–Fri., 10 A.M.–5 P.M. Sat., 1–5 P.M. Sun., free) is among the best museums in the state. Even if you don't think you're interested in boatbuilding or maritime history, you'll get caught up in the exhibits here. Historic watercraft and reconstructions and models of boats are on display here, well presented in rich historical and cultural context. There's also a lot to learn about the state's fishing history—not only pertaining to the fisheries themselves, but also to related occupations, such as the highly complex skill of net-hanging. Far from being limited to the few species of catches of today's fisheries, early North Carolina seamen also carried on a big business hunting sea turtles, porpoises, and even whales.

BEAUFORT

Across the street from the museum's main building, perched on the dock, is the **Harvey W. Smith Watercraft Center.** North Carolina mariners had for many generations an international reputation as expert shipbuilders, and even today, some builders continue to construct large, seaworthy vessels in their own backyards. This has always been done "by the rack of the eye," as they say here, which means that the builders use traditional knowledge handed down over the generations, rather than modern industrial methods. Their exceptional expertise is beautifully demonstrated by the craft in the museum and by boats still working the waters today. Here at the Watercraft Center, the Maritime Museum provides workspace for builders of full-size and model boats, and it teaches a vast array of classes in boatbuilding skills, both traditional and mechanized methods.

◖ Old Burying Ground

One of the most beautiful places in all of North Carolina, Beaufort's Old Burying Ground (Anne St., open daylight hours daily) is as picturesque a cemetery as you'd ever want to be buried in. It's quite small by the standards of some old Carolina towns, and crowded with 18th- and 19th-century stones. Huge old live oaks, Spanish moss, wisteria, and resurrection ferns, which unfurl and turn green after a rainstorm, give the Burying Ground an irresistibly gothic feel. Many of the headstones reflect the maritime heritage of this town, such as that of a sea captain whose epitaph reads, "The form that fills this silent grave/once tossed on ocean's rolling wave/but in a port securely fast/ he's dropped his anchor here at last."

Captain Otway Burns, an early privateer who spent much time in Beaufort, is buried here; his grave is easy to spot, as it is topped by a canon from his ship, the *Snap Dragon.* Nearby is another of the graveyard's famous burials, that of the "Little Girl Buried in a Barrel of Rum." This unfortunate waif is said to have died at sea and been placed in a cask of rum, to preserve her body for burial on land. Visitors often bring toys and trinkets to leave on her grave, which is marked by a simple

Old Burying Ground

© SARAH BRYAN

wooden plank. Though hers is the most gaudily festooned, you'll see evidence of this old tradition of funerary gifts on other graves here as well—most often, in this cemetery, coins and shells. This is a tradition found throughout the coastal South and the Caribbean, with roots tracing back to Africa. Feel free to add to her haul of goodies, but it's not karmically advisable to tamper with those already there.

Beaufort Historic Site

The Beaufort Historic Site (130 Turner St., 252/728-5225, www.beauforthistoricsite.org, $8 adults, $4 children) recreates life in late 18th- and early 19th-century Beaufort in several restored historic buildings. The 1770s "jump-and-a-half" (1.5-story) Leffers Cottage reflects middle-class life in its day, as a merchant, whaler, or—in this case—schoolmaster would have lived it. The Josiah Bell and John Manson Houses, both from the 1820s, reflect the graceful Caribbean-influenced architecture so prevalent in the early days of the coastal South. A restored apothecary shop, 1790s wooden courthouse, and a haunted 1820s jail that was used into the 1950s, are among the other important structures here. There are tours led by costumed interpreters, as well as driving tours of the old town in double-decker buses. Hours vary by season: 9:30 A.M.–5 P.M. Monday–Saturday March 1–November 31, plus 1–4 P.M. Sundays in June–August; 10 A.M.–4 P.M. Monday–Saturday December 1–February 28.

SPORTS AND RECREATION
Diving

North Carolina's coast is a surprisingly good place for diving. The **Discovery Diving Company** (414 Orange St., 252/728-2265, www.discoverydiving.com, $65–105/excursion) leads half- and full-day diving trips to explore the reefs and dozens of fascinating shipwrecks that lie at the bottom of the sounds and ocean near Beaufort.

Cruises and Wildlife Tours

Coastal Ecology Tours (252/247-3860, www.goodfortunesails.com, prices vary) runs very special tours on the *Good Fortune* of the Cape Lookout National Seashore and other island locations in the area, as well as a variety of half-day, day-long, overnight, and short trips, to snorkel, shell, kayak, and watch birds, and cruises to Morehead City restaurants, and other educational and fun trips. Prices range from $40 per person for a 2.5-hour dolphin-watching tour to $600 a night plus meals for an off-season overnight boat rental.

Lookout Cruises (600 Front St., 252/504-7245, www.lookoutcruises.com) carries sightseers on lovely catamaran rides in the Beaufort and Core Sound region, out to Cape Lookout, and on morning dolphin-watching trips.

Island Ferry Adventures (610 Front St., 252/728-7555, www.islandferryadventures.com, $10–15 adults, $5–8 children) runs dolphin-watching tours, trips to collect shells at Cape Lookout, and trips to see the wild ponies of Shackleford Banks.

Mystery Tours (600 Front St., 252 /728-7827 or 866/230-2628, www.mystery boattours.com, $15–50 adults, free–$25 children, some cruises for grownups only) offers harbor tours and dolphin-watching trips, as well as a variety of brunch, lunch, and dinner cruises, and trips to wild islands where children can hunt for treasure.

ACCOMMODATIONS

⟨ Outer Banks Houseboats (324 Front St., 252/728-4129, www.outerbankshouseboats.com) will rent you your own floating vacation home, drive it for you to a scenic spot, anchor it, and then come and check in on you every day during your stay. You'll have a skiff for your own use, but you may just want to lie on the deck all day and soak up the peacefulness. Rates run from $700 per weekend for the smaller houseboat, to $3,000 per week for the luxury boat, with plenty of rental options in between.

The **Inlet Inn** (601 Front St., 800/554-5466, www.inlet-inn.com) has one of the best locations in town, right on the water, near the docks where many of the ferry and tour boats land. If planning to go dolphin-watching or hop the ferry to Cape Lookout, you can get ready at a leisurely pace, and just step outside to the docks. Even in the high season, prices are quite reasonable.

The **Beaufort Inn** (101 Ann St., 252/728-2600, www.beaufort-inn.com) is a large hotel on Gallants Channel, along one side of the colonial district. It's an easy walk to the main downtown attractions, and the hotel's outdoor hot tub and balconies with great views make it tempting to stay in as well. The **Pecan Tree Inn** (116 Queen St., 800/728-7871, www.pecantree.com) is such a grand establishment that the town threw a parade in honor of the laying of its cornerstone in 1866. The house is still splendid, as are the 5,000-square-foot gardens. Catty-corner to the Old Burying Grounds is the **Langdon House Bed and Breakfast** (135 Craven St., 252/728-5499, www.langdonhouse.com). One of the oldest buildings in town, this gorgeous house was built in the 1730s on a foundation of English ballast stones. The **Red Dog Inn** (113 Pollock St., 252/728-5954, www.thereddoginnbb.com) is also in the historic district, half a block from the waterfront, and well-behaved dogs are welcome.

FOOD

Among the Beaufort eateries certified by Carteret Catch as serving local seafood are the **Blue Moon Bistro** (119 Queen St., 252/728-5800, www.bluemoonbistro.biz), **Sharpie's Grill and Bar** (521 Front St., 252/838-0101, www.sharpiesgrill.com), and **Aqua Restaurant** (114 Middle Ln. "behind Clawsons," 252/728-7777, www.aquaexperience.com).

If you're traveling with a cooler and want to buy some local seafood to take home, try the **Fishtowne Seafood Center** (100 Wellons Dr., 252/728-6644) or **Tripps Seafood** (1224 Harkers Island Rd., 252/447-7700).

◀ **Beaufort Grocery** (117 Queen St., 252/728-3899, www.beaufortgrocery.com, open for lunch and dinner every day but Tues., brunch on Sun., $20–36) is, despite its humble name, a sophisticated little eatery. At lunch it serves salads and crusty sandwiches, along with "Damn Good Gumbo" and specialty soups. In the evening the café atmosphere gives way to that of a more formal gourmet dining room. Some of the best entrées include boneless chicken breast sautéed with pecans in a hazelnut cream sauce; Thai-rubbed roast half duckling; and whole baby rack of lamb, served with garlic mashed potatoes, tortillas, and a margarita-chipotle sauce. Try the cheesecake for dessert.

The waterfront **Front Street Grill** (300 Front St., 252/728-4956, www.frontstreetgrillatstillwater.com) is popular with boaters drifting through the area, as well as diners who arrive by land. The emphasis is on seafood and fresh regional ingredients. Front Street Grill's wine list is extensive, and they have repeatedly won *Wine Spectator* magazine's Award of Excellence.

MOREHEAD CITY

Giovanni da Verrazano may have been the first European to set foot in present-day Morehead City when he sailed into Bogue Inlet. It wasn't until the mid-19th century that the town actually came into being, built as the terminus of the North Carolina Railroad to connect the state's overland commerce to the sea. Despite its late start, Morehead City has been a busy place. During the Civil War it was the site of major encampments by both armies. A series of horrible hurricanes in the 1890s, culminating in 1899's San Ciriaco Hurricane, brought hundreds of refugees from the towns along what is now the Cape Lookout National Seashore. They settled in a neighborhood that they called Promise Land, and many of their descendants are still here.

The Atlantic and North Carolina Railroad operated a large hotel here in the 1880s, ushering in Morehead's role as a tourist spot, and the bridge to the Bogue Banks a few decades later increased holiday traffic considerably.

Morehead is also an official state port, one of the best deepwater harbors on the Atlantic Coast. This admixture of tourism and gritty commerce gives Morehead City a likeable, real-life feel missing in many coastal towns today.

Sights

Morehead City's history is on display at **The History Place** (1008 Arendell St., 252/247-7533, www.thehistoryplace.org, 10 A.M.–4 P.M. Tues.–Sat.). There are many interesting and eye-catching historical artifacts on display, but the most striking exhibit is that of a carriage, clothes, and other items pertaining to Emeline Pigott, Morehead City's Confederate heroine. She was a busy girl all through the Civil War, working as a nurse, a spy, and a smuggler. The day she was captured, she was carrying 30 pounds of contraband hidden in her skirts, including Union troop movement plans, a collection of gloves, several dozen skeins of silk, needles, toothbrushes, a pair of boots, and five pounds of candy.

Entertainment and Events

Seafood is a serious art here. North Carolina's second-largest festival takes place in Morehead City every October, the enormous **North Carolina Seafood Festival** (252/726-6273, www.ncseafoodfestival.org). The city's streets shut down and over 150,000 visitors descend on the waterfront. Festivities kick off with a blessing of the fleet, followed with music, fireworks, competitions (like the flounder-toss), and, of course, lots and lots of food.

If you're in the area on the right weekend in November, you'll not want to deprive yourself of the gluttonous splendor of the **Mill Creek Oyster Festival** (Mill Creek Volunteer Fire Department, 2370 Mill Creek Rd., Mill Creek, 252/247-4777). Food, and lots of it, is the focus of this event. It's a small-town fete, a benefit for the local volunteer fire department, and the meals are cooked by local experts. You'll be able to choose from all-you-can-eat roasted oysters, fried shrimp, fried spot (a local fish), and more, all in mass quantities. The oysters may not be local these days (and few served on this coast are), but the cooking is very local—an authentic taste of one of North Carolina's best culinary traditions. Mill Creek is northwest of Morehead City on the Newport River.

Sports and Recreation

Many of this region's most important historic and natural sites are underwater. From Morehead City's **Olympus Dive Center** (713 Shepard St., 252/726-9432, www.olympusdiving.com), divers of all levels of experience can take charter trips to dozens of natural and artificial reefs that teem with fish, including the ferocious-looking but not terribly dangerous eight-foot-long sand tiger shark. There are at least as many amazing shipwrecks to choose from, including an 18th-century schooner, a luxury liner, a German U-boat, and many Allied commercial and military ships that fell victim to the U-boats that infested this coast during World War II.

Food

The **Sanitary Fish Market** (501 Evans St., 252/247-3111, www.sanitaryfishmarket.com) is probably Morehead City's best-known institution. The rather odd name reflects its 1930s origins as a seafood market that was bound by its lease and its fastidious landlord to be kept as clean as possible. Today it's a huge family seafood restaurant. Long lines in season and on weekends demonstrate its popularity. Of particular note are its famous hush puppies, which have a well-deserved reputation as some of the best in the state. Be sure to buy a Sanitary t-shirt on the way out; it'll help you blend in everywhere else in the state.

Captain Bill's (701 Evans St., 252/726-2166, www.captbills.com) is Morehead City's oldest restaurant, founded in 1938. Try the conch stew, and be sure to visit the otters that live at the dock outside. Another famous eating joint in Morehead City is **El's Drive-In** (3706 Arendell St., 252/726-3002), a tiny place across from Carteret Community College. El's has been around almost as many forevers as the Sanitary. It's most famous for its shrimp burgers, but serves all sorts of fried delights. **Mrs. Willis' Restaurant** (3114 Bridges St., 252/726-3741) is a popular home-style lunch and dinner spot. It's a sit-down restaurant, certainly not as casual as El's, but plenty laid-back just the same. Charcoal-grilled steaks are the specialty. **Cox's Restaurant** (4109 Arendell St., 252/726-6961) also has served down-home

BEAUFORT

cooking for many years, and is known for its friendly staff and coterie of local regulars.

For an old fashioned ladies' luncheon or afternoon tea, visit the tiny, five-table tearoom at the **Tea Clipper** (The History Place, 1012 Arendell St., 252/240-2800, www.theteaclipper.com, 11 A.M.–5 P.M. Tues.–Sat.). In addition to the many teas, you can order scones and desserts, and dainty quiche and sandwiches. The Tea Clipper shop, the mother ship of the little tearoom, has more than 120 teas of all kinds sold by the scoop.

HARKERS ISLAND

The Core Sound region, which stretches to the east-northeast of Beaufort many miles up to the Pamlico Sound, is a region of birds and boats. Like much of the Carolina coast, the marshes and pocosins here are visited by countless flocks of migratory birds on their ways to and from their winter quarters, as well as the many birds that live here year-round. Consequently, hunting has always been a way of life here, almost as much as fishing. In earlier generations (and to a much lesser extent today), men who fished most of the year did a sideline business in bird hunting; not only would they eat the birds they shot, but they made money selling feathers for ladies' hats, they trained bird dogs for their own and other hunters' use, and they served as guides to visiting hunters. Many Down Easterners also became expert decoy carvers. This art survives today, partly as art for art's sake, and also for its original purpose. Woodworking on a much grander scale has also defined the culture of this section, as it has bred generations of great boat-builders. Keep an eye out as you drive through Harkers Island, because you may see boats under construction in folks' backyards—not canoes or dinghies, but full-sized fishing boats.

To get to Harkers Island, follow U.S. 70 east from Beaufort, around the dogleg that skirts the North River. A little east of the town of Otway you'll see Harkers Island Road. Take a right on Harkers Island Road, and head south towards Straits. Straits Road will take you through the town by the same name, and then across a bridge over the Straits themselves, finally ending up on Harkers Island.

◖ Core Sound Waterfowl Museum

The Core Sound Waterfowl Museum (1785 Island Rd., Harkers Island, 252/728-1500, www.coresound.com, 10 A.M.–5 P.M. Mon.–Sat., 2–5 P.M. Sun., free), which occupies a beautiful modern building on Shell Point, next to the Cape Lookout National Seashore headquarters, is a community labor of love. The museum is home to exhibits crafted by members of the communities represented, depicting the Down East maritime life through decoys, nets, and other tools of the trades, everyday household objects, beautiful quilts and other utilitarian folk arts, and lots of other things held dear by the people who live and lived here. This is a sophisticated, modern institution, but its community roots are evident in touching details like the index-card labels, written in the careful script of elderly ladies, explaining what certain objects are, what they were used for, and who made them. For instance, just as Piedmont textile workers made and treasured their loom hooks, folks down here took pride in the hooks that they made to assist in the perennial off-season work of hanging nets. Baseball uniforms on display represent an era when one town's team might have to travel by ferry to its opponent's field. The museum hosts monthly get-togethers for members of communities Down East, a different town every month, which are like old home days. Families and long-lost friends reunite over home-cooked food, to reminisce about community history and talk about their hopes and concerns for the future.

The museum's gift shop has a nice selection of books and other items related to Down East culture. Be sure to pick up a copy of *The Harkers Island Cookbook* by the Harkers Island United Methodist Women. This cookbook has become a regional classic for its wonderful blend of authentic family recipes and community stories. You might also be able to find a Core Sound Christmas Tree, made by Harvey and Sons in nearby Davis. This old family fishery has made a hit in recent years manufacturing small Christmas trees out of recycled crab pots. It's a whimsical item, but it carries deep messages about the past and future of the Core Sound region.

Core Sound Decoy Carvers Guild

Twenty years ago, some decoy-carving friends Down East decided over a pot of stewed clams to found the Core Sound Decoy Carvers Guild (1575 Harkers Island Rd., 252/838-8818, www.decoyguild.com, call for hours). The Guild, which is open to the public, gives demonstrations, competitions, and classes for grown-ups and children, and has a museum shop that's a nice place to browse.

Events

The Core Sound Decoy Carvers Guild also hosts the **Core Sound Decoy Festival,** usually held in the early winter. Several thousand people come to this annual event—more than the number of permanent residents on Harkers Island—to buy, swap, and teach the art of making decoys.

Food

Captain's Choice Restaurant (977 Island Rd., 252/728-7122) is a great place to try traditional Down East chowder. Usually made of clams, but sometimes with other shellfish or fish, chowder in Carteret County is a point of pride. The point is the flavor of the seafood itself, which must be extremely fresh, and not hidden behind lots of milk and spices. Captain's Choice serves chowder in the old-time way—with dumplings.

VILLAGE OF CEDAR ISLAND

For a beautiful afternoon's drive, head back to the mainland, and follow U.S. 70 north.

You'll go through some tiny communities—Williston, Davis, Stacy—and, if you keep bearing north on Highway 12 when U.S. 70 heads south to the town of Atlantic, you'll eventually reach the tip of the peninsula, and the fishing village of Cedar Island. This little fishing town has the amazing ambience of being at the end of the earth. From the peninsula's shore you can barely see land across the sounds. The ferry to Ocracoke departs from Cedar Island, and it's an unbelievable two-hours-plus ride across the Pamlico Sound to get there. The beach here is absolutely gorgeous, and horses roam. They're not the famous wild horses of the Outer Banks, but they move about freely as if they were.

A spectacular location for bird-watching is the **Cedar Island National Wildlife Refuge** (on U.S. 70, east of the town Atlantic, 252/926-4021, www.fws.gov/cedarisland). Nearly all of its 14,500 acres are brackish marshland, and it's often visited in season by redhead ducks, buffleheads, surf scoters, and many other species. While there are trails for hiking and biking, this refuge is primarily intended as a safe haven for the birds.

Accommodations and Food

⟨ The Driftwood Motel (3575 Cedar Island Rd., 252/225-4861, www.clis.com/deg/drift2 .htm) is a simple motel in an incredible location, and since the ferry leaves from its parking lot, it's the place to stay if you're coming from or going to Ocracoke. There's also camping here, for $16 per tent and $18–20 for RV, with electricity, water, and sewer.

The Driftwood's **Pirate's Chest Restaurant** is the only restaurant on Cedar Island, so it's a good thing that it's a good one. Local seafood is the specialty, and dishes can be adapted for vegetarians.

Lower Outer Banks

The southern reaches of the Outer Banks of North Carolina comprise some of the region's most diverse destinations. Core and Shackleford Banks lie within the Cape Lookout National Seashore, a wild maritime environment populated by plenty of wild ponies but not a single human. On the other hand, the towns of Bogue Banks—Atlantic Beach, Salter Path, Pine Knoll Shores, Indian Beach, and Emerald Isle—are classic beach towns, with clusters of motels and restaurants, and even a few towel shops and miniature golf courses. Both areas are great fun, though, Cape Lookout especially so for eco-tourists and history buffs, and Bogue Banks for those looking for a day on the beach followed by an evening chowing down on good fried seafood.

◖ CAPE LOOKOUT NATIONAL SEASHORE

Cape Lookout National Seashore (Headquarters 131 Charles St., Harkers Island, 252/728-2250, www.nps.gov/calo) is an otherworldly place, 56 miles of beach on four barrier islands, a long tape of sand so seemingly vulnerable to nature that it's hard to believe there were once several busy towns on its banks. Settled in the early 1700s, the towns of the south Core Banks made their living in fisheries that might seem brutal to today's seafood eaters—whaling, and catching dolphins and sea turtles, among the more mundane species. Portsmouth, at the north end of the park across the water from Ocracoke, was a busy port of great importance to the early economy of North Carolina. Portsmouth declined slowly, but catastrophe rained down all at once on the people of the southerly Shackleford Banks, who were driven out of their own long-established communities to start new lives on the mainland when a series of terrible hurricanes hit in the 1890s.

Islands often support unique ecosystems. Among the dunes, small patches of maritime forest fight for each drop of fresh water, while ghost forests of trees that were defeated by advancing saltwater look on resignedly. Along the endless beach, loggerhead turtles come ashore to lay their eggs, and in the waters just off the strand, three other species of sea turtles are sometimes seen. Wild horses roam the beaches and dunes and dolphins frequent both the ocean and Sound sides of the islands. Other mammals, though, are all of the small and scrappy variety: raccoons, rodents, otters, and rabbits. Like all of coastal North Carolina, it's a great place for bird-watching, as it's located in a heavily traveled migratory flyway. (Pets are allowed, with leashes. The wild ponies on Shackleford Banks can pose a threat to dogs who get among them, and the dogs of course can frighten the horses, so be careful not to let them mingle should you and your dog find yourselves near the herd.)

Portsmouth Village

Portsmouth Village, at the northern tip of the Cape Lookout National Seashore, is a peaceful but eerie place. The village looks much as it did 100 years ago, the handsome houses and churches all tidy and in good repair, but with the exception of caretakers and summer volunteers, no one has lived here in nearly 40 years. In 1970, the last two residents moved away from what had once been a town of 700 people and one of the most important shipping ports in North Carolina. Founded before the Revolution, Portsmouth was a lightering station, a port where huge seagoing ships that had traveled across the ocean would stop, and have their cargo removed for transport across the shallow sounds in smaller boats. There is a visitors center located at Portsmouth, open varying hours April–October, where you can learn about the village before embarking on a stroll to explore the quiet streets.

In its busy history, Portsmouth was captured by the British during the War of 1812 and by the Yankees in the Civil War, underscoring its strategic importance. By the time of the Civil War, though, its utility as a waystation was already declining. An 1846 hurricane opened a new inlet at Hatteras, which quickly became a busy shipping channel. Then after abolition, the town's lightering trade was no longer profitable without slaves to perform much of the labor. The fishing and lifesaving businesses kept the town afloat for a couple more generations, but Portsmouth was never the same.

Once a year, an amazing thing happens. Boatloads of people arrive on shore, and the church bell rings, and the sound of hymn singing comes through the open church doors. At the Portsmouth Homecoming, descendants of the people who lived here come from all over the state and country to pay tribute to their ancestral home. They have an old-time dinner on the grounds with much socializing and catching up, and then tour the little village together. It's like a family reunion, with the town itself the family's matriarch. On the other 364 days of the year, Portsmouth receives its share of tourists and Park Service caretakers, but one senses that it's already looking forward to the next spring, when its children will come home again.

Shackleford Banks

The once-busy villages of Diamond City and Shackleford Banks are like Portsmouth in that, though they have not been occupied for many years, the descendants of the people who lived here retain a profound attachment to their ancestors' homes. Diamond City and nearby communities met a spectacular end. The hurricane season of 1899 culminated in the San Ciriaco Hurricane, a disastrous storm that destroyed homes and forests, killed livestock, flooded gardens with saltwater, and washed the Shackleford dead out of their graves. The Bankers saw the writing on the wall, and moved to the mainland en masse, carrying as much of their property as would fit on boats. Some actually floated their houses across Core Sound. Harkers Island absorbed most of the refugee population (many also went to Morehead City), and their traditions are still an important part of Down East culture. Daily and weekly programs held at the Light Station Pavilion and the porch of the Keepers' Quarters during the summer months teach visitors about the natural and human history of Cape Lookout, including what day-to-day life was like for the keeper of the lighthouse and his family.

Descendants of the Bankers feel a deep spiritual bond to their ancestors' home, and for many years they would return frequently, occupying fish camps that they constructed along the beach. When the federal government bought the Banks, it was made known that the fish camps would soon be off-limits to their deedless owners. The outcry and bitterness that ensued testified to the depth of the Core Sounders' love of their ancestral grounds. The Park Service may have thought that the fish camps were of no more importance than duck blinds or tents—ephemeral and purely recreational structures. But to the fish camps' owners, the Banks was still home, even if they themselves had been born on the mainland and never lived there for longer than a fishing season—the camps were their homes every bit as much as their actual residences on the mainland. Retaining their pride of spiritual, if not legal, ownership, many burned down their own fish camps rather than allow the Park Service to destroy them.

Cape Lookout Lighthouse

By the time you arrive at the 1859 Cape Lookout Lighthouse (visitors center, 252/728-2250), you'll probably already have seen it portrayed on dozens of brochures, menus, business signs, and souvenirs. With its striking diamond pattern, it looks like a rattlesnake standing at attention. Because it is still a working lighthouse, visitors are allowed in on only four dates each year, 10 A.M.–3:30 P.M. Visit Cape Lookout National Seashore's website (www.nps.gov/calo) for open house dates and reservation information. The allotted times fill up almost immediately.

Accommodations

Morris Marina (877/956-5688, www.capelook outconcessions, $65–100) rents cabins at Great Island and Long Point. Cabins have hot and cold water, gas stoves, and furniture, but in some cases visitors must bring their own generators for lights, as well as linens and utensils. Rentals are not available from December through March. Book well in advance.

CAMPING

Camping is permitted within Cape Lookout National Seashore, though there are no designated campsites or camping amenities. Everything you bring must be carried back out when you leave. Campers can stay for up to 14 days.

Getting There and Around

There is only one small part of Cape Lookout National Seashore that is accessible by car, the tip of Harkers Island, where the visitors center is located next to the Core Sound Waterfowl Museum. To get to the other side of the Sound, you'll have to catch one of several ferries that run to and from the Banks. Some carry vehicles, but others are passenger-only; fees vary, and some require reservations; most operate only from mid-March to early December; some will allow your pets, and others won't. Plan ahead, and be sure to leave time for unexpected changes in schedule.

The passenger ferry to Portsmouth departs from Ocracoke, and it's a relatively short hop across Ocracoke Inlet (Capt. Rudy Austin, 252/928-4361, passengers); but if you're trying to get to Portsmouth from mainland Carteret County, you'll first have to take the Cedar Island–Ocracoke ferry (NC Dept. of Transportation, 800/856-0343, www.ncdot .org/transit/ferry/routes, vehicles and passengers) across Pamlico Sound, a trip of more than two hours. One ferry goes to North Core Banks, departing from Atlantic (Morris Marina Kabin Kamps and Ferry Service, 877/956-6568, www.nps.gov/calo/playnyour-visit/ferry.htm, vehicles and passengers), and from Davis to Great Island on the South Core Banks (Great Island Cabins and Ferry Service, 877/956-6568, vehicles and passengers).

Four passenger ferries travel between Harkers Island and Cape Lookout Lighthouse and Shackleford Banks (Captain Jack's Ferry,

252/728-3575; Harkers Island Fishing Center, 252/728-3907; Island Ferry Adventures at Barbour Marina, 252/728-6181; and Local Yokel, 252/728-2759), and one Beaufort ferry goes to both the lighthouse and Shackleford Banks (Outer Banks Ferry Service, 252/728-2759). Other options for getting to Shackleford Banks are Morehead City's Waterfront Ferry Service (252/726-7678), and Beaufort's Island Ferry Adventures (252/728-7555) and Mystery Tours (252/728-7827).

Morris Marina and Ferry Service (877/956-6568) is Cape Lookout's main transportation and lodging concessionaire. In addition to ferries, they operate some vehicle shuttles on the Banks. Call with inquiries about specific routes. Some of the other ferries also run four-wheel-drive taxis from point to point within the National Seashore.

BOGUE BANKS

The beaches of Bogue Banks are popular tourist spots, but they have a typically North Carolinian, laid-back feel, a quieter atmosphere than the fun-fun-fun neon jungles of other states' beaches. The major attractions here, Fort Macon State Park and the North Carolina Aquarium at Pine Knoll Shores, are a bit more cerebral than, say, amusement parks and bikini contests. In the surfing and boating, bars and restaurants, and the beach itself, there's also a bustle of activity to keep things hopping. Bogue, by the way, rhymes with "rogue."

◖ North Carolina Aquarium

The North Carolina Aquarium at Pine Knoll Shores (1 Roosevelt Blvd., Pine Knoll Shores, 866/294-3477, www.ncaquariums.com, 9 A.M.–5 P.M. daily, until 9 P.M. every Thurs. in July, $8 adults, $7 seniors, $6 children 17 and younger) is one of the state's three great coastal aquariums. Here at Pine Knoll Shores, exhibit highlights include: a 300,000-gallon aquarium in which sharks and other aquatic beasts go about their business in and around a replica German U-Boat (plenty of originals lie right off the coast and form homes for reef creatures); a "jellyfish gallery" (they really can be beautiful); a pair of river otters; and many other wonderful animals and habitats.

Trails from the parking lot lead into the maritime forests of the 568-acre **Theodore Roosevelt Natural Area** (1 Roosevelt Dr., Atlantic Beach, 252/726-3775).

Fort Macon State Park

At the eastern tip of Atlantic Beach is Fort Macon State Park (2300 E. Fort Macon Rd., 252/726-3775, www.ncsparks.net/foma.html, 9 A.M.–5:30 P.M. daily, fort open 8 A.M.–6 P.M. Oct.–Mar., 8 A.M.–7 P.M. Apr., May, and Sept., and 8 A.M.–8 P.M. June–Aug., bathhouse area 8 A.M.–5:30 P.M. Nov.–Feb., 8 A.M.–7 P.M. Mar.–Oct., 8 A.M.–8 P.M. Apr., May, and Sept., and 8 A.M.–9 P.M. June–Aug., bathhouse $4/ day, $3 child). The central feature of the park is Fort Macon itself, an 1820s Federal fort that was a Confederate garrison for one year during the Civil War. Guided tours are offered, and there are exhibits inside the casemates. For such a stern, martial building, some of the interior spaces are surprisingly pretty.

Sports and Recreation

The ocean side of Bogue Banks offers plenty of public beach access. In each of the towns, from the northeast end of the island to the southwest end—Atlantic Beach, Pine Knoll Shores, Salter Path, Indian Beach, and Emerald Isle—there are parking lots, both municipal and private, free and for-fee.

Aside from the fort itself, the other big attraction at **Fort Macon** is the beach, which is bounded by the ocean, Bogue Sound, and Beaufort Inlet. Because there's a Coast Guard station on the Sound side, and a jetty along the Inlet, swimming is permitted only along one stretch of the ocean beach. A concession stand and bathhouse are located at the swimming beach.

Atlantic Beach Surf Shop (515 W. Fort Macon Rd., Atlantic Beach, 252/646-4944, www.absurfshop.com) gives individual ($50/ hour) and group ($40/hour) surfing lessons on the beach at Pine Knoll Shores. Lessons are in the morning and early afternoon. Call for reservations.

Accommodations

The **Atlantis Lodge** (123 Salter Path Rd., Atlantic Beach, 800/682-7057, www.atlantis lodge.com, $70–220) is an old, established, family-run motel. It has simple and reasonably priced efficiencies in a great beachfront location. Well-behaved pets are welcome for a per-pet-per-night fee. The **Clamdigger** (511 Salter Path Rd., Atlantic Beach, 800/338-1533, www.clam diggerramadainn.com, $40–260) is another reliable choice, with all oceanfront rooms. Pets are not allowed. The **Windjammer** (103 Salter Path Rd., Atlantic Beach, 800/233-6466, www.windjammerinn.com, $50–200) is another simple, comfortable motel, with decent rates through the high season.

Food

The **Channel Marker** (718 Atlantic Beach Causeway, Atlantic Beach, 252/247-2344) is an haute-er alternative to some of the old-timey fried seafood joints on Bogue Banks (which are also great—read on). Try the crab cakes with mango chutney, or the Greek shrimp salad. The extensive wine list stars wines from the opposite side of North Carolina, from the Biltmore Estate in Asheville.

White Swan Bar-B-Q and Chicken (2500-A W. Fort Macon Rd., Atlantic Beach, 252/726-9607) has been serving the Carolina trinity of barbecue, coleslaw, and hush puppies since 1960. They also flip a mean egg for breakfast.

The ◖ **Big Oak Drive-In and Bar-B-Q** (1167 Salter Path Rd., 252/247-2588, www.big oakdrivein.com) is a classic beach drive-in, a little red-white-and-blue-striped building with a walk-up counter and drive-up spaces. They're best known for their shrimpburgers ($4.95 large), a fried affair slathered with Big Oak's signature red sauce, coleslaw, and tartar sauce. Then there are the scallopburgers, oysterburgers, clamburgers, hamburgers, and barbecue, all cheap, and made for snacking on the beach.

THE DECLINE OF THE FISHING INDUSTRY

It's ironic that along the coast of North Carolina, where for centuries fishing has been more than a business – it's been an entire culture – relatively little of the seafood served in restaurants or sold in markets nowadays is actually caught by local fishermen. Sitting in a dockside restaurant, looking out at fishermen unloading their day's haul, you may be eating shrimp that were flown in from Thailand, or fish from Chile, or oysters from France. Like the textile industry, North Carolina's commercial fisheries have suffered tremendously from global trade. There is, however, a growing concern for promoting the interests of local fisheries before it's too late – if it's not already. **Carteret Catch** is an organization dedicated to the promotion of the fishing industry here in Carteret County. At their website (www.carteretcatch.org), you can find out which local restaurants and fish markets are buying seafood from the fishermen who live and work in this community, rather than from international wholesalers.

As recently as 10 years ago, the shores and riverbanks of eastern North Carolina were covered with fish houses. Often small, family-run operations, fish houses were the best places in the world for seafood lovers, who could buy their favorite fish and shellfish as soon as the boats were unloaded. Today, things are very different. For reasons both environmental and economic, the old-time seafood house is nearly extinct. Declines in popular species of fish and shellfish have hit North Carolina's fishermen, like others around the world, painfully hard. Concurrently, the skyrocketing value of land along the coast – and up the rivers and along the back creeks and marshes – often renders such a business unsustainable. Owners of fish houses are either run out of business by the exponential rise of their property taxes, or give in to the temptation to sell their waterfront lots for more money than they might have made in years of fishing.

This book will help you find some of the last remaining fish houses and seafood restaurants that still serve catches right off the docks. Though they have become so few and far between, the effort in finding traditional seafood houses is certainly worthwhile. You'll taste some of the freshest, best seafood in the world, and you'll be helping give a critically threatened traditional way of life a fighting chance.

Frost Seafood House (1300 Salter Path Rd., Salter Path, 252/247-3202) began in 1954 as a gas station and quickly became the restaurant that it is today. The Frost family catch their own shrimp and buy much of their other seafood locally. Be sure to request a taste of the "ching-a-ling sauce." Yet another community institution is the **Crab Shack** (140 Shore Dr., Salter Path, 252/247-3444). You'll find it behind the Methodist church in Salter Path. Operated by the Guthries (a family name that dates back to the dawn of time in this area, long before anyone thought of calling their home the "Crystal Coast"), the restaurant was wiped out in 2005 by Hurricane Ophelia, but they have since rebuilt, rolled up their sleeves, and plunged their hands back into the cornmeal.

WILMINGTON AND THE CAPE FEAR REGION

The Cape Fear region was and is very much a part of the Caribbean-basin culture that stretches up through the south Atlantic coast of North America—a world that reflects English, Spanish, and French adaptation to the tropics and, above all, to the profoundly transformative influence of the African cultures brought to the New World by captive slaves. Wilmington is part of the sorority that includes Havana, Caracas, Port au Prince, Santo Domingo, New Orleans, Savannah, and Charleston. Savannah, Charleston, and Wilmington are the main points of the Carolina Lowcountry, and like its closest sisters, Wilmington and the surrounding Cape Fear coast exhibits the richness of Afro-Caribbean culture in its architecture, cuisine, folklore, and speech.

Robeson County, along the South Carolina state line, is the geographic home of the Lumbee tribe, who are historically and spiritually tied to the beautiful blackwater Lumber River. The Lumbees are the largest tribe east of the Mississippi, yet many Americans have never heard of them. This is due in part to the fact that the government denies them federal recognition, a complex and highly contentious issue that casts a long shadow over much of the politics, economics, and history of this part of the state. A "non-reserved" tribe, the Lumbees have for centuries lived much as their white and African American neighbors have—a mostly rural existence, anchored in a profound devotion to the Christian faith. Their history is fascinating and often surprising, and can be explored by the traveler in and around the town of Pembroke.

© BRIAN LEON

HIGHLIGHTS

Wilmington Historic District: Wilmington's downtown reflects its glory days of commerce and high society. This is North Carolina's largest 19th-century historic district, a gorgeous collection of antebellum and late Victorian townhouses and commercial buildings, including many beautiful Southern iterations of the Italianate craze that preceded the Civil War (page 85).

Wrightsville Beach: North Carolina has many wonderful beaches, but few can compare with Wrightsville for its pretty strand, easy public access, clear waters, and overall beauty (page 88).

Hammocks Beach State Park: Accessible only by boat, one of the wildest and least disturbed Atlantic coast beaches, Bear Island is a popular stopover for migrating waterfowl and turtles (page 97).

Orton Plantation: Orton's formal gardens embody the aesthetic of "Southern Gothic," juxtaposing the romantic and largely imaginary idyll of the Old South with the mournful spookiness of moss-draped swamps, honking alligators, and the plantation's often tragic history. It's picturesque in the extreme (page 104).

Strike at the Wind: One of North Carolina's premier outdoor dramas tells the story of the Henry Berry Lowrie gang, Reconstruction-era outlaws and heroes of Lumbee history. For 30 years, the play has been acted every summer by members of the tribe (page 108).

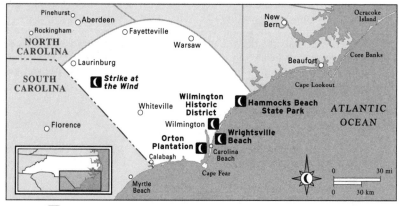

LOOK FOR ◖ TO FIND RECOMMENDED SIGHTS, ACTIVITIES, DINING, AND LODGING.

The area between Wilmington and Lumberton in the state's southeast corner is a strange, exotic waterscape (more so than a landscape) of seductively eerie swamps and backwaters. People from the Piedmont will turn up their noses at the swamps, claiming that they reek like rotten eggs and that the farmland's no good. But to those of us who are native to this corner of the Carolinas, our cypress knees and tannic creeks and nests of snakes and alligators make this a region of sinister but incomparable beauty—and swamp air the best aromatherapy there is. In this little band of coastal counties straddling the state line, within a 100-mile radius of Wilmington, we share the native habitat—the only one in the world—of the Venus flytrap, a ferocious little plant of rather ghastly beauty. It somehow seems like an appropriate mascot for these weird backwaters.

The greatest draw to this region, even more than colonial cobblestones and carnivorous plants, are the beaches of Brunswick, New Hanover, and Onslow Counties. Some of them, like Wrightsville and Topsail, are well known, and others remain comparatively secluded barrier island strands. In some ways the "Brunswick Islands," as visitors bureaus designate them, can be thought of as the northern edge of the famous Grand Strand area around Myrtle Beach, South Carolina. No square mile of this region could be mistaken for Myrtle Beach, though; even the beaches that are most liberally peppered with towel shops and miniature golf courses will seem positively bucolic in comparison. But those with an appreciation for Myrtle Beach's inimitable style, our own chaotically commercial, in-your-face Paris of the Pee Dee (one of the rivers that flows through the border region of the Carolinas), will be glad to know that it's only a few short miles away.

PLANNING YOUR TIME

Depending on which part of the Cape Fear area you're planning to explore, you have a range of good choices for your home base. Wilmington is an easy drive from pretty much anywhere in this region, giving ready access to the beaches to the north and south. It's so full of sights and activities that you'll probably want to stay here anyway and give yourself a day or more just to explore the city itself. If you're planning on visiting the beaches south of Wilmington, you might also want to consider staying in Myrtle Beach, South Carolina, which is about a 20 minutes' drive on U.S. 17 (with no traffic—in high season it's a very different story) from the state line. Farther inland, you'll find plenty of motels around Fayetteville and Lumberton, which are also a reasonable distance from Raleigh to make day trips.

HISTORY

The Cape Fear River, deep and wide, caught the attention of European explorers as early as 1524, when Giovanni de Verrazano drifted by, and two years later, when Lucas Vásquez de Ayllón and his men (including, possibly, the first African slaves within the present-day United States) had a walk-about before proceeding to their appointment for shipwreck near Winyah Bay in South Carolina. Almost a century and a half later, William Hilton and explorers from the Massachusetts Bay Colony had a look for themselves. They were either disgusted with what they saw or knew they'd found a really good thing and wanted to psych out anyone with thoughts of a rival claim, because they left right away, and on their way out posted a sign at the tip of the Cape to the effect of, "Don't bother, the land's no good."

The next summer, John Vassall and a group of fellow Barbadians attempted settlement, but within a few years they abandoned the area. It wasn't until 1726, when Maurice Moore made the banks of the river his own on behalf of a group of allied families holding a patent to the area, that European settlement took. Moore lay out Brunswick Town, and his brother Roger established his own personal domain at Orton. (Today, only the ballast-stone foundations of houses and walls of the Anglican church remain at Brunswick, but Roger's home at Orton still stands.) The machinations of the Moore brothers led to the demise, or at least disintegration, of the Cape Fear tribe, who had been clinging to their land with varying success since the first Europeans arrived. Maurice Moore, with the aid of Tuscaroras, drove away many of the tribe, and then the few who remained at a settlement within present-day Carolina Beach State Park were slaughtered by Roger Moore in 1725. He claimed, whether truthfully or not, that a band of Cape Fear had attacked Orton.

Brunswick was briefly an important port, but it was soon eclipsed by Wilmington, a new settlement up the river established by an upstart group of non-Moores. By the time of the Revolution, it was Wilmington that dominated trade along the river. Meanwhile, a large population of Scottish immigrants had since the 1730s been farming and making a living from the pine forests (manufacturing naval

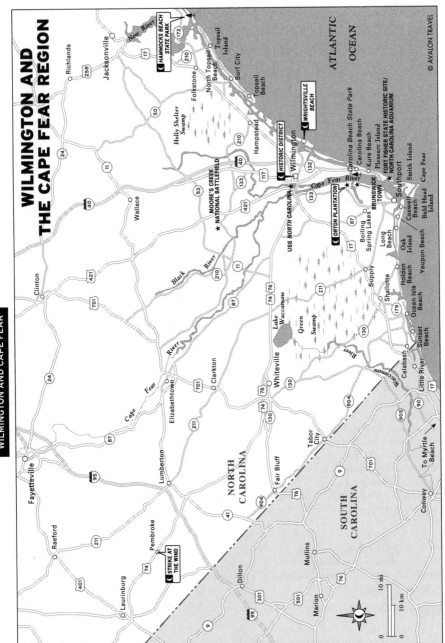

WILMINGTON AND CAPE FEAR

stores—tar, pitch, and turpentine) in the area around present-day Fayetteville.

The Lower Cape Fear region, particularly present-day Brunswick, New Hanover, Duplin, Bladen, and Onslow Counties, had a significantly larger slave population than most parts of North Carolina. The naval stores industry demanded a large workforce, and the plantations south of the river were to a large extent a continuation of the South Carolina Lowcountry economy, growing rice and indigo, crops that also led to the amassing of large populations of human chattel. All along the South Carolina and Georgia coasts, and into parts of Florida, these large communities of African-born and first-generation African American people established the culture now known as Gullah. Today the Gullah language and other aspects of the cultural heritage are most prominent around Charleston and on the islands just off the coast, and to a lesser extent in Savannah and points south, where a handful of communities still speak the Gullah language, a patois of English mixed with recognizably African vocabulary and grammar. The Gullah (sometimes called Geechee) accent, which has a heavy Caribbean resonance, can still be heard around Wilmington and the Brunswick Coast, in people who have never spoken any language but standard English. Aspects of Gullah traditions in cooking (gumbo, goobers/peanuts, okra), folklore (houses with steps, shutters, window panes, and roof-lines painted bright blue to keep bad luck away), and folk medicine (root doctoring) are still in evidence throughout the Lowcountry.

Another major cultural group in the Cape Fear region is that of the Lumbee tribe. Their origins have long been mysterious. While the federal government denies Lumbees the recognition necessary to receive the federal benefits due Native American tribes in the United States, and while they are sometimes identified by ethnologists as a "tri-racial isolate" (grouped with other Southern communities of unknown origins, like the Melungeons of Appalachia), there's no question that the tribe is of Native American heritage. It also seems that their ancestry includes European and African Americans,

leading to a variety of theories about their origin, including the especially persistent (though improbable) idea that they are descendants of the lost colonists of Roanoke. They've been variously called the Croatan Indians, Pembroke Indians, and Indians of Robeson County. In the days of slavery they were identified as Free People of Color, and the ever-evolving laws of the state concerning their civil rights long denied them the rights to vote or bear arms. Well into the 20th century the Lumbee were victims of segregation, and racism, both overt and vestigial, still places obstacles in the way of Lumbee advancement. Despite such hardships, a passionate devotion to the cause of education has produced a great many accomplished doctors, nurses, scholars, and other professionals who have in turn dedicated their careers and expertise to the well-being of their tribe.

The Lumbee also have a long history of resistance, and to the protection of their own land and rights. Most famously, the Lowry/Lowrie Band, outlaw heroes of the 19th century, defined the Lumbee cause for future generations. Another transformative moment in Lumbee history was the 1958 armed conflict near Maxton. Ku Klux Klan Grand Wizard "Catfish" Cole and about 40 other armed Klansmen held a rally here, at Hayes Pond. Local Lumbee, fed up with a recent wave of especially vicious intimidation at the hands of the Klan, showed up at the rally en masse—1,500 of them, all armed. The Lumbee shot out the one electric light and opened fire on the rally, causing the Klansmen to run like hell. The battle (which was won, incredibly, without a single death) was reported around the country, an energizing story for the cause of Native American rights, and a humiliation for the Ku Klux Klan.

In the late 20th and early 21st century, southeastern North Carolina's most prominent role is probably a military one. Fort Bragg, located in Fayetteville, is one of the country's largest Army installations, and the home base of thousands of the soldiers stationed in Iraq and Afghanistan. Nearby Pope Air Force Base is the home of the 43rd Airlift Wing, and at Jacksonville, the US Marine Corps' II Expeditionary Force, among other major divisions, are stationed at Camp Lejeune. Numerous museums in Fayetteville and Jacksonville tell the world-changing history of the military men and women of southeastern North Carolina.

INFORMATION AND SERVICES

The several area hospitals include: two in Wilmington, **Cape Fear Hospital** (5301 Wrightsville Ave., 910/452-8100, www.nhhn .org) and the **New Hanover Regional Medical Center** (2132 S. 17th St., 910/343-7000, www.nhhn.org); two in Brunswick County, **Brunswick Community Hospital** in Supply (1 Medical Center Dr., 910/755-8121, www .brunswickcommunityhospital.com) and **Dosher Memorial Hospital** in Southport (924 N. Howe St., 910/457-3800, www.dosher .org); two more in Onslow County, **Onslow Memorial Hospital** in Jacksonville (317 Western Blvd., 910/577-2345, www.onslow memorial.org) and the **Naval Hospital at Camp Lejeune** (100 Brewster Blvd., 910/451-1113, ej-www.med.navy.mil); and Fayetteville's **Cape Fear Valley Medical System** (1638 Owen Dr., 910/609-4000, www.cape fearvalley.com). Myrtle Beach's **Grand Strand Regional Medical Center** (809 82nd Pkwy., 843/692-1000, www.grandstrandmed.com) is not too far from the southernmost Brunswick communities. In an emergency, of course, calling 911 is the safest bet.

Extensive tourism and travel information is available from local convention and visitors bureaus: the **Wilmington/Cape Fear Coast CVB** (23 N. 3rd St., Wilmington, 877/406-2356, www.cape-fear.nc.us, 8:30 A.M.–5 P.M. Mon.– Fri., 9 A.M.–4 P.M. Sat., and 1–4 P.M. Sun.), and the **Brunswick County Chamber of Commerce** in Shallotte (4948 Main St., 800/426-6644, www.brunswickcountycham-ber.org, 8:30 A.M.–5 P.M. Mon.–Fri.).

GETTING THERE AND AROUND

Wilmington is the eastern terminus of I-40, more than 300 miles east of Asheville, approximately 120 miles east of Raleigh. The Cape Fear region is also crossed by a major north–south route, U.S. 17, the old Kings Highway of colonial times. Wilmington is roughly equidistant along U.S. 17 between Jacksonville to the north and Myrtle Beach, South Carolina, to the south; both cities are about an hour away. Wilmington International Airport serves the region with flights to and from East Coast cities. For a wider selection of routes, it may be worthwhile to consider flying into Myrtle Beach or Raleigh, and renting a car. If driving to Wilmington from the Myrtle Beach airport, add another half-hour or hour to get through Myrtle Beach traffic (particularly in the summer), as the airport there is on the southern edge of town. If driving from Raleigh-Durham International Airport, figure on the trip taking at least 2.5 hours. There is no passenger train service to Wilmington.

Topsail and Jacksonville are an easy drive on U.S. 17, as are the southerly Brunswick County beaches like Holden, Ocean Isle, and Sunset. The beaches and islands along the Cape itself, due south of Wilmington, are not as close to U.S. 17. They can be reached by taking U.S. 76 south from the city, or by ferry from Southport. The **Southport-Fort Fisher Ferry** (800/293-3779 or 800/368-8969) is popular as a sightseeing jaunt as well as a means simply to get across the river. It's a 30-minute crossing; most departures are 45 minutes apart, 5:30 A.M.–7:45 P.M. from Southport (until 6:15 P.M. in the winter), and 6:15 A.M.–8:30 P.M. leaving Fort Fisher (until 7 P.M. in the winter). For most vehicles, the fare is $5, but if you're driving a rig that's more than 20 feet long, boat trailers and the like included, the price can be as high as $15. It's $1 for pedestrians, $2 for bicycle riders, and $3 for folks on motorcycle. Pets are permitted if leashed or in a vehicle, and there are bathrooms on all ferries.

Wave Transit (910/343-0106, www.wave transit.com), Wilmington's public transportation system, operates buses throughout the metropolitan area and trolleys in the historic district. Fares are very low—$1 max, one-way. If you're planning on exploring outside the city, though, your best bet is to go by car.

Wilmington

In many cities, economic slumps have an unexpected benefit: historic preservation. With Wilmington's growth at a standstill in much of the 20th century, there was no need to replace the old buildings and neighborhoods. As a result, downtown Wilmington has remained a vast museum of beautiful architecture from its early days, and that historic appeal accounts for much of its popularity today as a tourist destination.

The city is once again ascendant, an ever more desirable place to live as well as to vacation. Hollywood noticed the little city a couple of decades ago, and Wilmington has become one of the largest film and TV production sites east of Los Angeles. *Dawson's Creek, Matlock,* and *One Tree Hill* are just some of the well-known series filmed here, and noteworthy movies filmed at least partly in Wilmington include *Forrest Gump, Sleeping with the Enemy, I Know What You Did Last Summer,* and many more (though not, ironically, either version of *Cape Fear*). It's not unlikely that, strolling through city, you'll happen on a film crew at work.

HISTORY

Incorporated in 1739, Wilmington was strategically situated for maritime commerce. Its deepwater port made it a bustling shipping center for the export of lumber, rice, and naval stores (turpentine and tar tapped from the now nearly vanished longleaf pine forests). Businessmen came to Wilmington from around the world, especially from Barbados, Scotland and northern Europe, and from the American colonies to the north. A fair number of New Englanders settled here, Nantucketers and other seafaring Yankees. In 1840, Wilmington became the eastern terminus of the 161-mile Wilmington and Weldon Railroad, which was at that time the longest railroad in the world. Now linking the commerce of land and sea with unprecedented efficiency, Wilmington's population exploded to almost 10,000 by 1860, making it the largest city in North Carolina.

During the War Between the States, the Wilmington and Weldon line was one of the crucial Confederate arteries for trade and transport, and Wilmington's port was a swarming hive of blockade runners. Its fall to the Union at the late date of January 1865 was a severe blow to the sinking Confederacy. Commerce allowed the city to weather the Civil War and Reconstruction, and it continued to grow and flourish. By 1890, the population had grown to 20,000. This was not an easy era socially, though, and tensions between white and black and Democrat and Republican Wilmingtonians exploded in the 1898 Wilmington Race Riot, one of the uglier incidents in the state's history. During the riot, a mob of white Democrats overthrew the city's Republican government, destroyed the black newspaper, the *Daily Record,* and murdered at least 22 African American citizens, leading to a radically accelerated revocation of the civil rights gained by African Americans in North Carolina during Reconstruction.

In the early 20th century, North Carolina's economic pulse was increasingly to be found in the Piedmont, with its textile and manufacturing boom. In 1910, Charlotte surpassed Wilmington in population. Economically, the darkest hour came in 1960, with the relocation of the Atlantic Coast Line headquarters to Florida. The old port city experienced a slow decline in vitality throughout the 20th century. Today Wilmington is a city of about 100,000 people, with ever-increasing cachet and economic vitality as a retirement and vacation destination.

SIGHTS
◖ Historic District

Wilmington is to 19th-century architecture what Asheville is to that of the early 20th century. Having been the state's most populous city until around 1910, when Charlotte and its Piedmont neighbors left the old port city in their wake, Wilmington's downtown reflects

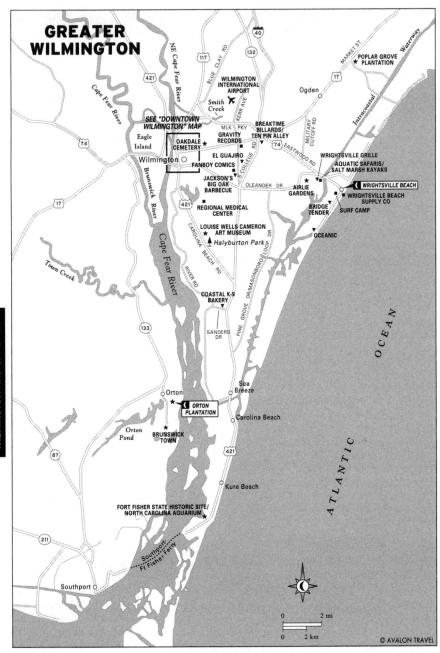

© JIMMY MCDONALD
Wilmington riverfront

on the property: the slave quarters. This confined but rather handsome two-story brick building is one of the few surviving examples in this country of urban slave dwellings. Extensive renovations are underway to restore the quarters to its early appearance.

The **Burgwin-Wright House** (224 Market St., 910/762-0570, www.burgwinwrighthouse .com, tours 10 A.M.–3:30 P.M. Tues.–Sat., closed in January, $6 adults, $3 children under 12) has an oddly similar history to that of the Bellamy Mansion, despite being nearly a century older. John Burgwin (the emphasis is on the second syllable), a planter and the treasurer of the North Carolina colony, built the house in 1770 on top of the city's early jail. Soon thereafter, Wilmington became a theater of war, and the enemy, as was so often the case, took over the finest dwelling in town as its headquarters. In this case the occupier, who had a particularly fine eye for rebel digs, was Lord Cornwallis, then on the last leg of his campaign before falling into George Washington's trap. The Burgwin-Wright House is, like the Bellamy Mansion, a vision of white-columned porticoes shaded by ancient magnolias, but the architectural style here is a less ostentatious, though no less beautiful, 18th-century form, the mark of the wealthy merchant and planter class in the colonial South Atlantic/Caribbean world. Seven terraced sections of garden surround the house; they are filled with native plants and many original landscape features, and make an intoxicating setting for an early spring stroll.

Yet another beautiful home in the historic district is the **Zebulon Latimer House** (126 S. Third St., 910/762-0492, www.latimerhouse .org, 10 A.M.–4 P.M. Mon.–Fri., noon–5 P.M. Sat., $8 adults, $4 if touring with a docent). The Latimer House is several years older than the Bellamy Mansion, but in its day was a little more fashion-forward, architecturally speaking. Mr. Latimer, a merchant from Connecticut, preferred a more urban expression of the Italianate style, a blocky, flat-roofed design with cast-iron cornices and other details that hint at the coming decades of Victorian aesthetics. Also located on the grounds is a

its glory days of commerce and high society. This is North Carolina's largest 19th-century historic district, a gorgeous collection of antebellum and late Victorian townhouses and commercial buildings, including many beautiful Southern iterations of the Italianate craze that preceded the Civil War.

The **Bellamy Mansion** (503 Market St., 910/251-3700, www.bellamymansion .org, hourly tours 10 A.M.–5 P.M. Tues.–Sat., 1–5 P.M. Sun., $10 adults, $4 children under 12) is a spectacular example of Wilmington's late-antebellum Italianate mansions. This enormous white porticoed house ranks among the loveliest Southern city houses of its era. Built by planter Dr. John Bellamy just before the outbreak of the Civil War, the house was commandeered by the Yankees after the fall of Fort Fisher, and a trip to Washington and a pardon granted personally by President Andrew Johnson, a fellow North Carolinian, were required before Dr. Bellamy could pry his home out of Federal hands. In addition to the mansion, another highly significant building stands

WILMINGTON AND CAPE FEAR

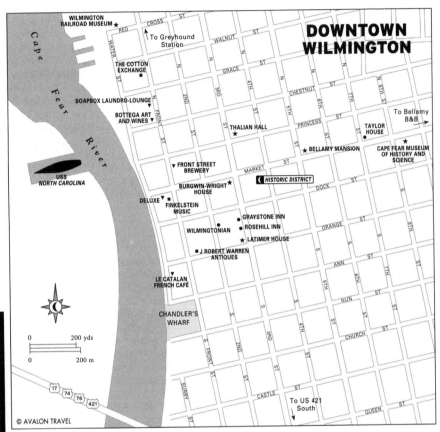

very interesting two-story brick slave dwelling. The Latimer House is the headquarters of the Lower Cape Fear Historical Society, whose archive of regional history is important to genealogists and historic preservationists.

If you'd like to visit the Bellamy Mansion, Latimer House, and Burgwin-Wright House, be sure to buy a **three-house ticket** at the first house you visit. At $21, it will save you several bucks over what you'd pay were you to buy a ticket at each stop.

Wrightsville Beach

Wrightsville Beach, just outside of Wilmington, is easily one of the nicest beaches in the Carolinas, which is a linear kingdom of beautiful strands. The beach is wide and easily accessible, visitor- and family-friendly, and simply beautiful. The water at Wrightsville often seems to be a brighter blue than one is accustomed to seeing this far north on the Atlantic coast, lending the feeling of a tropical coast. Wrightsville enjoys warm summertime water temperatures, a very large strand, and lots of lodging and rental choices along the beach. Numerous public beach access points (searchable at www.townofwrightsville beach.com/accesspoints.htm), some wheelchair-accessible and some with showers and/or bathrooms, line Lumina Avenue. The largest public parking lot, with 99 spaces, is at Beach Access #4, 2398 Lumina Avenue; #36 at 650

Lumina Avenue also has a large lot. They all fill up on busy days, but if you press on from one access point to the next, you'll eventually find a spot.

Historic Sights Around Wilmington
POPLAR GROVE PLANTATION
North of the city, about halfway between Wilmington and Topsail, is Poplar Grove Plantation (10200 U.S. 17 N., 910/686-9518, www.poplargrove.com, 9 A.M.–5 P.M. Mon.–Sat., noon–5 P.M. Sun, $8 adults, $7 seniors, $5 children ages 6–15). This antebellum peanut plantation features a beautiful 1850 big house, a restored tenant farmer's cabin, and other dependencies, as well as an extensive network of hiking trails through coastal forests and wetlands. In May, the plantation fills up with antique dealers and shoppers for the **Down Home Antique Fair.**

MOORE'S CREEK NATIONAL BATTLEFIELD
Not surprisingly, given its importance as a maritime center, the environs of Wilmington have seen much military action over the last 300 years. About 20 miles northwest, outside the town of Currie near Burgaw, is the Moore's Creek National Battlefield (40 Patriots Hall Dr., Currie, 910/283-5591, www.nps.gov/mocr, 9 A.M.–5 P.M. daily except Thanksgiving, Christmas, and New Year's Day). The site commemorates the brief and bloody skirmish of February 1776 in which a Loyalist band of Scottish highlanders, kilted and piping, clashed with Patriot colonists. The revolutionaries fired on the Scotsmen with cannons as they crossed a bridge over Moore's Creek, which they'd previously booby-trapped, greasing it and removing planks. About 30 of the Crown's soldiers died, some drowning after they were blown off the bridge. Important as a moment in the American Revolution, this was also a noteworthy occasion in Scottish military history as well: it was the last major broadsword charge in Scottish history, led by the last Scottish clan army.

USS *NORTH CAROLINA*
Docked in the Cape Fear River, across from the Wilmington waterfront at Eagles Island, is the startling gray colossus of the battleship USS *North Carolina* (Eagles Island, 910/251-5797, www.battleshipnc.com, 8 A.M.–8 P.M. daily Memorial Day–Labor Day, 8 A.M.–5 P.M. daily Labor Day–Memorial Day, $9.50 adults, $5 ages 12 and under). This decommissioned World War II warship, which saw service at Guadalcanal, Iwo Jima, and many other important events in the Pacific theater, is a floating monument to the nearly 10,000 North Carolinians who died in WWII, and a museum of what life was like in a floating metal city.

Tours are self-guided, and include nine decks, the gun turrets and bridge, crew quarters, the sick deck, and the Roll of Honor display of the names of North Carolina's wartime dead. Allow yourself at least two hours to see it all. Visitors prone to claustrophobia might wish to stay above deck. The passageways and quarters below are close, dark, and very, very deep; from the heart of the ship it can take quite a while to get back out, and on a busy day the crowds can make the space seem even more constricted. (Just imagine how it would have felt to be in this ship in the middle of the Pacific, with nearly 2,000 other sailors aboard.)

The battleship is also one of North Carolina's most famous haunted houses, as it were—home to several ghosts who have been seen and heard on many occasions. The ship has been featured on the Sci-Fi Channel and on the ghost hunting show *TAPS,* and is the subject of extensive writing and paranormal investigation. Visit www.hauntednc.com to hear some chilling unexplained voices caught on tape.

OAKDALE CEMETERY
In the mid-19th century, as Wilmington was bursting at the seams with new residents, the city's old cemeteries were becoming overcrowded with former residents. Oakdale Cemetery (520 N. 15th St., 910/762-5682, www.oakdalecemetery.org, 8 A.M.–5 P.M. daily year-round) was founded a ways from downtown to ease the subterranean traffic jam. It

was designed in the park-like style of grave-yards that was popular at that time, and soon filled up with splendid funerary art—weeping angels, obelisks, willows—to set off the natural beauty of the place. (Oakdale's website has a primer of Victorian grave art symbolism.) Separate sections were reserved for Jewish burials and for victims of the 1862 yellow fever epidemic. It's a fascinating place for a quiet stroll.

Museums

CAPE FEAR MUSEUM OF HISTORY AND SCIENCE

The Cape Fear Museum of History and Science (814 Market St., 910/798-4370, www.capefearmuseum.com, 9 A.M.–5 P.M. Mon.–Sat., 1–5 P.M. Sun., closed Tues. Labor Day–Memorial Day, $6 adults, $5 students and seniors, $3 children 3–17) has exhibits about the ecology of the Cape Fear and its human history. Special treats are exhibits about giant native life forms, including the prehistoric ground sloth and Michael Jordan.

LOUISE WELLS CAMERON ART MUSEUM

The Louise Wells Cameron Art Museum (3201 S. 17th St., 910/395-5999, www.cameronartmuseum.com, 11 A.M.–5 P.M. Tues.–Thurs., Sat. and Sun., 11 A.M.–9 P.M. Fri., $8 adults, $5 students and members, $3 children 2–12) is one of the major art museums in North Carolina, a very modern gallery with a good permanent collection of art of many media, with a special emphasis on North Carolina artists. Masters represented include Mary Cassatt and Utagawa Hiroshige. Special exhibits change throughout the year.

WILMINGTON RAILROAD MUSEUM

The Wilmington Railroad Museum (505 Nutt St., 910/763-2634, www.wilmingtonrailroadmuseum.org, 10 A.M.–5 P.M. Mon.–Sat., 1–5 P.M. Sun. Apr. 1–Sept. 30, closed Sun. Oct.–Mar., $6 adults, $5 seniors and military, $3 ages 2–12) explores a crucial but now largely forgotten part of this city's history: its role as a railroad town. In 1840, Wilmington became the terminus for the world's longest continuous rail line, the Wilmington and Weldon. The Atlantic Coast Line Railroad (into which the W&W had merged around 1900) kept its headquarters at Wilmington until the 1960s, when it moved its offices, employees, and a devastatingly large portion of the city's economy, to Florida. All manner of railroad artifacts are on display in this great little museum, from timetables to locomotives. A classic iron horse, steam engine #250, sits on the track outside and has been restored beautifully.

Gardens and Parks

AIRLIE GARDENS

Airlie Gardens (300 Airlie Rd., 910/798-7700, www.airliegardens.org, 9 A.M.–5 P.M. Mon.–Sat. Jan. 2–Mar. 19, 9 A.M.–5 P.M. daily Mar. 20–Dec. 31, longer hours in Apr. and May, $5 adults, $3 children 6–12, no pets) is most famous for its countless azaleas, but this 100-year-old formal garden park has many remarkable features, including an oak tree believed to be nearly 500 years old, and the Minnie Evans Sculpture Garden and Bottle Chapel. Evans, a visionary African American artist whose mystical work is among the most prized of all "outsider art," was the gatekeeper here for 25 of her 95 years. Golf cart tours are available with 48 hours notice for visitors who are not mobile enough to walk the gardens. On second Saturdays, New Hanover County residents can get in free.

HALYBURTON PARK

A more natural landscape for hiking and biking is Halyburton Park (4099 S. 17th St., 910/341-7855, www.halyburtonpark.com, park open dawn–dusk daily, nature center 9 A.M.–5 P.M. Mon.–Sat.). The 58 acres of parkland, encircled by a 1.3-mile wheelchair-accessible trail and crisscrossed by interior trails, gives a beautiful glimpse of the environment of sandhills, Carolina bays (elliptical, often boggy depressions), and longleaf pine and oak forest that used to comprise so much of the natural landscape of this area.

ANOLES OF CAROLINA

During your visit to the Wilmington area, you'll almost certainly see anoles. These are the tiny green lizards that skitter up and down trees and along railings – impossibly fast, beady-eyed little emerald beasts. Sometimes called "chameleons" by the locals, anoles can change color to camouflage themselves against their backgrounds. They also like to puff out their crescent-shaped dewlaps, the little scarlet pouches under their chins, when they're courting, fighting, or otherwise advertising their importance.

Explorer John Lawson was quite taken with them, as he describes in his 1709 *A New Voyage to Carolina.*

> Green lizards are very harmless and beautiful, having a little Bladder under their Throat, which they fill with Wind, and evacuate the same at Pleasure. They are of a most glorious Green, and very tame. They resort to the Walls of Houses in the Summer Season, and stand gazing on a Man, without any Concern or Fear. There are several other Colours of these Lizards, but none so beautiful as the green ones are.

NEW HANOVER COUNTY ARBORETUM

The New Hanover County Arboretum (6206 Oleander Dr., 910/452-6393), also a popular walking spot, is a Cooperative Extension horticulture laboratory that showcases native plants and horticultural techniques in a varied five-acre garden setting.

ENTERTAINMENT AND EVENTS
Performing Arts

Thalian Hall (310 Chestnut St., 800/523-2820, www.thalianhall.com) was built in the mid-1850s and today is the last standing theater designed by the prominent architect John Montague Trimble. At the time of Thalian Hall's opening, fully one-tenth of the population of Wilmington could fit into the Thalian opera house, and the combination of the grand facility and Wilmington's longstanding love of the arts made this an important stop for many artists and productions touring the country in those days. It is still a major arts venue in the region, hosting performances of classical, jazz, bluegrass, and all sorts of other music, as well as ballet, children's theater, and more. Its resident theater company is the **Thalian Association** (910/251-1788, www.thalian .org), which traces its roots back to 1788 and has been named the official community theater company of North Carolina.

Also making its home at Thalian Hall is **Big Dawg Productions** (http://bigdawgproductions.com). They put on a variety of plays and musicals throughout the year, of all genres, and host the wonderful **New Play Festival**, a festival of first-time productions of work by authors under the age of 18. In the more than a dozen years of this festival, many works have premiered here that have gone on to much wider audiences and acclaim. Another Thalian company for nearly 25 years, the **Opera House Theatre Company** (910/762-4234, www .operahousetheatrecompany.net) has produced one varied season after another of big-name musicals and dramas, as well as the work of North Carolinian and Southern playwrights. Rounding out the companies who perform at Thalian Hall is **Stageworks Youth Theater,** a community company of 10- to 17-year-old actors. Their productions "are not 'kiddie theater,'" as they write, "but substantial dramas, comedies, and musicals."

Festivals

Wilmington's best-known annual event is the **Azalea Festival** (910/794-4650, www.nc azaleafestival.com), which takes place in early April at venues throughout the city. It centers around the home and garden tours of Wilmington's most beautiful—and, at this time of year, azalea-festooned—historic sites. There is a dizzying slate of events, including a parade, circus, gospel concerts, shag and step competitions, even boxing matches. And like any self-respecting Southern town, it crowns royalty—in this case, the North Carolina Azalea Festival Queen, as well as its Princess, and the Queen's court, and a slate of cadets to escort all the Queen's ladies in waiting, and a phalanx of over 100 Azalea Belles. The Azalea Festival draws over 300,000 visitors, so book your accommodations well in advance; and if you're traveling through the area in early April but aren't coming to the festival, be forewarned, this will be one crowded town.

For all that Wilmington has become such a magnet for Hollywood, there's also a passion here for independent films. November's **Cucalorus Film Festival** (910/343-5995, www.cucalorus.org) has, over the course of a dozen years, become an important festival that draws viewers and filmmakers from around the world. Roughly 100 films are screened during each year's festival, which takes place at Thalian Hall and at the small Jengo's Playhouse (815 Princess St.) where the Cucalorus Foundation gives regular screenings throughout the year.

North of Wilmington, towards Topsail, the town of Hampstead has held its annual **North Carolina Spot Festival** (www.ncspotfestival.com) for nearly 50 years. The spot is a small fish that's a traditional favorite food on this coast, and in the fourth weekend of September hundreds of people gather here to deep-fry and gobble them up. There are bands and a pageant, but the fun centers around eating. It's a great little down-home festival.

Nightlife

The **Soap Box Laundro-Lounge** (255 N. Front St., 910/251-8500, www.soapboxlaundrolounge.com) has 11 washing machines, four dryers, and a good, long folding table. So what's it doing in the "Nightlife" section? It's also an important indie music venue (great bands, all kinds of music), a bar, a pool hall, and the setting of Monday-night Heavy Metal Bingo. ("No perfume scent down here, just the smell of PBR and ink.")

Bottega Art and Wines (208 N. Front St.,

910/763-3737, www.bottegagallery.com) is an innovative, energetic gallery/venue/art space/ wine bar. It's a gallery of contemporary art, to a large extent but not exclusively abstract, with frequently changing exhibitions. It's a serious wine bar, with a list a mile long of mainly American, Italian, and organic wines and beers, and a selection of nice hors d'oeuvres. It's also a venue for a rich slate of music performances and poetry readings, and hosts arts gatherings like writers' forums and art discussion groups. At the time of this writing, Bottega has announced that they're planning a spelling bee. It's bound to be unique and well worth checking out.

Breaktime Billiards/Ten Pin Alley (127 S. College Rd., 910/452-5455, www.breaktimetenpin.com, billiards and bowling 11 A.M.–2 A.M. daily, lounge 6 P.M.–2 A.M. Mon.–Fri., 11 A.M.–2 A.M. Sat. and Sun.) is a 30,000-square-foot entertainment palace. It consists of Breaktime Billiards, with 24 billiard tables and one regulation-size snooker table; Ten Pin Alley, with 24 bowling lanes and skee-ball; and in between them, the Lucky Strike Lounge, a full bar and snack shop with all manner of video games, and which hosts soft-tip dart and foosball tournaments. Put in an order for a meal and a beer or cocktail, and the staff will bring it to you if you're in the middle of a game.

Front Street Brewery (9 N. Front St., 910/251-1935, www.thefrontstreetbrewery .com, 11:30 A.M.–midnight Mon.–Wed., 11:30 A.M.–2 A.M. Thurs.–Sat., 11:30 A.M.– 10 P.M. Sun., late-night menu starts at 10:30 P.M.) serves lunch and dinner, but what is most special is their menu of beers brewed on-site. They serve their own pilsner, IPA, and lager, Scottish and Belgian ales, and their specialty River City Raspberry Wheat ale. The space has an attractive dark-paneled saloon decor, and plenty of seating areas to choose from, depending on whether you're looking for a sit-down meal or simply to gab over beer with friends.

SHOPPING
Shopping Centers

The buildings of **The Cotton Exchange** (Front and Grace Sts., 910/343-9896, www.shopcottonexchange.com) have housed all manner of businesses in over a century and a half of continuous occupation: a flour and hominy mill, a Chinese laundry, a peanut cleaning operation (really), a "mariner's saloon" (we'll say no more about that), and, of course, a cotton exchange. Today they're home to dozens of boutiques and restaurants, and lovely little specialty shops selling kites, beads, and spices.

Antiques and Consignment Stores

An especially intriguing shop is **J. Robert Warren Antiques** (110 Orange St., 910/762-6077, www.jrobertwarrenantiques.com), which occupies an 1810 townhouse downtown. Warren specializes in fine and rare antiques from North Carolina, like furniture from the early masters, the work of colonial silversmiths, prints and paintings of early Carolinians and Carolina scenes, nautical hardware from old ships, and much more.

The **Ivy Cottage** (3020/3030/3100 Market St., 910/815-0150, www.twocottages.com, 10 A.M.–6 P.M. Mon.–Sat., 1–5 P.M. Sun., hours vary in the winter) is generally described as a "consignment store," but that title doesn't begin to do justice to the strange, overwhelmingly varied nature of this wonderful store. Its four buildings and two gardens are overflowing, from folk pottery and antique ephemera to $40,000 antique diamond bracelets. Their website takes a stab at summing it all up: "classic furniture and home accessories, antiques, china, crystal, silver, fine jewelry, oriental carpets, art work and yard and garden items"—but really to understand, you'll have to see for yourself. Allow yourself plenty of time.

Books and Comics

Wilmington has quite a few nice bookstores, both retail and used. **McAllister & Solomon** (4402-1 Wrightsville Ave., 910/350-0189, www.mcallisterandsolomon.com) stocks over 20,000 used and rare books, a great treat for collectors to explore. **Two Sisters Bookery** (318 Nutt St., Cotton Exchange, 910/762-4444, www.twosisters.booksense.com, 10 A.M.–6 P.M. Mon.–Sat., noon–6 P.M. Sun.) is a nice little independent bookseller at the Cotton Exchange, with an inventory covering all genres and subject matters, and a calendar full of readings by favorite authors. Also excellent is **Pomegranate Books** (4418 Park Ave., 910/452-1107, www.pombooks.net, 10 A.M.–6 P.M. Mon.–Sat.), which has a progressive bent and a wide selection of good reads.

Fanboy Comics (3901-A Wrightsville Ave., 910/452-7828, www.fanboycomics.biz, 11 A.M.–9 P.M. Mon.–Wed., 11 A.M.–11 P.M. Thurs.–Sat., noon–9 P.M. Sun.) specializes in buying and selling Silver and Bronze Age superhero comics, a period beginning in the 1950s, and ending, at least in terms of Fanboy's stock, around 1977. The Silver and Bronze Ages have many defining characteristics, among which are graphic and technical innovations, the gradual transformation of two-dimensional superheroes into more fully developed characters with human problems and cares, and the introduction of science fiction and, eventually, '70s noir storylines. Fanboy carries an amazing stock, and they also host frequent gaming events and tournaments.

Galleries and Art Studios

An unusual retail art gallery is found between Wilmington and Wrightsville, the 23,000-square-foot **Racine Center for the Arts** (203 Racine Dr., 910/452-2073, www.racinecenter.com). In addition to the sales gallery, it has art space for classes in pottery, stained glass, and other crafts, and operates the Firebird Paint Your Pottery and Art Studio. Visitors can show up at the Firebird without reservations, and go right to work on their own pottery and mosaics with the help of staff.

Music

Finkelstein Music (6 South Front St., 910/762-5662) is a family business that has been at this site, a great old commercial building on a busy downtown corner, for over 100 years. It began as a dry good store, but gradually evolved into today's music store, which carries a great selection of guitars, electric basses, and percussion.

Gravity Records (125-1 S. Kerr Ave., 910/392-2414, www.gravity-records.com) is a record store with a wide selection of all sorts of music. They sell CDs and DVDs, but the focus is on LP records. They've got a huge stock of vinyl, and they also sell and service turntables. Another good choice is **Yellow Dog Discs** (341-12 S. College Rd., 910/792-0082, www.myspace.com/yellowdogdiscs), a buy/sell/trade store for CDs, DVDs, LPs, games, and posters. Their motto is "Skip free, guaranteed."

For Dogs

Coastal K-9 Bakery (5905 #9 Carolina Beach Rd., 866/794-4014, www.coastalk9bakery.com, 10 A.M.–6 P.M. Mon.–Sat., 1–5 P.M. Sun.) sells fresh-baked gourmet dog treats, including various organic and hypoallergenic goodies, Carolina barbecue biscuits, liver brownies, and even vegetarian bacon bits.

SPORTS AND RECREATION
Surfing

Wrightsville Beach is a very popular destination for East Coast surfers and is home to several surfing schools. **Surf Camp** (530 Causeway Dr., 866/844-7873, www.wbsurfcamp.com) is probably the area's largest surfing instruction provider. They teach a staggering number of multi-day camps; one-day courses; kids-only, teenagers-only, women-only, and whole-family offerings; and classes in safety as well as technique. **Wrightsville Beach Supply Company** (1 N. Lumina Ave., 910/256-8821, www.wbsupplyco.com) has a retail store, and offers surf classes in the summertime (8–10 A.M. daily, $45 including board rental) and private lessons ($60) arranged according to the customer's schedule. **Crystal South Surf Camp** (Public access #39 on the beach, 910/395-4431, www.crystalsouthsurfcamp.com) is a family-run operation that gives group and individual five-day instruction for all ages.

Other Water Sports

Salt Marsh Kayaks (Shop 222 Old Causeway Dr., rental facility 275 Waynick Blvd., 866/655-2925, http://saltmarshkayakcompany.com), rents kayaks (sit-insides and sit-on-tops, singles and tandems) and sailboats, gives classes in sailing and kayaking, and guides tours through some of the area's most interesting waterscapes. **II Dolphins Sailing School** (222 Old Causeway Dr., 910/619-1646, www.iidolphins.com), which operates out of the Salt Marsh Kayaks storefront, teaches courses from Keelboat Sailing 101 to more advanced classes in navigation. They also run evening ocean cruises ($50 individuals, $95 couples, $45 children under 13) departing from the Blockade Runner docks.

Aquatic Safaris (6800-1A Wrightsville Ave., 910/392-4386, www.aquaticsafaris.com, in-season 9 A.M.–6 P.M. Mon.–Thurs., 9 A.M.–7 P.M. Fri., 6:30 A.M.–6 P.M. Sat., 6:30 A.M.–5 P.M. Sun., out of season 10 A.M.–6 P.M. Mon.–Fri., 10 A.M.–5 P.M. Sat., noon–4 P.M. Sun.) runs charter diving trips to shipwrecks (some sunken for artificial reefs, some scuttled during WWII when U-boats were a frequent sight here) and other underwater environments. They also teach dive classes and rent equipment.

ACCOMMODATIONS

Wilmington overflows with historic bed-and-breakfasts. The ◖ **Wilmingtonian** (101 S. Second St., 910/343-1800, www.thewilmingtonian.com, $87–325/night) is a complex of five buildings, four of which are renovated historic structures, from the 1841 de Rosset House to a 1950s convent. The de Rosset House is an utterly fabulous Italianate mansion, one of the most recognizable buildings in Wilmington. For $325 ($250 out of season), you can stay in the Cupola Suite, a spectacular aerie with a panoramic view of the port. The **Rose Hill Inn** (114 S. Third St., 800/815-0250, www.rosehill.com, $90–200) occupies a pretty 1848 residence three blocks from the river. The flowery high-B&B-style decor suits the house well, making for elegant but comfy quarters. The **Taylor House** (14 N. Seventh St., 800/382-9982, www.taylor housebb.com, $125–140) is an absolutely lovely 1905 home—rather subdued in design when compared to some of the architectural manifestos nearby, but in a very attractive way. The pretty, sunny rooms promise relaxation. The famous **[** **Graystone Inn** (100 S. Third St., 888/763-4773, www.graystone inn.com, $159–379) was built in the same year as the Taylor House, but its builder, the widow Elizabeth Bridgers, had a very different aesthetic. The splendor of the palace first known as the Bridger House reflects the fortune of Mrs. Bridgers' late husband, a former Confederate congressman and one of the most influential figures in Wilmington's days as a railroad center.

These are by no means the only excellent bed-and-breakfast inns in Wilmington; the city is full of them. Check in with the **Cape Fear Convention and Visitors Bureau** (www.cape fear.nc.us) for a comprehensive listing. For those who prefer the privacy of a non-B&B setting, there are many chain motels, as well as small, family-run establishments, ranging from the most basic to luxurious accommodations.

FOOD
Continental
Le Catalan French Café (224 S. Water St., 910/815-0200, www.lecatalan.com, from 11:30 A.M. for lunch and dinner Tues.–Sat., and Sun. in the summer), couldn't have a nicer location, on the Riverwalk in the old downtown. They serve wonderful classic French food—quiches and *feuilletés*, beef bourguignonne on winter Fridays, and a chocolate mousse for which they are famous. Their greatest draw, though, is the wine list (and attached wine store). The proprietor, Pierre Penegre, is a Cordon Bleu–certified oenologist, and is frequently on hand to make recommendations.

Seafood
Wrightsville Beach's **Bridge Tender** (1414 Airlie Rd., Wilmington, 910/256-4519, www.the bridgetender.com, lunch 11:30 A.M.–2 P.M. daily, dinner from 5 P.M. daily, bar open all day, $20–35) has been in business for over 30 years and is an icon of the local restaurant scene. The atmosphere is simple and elegant, with a dockside view. Entrées focus on seafood and angus beef, with an extensive à la carte menu from which you can create delicious combinations of your favorite seafood and the Bridge Tender's special sauces. A sushi menu rounds out the appetizers, and a long wine list complements everything.

When you see a restaurant set in a really beautiful location, you dearly hope the food is as good as the view. Such is the case at Wrightsville's **Oceanic** (703 S. Lumina, Wrightsville Beach, 910/256-5551, www .oceanicrestaurant.com). The Wilmington *Star-News* has repeatedly voted it the Best Seafood Restaurant in Wilmington, and it receives similar word-of-mouth accolades right and left. It occupies a big old house right on the beach, with a wraparound porch and a pier. For an extra-special experience, ask for a table on the pier.

The relatively new **Wrightsville Grille** (6766 Wrightsville Ave., Suite J at Galleria Shopping Center, Wrightsville Beach, 910/509-9839) is roundly praised for its crab cakes ($20 for two), known for being super-hefty and having a high crab-to-breading ratio. The menu has a lot of casual café favorites, burgers and sandwiches, as well as extensive seafood and meat selections, and a daily "Chocoholic Special."

Southern and Barbecue
In business since 1984, **[** **Jackson's Big Oak Barbecue,** (920 S. Kerr Ave., 910/799-1581, all dishes under $8) is an old favorite. Their motto is, "We ain't fancy, but we sure are good." Good old vinegary, Eastern North Carolina–style pork barbeque is the main item, though you can pick from Brunswick stew, fried chicken, and a mess of country vegetables. You'll get hush puppies and cornsticks at the table, but it will be worth your while not to fill up too fast—the cobblers and banana pudding are great.

Another star of Southern cooking is **Casey's Buffet Barbecue and Home Cookin'** (5559 Oleander Dr., 910/798-2913, lunch Tues.–Sat., dinner Wed.–Sun.). Here you can feast on barbecue and Brunswick stew, fried chicken and catfish, okra and collard greens. Adventurous Yankees might want to venture into the Southern culinary backwoods and try chitterlings (pronounced "chitlins," of course) and chicken gizzards. The folks at the next table are enjoying them, so why not you?

Eclectic American
Keith Rhodes, a Wilmington native and chef of **Deluxe** (114 Market St., 910/251-0333, www.deluxenc.com, $16–35) beat out 69 other top chefs to win first place in the Goodness Grows championship, a statewide title. The menu at Deluxe features stunning high-gourmet creations that pay homage to down-home Southern cooking, including confit of bobwhite quail on apple corn-cake and a bed of braised collards, buttermilk-fried crispy calamari, and white soy-molasses grilled lamb chops. Deluxe deserves additional gold stars for two special features: excellent vegetarian selections and menu descriptions that identify locally caught and grown ingredients.

Flaming Amy's Burrito Barn (4002 Oleander Dr., 910/799-2919, www.flaming amysburritobarn.com, 11 A.M.–10 P.M. daily) is, in their own words, "Hot, fast, cheap, and easy." They've got a long menu with 20 specialty burritos (Greek, Philly steak, Thai), eight fresh salsas, and bottled and on-tap beers. It's very inexpensive—you can eat well for under $10, drinks included. Frequent special promotions include Tattoo Tuesdays; if you show the cashier your tattoo (come on, we all know you've got one), you can take 10 percent off your meal.

Latin American
There are certain elements that every good Cuban restaurant must possess, and if any one of them isn't just right, you should question the whole menu. It must have good, authentic Cuban coffee, Cuban bread (sort of like French bread, but ineffably different), *maduros* (fried sweet plantains), and flan. Even though none of these is a main dish, every good Cuban cook worth his or her salt knows the secrets to these all-important details. **El Guajiro** (1015-A S. Kerr Ave., 910/397-9253, 10 A.M.–7:30 P.M. Mon.–Sat., $5–10) gets them all right. You won't go wrong with the *ropa vieja* and classic Cuban sandwiches, but anything you order from Guajiro's menu is bound to be good.

El Sombrero Azul (127 S. College Rd., 910/791-4250) serves down-home Salvadoran food, a savory cuisine that shares a lot of elements with Mexican food, but with many subtle and delicious differences. They make their own tortillas at Sombrero Azul, which demonstrates their commitment to authenticity and flavor. Onion-festooned pork chops, tamales, and *pastelitos* are all great choices. The restaurant used to be called Cocina de Carmen, and you might still hear it recommended by that name.

Asian
◖ **Double Happiness** (4403 Wrightsville Ave., 910/313-1088, lunch and dinner) is a very popular Chinese and Malaysian restaurant, known for serving traditional dishes that are a refreshing departure from the standard canon of American Chinese restaurants. The setting is original too, without, as one local food critic wrote, "a buffet or glamour food photos over a hospital-white take-out counter." You can choose between regular booths and traditional floor seating. If you're lucky, you might be present when the chef decides to send around rice balls, a sweet dessert snack, for everyone on the house.

NORTH OF WILMINGTON
Topsail Island
In the manner of an old salt, Topsail is pronounced "Tops'l." The three towns on Topsail Island—Topsail Beach, North Topsail Beach, and Surf City—are popular beach communities; they're less commercial than some of their counterparts elsewhere along the coast, but still destinations for throngs of visitors in the summer months. A swing bridge gives access to the

island at Surf City (the bridge opens around the beginning of each hour, so expect backups) and a high bridge between Sneads Ferry and North Topsail.

Among Topsail's claims to fame is its importance in the conservation of sea turtle populations. The **Karen Beasley Sea Turtle Rescue and Rehabilitation Center** (822 Carolina Ave., Topsail Beach, www.seaturtlehospital .org, visiting hours 2–4 P.M. Mon., Tues., and Thurs.–Sat. in June, July, and Aug.) treats sea turtles that have been injured by sharks or boats, or are ill or stranded. Its 24 enormous tubs, which look something like the vats at a beer brewery, provide safe places for the animals to recover from their injuries and recoup their strength before being released back into the ocean. Guardian angels from the hospital also patrol the full shoreline of Topsail Island every morning in the summertime, before the crowds arrive, to identify and protect any new clutches of eggs that were laid overnight. Founder Jean Beasley has been featured as a Hero of the Year on the Animal Planet channel. Unlike most wildlife rehabilitation centers, this hospital allows the public to tour the facilities (during limited summer hours) and catch a glimpse of the patients.

Also at Topsail Beach is the **Missiles and More Museum** (720 Channel Ave., 910/328-8663, www.topsailmissilesmuseum .org). This little museum commemorates a rather peculiar chapter in the island's history: when it was used by the U.S. government for a project called Operation Bumblebee. During Operation Bumblebee, Topsail was a proving ground for missiles, and the work done here led to major advancements in missile technology and the development of a precursor of the ram jet engine used later in supersonic jet design. Exhibits include real warheads left over from the tests, and even one that washed up on the beach 50 years after being fired out to sea. Especially interesting to lovers of projectiles will be the 1940s color film of missile firings here at Topsail.

Jacksonville

Jacksonville is best known as the home of

Camp Lejeune, a massive Marine installation that dates to 1941. Lejeune is the home base of the II Marine Expeditionary Force, and of MARSOC, the Marine Corps division of U.S. Special Operations Command. The nearly 250 square miles that comprise the base include extensive beaches, where servicemen and women receive training in amphibious assault skills.

Construction has begun for the Museum of the Marine (www.mcmuseum.com), a major commemorative museum that will explore the history of this branch of the military, with particular focus on the contributions of Marines from and trained in North Carolina.

Camp Johnson, a satellite installation of Camp Lejeune, used to be known as Montford Point, and was the home of the famous African American Montford Point Marines. Their history, a crucial chapter in the integration of the United States Armed Forces, is paid tribute to at the **Montford Point Marine Museum** (Building 101, East Wing, Camp Gilbert Johnson, 910/450-1340, www.montfordpoint marines.com, 11 A.M.–2 P.M. and 4–7 P.M., Tues. and Thurs., and 11 A.M.–4 P.M. Sat.).

🄲 Hammocks Beach State Park

At the very appealing little fishing town of Swansboro you'll find the mainland side of Hammocks Beach State Park (1572 Hammocks Beach Rd., 910/326-4881, http://ncparks.gov/ Visit/parks/habe, 8 A.M.–6 P.M. daily Sept.– May, 8 A.M.–7 P.M. daily June–Aug.). Most of the park lies on the other side of a maze of marshes, on Bear and Huggins Islands. These wild, totally undeveloped beaches are important havens for migratory waterfowl and nesting loggerhead sea turtles. Camping is permitted on Bear Island, in reserved and first-come sites, with restrooms and showers available nearby. A private boat or **passenger ferry** (910/326-4881, $5 adults, $3 seniors and children) are the only ways to reach the islands. The ferry's schedule varies by days of the week and season: Wed.–Sat. May and Sept. and Fri.– Sat. Apr. and Oct., departs from the mainland every half-hour 9:30 A.M.–4:30 P.M., departs from the island every hour 10 A.M.–5 P.M.;

Mon.–Tues. Memorial Day–Labor Day departs from the mainland every hour 9:30 A.M.–5:30 P.M., departs from the island every hour 10 A.M.–6 P.M.; Wed.–Sun. Memorial Day–Labor Day departs from the mainland every half-hour 9:30 A.M.–5:30 P.M., departs from the island every half-hour 10 A.M.–6 P.M.

The Southern Coast

From the beaches of Brunswick and New Hanover County to the swampy, subtropical fringes of land behind the dunes, this little corner of the state is incredibly special—and is one of the most beautiful parts of North Carolina.

There are a string of beaches here, starting with Carolina Beach and Kure, just south of Wilmington, and descending through the "Brunswick Islands," as they are designated in tourist literature. Most of these beaches are low-key, quiet family beaches, largely lined with residential and rental properties. They're crowded in the summertime, of course, but are still much more laid-back than Myrtle Beach, over the state line to the south, and even Wrightsville and some of the "Crystal Coast" beaches.

You'll see some distinctive wildlife here, too. The first you'll notice, more likely than not, is the ubiquitous green anole (called "chameleons" by many locals). These tiny lizards, normally a bright lime green, but able to fade to brown when invisibility is called for, are everywhere—skittering up porch columns and along balcony railings, peering at you around corners, hiding between the fronds of palmetto trees. The males put on a big show by puffing out their strawberry-colored dewlaps. Generations of Lowcountry children have spent thousands of frustrated hours trying to catch them, usually with next to no success. If you catch them from the front, they'll bite (albeit rather harmlessly), and if you catch them from behind, they'll be only too happy to cede to you their writhing tails, while the rest of them keeps running. But from a respectful distance, they're amusing companions all along one's outdoor sojourns in this region.

This is also the part of the state where the greatest populations of alligators live. Unlike anoles, who threaten but can't back it up, alligators are nonchalant creatures who rarely appear better than comatose, but they are genuinely deadly if crossed. All along river and creek banks, bays, and swamps, you'll see their scaly hulks basking motionless in the sun. While canoeing or kayaking, you might only be able to see the little arcs of their eyes and nostrils poking out from underwater, and maybe the scaly ridges of their backs and tails. They may just as easily be totally submerged, floating underwater and thinking sinister thoughts. Be careful where you step, and avoid wading or swimming in fresh water. Above all, keep small children and pets well clear of anywhere a gator might lurk. That said, alligators are some of the most thrillingly strange animals to be found anywhere in the United States, and the herp-fancier, against better judgment, is bound to find them brutishly lovable.

In certain, highly specialized environments—mainly in and around Carolina bays that offer both moistness and nutrient-poor soil—the Venus flytrap and other carnivorous plants thrive. To the average fly, these are more threatening than an alligator any day. The flytrap and some of its cousins are endangered, but in this region—and nowhere else in the world—you'll have plenty of opportunities to see them growing and gorging.

KURE BEACH

Kure is a two-syllable name: pronounced "Kyur-ee," (as in Madame, but not "curry"). This is a small beach community, not an extravaganza of neon lights and shark-doored towel shops. Most of the buildings on the island are houses, both rental houses for vacationers and the homes of Kure Beach's year-round residents. The beach itself, like all North Carolina ocean beaches, is public.

Carolina Beach State Park

Just to the north of Kure is Carolina Beach State Park (1010 State Park Rd. off of 421, Carolina Beach, 910/458-8206, www.ncparks .gov/Visit/parks/cabe/main.php). Of all the state parks in the coastal region, this may be the one with the greatest ecological diversity. Within its boundaries are coastal pine and oak forests, pocosins between the dunes, saltwater marshes, a 50-foot sand dune, and limesink ponds; of the limesink ponds, one is a deep cypress swamp, one is a natural garden of water lilies, and one an ephemeral pond that dries into a swampy field every year, an ideal home for the many carnivorous plants that live here. You'll see Venus flytraps and their ferocious cousins here, but please resist the urge to dig or pick them, or to tempt them with your fingertips. Sort of like stinging insects that die after delivering their payload, the flytraps' traps can wither and fall off once they're sprung.

The park has 83 drive-to/walk-in campsites, each with a grill and picnic table. Two are wheelchair-accessible. Restrooms and hot showers are nearby. Camping is $15 per night, $10 per night for campers over the age of 62.

Fort Fisher State Historic Site

At the southern end of Kure Beach is Fort Fisher State Historic Site (1000 Loggerhead Rd. off of U.S. 421, 910-458-5798, www.ncparks.gov/Visit/parks/fofi/main.php, 8 A.M.–9 P.M. June–Aug., 8 A.M.–8 P.M. Mar.–May and Sept.–Oct., 8 A.M.–6 P.M. Nov.–Feb.). Fort Fisher was a Civil War earthwork stronghold designed to withstand massive assault. Modeled in part upon the Crimean War's Tower of Malakhoff, Fort Fisher's construction was an epic saga in itself, as hundreds of Confederate soldiers, African American slaves, and conscripted Lumbee Indiands were brought in to build what became the Confederacy's largest fort. After the fall of Norfolk in 1862, Wilmington

© JIMMY MCDONALD

Carolina Beach

became the most important open port in the South, a vital harbor for blockade-runners and military vessels. Fisher held until nearly the end of the War. On Christmas Eve of 1864, U.S. General Benjamin "The Beast" Butler attacked the fort with 1,000 men, but was repulsed—a retreat that led to his being relieved of his command. A few of weeks later, in January 1865, Fort Fisher was finally taken, but it required a Yankee force of 9,000 men and 56 ships in what was to be the largest amphibious assault until World War II. Without its defenses at Fort Fisher, Wilmington soon fell, hastening the end of the war, which came only three months later. Thanks to the final assault by the Union forces, and a century and a half of subsequent winds, tides, and hurricanes, not a great deal of the massive earthworks survives. But the remains of this vitally important Civil War site are preserved in an oddly peaceful and pretty seaside park, which contains a restored gun emplacement and a visitors center with interpretive exhibits.

Also at Fort Fisher is a branch of the **North Carolina Aquarium** (910/458-8257, 9 A.M.–5 P.M. daily year-round, until 9 P.M. Thurs. in summer, $8 adults, $7 seniors, $6 under 17). Like its sisters at Roanoke and Pine Knoll Shores, this is a beautiful aquarium that specializes in the native marine life of the North Carolina waters. It's also a center for marine biology and conservation efforts, assisting in the rescue and rehabilitation of sea turtles, marine mammals, freshwater reptiles, and other creatures of the coast.

Accommodations

The beaches of the Carolinas used to be lined with boarding houses, the old-time choice in lodging for generations of middle-class tourists. They were sort of a precursor to today's bed-and-breakfasts, cozy family homes where visitors dined together with the hosts and were treated not so much like customers as houseguests—which is just what they were. Hurricane Hazel razed countless guesthouses when it pummeled the coast in 1954, ushering in the next epoch, that of the family motel. The

Beacon House (715 Carolina Beach Ave. N., 877/232-2666, www.beaconhouseinnb-b.com, breakfast not included, some pets permitted in cottages with an extra fee) at Carolina Beach, just north of Kure, is a rare survival from that era. The early-1950s boarding house has the typical upstairs and downstairs porches, and dark wood paneling indoors. (Nearby cottages are also rented by the Beacon House.) The price is much higher than it was in those days (now $150 and up in the high season, much less in the off-season), but you'll be treated to a lodging experience from a long-gone era.

BALD HEAD ISLAND

Bald Head Island, an exclusive community where golf carts are the only traffic, is a two-mile, 20-minute ferry ride from Southport. More than eighty percent of the island is designated as a nature preserve, and at the southern tip stands "Old Baldy," the oldest lighthouse in North Carolina.

Sights

The **Bald Head Island Lighthouse** (910/457-7481, www.oldbaldy.org, 10 A.M.–4 P.M. Tues.–Sat., 11 A.M.–4 P.M. Sun., call for winter hours, $3 to climb) was built in 1818, replacing an even earlier tower that was completed in 1795. Despite being the newcomer at Bald Head, the 109-foot lighthouse is the oldest such structure surviving in North Carolina. A visit to the lighthouse includes a stop next door at the **Smith Island Museum** housed in the lighthouse keeper's home. The development of Smith Island (of which Bald Head is the terminus) allowed almost 17,000 acres to be set aside as an ecological preserve. The Old Baldy Foundation leads **historic tours** (910/457-5003, 10:30 A.M. Tues.–Sat., $40, $30 guests of island establishments) of Bald Head, departing from Island Ferry Landing, a short walk from the lighthouse.

Food

A popular eatery on Bald Head is **Eb and Flo's Steam Bar** (910/457-7217, closed Wed. and in the winter, $10–20). It's on the waterfront, with the lighthouse behind it and a dining room/deck view over Long Bay to Fort Caswell. The seafood steamer pot is the specialty, and there is also a selection of burgers and sandwiches.

SOUTHPORT

Without a doubt one of North Carolina's prettiest towns, Southport is an 18th-century river town whose port was overtaken by Wilmington in importance—and hence it has remained small and quiet. It was the Brunswick County seat until the late 1970s, when that job was outsourced to Bolivia. (Bolivia, North Carolina, that is.) There have been plans in the works for the construction of an enormous international port here, and should that ever come to pass, this peaceful riverbank will be irrevocably changed. Given Southport's history—which has included several eras when the town seemed just on the brink of large-scale growth and importance in the world of international trade—it may be that the North Carolina International Port will go the way of Southport's other pipe dreams. In the meantime, it's a wonderfully charming place, with block upon block of beautiful historic houses and public buildings. The old cemetery is a gorgeous spot, and in it you'll find many tombstones that bear witness to the town's seafaring history—epitaphs for sea captains who died while visiting Smithville (Southport's original name), and stones carved with pictures of ships on rolling waves.

Sights

The **North Carolina Maritime Museum at Southport** (116 N. Howe St., 910/457-0003, 9 A.M.–5 P.M. Mon.–Fri., 10 A.M.–5 P.M. Sat., and 1–5 P.M. Sun., $2 adults, $1 over 62, free under 16) is a smaller, storefront branch of the Maritime Museum at Beaufort, where you can learn about the seafaring history of the Carolina coast. Among the many topics of interest here is the life of pirate Stede Bonnet, whose girly surname belies his infamous life of crime. Bonnet, who spent much time in the Southport area, was by turns the pillaging buddy and bitter rival of Blackbeard. Other cool displays in the museum include a section

© SARAH BRYAN

an old jail in Southport

© SARAH BRYAN

Southport's old cemetery provides a glimpse into the past.

of a 2,000-year-old, 54-inch Indian canoe, and an 8-foot jawbone of a whale.

Events

Southport hosts the state's best-known **Fourth of July celebration** (910/457-6964, www.nc4thofjuly.com), attended each year by up to 50,000 people. (That's approximately 20 times the normal population of the town.) In addition to the requisite fireworks, food, and music, the festival features a special tribute to veterans, a flag retirement ceremony (that is, folks bring their old and worn-out flags), and a naturalization ceremony for new Americans.

Shopping

There are two irresistible pet boutiques in Southport, where you can pick up treats for your canine traveling companion or presents to bring back to your pets at home. **Zeetlegoo's Pet and People Store** (1635 N. Howe St., 910/457-5663, www.zeetlegoo.com, 10 A.M.–6 P.M. Mon.–Fri., 10 A.M.–4 P.M. Sat.) sells toys and treats for cats, dogs, and exotics,

as well as leashes, cat furniture, and health products. Timber, a golden retriever mix, and Sammy, a cream-colored cat, are the resident product testers. **Cool Dogs & Crazy Cats** (310 N. Howe St., 910/457-0115, www.cooldogscrazycats.com) has a selection of fresh-baked biscuit delicacies, organic catnip, supplies and toys for cats and dogs, and jewelry and other items for their human customers.

Accommodations

Lois Jane's Riverview Inn (106 W. Bay St., 800/457-1152, www.loisjanes.com, $93–143 depending on season) is a Victorian waterfront home built by the innkeeper's grandfather. The rooms are comfortably furnished, bright and not frou-frou, and the Queen Deluxe Street, a cottage behind the inn, has its own kitchen and separate entrance. The front porch of the inn gives a wonderful view of the harbor. At the same location is the **Riverside Motel** (106 W. Bay St., 910/457-6986, www.riverside-motelinc.com, $65–75), which also has a front porch with a fantastic panorama of the shipping channel. Another affordable option is the **Inn at River Oaks** (512 N. Howe St., 910/457-1100, www.theinnatriveroaks.com, $65–135), a motel-style inn with very simple suites.

The **Inn at South Harbour Village** (South Harbour Village, 800/454-0815, www.southharbourvillageinn.com, $120–370, two-night minimum in high season) is a waterfront hotel in a development between Southport and Oak Island. The nine condo-style luxury suites have efficiency kitchens and dining rooms, inviting extended stays. The property overlooks the Intracoastal Waterway and South Harbour marina.

At Oak Island, west of Southport, **Captain's Cove Motel** (6401 E. Oak Island Dr., Oak Island, 910/278-6026, www.realpages.com/captainscove, avg. $65) is a long-established family motel one block from the beach. The **Island Resort and Inn** (500 Ocean Dr., Oak Island, 910/278-5644, www.islandresortandinn.com, $75–190 depending on season) is a beachfront property with standard motel rooms and one- and two-bedroom apartment suites.

© KEITH M. MORGAN

Yacht Basin Provision Company

The **Ocean Crest Motel** (1417 East Beach Dr., Oak Island, 910/278-3333, www.ocean-crest-motel.com, $65–155 depending on season) is a large condo-style motel, also right on the beach.

Food

The **❰ Yacht Basin Provision Company** (130 Yacht Basin St., 910/457-0654, $10–20) is a popular Southport seafood joint with a super-casual atmosphere. Customers place their orders at the counter and serve themselves drinks (on an honor system), then seat themselves dockside to await the arrival of their chow. Most popular here are the conch fritters and grouper salad sandwich, but anything you order will be good.

OCEAN ISLE

Ocean Isle is the next-to-most-southerly beach in North Carolina, separated from South Carolina only by Bird Island and the town of Calabash. In October, Ocean Isle is the site of the **North Carolina Oyster Festival** (www.brunswickcountychamber.org/OF-nc-oyster-festival.cfm), a huge event that's been happening for nearly 30 years. In addition to an oyster stew cook-off, surfing competition, and entertainment, this event features the North Carolina Oyster Shucking Competition. Oyster shucking is not so picayune a skill as it might sound. In the not-that-long-ago days when North Carolina's seafood industry was ascendant, workers—most often African American women—lined up on either side of long work tables in countless oyster houses along the coast and the creeks, and opened and cut out thousands of oysters a day. A complex occupational culture was at work in those rooms, one that had its own vocabulary, stories, and songs. The speed at which these women worked was a source of collective and individual pride, and the fastest shuckers enjoyed quite a bit of prestige among their colleagues. High-speed shucking is a skill that's well remembered by many Carolinians who might now be working at Wal-Mart, rather than in the old dockside shacks and warehouses. The state shucking championship is the time when some of the best shuckers prove that although

North Carolina may have changed around them, they haven't missed a beat.

SOUTH ALONG U.S. 17

U.S. 17 is an old colonial road—in fact, its original name, still used in some stretches, is the King's Highway. George Washington passed this way on his 1791 Southern tour, staying with the prominent planters of this area and leaving in his wake the proverbial legends about where he lay his head of an evening. Today, the King's Highway, following roughly its original course, is still the main thoroughfare through Brunswick County into South Carolina.

◖ Orton Plantation

Gardens adorn the relentlessly beautiful grounds of an early 18th-century rice plantation (9149 Orton Rd. SE, Winnabow, 910/371-6851, www.ortongardens.com, 8 A.M.–6 P.M. spring and summer, 10 A.M.–5 P.M. fall and winter, closed Dec.–Feb., $9 adults, $8 seniors, $3 children). The centerpiece of the estate is the 1735 house, with circa-1840 additions; it's a quintessential white-columned antebellum palace, and a dead-ringer for *Gone with the Wind*'s Twelve Oaks. (The house is still a home, and is not open to the public.) A tragic history underlies the plantation's beauty, beginning with the extermination of the local native tribe that tried to repulse white encroachment by destroying the first house on this site. The Lowcountry rice plantation was one of the most complex, labor-intensive kinds of antebellum industry, and Orton, no exception, was home to a large slave community. Yankees occupied it during the Civil War and used the house as a hospital. This was a blessing in disguise, as it probably saved the house from being burned, the fate of many of the other great plantations along and near the King's Highway.

It was in the early 20th century that the formal gardens came into being, the project of Mrs. Luola Sprunt. Many of the massive live oaks, which look like they've been here for centuries, were actually planted in this era. Orton is perhaps the state's most famous azalea

garden, an amazing spectacle of color in the gentle Lowcountry springtime. Swamps and river marshes sidle up to the gardens, and are home to many species of water birds, and—mind where you walk along the water's edge—a population of fat and happy alligators.

Brunswick Town and Fort Anderson

Nearby to Orton is the Brunswick Town/Fort Anderson State Historic Site (8884 St. Philip's Rd. SE, Winnabow, 910/371-6613, www.ah.dcr.state.nc.us/sections/hs/brunswic/brunswic.htm, 10 A.M.–4 P.M. Tues.–Sat.), the site of what was a bustling little port town in the early and mid-1700s. In its brief life, Brunswick saw quite a bit of action. It was attacked in 1748 by a Spanish ship, which, to residents' delight, blew up in the river. (One of that ship's cannons was dragged out of the river about 20 years ago and is on display here.) In 1765, the town's refusal to observe royal tax stamps was a successful precursor to the Boston Tea Party eight years later. But by the end of the Revolutionary War, Brunswick Town was solid gone, burned by the British but having been made obsolete anyway by the growth of Wilmington. Today nothing remains of the colonial port except for the lovely ruins of the 1754 St. Philip's Anglican Church and some building foundations uncovered by archaeologists. During the Civil War, Fort Anderson was built upon this site, sand earthworks that were part of the crucial defenses of the Cape Fear, protecting the blockade-runners who came and went from Wilmington. Some of the walls of that fort also survive. A visitors center at the historic site tells the story of this surprisingly significant stretch of riverbank, and the grounds, with the town's foundations exposed and interpreted, are an intriguing vestige of a forgotten community.

Nature Preserves

The Nature Conservancy's **Green Swamp Preserve** (NC 211, 5.5 miles north of Supply, Nature Conservancy regional office 910/395-5000, www.nature.org/wherewework/

© SARAH BRYAN

fiddler crab – actual size about 2.5 inches – on the marsh at Calabash

northamerica/states/northcarolina/preserves/art5606.html) contains nearly 16,000 acres of some of North Carolina's most precious coastal ecosystems, the longleaf pine savanna and evergreen shrub pocosin. Hiking is allowed in the preserve, but the paths are primitive. It's important to stay on the trails and not explore in the wilds because this is an intensely fragile ecosystem. In this preserve are communities of rare carnivorous plants, including the monstrous little pink-mawed Venus flytrap, four kinds of pitcher plant, and sticky-fingered sundew. It's also a habitat for the rare red-cockaded woodpecker, which is partial to diseased, old-growth longleaf pines as a place to call home.

The Nature Conservancy maintains another nature preserve nearby, the **Boiling Spring Lakes Preserve** (off of NC 87, Boiling Spring Lakes, trail begins at Community Center, Nature Conservancy regional office 910/395-5000, www.nature.org/wherewework/northamerica/states/northcarolina/preserves/art12787.html). Brunswick County contains the state's greatest concentration of rare plant species, and the most diverse plant communities anywhere on the East Coast north of Florida. This preserve is owned by the Plant Conservation Program, and includes over half the acreage of the town of Boiling Spring Lakes. The ecosystem here is made up of Carolina bays, pocosins, and longleaf pine forests. Like the Green Swamp Preserve, many of the species here are dependent on periodic fires in order to propagate and survive. The Nature Conservancy does controlled burning at both sites to maintain this rare habitat.

Calabash and Vicinity

The once tiny fishing village of Calabash, just above the South Carolina line, was founded in the early 18th century as Pea Landing, a shipping point for the bounteous local peanut crop. Calabashes, a kind of gourd, were used as dippers in the town supply of drinking water, and when the settlement was renamed in 1873, it was supposedly for that reason that it became Calabash. In the early 1940s, a style of restaurant seafood was developed here that involves deep-frying lightly battered fish and shellfish.

© SARAH BRYAN

Calabash marshes

As the style caught on and more restaurants were built here, the term "Calabash-style seafood" was born. Jimmy Durante was fond of dining in Calabash, and some will claim that it was in tribute to food here that he signed off on his shows saying, "Good night, Mrs. Calabash, wherever you are." Though Calabash seafood is advertised at restaurants all over the country now, this little town has more than enough restaurants of its own to handle the yearly onslaught of tourists in search of an authentic Calabash meal.

Indigo Farms (1542 Hickman Rd. NW, Calabash, 910/287-6794, 8 A.M.–5 P.M. Mon.–Sat., longer in the warm months), three miles above the South Carolina line in Calabash, is a superb farm market, selling all manner of produce, preserves, and baked goods. They also have corn mazes and farm activities in the fall, and are a training site for porcine contestants in the prestigious local NASPIG races.

Sunset Beach, the southernmost of the Brunswick County beaches, is a wonderfully small-time place, a cozy town that until 2008 could only be reached via a one-lane pontoon bridge. One of the area's most popular restaurants is located just on the inland side of the bridge to Sunset Beach. **Twin Lakes Seafood Restaurant** (102 Sunset Blvd., 910/579-6373, http://twinlakesseafood.com) was built almost 40 years ago by Clarice and Ronnie Holden, both natives of the area. Clarice was born into a cooking family, the daughter of one of the founders of the Calabash restaurant tradition. Twin Lakes serves fresh, locally caught seafood, a rarity in this time and place. In-season and on weekends, expect long lines.

In the nearby town of Shallotte (pronounced "Shuh-LOTE"), **Holden Brothers Farm Market** (5600 Ocean Hwy. W., 910/579-4500) is a popular source for local produce. The peaches in season are wonderful, and the variety of homemade canned goods and pickles are worth the trip.

Points Inland from Wilmington

Moving inland from the Wilmington area, you will pass first through a lush world of wetlands distinguished by the peculiar Carolina bays. Not necessarily bodies of water, as the name would suggest, the bays are actually ovoid depressions in the earth, of unknown and much-debated origin. They are often water-filled, but by definition are fed by rainwater rather than creeks or groundwater. They create unique environments, and are often surrounded by bay laurels (hence the name), and guarded by a variety of carnivorous plants.

The next zone, bounded by the Waccamaw and Lumber Rivers, is largely made up of farmland and small towns. This was for generations prime tobacco country, and that heritage is still very much evident in towns like Whiteville, where old tobacco warehouses line the railroad tracks. Culturally, this area—mostly in Columbus County, extending a little ways into Robeson to the west and Brunswick to the east—is of a piece with the three counties in South Carolina with which it shares a border—Horry, Marion, and Dillon. Many of the same family names are still to be found on either side of the state line.

The area around the Lumber River, especially in Robeson County, is the home of the Lumbee, native peoples with an amazing heritage of devotion to faith and family, and steadfast resistance to oppression. If you turn on the radio while driving through this area, you'll likely find Lumbee gospel programming, and get a sense of the cadences of Lumbee English. The characteristics that make it different from the speech of local whites and African Americans are very subtle, but certain hallmarks of pronunciation and grammar (which include the sub-variations of different families and towns within the community) distinguish the tribe's speech as one of the state's most distinctive dialects.

At the edge of the region covered in this chapter is Fayetteville. From its early days as the center of Cape Fear Scottish settlement to its current role as one of the most important military communities in the United States, Fayetteville has always been one of the most significant of North Carolina's cities.

ALONG HIGHWAY 74

A little ways inland from Calabash, the countryside is threaded by the Waccamaw River, a gorgeous, dark channel full of cypress knees and dangerous reptiles. (The name is pronounced "WAW-cuh-MAW," with slightly more emphasis on the first syllable than the third.) It winds its way down from Lake Waccamaw through a swampy little portion of North Carolina, crossing Horry County, South Carolina (unofficial motto: "The H is silent"), before joining its fellow North Carolina natives, the Pee Dee and Lumber Rivers, to let out in Winyah Bay at the colonial port of Georgetown. Through the little toenail of North Carolina that the Waccamaw crosses, it parallels the much longer Lumber River, surrounding the very rural Columbus County and part of Robeson County in an environment of deep, subtropical wetlands.

Sights

Pembroke is the town around which much of the Lumbee community revolves, and at the center of life here is the University of North Carolina at Pembroke. Founded in 1887 as the Indian Normal School, UNCP's population is now only about one-quarter Native American, but it's still an important site in North Carolina's native history. The **Museum of the Native American Resource Center** (Old Main, UNCP, 910/521-6282, www.uncp .edu/nativemuseum, 8 A.M.–noon and 1–5 P.M. Mon.–Sat., free) is on campus, occupying Old Main, a 1923 building that's a source of pride for the Pembroke community. The Resource Center has a small but very good collection of old artifacts and contemporary art by members of Native American tribes across the country.

WILMINGTON AND CAPE FEAR

Laurinburg's **John Blue House** (13040 X-way Rd., 910/276-2495, www.johnblue cottonfestival.com) is a spectacle of Victorian design, a polygonal house built entirely of heart pine harvested from the surrounding property, and done up like a wedding cake with endless decorative devices. John Blue, the builder and original owner, was an inventor of machinery used in the processing of cotton. A pre–Civil War cotton gin stands on the property, and is used for educational demonstrations throughout the year. This is the site of the **John Blue Cotton Festival,** an October event that showcases not only the ingenuity of the home's famous resident, and the process of ginning cotton, but also lots of local and regional musicians and other artists.

◖ Strike at the Wind

For more than 30 years, the Lumbee tribe has put on a production of the play *Strike at the Wind* (North Carolina Indian Cultural Center, 638 Terry Sanford Rd., Pembroke, 910/521-0835, www.strikeatthewind.com, July 7–Aug. 26, Fri. and Sat., show begins at 8 P.M., play at 8:30 P.M., $12 adults, $6 ages 6–13 and over 61, $2 parking), which takes place in the outdoor Adolph Dial Amphitheater on the banks of the Lumber River. (Adolph Dial was one of the greatest scholars of Lumbee history.) The play, which tells the story of Henry Berry Lowry and his gang, is acted by members of the Lumbee tribe, as well as white and African American cast members, and while a few of the cast are professional actors, most are people from the surrounding area who are simply passionate about their history and want to be part of its most famous public portrait. The music for the play was composed by songwriter Willie French Lowery, himself an important artistic ambassador of the Lumbee tribe.

HENRY BERRY LOWRY

In some places, the Civil War didn't end the day Lee surrendered, but smoldered on in terrible local violence. One such place was the Lumbee community of Robeson County, in the days of the famous Lowry Band.

Then as now, Lowry (also spelled Lowrie) was a prominent name in the tribe. During the Civil War, Allen Lowry led a band of men who hid out in the swamps, eluding conscription into the backbreaking corps of semi-slave labor that was forced to build earthenworks to defend Wilmington. When the war ended, violence against the Lumbees continued, and the Lowry Band retaliated, attacking the plantations of their wartime pursuers. Allen Lowry and his oldest son were captured in 1865 and executed. Henry Berry Lowry, the youngest son, inherited the mantle of leadership.

For the next several years, long after the end of the Civil War, the Lowry Band was pursued relentlessly. Arrested and imprisoned, Lowry and his band escaped from prison in Lumberton and Wilmington. Between 1868 and 1872,

the state and federal governments tried everything – putting a bounty on Lowry's head, even sending in a federal artillery battalion. After an 11-month campaign of unsuccessful pursuit, the federal soldiers gave up. Soon afterwards, the Lowry Band emerged from the swamps, raided Lumberton, and made off with a large amount of money. This was the end of the road for the Lowry Band, though, and one by one its members were all killed in 1872 – except, perhaps, Henry Berry. It's unknown whether he died, went back into hiding, or left the area altogether. As befits a legend, he seems simply to have disappeared.

Henry Berry Lowry is a source of fierce pride to modern Lumbees, a symbol of the tribe's resistance and resilience. Every summer, members of the tribe perform in the long-running outdoor drama **Strike at the Wind,** which tells the story of the Lowry Band. Another vivid retelling of the story is the 2001 novel *Nowhere Else on Earth,* by Josephine Humphreys.

Entertainment and Events

Several of the state's big agricultural festivals are held in this area. If you're in the little town of Fair Bluff in late July, you might be lucky enough to witness the coronation of the newest Watermelon Queen. The **North Carolina Watermelon Festival** (910/212-0013, www.nc watermelonfestival.com) began as an annual competition between two friends, local farmers whose watermelons grew to over 100 pounds. The two-man competition expanded into this festival that celebrates watermelon-growing throughout the state, and in which a new court of watermelon royalty is crowned every year.

In Tabor City, there's a famous **Yam Festival** (www.discovercolumbuscounty.org) in October, during which the tiny town's population sometimes quadruples. Yam partisans crown their own royal court during this festival. Then when spring rolls back around, Chadbourn holds its annual **Strawberry Festival** (http://ncstrawberryfestival.com), at which the coronation of the Strawberry Queen takes place. If this seems a strange sort of royalty, bear in mind that across the South Carolina line, they have a Little Miss Hell Hole Swamp competition.

All of North Carolina, and in particular the Cape Fear region in the southeast, has a great deal of Scottish ancestry and heritage. In the small town of Red Springs in Robeson County, a small Presbyterian school, Flora Macdonald College, operated for many years. Though it's now been closed for a generation, its grounds and lovely gardens are listed in the National Register of Historic Places and are the setting of the annual **Flora Macdonald Highland Games** (200 South College St., Red Springs, 910/843-5000, www.capefearscots.com). Like its counterpart to the west at Grandfather Mountain, these Highland Games are a fun celebration of Celtic culture. The festival includes piping competitions, sheepdog competitions, food, dancing, and of course the traditional feats of highland athleticism like tossing the caber.

Sports and Recreation

Several beautiful state parks line the Waccamaw and Lumber Rivers. **Lake Waccamaw State Park** (1866 State Park Dr., Lake Waccamaw, 910/646-4748, http://ncparks.gov/Visit/parks/lawa/main.php) encompasses the 9,000-acre lake of that name. The lake is technically a Carolina bay, a mysterious geological feature of this region. Carolina bays are large, oval depressions in the ground, many of which are boggy and filled with water, but which are actually so-named because of the bay trees that typically grow in and around them. Lake Waccamaw has geological and hydrological characteristics that make it unique even within the odd enough category of Carolina bays. Because of its proximity to a large limestone deposit, the water is more neutral than its usually very acidic cousins, and so it supports a greater diversity of life. There are several aquatic creatures that live only here, with great names like the Waccamaw fatmucket and silverside (a mollusk and a fish, respectively). The park draws many boaters and paddlers, naturally, though the only available launches are outside the property. Primitive campsites are available in the park for $9/night.

Singletary Lake State Park (6707 Hwy. 53 E., Kelly, 910/669-2928, www.ncparks .gov/Visit/parks/sila/main.php), north of Lake Waccamaw in Kelly, centers around one of the largest of the Carolina bays, the 572-acre Singletary Lake, which lies within the Bladen Lakes State Forest. There is no individual camping here, though there are facilities for large groups—including the entrancingly named Camp Ipecac—which date from the Civilian Conservation Corps era. There is a nice one-mile hiking trail, the CCC-Carolina Bay Loop Trail, and a 500-foot pier extending over the bay. Some of the cypress trees here are estimated to have been saplings when the first Englishmen set foot on Roanoke Island.

Lumber River State Park (2819 Princess Ann Rd., Orrum, 910/628-4564, http://nc-parks.gov/Visit/parks/luri/main.php) has 115 miles of waterways, with numerous put-ins for canoes and kayaks. The river, referred to as the Lumber or Lumbee River, or, in areas farther upstream, as Drowning Creek, traverses both the coastal plain region and the eastern edge of the Sandhills. Camping is available here for $9 per night at unimproved walk-in and canoe-in sites.

Yogi Bear's Jellystone Park (626 Richard Wright Rd., 877/668-8586, www.taborcity jellystone.com), formerly known as Daddy Joe's, is a popular campground with RV and tent spaces, rental cabins, and yurts. The facilities are clean and well maintained, and there are tons of children's activities on-site. Some of the camping is in wooded areas, but for the most part expect direct sun and plan accordingly.

In Fair Bluff is **River Bend Outfitters** (1206 Main St., 910/649-5998, www.whiteville .nc/rbo), a canoe and kayak company that specializes in paddling and camping trips along the beautiful blackwater Lumber River.

Food

If you pass through Tabor City, don't neglect to have a meal at the **(C Todd House** (102 Live Oak St., 910/653-3778), which has been serving fine country cooking since 1923. The Todds are one of the oldest families in the area along the state line, and the first in the restaurant business was Mrs. Mary Todd, who took to cooking meals for visiting tobacco buyers. (This area lived and died by tobacco for generations.) Through her daughter's time, and a couple of subsequent owners, the Todd House has continued to serve famously good barbecue, fried chicken, and other down-home specialties. Their wonderful pies are available for purchase, so pick one up for the road.

FAYETTEVILLE

Fayetteville is North Carolina's sixth-largest city, and in its own quiet way has always been one of the state's most powerful engines of growth and change. In the early 1700s, it became a hub for settlement by Scottish immigrants, who helped build it into a major commercial center. From the 1818 initiation of steamboat travel between Fayetteville and Wilmington along the Cape Fear—initially a voyage of six days!—to the building of the Plank Road, a huge boon to intrastate commerce, Fayetteville was well

downtown Fayetteville

connected to commercial resources all through the Carolinas.

At a national level, Fayetteville serves as the location of two high-level military installations. Fort Bragg is the home of the XVIII Airborne Corps, the 82nd Airborne, the Delta Force, and the John F. Kennedy Special Warfare Center and School. As such, it's also the home of many widows and children of soldiers who have died in Iraq and Afghanistan. Pope Air Force Base is nearby, the home of the 43rd Airlift Wing, and its Maintenance, Support, and Operations Groups.

Sights

The **Fayetteville Museum of Art** (839 Stamper Rd., 910/485-5121, www.fayetteville museumart.org, 10 A.M.–5 P.M. Mon.–Fri., 1–5 P.M. Sat. and Sun., closed state holidays) is one of North Carolina's major galleries. Featuring art from a variety of media, and an expansive view of the nature of art, the museum provides a valuable resource for art education and inspiration in the region.

The **Museum of the Cape Fear Regional Complex** (801 Arsenal Ave., 910/486-1330, http://ncmuseumofhistory.org/osm/mcf.html, 10 A.M.–5 P.M. Tues.–Sat., 1 P.M.–5 P.M. Sun.) has three components, each telling different stories of Fayetteville's history. The museum itself has exhibits on the history and prehistory of the region, including its vital role in developing transportation in the state, as well as its centrality as a military center. There is an 1897 house museum, the Poe House, which belonged to a Mr. Edgar Allen Poe—not Edgar Allan the writer, but Edgar Allen, a brickyard owner. The third section is the 4.5-acre Arsenal Park, the site of a federal arms magazine built in 1836, claimed by the Confederacy in 1861, and destroyed by General Sherman in 1865.

The **Airborne and Special Operations Museum** (100 Bragg Blvd., 910/643-2766, www.asomf.org, 10 A.M.–5 P.M. Tues.–Sat., noon–5 P.M. Sun., closed Mon. except for federal holidays, free admission, $4 for theater and motion simulator) is an impressive facility that presents the history of Special Ops paratroopers, from the first jump in 1940 to the divisions' present-day roles abroad in peacekeeping missions and war. In the museum's theater you can watch an amazing film of what it looks like when a paratrooper makes the jump, and the 24-seat Pitch, Roll, and Yaw Vista-Dome Motion Simulator makes the experience even more exciting.

The **JFK Special Warfare Museum** (Building D-2502, Ardennes and Marion Sts., Fort Bragg, 910/432-4272, www.jfkwebstore.com/index.php, ID required to get onto the base) tells the story of further amazing facets of the U.S. military, including Special Ops and Psychological Ops. The museum focuses on the Vietnam War era, but chronicles unconventional warfare from colonial times to the present.

Going back a good bit further in time, the **Fayetteville Independent Light Infantry Armory and Museum** (210 Burgess St., 910/433-1612, open by appointment, free) displays artifacts from the history of the Light Infantry. The FILI is still active, dedicated as North Carolina's official historic military command, a ceremonial duty. But in its active-duty days, which began in 1793, FILI had some exciting times, particularly during the Civil War. In addition to the military artifacts, this museum also exhibits a carriage in which the Marquis de Lafayette was shown around Fayetteville—the only one of the towns bearing his name that he actually visited.

The 79-acre **Cape Fear Botanical Garden** (536 N. Eastern Blvd., 910/486-0221, www.capefearbg.org, 10 A.M.–5 P.M. Mon.–Sat., noon–5 P.M. Sun., closed Sun. mid-Dec.–Feb., $5 adults, $4 military and AAA, free under 12, everyone free first Sat. of every month and entire month of April) is one of the loveliest horticultural sites in North Carolina. The camellia and azalea gardens are spectacular sights in the early spring, but the variety of plantings and environments represented makes the whole park a delight. Along the banks of the Paw Paw River and Cross Creek, visitors will find dozens of garden environments, from lily gardens and hosta gardens, to woods and a bog, and an 1880s farmhouse garden. Without a doubt, this is the prettiest place in Fayetteville.

Cross Creek Cemetery (North Cool Spring and Grove Sts., 800/255-8217, dawn–dusk daily) is an attractively sad spot, the resting place of many Scots men and women who crossed the ocean to settle the Cape Fear. Though people of all kinds and times are buried here, it is the oldest section that is most poignant, where one stone after another commemorates Mr. or Mrs. Mac-So-and-So, Late of Glasgow or Perth, Merchant in this Town. One can feel the invisible ties of kith and kin that led these early immigrants to band together for comfort in the New World. (While strolling this cemetery, and especially when pausing to read a stone, beware of extraordinarily fast-moving fire ants.)

Entertainment and Events

The **Cameo Theatre** (225 Hay St., 910/486-6633, www.cameoarthouse.com) is a cool old early-20th-century movie house, originally known as the New Dixie. Today it is

WILMINGTON AND CAPE FEAR

"Fayetteville's alternative cinematic experience," a place for independent and art house movies.

The **Cape Fear Regional Theatre** (1209 Hay St., 910/323-4233, www.cfrt.org) began in 1962 as a tiny company with a bunch of borrowed equipment. Today it is a major regional theater with a wide reputation. Putting on several major productions each season, with a specialty of popular musicals, it draws actors and directors from around the country, but maintains its heart here in the Fayetteville arts community. The **Gilbert Theater** (116 Green St., entrance on Bow St., above Fascinate-U Museum, 910/678-7186, www.gilberttheater.com) is a small company that puts on a variety of productions throughout the year, with special emphasis on classic drama and multicultural offerings. Tickets are $10 and seating is on a first-come basis.

Fayetteville's late-April **Dogwood Festival** features rock, pop, and beach music bands; a dog show; a recycled art show; a "hogs and rags spring rally"; and the selection and coronation of Miss, Teen Miss, Young Miss, and Junior Miss Dogwood Festival.

Accommodations and Food

Fayetteville's lodging options are by and large chain motels, a multitude of which can be found at the Fayetteville exits off of I-95. You'll generally find a pretty reasonable deal at the old standards, but if you'd like to stay somewhere with more personality, Wilmington and Raleigh are both easily accessible.

Likewise, the city's dining choices tend towards the highway chains. There are some exceptions, though. The **(Hilltop House** (1240 Fort Bragg Rd., 910/484-6699, www.hilltophousenc.com, lunch 11 A.M.–2 P.M.

Mon.–Sat., supper 5 P.M.–9 P.M. Mon.–Thurs. and 5 P.M.–10 P.M. Fri. and Sat., Sun. brunch 10:30 A.M.–2:30 P.M., complimentary wine tasting every Tues. night, $15–25) serves hearty fare in an elegant setting, and was recognized in 2007 with a Wine Spectator Award for Excellence—not surprising, given that the Hilltop House has a 74-page wine list. More casual is the **Mash House** (4150 Sycamore Dairy Rd., 910/867-9223, www.themashhouse.com, $8–16), which has a good variety of pizzas and sandwiches, as well as heavier entrées and a selection of good homemade brews.

Information and Services

Cape Fear Valley Health Services (1638 Owen Dr., 910/609-4000, www.capefearvalley.com) is a large hospital complex with acute care services, a major cardiac care program, and everything else one would expect from an important regional hospital.

The website of the **Fayetteville Area Convention and Visitors Bureau** (www.visitfayettevillenc.com) is an excellent source of tourist information for this city. There you'll find not only the basics about what, where, and how much, but detailed driving tours, extensive historical information, and much more.

Getting There and Around

Fayetteville Regional Airport (400 Airport Rd., 910/433-1160, flyfay.ci.fayetteville.nc.us) has daily flights to and from Charlotte (US Airways Express) and Atlanta (ASA, Delta Connections). The city is served by **Amtrak** (472 Hay St., 800/872-7245, www.amtrak.com, 10 A.M.–5:45 P.M. and 10 P.M.–5:45 A.M. daily) via the Palmetto and Silver Service lines. It's also a short hop off of I-95.

RALEIGH AND THE TRIANGLE

The title "Triangle," long used to describe the Raleigh-Durham-Chapel Hill area, referred originally to the three major universities here, the University of North Carolina (Chapel Hill), Duke University (Durham), and North Carolina State University (Raleigh). It makes sense geographically to group these two cities and one big town together as one region; in a satellite image, the Triangle is an unbroken sprawl of humanity. But Raleigh, Durham, and Chapel Hill are very different places.

That said, there is a spirit that unites the communities of the Triangle. The concentration of colleges here—there are over a dozen institutions of higher learning, including several prominent historically black universities—make for a highly educated population. By some counts, there are more PhDs per capita in the Triangle than anywhere else in the United States.

The Triangle has a deeply liberal bent, to the consternation and puzzlement of much of the rest of this reddish state. Senator Jesse Helms famously remarked that there was no need to build a zoo in North Carolina, because putting a fence around Chapel Hill would serve the same purpose. The Chapel Hill area is the epicenter of progressive politics here, most intensely concentrated in the emphatically left-wing little town of Carrboro. In 2004, Carrboro officially celebrated Dennis Kucinich Day; granted, this was in part because this leftmost of leftist candidates was the first presidential contender ever to deliver a stump speech in Carrboro, but he was received by 900 adoring supporters and serenaded with peace chants

HIGHLIGHTS

◖ North Carolina Museum of Natural Sciences: Get breathtakingly close to massive whale and dinosaur skeletons and discover the many ecosystems of our state in this excellent nature museum (page 116).

◖ North Carolina Museum of History: North Carolina boasts centuries of remarkable history, literature, art, and sports, and there's no better place to explore it all than here at the Museum of History (page 116).

◖ North Carolina Museum of Art: The Museum of Art has amazingly varied collections, encompassing art from ancient Greece, Egypt, and the Americas, to Judaica, pop art, and 18th- and 19th-century American and European masters (page 117).

◖ Historic Stagville: One of the South's largest enslaved populations lived and worked on this plantation immediately prior to the Civil War, and the story of their community is preserved here (page 129).

◖ Full Frame Documentary Festival: This annual Durham shindig has become a festival of international importance, where new documentary work premieres and icons of the art form mingle with fans (page 131).

◖ Carolina Basketball Museum: Few sports fans would dispute that University of North Carolina's basketball program has one of the greatest, if not the greatest, collegiate

LOOK FOR ◖ TO FIND RECOMMENDED SIGHTS, ACTIVITIES, DINING, AND LODGING.

athletic traditions in American sports. On the UNC campus, this new museum celebrates the pride of Chapel Hill (page 139).

and protest songs. Carrboro was also North Carolina's first municipality to elect an openly gay mayor, and the first to extend the benefits of domestic partnership to gay couples.

The Triangle area ranks with New Orleans and Oxford, Mississippi, as one of the literary capitals of the South. UNC's Creative Writing Program has a lot to do with the concentration of fine writers here, but the whole region is full of talent, and has been home to writers from Thomas Wolfe to Charles Kuralt to David Sedaris. The music scene is just as rich,

with great symphonies and chamber groups, a century-old blues tradition, and probably more old-time string band musicians than anywhere outside the mountains. If you like alternative country, you'll find a live music scene that rivals those of Austin and Nashville.

PLANNING YOUR TIME

The ground covered in this chapter is best approached as three destinations, for the purpose of laying out a practical itinerary. Moving from east to west, Wilson and other

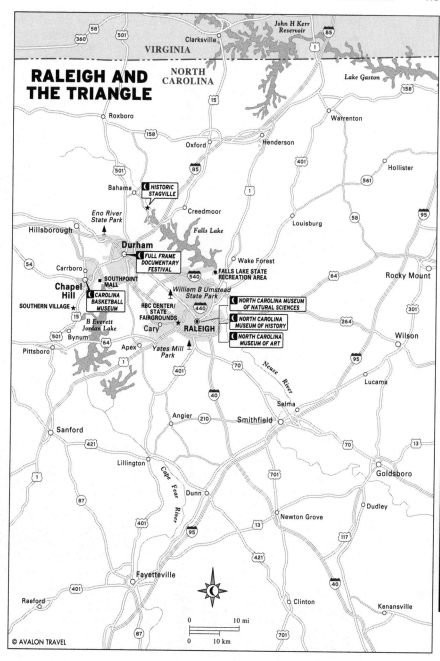

RALEIGH AND
THE TRIANGLE

towns east of I-95 are an easy drive from Raleigh—an hour, more or less, depending on traffic—but there's a fair amount of road to drive in between them, so this region merits at least a day of its own. Raleigh itself calls for another full day, as it is large and flows in all directions, with the suburbs like Zebulon, Cary, and Wake Forest all radiating from the 440 Beltline. Durham and Chapel Hill are only nine miles apart, so together they form home base for the third region of this chapter. Carrboro is so closely linked to Chapel Hill—it's actually difficult to tell exactly which block of Franklin/Main Street demarcates their respective city limits—that they're treated here as if they were one town. Hillsborough is an easy drive from both Chapel Hill and Durham, and Pittsboro is about 20 minutes south of Chapel Hill.

If you decide to choose one town in the Triangle to stay at night while exploring the whole area during the day, Durham is the most centrally located of the three. That said, though, Highways 40 and 70 link the whole Triangle area quite efficiently, and there are few points mentioned in this chapter that are more than half an hour's drive from any other given destination.

Raleigh and Vicinity

Loyal watchers of the *Andy Griffith Show* know that when trouble comes to Mayberry, it comes from one of two places: Up North or Raleigh. Although many of that show's observations about North Carolinians are right on target, this is one that, at the risk of committing heresy, I must dispel. Raleigh is no hive of citified depravity. As the home of our state government and several universities, Raleigh is a spark that helps power the cultural engine of the rest of the state.

North Carolina State University is here, as are two prominent historically black universities, Shaw and Saint Augustine's, and two small women's colleges, Peace and Meredith. The North Carolina Museum of History and the Natural Sciences Museum are excellent, as is the North Carolina Museum of Art. Like so much of North Carolina, there is a lot of good music (of all kinds) to be heard in Raleigh, and the city's New Year's Eve/First Night celebration, which takes place at venues throughout the downtown, is really special.

SIGHTS
◖ North Carolina Museum of Natural Sciences

The North Carolina Museum of Natural Sciences (Bicentennial Plaza, 11 W. Jones St., 877/462-8724, www.naturalsciences.org,

9 A.M.–5 P.M. Mon.–Sat., noon–5 P.M. Sun., 9 A.M.–9 P.M. first Fri. of every month, free) hosts national traveling exhibitions, and is home to excellent permanent exhibits. "Mountains to the Sea" is a re-creation of the regional environments of the state, populated with live and mounted animals and plants. Stars of "Prehistoric North Carolina" include the world's only publicly displayed skeleton of an *Acrocanthosaurus,* a 38-foot, 4.5-ton predatory dinosaur, and the remains of "Willo," a 66-million-year-old, small vegetarian dinosaur, whose fossilized heart is a miraculous boon to paleontology. The whales whose skeletons hang in the Coastal Carolina exhibit are celebrities, each with its own interesting story, including "Trouble," a sperm whale who washed up at Wrightsville Beach in 1928, and "Mayflower," a right whale killed in a legendary 1874 struggle with Carolina whalers off of Shackleford Banks. Visitors can also walk among hummingbirds and butterflies in the Living Conservatory, a top-floor tropical forest, and work among museum collections in the public Naturalist Center.

◖ North Carolina Museum of History

Across Bicentennial Plaza is the North Carolina Museum of History (5 E. Edenton

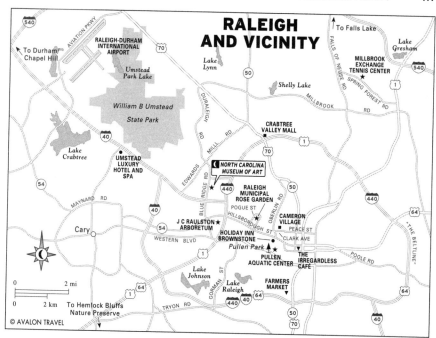

St., 919/807-7900, http://ncmuseumofhistory.org, 9 A.M.–5 P.M. Tues.–Sat., noon–5 P.M. Sun., free). Here visitors learn about the history of the state's exemplary military, from the Revolution to Iraq; about the musicians and genres that make this state one of the wellsprings of American music; about the handicrafts, from pottery to textiles to furniture, created by centuries of renowned artisans; and about medicine in North Carolina, from traditional African American root medicine and Indian herbs to the pharmaceuticals and technology that draw patients and researchers from around the world. You can also see a uniform worn by Harlem Globetrotter (and Wilmington native) Meadowlark Lemon and a stock car driven by Carolina legend Richard Petty. The Museum of History hosts concerts and many educational events throughout the year.

North Carolina Museum of Art

The North Carolina Museum of Art (2110 Blue Ridge Rd., 919/839-6262, http://ncartmuseum .org, 9 A.M.–5 P.M. Sat. and Tues.–Thurs., 9 A.M.–9 P.M. Fri., 10 A.M.–5 P.M. Sun., free) is just outside the Beltline. Its collections are of the highest quality, and include masterpieces of art from all eras and regions of the world, from ancient Egyptian, Greek, Roman, and pre-Columbian American art to the work of Botticelli, Giotto, and Raphael; Monet; Copley, Cole, Homer, Eakins, and Chase; Georgia O'Keefe and Thomas Hart Benton, and many, many more. The gallery is also home to one of the nation's two Jewish ceremonial art collections, and to collections of 19th- and 20th-century African art.

Historic Homes

The 1770s **Joel Lane Museum House** (corner of St. Mary's and W. Hargett Sts., 919/833-3431, 10 A.M.–2 P.M. Tues.–Fri., 1–4 P.M. Sat. Mar.–mid-Dec., $5 adult, $4 senior, $2 child six and over) is Wake County's oldest standing home. Costumed docents lead tours of the house and period gardens.

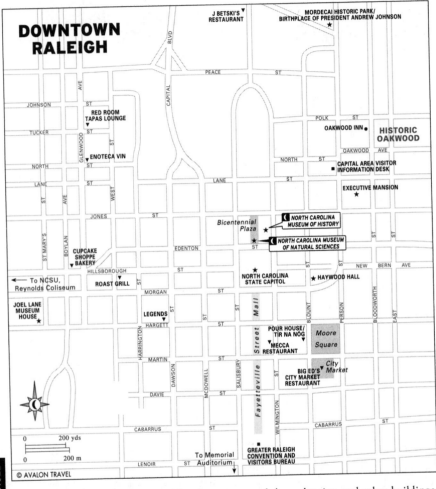

DOWNTOWN RALEIGH

J BETSKI'S RESTAURANT

MORDECAI HISTORIC PARK/
BIRTHPLACE OF PRESIDENT ANDREW JOHNSON

PEACE ST

CAPITAL BLVD

JOHNSON ST

RED ROOM
TAPAS LOUNGE

TUCKER ST

GLENWOOD ST

ENOTECA VIN

NORTH ST

LANE ST

WEST ST

AVE

ST MARY'S ST

BOYLAN ST

JONES ST

CUPCAKE
SHOPPE
BAKERY

HILLSBOROUGH ST

← To NCSU,
Reynolds Coliseum

ROAST GRILL

MORGAN ST

JOEL LANE
MUSEUM
HOUSE

LEGENDS

HARGETT ST

HARRINGTON ST

DAWSON ST

MARTIN ST

McDOWELL ST

DAVIE ST

CABARRUS ST

0   200 yds
0   200 m

© AVALON TRAVEL

LENOIR ST

POLK ST

OAKWOOD INN

HISTORIC
OAKWOOD

OAKWOOD AVE

NORTH ST

CAPITAL AREA VISITOR
INFORMATION DESK

LANE ST

EXECUTIVE MANSION

Bicentennial
Plaza

NORTH CAROLINA
MUSEUM OF HISTORY

NORTH CAROLINA MUSEUM
OF NATURAL SCIENCES

EDENTON ST

NEW BERN AVE

NORTH CAROLINA
STATE CAPITOL

HAYWOOD HALL

Fayetteville Street

Mall

SALISBURY ST

BLOUNT ST

PERSON ST

BLOODWORTH ST

EAST ST

POUR HOUSE/
TIR NA NÓG

MECCA
RESTAURANT

Moore
Square

BIG ED'S
CITY MARKET
RESTAURANT

City
Market

WILMINGTON ST

CABARRUS ST

To Memorial
Auditorium

GREATER RALEIGH
CONVENTION AND
VISITORS BUREAU

The 1799 **Haywood Hall** (211 New Bern Pl., 919/832-8357, 10:30 A.M.–1:30 P.M. Thurs. only, free) is another of Raleigh's oldest standing buildings. Built for the state's first elected treasurer and his family, the house and gardens are open to the public and feature a historic doll collection. A fee is charged for tours.

Mordecai Historic Park (corner of Mimosa St. and Wake Forest Rd., 919/857-4364, www.raleighnc.gov/mordecai, $5 adults, $3 seniors, $3 youth 7–17) includes a late 18th-/early 19th-century plantation house and restored dependencies, and other buildings, including the birthplace of President Andrew Johnson. The park grounds are open daily dawn–dusk, and the house is open for hourly tours 10 A.M.–4 P.M. Tuesday–Saturday and 1–4 P.M. on Sunday.

Still more historic homes can been seen in Raleigh's historic **Oakwood neighborhood,** which is listed on the National Register of Historic Places. This mostly late 19th-century neighborhood is bounded by Franklin, Watauga, Linden, Jones, and Person Streets, and self-guided walking/driving tour brochures can be picked up at the Capital Area Visitor Information center inside the Museum of History.

Other Sights

The **North Carolina State Capitol** (1 E. Edenton St., 866/724-8687, www.ncstatecapitol .com, 8 A.M.–5 P.M. Mon.–Fri., 10 A.M.–4 P.M. Sat., 1 A.M.–4 P.M. Sun., free) and the **Executive Mansion** (200 N. Blount St., 919/807-7950) built in the 1830s and 1890s, respectively, are lovely examples of Victorian architecture. The Greek Revival capitol building has been restored to its antebellum appearance. Be alert when you visit the library; this is where the capitol's many ghosts are most active. Guided tours last approximately 45 minutes. The Executive Mansion was described by FDR as possessing "the most beautiful governor's residence interior in America." Tours are available, but the hours vary by season and state functions—it is still the home of our governor,

and it wouldn't do if you were to walk in unannounced, and find the governor and cabinet dancing with lampshades on their heads. (Work goes on here too.)

The **J. C. Raulston Arboretum** (4415 Beryl Rd. across from Capitol City Lumber Company, 919/515-3132, www.ncsu.edu /jcraulstonarboretum, 8 A.M.–8 P.M. daily Apr.–Oct., 8 A.M.–5 P.M. Nov.–Mar., free) is a free public garden focused on the development of ornamental plants suitable to the Southern climate, where one can visit highly specialized areas devoted to white flowers, roses, and border plants. (The 300- by 18-foot perennial border may cause a serious case of yard envy.) The **Raleigh Municipal Rose Garden** (301 Pogue St. near NCSU) is home to over 1,000 roses of 60 varieties. Carolina roses are blessed with an extra-long growing season, and the Municipal Rose Garden also features bulbs and other ornamental plants, so a visit to the garden is special most any time of year. Another place for a scenic walk is **Historic Yates Mill County**

COURTESY OF ONCLE BERNARD ON FLICKR.COM

Yates Mill

Park (4620 Lake Wheeler Rd., 919/856-6675, 8 A.M.–sunset daily), a few miles south of downtown. The gristmill that presides over the mill race here is nearly two centuries old. Hiking trails surround the millpond.

ENTERTAINMENT AND EVENTS
Performing Arts

The **North Carolina Symphony** (919/733-2750, www.ncsymphony.org), a full-time, 65-member orchestra under the direction of conductors Grant Llewellyn and William Henry Curry, tours throughout the state and beyond. Its home venue in Raleigh is the wonderful Meymandi Concert Hall at **Progress Energy Center** (2 E. South St., 919/831-6060). The **North Carolina Opera** (919/792-3850, www.operanc.com) has its home stage at Memorial Auditorium, also in the Progress Energy Center. The Opera's rehearsals, held at a nearby church, are sometimes open to the public—see their website for details.

The **Time Warner Cable Music Pavilion at Walnut Creek** (3801 Rock Quarry Rd., 919/831-6400) is probably the top local music venue, attracting whomever is topping the pop and country charts at any given moment. Given the stature of the artists who play here, concerts can sell out very quickly. The **Lincoln Theatre** (126 E. Cabarrus St., 929/821-4111, www.lincolntheatre.com, doors open at 9 P.M., all ages admitted, $2 surcharge for guests under 18) is another important local performing arts institution, where major rock, blues, jazz, and other bands fill the schedule.

Nightlife

The best place to find out what's going on at Triangle-area clubs on any given night of the week is the *Independent Weekly,* a free newspaper that's available at restaurants and shops throughout the region. By state law, establishments that serve liquor and make no more than 30 percent of their revenue from food must be private-membership clubs, but every club has ways of getting first-time visitors through the doors. Some clubs must be joined a few days in advance, while others accept applications with nominal dues at the door. Raleigh's popular nightspots are dance clubs, lots of live music venues, and gay clubs with great drag events.

The **Pour House Music Hall** (224 S. Blount St., 919/821-1120, www.the-pourhouse.com) is a great venue, with alternative country, rock and roll, bluegrass, and all sorts of other bands on the schedule. Visitors must print the membership form from the website, fill it out, and bring it to the door with $1. For Irish ambiance, visit **Tír Na Nóg Irish Pub and Restaurant** (218 S. Blount St., 919/833-7795, www.tirnanogirishpub.com) and the **Hibernian Restaurant and Bar** (311 Glenwood Ave., 919/833-2258, www.hibernianpub.com).

Legends (330 W. Hargett St., 919/831-8888, www.legends-club.com, 9 P.M.–"until…" daily) is one of the most popular gay and lesbian clubs in the state, a fun bar that is also ground-zero for the area's pageant circuit. Call for membership details. Nearby, are other popular gay nightspots, **Capitol Corral** (313 Hargett St., 919/755-9599, www.cc-raleigh.com, ages 18 and over), open for more than 30 years and **Flex Club** (2 South West St., 929/832-8855, www.flex-club.com, Mon.–Sat. from 5 P.M., Sun. from 2 P.M., membership $15), which is primarily a men's bar.

For Latin dancing and delicious Spanish food, try the **Red Room Tapas Lounge** (510 Glenwood Ave. S., 919/835-1322, www.redroomraleigh.com, 5 P.M.–midnight Sun.–Wed., 5 P.M.–2 A.M. Thurs.–Sat.). **Berkeley Café** (217 W. Martin St., 919/821-0777, call for hours) serves both lunch and dinner, and stays open late with music by well-known rock-and-roll and alternative bands.

The **Players' Retreat** (105 Oberlin Rd., 919/755-9589, www.playersretreat.net) has been a favorite Raleigh bar since 1951. **Mitch's Tavern** (2426 Hillsborough St., 919/821-7771, 11 A.M.–2 A.M. Mon.–Sat., 5 P.M.–midnight Sun.) and **Sammy's Tap and Grill** (2235 Avent Ferry Rd., 919/755-3880, www.sammys

ncsu.com) are great places to watch ACC sports, if you can find a seat. Other choices for sports bars include **Skybox Grill and Bar** (3415 Wake Forest Rd., 919/872-2323, www.skyboxgrillandbar.com) and either Raleigh location of the **Carolina Ale House** (512 Creekside Dr., 919/835-2222; 4512 Falls of Neuse Rd., 919/431-0001).

Goodnight's Comedy Club (861 W. Morgan St., 919/828-5233, www.ticketbiscuit.com/goodnightscomedy) has a national reputation as a great place to see major and emerging stand-up comedians. **Comedy Worx** (431 Peace St., 919/829-0822, www.comedyworx.com) is a venue for competitive improv, in which the audience decides what the performers will do and who does it best.

Fairs and Festivals

The 10-day **North Carolina State Fair** (1025 Blue Ridge Rd., 919/821-7400, www.ncstatefair.org), held each October, is the nation's largest agricultural fair, with an annual attendance of about 800,000. Plan on going back several times to take it all in. It has everything one wants in an agricultural fair: livestock and produce competitions, (big-name) bluegrass concerts, carnival rides, fighter jet flyovers, and lots and lots of deep-fried food.

Raleigh ends the year right with the **First Night** (919/832-8699, www.firstnightraleigh.com) celebration. From dusk until midnight, when the Raleigh Acorn drops, the downtown stays open on New Year's Eve for a night of music—including many of the best home-grown jazz, rock-and-roll, traditional, country, and blues bands and performers—at a variety of wonderful venues. First Night also features art exhibits, dance competitions, magic shows, and the appearance of an "Animal of the Hour" at the Museum of Natural Sciences. The atmosphere is romantic and elegant for adults, but there is a great deal of fun for children as well. The downtown streets, still twinkly with Christmas lights, are closed off to allow for relaxed pedestrian traffic. The First Night Tram offers comfortable transportation between venues for those who prefer to ride.

SHOPPING

Cameron Village (Oberlin Rd. between Hillsborough St. and Wade Ave.) was one of the earliest shopping centers in the Southeast, a planned commercial neighborhood built on the grounds of the old Cameron plantation in the late 1940s. Their motto was, "Shop as you please, with the greatest of ease, in the wonderful Cameron Village!" The complex opened with three stores, but today there are dozens. It tends towards independent boutiques and high-end chains, and is a fun place to splurge. Some of the notable shops are **Tookie's Toys** (2028 Cameron St., 919/828-5574, 10 A.M.–7 P.M. Mon.–Fri., 10 A.M.–6 P.M. Sat., noon–5 P.M. Sun.); the **Seagrove Pottery** store (443-B Daniels St., 919/831-9696, 10 A.M.–6 P.M. Mon.–Fri., 1–5 P.M. Sun.) which sells, of course, pottery from Seagrove; **Uniquities** (450 Daniels St., 919/832-1234, 10 A.M.–7 P.M. Mon.–Sat., 1–6 P.M. Sun.), a great women's clothing boutique; and the **Junior League Bargain Box** (401 Woodburn Ave., 919/833-7587, 10 A.M.–6 P.M. Mon.–Sat.), a nice thrift shop.

The 1914 **City Market** (303/200 Blake St., www.citymarketraleigh.com) complex is another collection of nifty little shops and restaurants in a historic setting. **Crabtree Valley Mall** (Glenwood Ave./70 at 440) is the main conventional shopping mall in Raleigh.

SPORTS AND RECREATION
Spectator Sports

North Carolina State University is the southern terminus of Tobacco Road, the zone of legendary college sports traditions in the Atlantic Coast Conference. Though the UNC-Duke rivalry may score more media attention, **Wolfpack athletics** (www.gopack.com) is nothing to sniff at. Men's basketball games take place at the 20,000-seat **RBC Center** (1400 Edwards Mill Road, 919/861-2300, www.rbccenter.com) and football is next door at **Carter-Finley Stadium** (4600 Trinity Rd., 919/865-1510). Women's basketball and other Wolfpack sporting events take place at **Reynolds Coliseum** (2411 Dunn Ave.,

© WENDY MOODY

Raleigh Farmers Market

919/515-2100) and **Doak Field** (1081 Varsity Dr., 919/515-2100).

During hockey season, the RBC Center is home to the **Carolina Hurricanes** (http://hurricanes.nhl.com). North Carolina may seem an unlikely place for an NHL franchise, but the Canes proved themselves in the 2005–2006 season, beating the Edmonton Oilers to win the Stanley Cup. Tickets can be purchased in person at the Time Warner Cable Box Office inside the RBC Center (919/861-2323, no sales by phone) or through Ticketmaster (www.ticketmaster.com).

We North Carolinians love our "sports entertainment," and for those who don't fancy wrestling, there's roller derby. Women's roller derby is making a national comeback, and the cities of the Carolinas are blessed with some bruisers. Raleigh-based **Carolina Rollergirls** (www.carolinarollergirls.com) is a Women's Flat Track Derby Association league that currently consists of three teams: the Debutante Brawlers, the Tai Chi-tahs, and the Trauma Queens. Derbies take place at Dorton Arena on the State Fairgrounds (1025 Blue Ridge Blvd., 919/821-7400). Tickets are available from Schoolkids Records in Raleigh (2712-100 Hillsborough St., 919/821-7766, www.schoolkidsrecords.com, 10 A.M.–9 P.M. Mon.–Sat. and noon–7 P.M. Sun.) and other enlightened establishments.

Outdoor Recreation

William B. Umstead State Park (8801 Glenwood Ave., 919/571-4170, www.ils.unc.edu/parkproject/visit/wium/do.html), between Raleigh and Durham, offers 20 miles of hiking trails, boat rentals (availability varies by season), and mountain bike trails. The deep forests and creek banks feature flora normally found at higher elevations, including mountain laurel, and are frequented by a variety of wildlife. The Crabtree Creek entrance, where you'll find the visitors center, is 10 miles northwest of Raleigh off of U.S. 70.

If your canoe or kayak is already strapped onto your car and all you need is a place to put in, try the **Neuse River Canoe Trail.** Over a stretch of 17 miles of the Neuse, you can choose from five different launches, beginning at the Falls Lake Dam. Visit www.raleigh-nc/parks&rec for downloadable maps of the river.

Indoor Athletics

Millbrook Exchange Tennis Center (1905 Spring Forest Road, 919/872-4128) has 23 public hard-surface courts, a pro shop, and many other amenities. The **Pullen Aquatic Center** (410 Ashe Avenue, 919/831-6197) has an Olympic-size pool and extensive programs. Several area skating facilities are available for ice, roller, and in-line skating, including the **Raleigh IcePlex** (2601 Raleigh Blvd., 919/878-9002, www.iceplex.com).

ACCOMMODATIONS

Raleigh is still catching up to other North Carolina cities when it comes to small, non-chain hotels. There are dozens of chain motels around the city, concentrated near the airport and downtown, and at various exits off of I-40 and U.S. 70. But for individualized service, your best choice in Raleigh is a bed-and-breakfast.

Raleigh's best-known B&B is the **Oakwood Inn** (411 N. Bloodworth St., 919/832-9712, www.oakwoodinnbb.com, from $140). Housed in the 1871 Raynor-Stronach House, it's listed in the National Register of Historic Places and is one of only four of the original 11 houses remaining in the historic Oakwood neighborhood. If you're hoping to attend a theater production while in Raleigh, the Oakwood can set you up with a special package, subject to availability. Innkeepers Gary and Doris Jurkiewicz have won a slew of awards for the inn's excellence and their hospitality.

Cameron Park Inn (211 Groveland Ave., 919/835-2171 or 888/257-2171, www.cameronparkinn.com, from $139) is a 1916 home in the Cameron Park historic district, located in the North Carolina State/Cameron Village area. The wide porch and lush English garden are mellow retreats after a day in the city. Not far from Cameron Village is the 1920s bunga-low **Woodburn Cottage** (117 Woodburn Rd., 919/828-2276, www.woodburncottage.com, from $129), with two large rooms comfortably furnished in the arts-and-crafts style and with spa-like bathtubs.

If you don't need to stay inside the city limits and are craving some pampering, **Umstead Luxury Hotel and Spa** (100 Woodland Pond, Cary, 866/877-4141, www.theumstead.com, from $299) in Cary shouldn't be missed. This new in 2007 establishment is quickly earning a reputation as one of the most luxurious hotels in North Carolina. The Umstead's 14,000-square-foot spa has an incredible menu of services: 10 different specialized massages; many facial, manicure, and pedicure choices; milk, mineral, and aromatherapy baths; and a long list of body therapies and Asian body care rituals. There's also a three-acre lake on the property, a 24-hour fitness center, and an outdoor heated pool. Guests have tee privileges at the Prestonwood Country Club, about 10 minutes away.

Other than bed-and-breakfasts, there are few choices for lodging in Raleigh that aren't of the standard national chains. Plenty of motels ring and radiate from the Beltline, especially near Raleigh-Durham International Airport on I-40. Downtown choices tend to be more expensive than lodging in the outlying areas. The **Clarion State Capitol** (320 Hillsborough St., 919/832-0501, www.raleighclarion.com, from $85) gets mixed reviews, but the location is very convenient to all the downtown sights. The **Sheraton Raleigh** (421 S. Salisbury St., 919/834-9900, from $120) is also in the heart of the city, and the **Holiday Inn Brownstone** (1707 Hillsborough St., 919/828-0811, www.brownstonehotel.com, from $100) is convenient to both downtown and North Carolina State.

FOOD
Eclectic American

One of the most popular eateries in the Triangle since the 1970s, **The Irregardless Café** (901

W. Morgan St., 919/833-8898, www.irregardless .com, lunch 11:30 A.M.–2:30 P.M. Tues.– Fri., dinner 5:30–10:30 P.M. Tues.– Thurs., 5:30–10 P.M. Fri. and Sat., brunch 10 A.M.–2 P.M. Sun., $15–25) began as a strictly vegetarian café, and has since expanded to include omnivorous fare—in fact, most of the entrées are now seafood and chicken dishes, but it still serves some good vegetarian and even vegan chow. From the long list of desserts, try the pear and almond caramelized tart and the vegan chocolate mocha raspberry cake. The *New York Times* calls Irregardless "the place to eat when you're in Raleigh," and plenty of locals agree.

It's not unusual for a major museum to have a small café or snack bar tucked away between galleries. What is unusual is for a museum café to be a destination in itself— somewhere that diners will want to visit even if they don't plan to see the exhibits. The North Carolina Museum of Art's **◖ Blue Ridge: A Museum Restaurant** (North Carolina Museum of Art, 2110 Blue Ridge Rd., 919/664/6838, www.ncartmuseum.org/ restaurant.shtml, 11:30 A.M.–2 P.M. Tues.– Sat., 10:30 A.M.–2:30 P.M. Sun., $8–12) is such a case. Husband-and-wife team Andy (head chef) and Jennifer (pastry chef) Hicks have made Blue Ridge famous with such dishes as their pan-fried, pecan-crusted pork cutlets in a mustard-chardonnay reduction, and their "Hunt Scene Breakfast"—grilled wild boar sausage and Manchego grits, with wild mushroom, roasted tomato, and rosemary ragout.

Enoteca Vin (410 Glenwood Ave., Suite 350, 919/834-3070, www.enotecavin.com, 5:30–10:30 P.M. Tues.–Sat., 11 A.M.–2:30 P.M. Sun., $15–20), a "wine-focused restaurant serving eclectic new American food," wins awards and acclaim right and left. The menu focuses on fresh and local ingredients, and is designed to complement the carefully chosen international wine list.

Lilly's Pizza (1813 Glenwood Ave., 919/833-0226, www.lillyspizza.com, 11 A.M.–10 P.M. Sun.–Wed., 11 A.M.–11 P.M.

Thurs., 11 A.M.–midnight Fri.–Sat., under $10) is a locally owned, one-of-a-kind parlor that's been around for more than 15 years. They use lots of organic local ingredients, even in the homemade crusts. You can choose favorite ingredients for a custom pie, or have an equally tasty calzone, stromboli, or lasagna.

Bogart's American Grill (510 Glenwood Ave., 919/832-1122, www.bogartsamerican grill.com, $10–25) is a casual spot, and is a local favorite for burgers and sandwiches—as well as serious rotisserie and seafood choices.

Hayes Barton Café and Dessertery (2000 Fairiew Rd., 919/856-8551, http://hayesbarton-cafe.com, lunch 11:30 A.M.–2 P.M. Tues.–Sat., dinner 6–9 P.M. Wed.–Thurs. and 6–9:30 P.M. Fri.–Sat.) also serves up a good burger and plenty of other choices, but the real treat at this 1940s-themed restaurant is the long, long list of cakes and pies.

Asian

Waraji Japanese Restaurant (5910 Duraleigh Rd., 919/783-1883, www.warajires-taurant.com, lunch 11:30 A.M.–2 P.M. Mon.– Fri., dinner 5:30–9:30 P.M. Mon.–Thurs., 5:30–10:30 P.M. Fri. and Sat., $10–40) occupies a very spare storefront in a strip mall, a setting belying the uniqueness of this very serious sushi restaurant. Dozens of traditional and imaginative specialty rolls are served, along with tempura, udon, and various familiar Japanese entrées.

Sawasdee Thai Restaurant (3601 Capital Blvd., Suite 107, 919/878-0049, http://sawasdee restaurant.com, lunch 11:30 A.M.–2:30 P.M. Mon.–Fri., dinner 5–9 P.M. Sun.–Thurs., 5–10 P.M. Fri.–Sat., under $15) has a promising system for identifying the relative hotness of its food; it uses the scale of "spicy," "extra spicy," and "make you cry." Many a vegetarian has discovered sorrowfully that favorite Thai dishes have hidden animal products, such as oyster or fish sauce, but Sawasdee is happy to cater to vegetarian diets. Just ask your server if what you want to order can be made purely vegetarian, and he or she will be glad to advise.

European

J. Betski's Restaurant (10 W. Franklin St., Suite 120, 919/833-7999, www.jbetskis.com, 5:30–10 P.M. Mon.–Thurs., 5:30–10:30 P.M. Fri. and Sat., late-night menu 11 P.M.–1 A.M. Fri. and Sat., $17–20) gets high praise in these parts for traditional German and Polish cuisine, including great pierogis and kielbasa, rich strudel and gingerbread desserts, and a wide selection of German wines and beers.

518 West (518 W. Jones St., 919/829-0248, www.518west.com, 11:30 A.M.–9:30 P.M. Mon., 11:30 A.M.–10 P.M. Tues.–Thurs., 11:30 A.M.–10:30 P.M. Fri.–Sat., brunch 10:30 A.M.–2 P.M. and dinner 5–9 P.M. Sun.) serves fresh pasta, wood-fired pizza, and many standard and special Italian dishes (including vegetarian choices). Diners with picky children will be relieved to spot hot dogs and french fries on the kids' menu. Another great place for Italian is **Vivace** (4209 Lassiter Mill Rd., Suite 115, 919/787-7747, www.vivaceraleigh.com, 11 A.M.–10 P.M. Mon.–Thurs., 11 A.M.–11 P.M. Fri.–Sat., 11 A.M.–9 P.M. Sun., $10–30), which has a dining room as stylish as the food is delicious. The wine list is unbelievable.

Middle Eastern

More than 30 years ago, **Neomonde Baking Company** (3817 Beryl Rd., 919/828-1628, www.neomonde.com, 10 A.M.–9 P.M. Mon.–Sat., 10 A.M.–7 P.M. Sun., under $10) was founded in Raleigh by four brothers who had newly emigrated from Lebanon. The superior quality of the baked-on-site bread at Neomonde is due to the brothers' having grown up in a family that made its bread from scratch—starting not with flour, but with planting the wheat field. Many favorite and less familiar Middle Eastern snacks and sandwiches are on the menu at Neomonde.

Southern

Big Ed of **Big Ed's City Market Restaurant** (220 Wolfe St., 919/836-9909, 7 A.M.–2 P.M. Mon.–Fri., 7 A.M.–noon Sat., approx. $10 lunch, cash only) has made some remarkable claims about his food over the years—asserting that a Big Ed's breakfast will make a tadpole slap a whale, and that the biscuits alone will empower a poodle to pull a freight train. It's not certain that those exact hypotheses have been put to the test, but the crowds at Big Ed's for breakfast and lunch suggest that the claims might not be purely rhetorical. The joint specializes in pork products—bacon, country ham, barbecue—and in-season regional vegetables. If you visit for breakfast, you'll be able to order the classic Southern breakfast: ham, grits, and biscuits with red-eye gravy. Now you're in North Carolina.

Greek-American restaurateur families have had a strong influence on Southern cuisine for more than a century, often opening the first restaurants in small towns, and mastering the arts of frying chicken and boiling greens. Raleigh's **Mecca Restaurant** (13 E. Martin St., 919/832-5714, 7:30 A.M.–7 P.M.) was opened in 1930 by the Dombalis family, and has become such a local institution—particularly a favorite of state government officials and workers—that when it celebrated its 75th anniversary, the whole city celebrated Mecca Restaurant Day. At the Mecca's lunch counter, you can order up most any Southern classic you can think of, including eastern North Carolina barbecue and fried trout, as well as their popular hamburgers. There's also assorted Mediterranean fare.

Another such case is the Poniros family's **Roast Grill** (7 South West St., 919/832-8292, www.roastgrill.com, 11 A.M.–4 P.M. Mon.–Sat., under $5), which has been serving hot dogs since 1940. You can get a hot dog (blackened to your specifications), chili, a glass-of-bottle Coke or beer, pound cake, and/or baklava. That's it—unless the Christmas parade is going by outside, in which case you may also have hot chocolate or coffee. Whatever you do, don't ask for condiments! They admonish customers, "A WORD OF WARNING!!—WE DO NOT SERVE: French Fries, Potato Chips, Ketchup, Cheese, Kraut, Pickles, Relish, Mayonnaise!! We feel them to be terribly unnecessary and truly demeaning to the passions of a great hot dog connoisseur!" It may sound Spartan, but Raleigh diners have been coming back for almost 70 years.

Bakeries

Raleigh has its very own "cupcake boutique," the **Cupcake Shoppe Bakery** (104 Glenwood Ave., 919/821-4223, www.thecupcakeshop-peraleigh.com, 10 A.M.–8 P.M. Tues.–Thurs., 10 A.M.–11 P.M. Fri.–Sat., $2.25–$2.75/each, $28/mixed dozen). They bake fresh batches daily of at least a dozen flavors, from basic chocolate and vanilla cupcakes with chocolate and vanilla icing, to red velvet cupcakes with cream cheese icing, to dark chocolate cupcakes with espresso buttercream icing. An especially nice touch is that the shop is open late on weekends, allowing for quick satisfaction of cravings after dinner and a movie. Another lovely bakery in Raleigh is **Plaisirs de France** (5635 Creedmoor Rd., 919/788-0379), specializing in croissants, éclairs, and other French delicacies.

INFORMATION AND SERVICES

The main hospital in Raleigh is **WakeMed** (3000 New Bern Ave., 919/350-8900), though Rex Healthcare and Duke Health also operate hospitals here. If you have an emergency, call 911 and let the EMTs decide which one is closest. There is at least one 24-hour pharmacy, **CVS** (3914 Capital Blvd., 919/876-5600).

Travelers' information can be found at the **Greater Raleigh Convention and Visitors Bureau** (One Bank of America Plaza/421 Fayetteville St., 800/849-8499, www.visit raleigh.com), at the **Capital Area Visitor Information desk** in the lobby of the Museum of History (5 E. Edenton St., 866/724-8687), the **Greater Raleigh Chamber of Commerce** (800 S. Salisbury St., 919/664-7000, www.ra-leighchamber.org), and the state **Department of Tourism** (301 N. Wilmington St., First Floor, 800/847-4862, www.visitnc.com).

For international travelers, Raleigh-Durham International Airport contains **TRAVELEX outlets** in Terminals A and C (919/840-0366, 7 A.M.–8 P.M. daily Terminal A., 2:30–6 P.M. daily Terminal C).

GETTING THERE AND AROUND

I-40 and U.S. 70 are the main highways to and through town. The Raleigh Beltline, I-440, forms a loop around the city, with I-40, U.S. 70, and U.S. 64 radiating out in all directions. I-40 is the quickest route to Chapel Hill, to the west, and to I-95 in the east. I-40 and U.S. 70 are both good routes to Durham. U.S. 64 goes to Wilson, and on the other side of the city joins with U.S. 1 headed southeast towards Sanford and the Sandhills.

Raleigh-Durham International Airport (RDU) (www.rdu.com) is one of the main air hubs in North Carolina, and the primary airport in the Triangle. It's located 15 minutes from Raleigh, off of I-40, and is a point of transit for most major national airlines. The Raleigh **Amtrak** station (www.amtrak.com) is located at 320 West Cabarrus Street, and there's also a station at 211 North Academy Street in Cary.

Raleigh's **CAT** system (Capital Area Transit, 919/485-7433, www.gotriangle.org) spreads its filaments all over the city, both inside and outside the Beltline, and links readily to other major transportation hubs. Many taxi and driver services are available, including **Yellow Cab** (919/875-1821), **Alliance Concierge** (919/815-6953), and **Blue Diamond Limousines and Sedans** (919/772-9595).

RALEIGH SUBURBS

Raleigh is girded by extensive suburbs and old-towns-turned-bedroom-communities—Apex, Zebulon, Fuquay-Varina, Cary—home to many of the new arrivals who work in the tech sector. (Bless their hearts, when they're not listening we maintain that "Cary" is an acronym for "Containment Area for Relocated Yankees.")

The small town of **Wake Forest** in northern Wake County is the original home of the university of the same name, but if you're looking for the Demon Deacons nowadays you'll have to try Winston-Salem, a couple of hours west. Nevertheless, Wake Forest is an attractive town with pretty historic architecture—including the pre-1820 **Calvin Jones House** (440 N. Main St., 919/556-2911, www.wake forestbirthplace.org)—as well as cafés, shops, and **Falls Lake State Recreation Area** (headquarters 13304 Creedmoor Rd., www.ncparks .gov/Visit/parks/fala/main.php).

Zebulon, just east of Raleigh, is the home of the **Carolina Mudcats** (www.gomudcats.com), a double-A affiliate of the Florida Marlins. The Mudcats' **Five County Stadium** (1501 NC Highway 39, 919/269-2287, www.gomud cats.com) is a great place to watch serious baseball in an affordable, cozy small-town setting.

Cary, to the southwest of Raleigh, is in many ways the quintessence of the suburban growth experienced in the Raleigh-Durham region in the last couple of decades, but Cary actually has plenty of history to its name; you can explore the old **Page-Walker Hotel** (119 Ambassador Loop, 919/460-4963, 10 A.M.–9:30 P.M. Mon.–Thurs., 10 A.M.–5 P.M. Fri., 10 A.M.–1 P.M. Sun.), now a local heritage museum. You can also catch a **Carolina Railhawks** (http://carolinarail hawks.com) pro soccer game, and try chum-chum or sandesh at the **Mithai House of Indian Desserts** (744-F E. Chatham St., 919/469-9651, www.mithaius.com, 11:30 A.M.–5:30 P.M. Mon., 11 A.M.–9 P.M. Tues.–Sun.).

Durham

Home of Duke and North Carolina Central University, Durham is an exciting place. Major arts festivals, most notably the Full-Frame Documentary Festival and the American Dance Festival, bring tens of thousands of visitors to Durham every year. Duke University's famous Blue Devils are one of the nation's dominant basketball teams, and NCCU's Eagles are a football powerhouse. There's a great deal of literary activity too, and one of the best selections of bookstores in the region.

Formerly abuzz with cigarette-rolling factories, Durham has met the demise of the tobacco industry—to which it owes its existence—with grace. Many of the long brick warehouses, formerly factories for such brands as Lorillard and Winston and American Tobacco, have been transformed into attractive restaurants and public venues. The American Tobacco Historic District ensures that the city's smoky origins won't be forgotten.

Durham is also an important center of urban African American heritage, and was referred to in the early 20th century as the Capital of the Black Middle Class. North Carolina Central University is a historically African American school, and though it's often overshadowed by nearby Duke, UNC, and NC State, it is one of our state's major educational institutions.

Next to NCCU's campus is Hayti, an African American neighborhood where in the days of segregation black Durhamites maintained their own bustling commercial district. Blind Boy Fuller, Reverend Gary Davis, and other Carolina blues legends did stints here as street performers, and a historical marker next to the Hayti Heritage Center commemorates their time in Durham.

DUKE UNIVERSITY

Duke University is often thought of as a sort of Southern Ivy League school, and the reputation is justly deserved, for its students are among the academic (and athletic) elite in the country. The architecture of the Duke campus—much of it designed by turn-of-the-century African American architect Julian Abele—is done up in dark, gothic stonework, and really does feel like an island that floated away from some northeastern state and accidentally came to rest here in North Carolina. Originally called Trinity College and located in Randolph County, it came to Durham and became Duke University under the auspices of the Duke family, tobacco barons who were responsible for, among other things, the university's early policy of admitting female students. It continues to be a leading light in the world of academia.

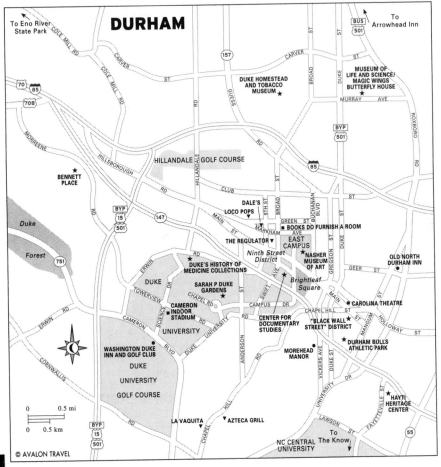

Duke's **Center for Documentary Studies** (1317 W. Pettigrew Street. 919/660-3663, http://cds.aas.duke.edu, gallery hours 9 A.M.–7 P.M. Mon.–Thurs., 9 A.M.–5 P.M. Fri., 11 A.M.–4 P.M. Sat., and 1–5 P.M. Sun.) is an invaluable resource to artists, documentarians, and educators throughout the region, as well as a fascinating place to visit when you're in town. Occupying the Lyndhurst House, a handsome old home on Pettigrew Street within easy walking distance of the 9th Street shops and restaurants, CDS includes a gallery, teaching facilities, and extensive darkrooms and labs.

The gallery, which is open to the public, showcases documentary screenings and cutting-edge photography and multimedia work. It's a fun stop for anyone intrigued by today's documentary renaissance.

The Nasher Museum of Art (2001 Campus Dr., 919/684-5135, www.nasher.duke.edu, 10 A.M.–5 P.M. Mon.–Sat., until 9 P.M. Thurs., noon–5 P.M. Sun., $5 adults, $4 seniors, $3 non-Duke students, and free to Duke students, Durham residents, and visitors under 16) is home to extensive collections of ancient and medieval art, including one of the largest collections of pre-Columbian Latin American art in the United States. The building is a stunningly modern creation by architect Rafael Viñoly. At the museum café, the art of cooking is on display in the work of contemporary Southern chef Amy Tornquist, whose fare is as much a part of the Nasher's artistic mission as the presentation of paintings and sculpture.

Adjoining the grounds of the Nasher are the **Sarah P. Duke Gardens** (919/684-3698, www.hr.duke.edu/dukegardens, 8 A.M.–dusk daily, free), 55 acres of some of the finest landscaping and horticultural arts to be seen in the Southeast.

While on campus, check out **Duke's History of Medicine Collections** (103 Seeley G. Mudd Building, Duke University Medical Center Library), where you'll find antique medical equipment and the nation's largest collection of miniature ivory mannequins. In the lobby of the Mary Duke Biddle Music Building, on East Campus, is the **Eddy Collection of Music Instruments,** over 500 instruments that date from the last three centuries.

NORTH CAROLINA CENTRAL UNIVERSITY

North Carolina Central University was founded in 1910, the first public liberal arts college for African Americans in the United States. Still a predominantly black institution, Central is one of the state's great universities, and as important to the history and vitality of the city as Duke, its much larger neighbor.

The **North Carolina Central University Art Museum** (NCCU campus, Lawson St. between Fine Arts and Music buildings, 919/560-6211, 9 A.M.–5 P.M. Tues.–Fri., 2–5 P.M. Sun., free) specializes in the work of 19th- and 20th-century African American artists. The collections include work by such prominent and varied masters as Romare Bearden, Jacob Lawrence, Henry Ossawa Tanner, and Minnie Evans.

Inside the William Jones Building on Central's campus is a display of the Durham **Woolworth lunch counter,** site of a 1960 sit-in attended by Dr. Martin Luther King, Jr.,

which signaled a sea-change in the civil rights movement.

AFRICAN AMERICAN HERITAGE SIGHTS

Sights of importance to African American history are found throughout Durham. **St. Joseph's Performance Hall** and the **Hayti Heritage Center** (804 Old Fayetteville St. 919/683-1709, www.hayti.org, 10 A.M.–5 P.M. Mon.–Fri., 10 A.M.–3 P.M. Sat.) celebrate the historic African-American community of Hayti—pronounced "Hay-tye," rhymes with "necktie"—the former St. Joseph's AME Church sanctuary is a special venue for the performing arts in Durham, and the Heritage Center houses an art gallery, dance studio, and community meeting space. Also on Fayetteville Street is **White Rock Baptist Church** (3400 Fayetteville St., 919/688-8136, www.whiterockbaptistchurch.org), home of a congregation founded in 1866. Dr. King spoke here in 1960 after participating in the Woolworth sit-in.

The neoclassical revival-style **Mechanics and Farmers Bank** building (116 W. Parrish Street, downtown) stands at the heart of a district known in the early 20th century as **Black Wall Street.** Mechanics and Farmers Bank and "the Mutual," **North Carolina Mutual Life Insurance Company** (411 W. Chapel Hill St., 919/682-9201, www.ncmutuallife.com), were the flagships of Durham's African American commercial establishment. The history of the Mutual is chronicled in the Heritage Room at its modern-day location on West Chapel Hill Street.

◖ Historic Stagville

About 15 minutes north of downtown Durham, Historic Stagville (5828 Old Oxford Hwy., 919/620-0120, www.historicstagvillefoundation.org, 10 A.M.–4 P.M. Tues.–Sat., hourly tours most days 10 A.M.–3 P.M.) preserves part of what was a staggeringly large plantation system. The Cameron-Bennehan family's holdings totaled nearly 30,000 acres in 1860, and the 900 African Americans who worked the land were one of the South's largest slave communities. Historic Stagville includes 71 acres of the original plantations, with several notable vernacular structures including two-story timber-frame slave quarters, a massive hipped-roof barn built in 1860, and the late 18th-century Bennehan plantation house. Interpretation of the Stagville site acknowledges the centrality of the African American experience here, and tries to reconstruct, through documentary evidence, archaeology, and folklore, what life may have been like for the slave community. One of the main events on Stagville's calendar is its **Juneteenth Celebration,** an event celebrated in parts of the South for generations, marking the arrival of the news of emancipation. Stagville's Juneteenth features music, food, crafts, and interpretation by costumed guides.

OTHER SIGHTS

A different side of 19th-century Durham life is presented at the **Duke Homestead and Tobacco Museum** (2828 Duke Homestead Rd., 919/477-5498, www.dukehomestead.nc historicsites.org, Tues.–Sat., hours vary, free). Here the patriarch of Durham's tobacco industry, Washington Duke, began his career as a humble tobacco farmer. Discovering the popularity of bright leaf tobacco among Union soldiers, he began processing large quantities of it (at one point wrapping the product in labels that read, ironically, "Pro Bono Publico"). This was the beginning of North Carolina's meteoric rise to the top of the world tobacco market, an economy that transformed the state and made the city of Durham what it is today. Throughout the year, the Duke Homestead displays and demonstrates period techniques in tobacco culture.

Bennett Place (4409 Bennett Memorial Rd., 919/383-4345, www.bennettplace.nchist-oricsites.org, 10 A.M.–4 P.M. Tues.–Sat., free) is a historic site that commemorates the meeting of Confederate General Joseph Johnston and Union General William Tecumseh Sherman in April 1865. In the last days of the Civil

Sarah P. Duke Gardens

© CHRIS LAWRENCE

War, when Jefferson Davis was fleeing south to Georgia and Abraham Lincoln was dead, Johnston and Sherman had a series of negotiations here that led to the surrender of all the Confederate forces in the Carolinas, Georgia, and Florida.

The **North Carolina Museum of Life and Science** (433 Murray Ave., 919/220-5429, www.ncmls.org, 10 A.M.–5 P.M. Tues.–Sat., noon–5 P.M. Sun., $9.50 adults, $8.50 ages 65 and over and military personnel, $7.50 ages 3–12), home of the **Magic Wings Butterfly House** and **Bayer Crop Science Insectarium,** is the perfect place for children who enjoy meeting strange bugs, climbing inside tornadoes, and taking a trip on a locomotive to see red wolves. Grayson's Café, inside the museum, is open until 4 P.M. every day that the museum is open.

For the truly adventurous, there is no better way to see Durham than by open air. Pilot Mike Ratty takes one or two passengers at a time for **sightseeing flights** (www.carolinabarnstormers.com) in a 1940s biplane in the spring, fall, and winter. The price is high—$100 for 25-minute rides, $200 for an hour—but the experience is unforgettable.

ENTERTAINMENT AND EVENTS
Full Frame Documentary Festival

April brings the Full Frame Documentary Festival (www.fullframefest.org) which, before it had celebrated its 10th year, had already been identified by the *New York Times* as the premier documentary film festival in the United States. Venues throughout downtown host screenings, workshops, panels, and soirees, where documentary fans and aspiring filmmakers can mingle with the glitterati of the genre.

Other Festivals

February's **Black Diaspora Film Festival** (www.hayti.org/film) takes place at the Hayti Heritage Center. Films about the African and African-American experience are screened and discussed in a stimulating event that is free to the public.

The **Grady Tate Jazz Festival** (www.nccu.edu) takes place in April at North Carolina Central University. North Carolina was home to such jazz legends as Thelonious Monk and John Coltrane, and Central has a widely respected jazz program, so it's only fitting that Durham should host this prestigious event.

For six weeks every summer, Durham is the site of the **American Dance Festival** (www.americandancefestival.org), an internationally known event where the world's best choreographers often premiere new work. Durhamites and the visitors who come from around the world to ADF are one step ahead of the audiences in New York.

One of the region's most popular music festivals is the **Festival for the Eno** (www.enoriver.org/festival), which takes place every Fourth of July weekend. The festival is held on the banks of the Eno River, so you can listen to the performances from the comfort of your inner tube while floating in the river. In addition to showcasing dozens of excellent world, folk, and bluegrass bands, the Festival for the Eno is a great place for browsing the work of many of North Carolina's craftspeople. The beautiful images used to promote each year's festival are collected by festival-goers in the Triangle.

August's **North Carolina Gay and Lesbian Film Festival** (www.carolinatheater.org) is the second-largest such event in the Southeast. Approximately 10,000 visitors attend the festival every year to watch new work by up-and-coming LGBT filmmakers at Durham's Carolina Theater.

The **Bull Durham Blues Festival** (www.hayti.org/blues) is put on by the Hayti Heritage Association in September. Now more than 20 years old, the festival brings modern blues artists from around the region and around the world to celebrate Durham's history as a gathering place for some of the greatest Piedmont-style blues musicians. The oldest old-timers still remember Reverend Gary Davis, Blind Boy Fuller, and other important figures in early blues busking on the street corners of Durham when the tobacco markets were in full swing.

Nightlife

The **All People's Grill** (6122 Guess Rd., 919/620-9591, www.allpeoplesgrill.com) has been serving Southern soul food and great blues music for generations. While gobbling up on-the-money collard greens and fried chicken, you can hear some of the top blues artists of this region, many of them on the roster of the Music Maker Relief Foundation (www.music maker.org), a regional organization that promotes blues musicians to ensure that they are able to make a living playing and so carry on their art. Check the All People's website for upcoming shows.

Bingo parlors dot the landscape, but Durham is one of the few places where you can be part of the craze that is **Drag Bingo** (www.dragbingo.com, $15 in advance, $17 at the door). Once a month, tickets go on sale—and sell out fast—for a bingo event to benefit area HIV/AIDS services. It's an incredibly fun scene—a mixture of gay and straight, folks in drag and in their usual attire, covetable prizes, a little bit of raunchy humor, and a lot of money going to a great cause.

James Joyce Irish Pub (912 W. Main St., 919/683-3022, www.jamesjoyceirishpub.com, opens 11:30 A.M. Mon.–Sat. and noon on Sun., music starts at 10 P.M. Fri.–Sat.) is a favorite local bar, established by a Durhamite originally from County Kerry. Here you can drink a lovely pint while listening to live music—or watching Duke basketball, rugby, or a football (as in soccer) match.

SHOPPING
Malls and Shopping Districts

Brightleaf Square (corner of Main St. and Gregson St., www.historicbrightleaf.com), handsome circa-1900 warehouses of the American Tobacco Company, are no longer hives of cigarette rollers, but have evolved into the flagship of Durham's post-tobacco-industry revitalization. Over a dozen restaurants now occupy the old industrial bays, side-by-side with diverse and interesting retailers.

The **Streets at Southpoint** (Fayetteville St. at I-40, www.streetsatsouthpoint.com) is a traditional shopping mall—with movie theaters, food court, and all. In addition to the usual anchor department stores and mall chains, Southpoint features a nice selection of upscale clothing shops, and has one of only three **Apple stores** in North Carolina.

The core of the **Ninth Street district** of Durham, adjacent to the Duke campus, are the blocks between Main Street and Hillsborough Road/Markham Avenue. Here you'll find many small (and very good) eateries and an eclectic mix of shops.

Books

The Regulator (720-Ninth St., 919/286-2700, 9 A.M.–9 P.M. Mon.–Sat., 10 A.M.–6 P.M. Sun.) is one of the Triangle area's favorite bookshops. It hosts readings by important authors from around the world, and has a periodicals section that carries a nice and eccentric selection of literary journals and homemade zines.

The Know (2520 Fayetteville St., 919/682-7223) specializes in African American fiction and history, and Afrocentric literature and philosophy. On Friday nights, the store bustles with jazz fans who come to hear Yusuf Salim, a legendary Durham pianist.

Wentworth and Leggett Rare Books and Prints (Brightleaf Square, 905 W. Main St., 919/688-5311, www.wentworthleggettbooks .com, 11 A.M.–7 P.M. Mon.–Sat., call ahead Sun. and Nov. and Dec.) is an antiquarian dealer, also specializing in old prints, maps, postcards, and magazines. The downtown **Book Exchange** (107 W. Chapel Hill St., 919/682-4662) is a secondhand-book lover's paradise—a warren of shelves, difficult to navigate for the overflow books stacked all around.

Other good area bookstores are **Books Do Furnish A Room** (1809 W. Markham Ave., 919/286-1076, www.booksdofurnish aroom.com, 10 A.M.–6 P.M. most days), for new books, and the Durham branch of **Nice Price Books** (811 Broad St., 919/416-1066, 10 A.M.–10 P.M. Mon.–Sat., noon–10 P.M. Sun.) for used books and music.

SPORTS AND RECREATION
Hiking, Biking, and Water Sports

Durham is loaded with choices for hikers, joggers, and bikers. The Eno River is surrounded by thousands of acres of parkland, much of which is marked for hiking. **Eno River State Park** (6101 Cole Mill. Rd., 919/383-1686), northwest of Durham, offers hiking, canoeing (Class I–III rapids), and camping in the beautiful and wild river valley. See the Eno River Association website (www.enoriver. org) for information on more places and ways to enjoy the river. **Frog Hollow Canoe and Kayak** (919/949-4315, www.froghollowoutdoors.com, 10 A.M.–6 P.M. Wed.–Fri., 9 A.M.–6:30 P.M. weekends, by reservation only) rents boats and guides tours. During the warm months, you have the leisurely option of **Wafting the Eno** (919/471-3802, www.wafter. org, $12, reservations required). These guided float trips take off from West Point Park at 10 A.M. and 3:30 P.M., and at 9 P.M. when there's a full moon.

The **American Tobacco Trail** (www.triangle trails.org/ATT.HTM) is comprised of 12 miles of walking, hiking, and biking trails throughout Durham, including through the downtown. The trail will eventually be 22 miles long. **Tobacco Trail Bicycle Rentals** (4704 Fayetteville Rd., 919/389-3437, www.tt bikes.com) offers rentals of bicycles of all kinds for $7 per hour and up, as well as guided tours of the American Tobacco Trail by appointment. The **Carolina Tarwheels** (919/687-5066, www.tarwheels.org), a weekend biking club, welcomes newcomers and visitors.

Golf

Golfers have several good public courses to choose from in the area, including **Hillandale Golf Course** (1600 Hillandale Road, 919/286-4211 or 800/367-2582, www.hillandale golf.com) and **Lakeshore Golf Course** (4621 Lumley Road, 596-2401). The **Golf Center** (4343 Garrett Rd., 919/403-2255, 10 A.M.–10 P.M. daily), has a fully lit driving range, PGA and LPGA teaching pros, and a huge pro shop.

Indoor Recreation

The **Vertical Edge Climbing Center** (2422-D U.S. 70 East, behind Kawasaki-Suzuki, 919/596-6910, www.verticaledgeclimbing.com) is a full-service, indoor rock- and wall-climbing gym, with instruction and plenty of activity for experts as well as first-time climbers.

With locations throughout piedmont North Carolina, including at Northgate Mall in Durham, **Game Frog Café** (1058 West Club Blvd., Space 111, 919/286-0200, www.game frog.net) is a super-cool environment for gaming. Hundreds of Xbox, PS2, GameCube, and PC games are available for individual and tournament play. Rates vary by location, but an hour costs about $7, with discounts for multihour and even all-day passes. Games rated Mature are restricted; no one under 13 may play them, and all underage gamers must provide a parental consent form, which can be downloaded from the website.

Spectator Sports

Thanks to the exploits of a demon and a smoke-snorting steer, Durham is probably even better known for its sports tradition than its history as a tobacco dynamo.

The NCAA Division-1 **Duke Blue Devils** embody the gold standard in college basketball, and excel in many other sports. Their history is chronicled in the **Duke Sports Hall of Fame** (Towerview Rd., 919/613-7500), inside Cameron Indoor Stadium. Coach Mike Krzyzewski—that's pronounced "Shuh-shev-skee," but you can call him Coach K—has shepherded the men's basketball team since 1980, leading them to a phenomenal number of championships. His resemblance to the Duke mascot is equally phenomenal. Duke has turned out some of the greatest basketball players of the last 20 years, including Grant Hill, Christian Laettner, and J. J. Reddick. Not surprisingly, it is extremely difficult to come by Duke basketball tickets. See the *Scoring ACC Basketball Tickets* sidebar for strategies.

Duke students are famous for living in tents for months on end outside Cameron Indoor Stadium, waiting first to buy tickets and then to

SCORING ACC BASKETBALL TICKETS

If you're visiting the Triangle during college basketball season and are hoping to catch a game in person, don't count on being able to buy a ticket at the box office. In fact, count on not being able to. The 20,000-seat Dean Dome, UNC's Dean E. Smith Center, routinely sells out for men's in-conference games, and the RBC Centura Center, the NC State Wolfpack men's 20,000-seat home arena, often does as well. Duke plays at the comparatively quaint Cameron Indoor Stadium, and its 9,000 seats are the hardest of all to obtain. Tickets for women's games, which at UNC and NCSU take place on the older, smaller courts, are much less difficult to come by, though ACC games sometimes sell out, and the Duke/UNC women's games always do. The most prized and scarce treasure of all is a ticket to the Duke/UNC men's game. Unless a current student of one of the schools really, really likes you, or you're a major benefactor with a classroom building named in your honor, your chances of paying face value for a ticket are slim to none. So get out your wallet.

During basketball season, tickets appear on eBay, Craigslist, and ticket-scalping search engines. Really good tickets will probably go on the auction block well in advance of the game, and are fought over fiercely. If you wait until the day of a game, there's a chance of finding a seller who has just that day decided not to use his or her own tickets, and wants to get rid of them fast. To win these, you've got to stay alert and act fast. Prices vary from game to game depending on the teams' respective records that season and the heat of the rivalry. For a minor out-of-conference game, such as are played early in the season — the Wolfpack versus the Flying Menace of Snickelfritz County Community College, let's say — you should be able to get a reasonably good ticket for $10–20 above face value and without much difficulty, if the game sells out at all. For a sold-out game between ACC teams, prices go up steeply. Expect to pay three or more times the face value for a good seat at an in-conference game of minor importance. For an important ACC game, the worst seats in the house could be over $100, the good seats $200–300 and up. If you want to go to a UNC/Duke game, seats up in the rafters will be in the hundreds, and a good seat could easily set you back $1,000...or more.

Scalping is illegal in North Carolina. It's also pretty common. On game day, the scalpers are the people hanging around outside the arena, or on nearby street corners, holding signs that say "Need Tickets." Technically, they probably will buy tickets if you're selling, but "Need Tickets" is code for "Got Tickets." If you ask one of them if he has a ticket, he'll ask cagily what you're looking for. Draw your line in the sand — you want a really good ticket for not a lot of money. If you ask for courtside seats for $20 each, you'll only get laughter and lose your bargaining chips, but if you start not too far from the bounds of reason, he'll talk business. Be firm, and be willing to turn down a best offer. There's another scalper just a few steps away. If you don't mind missing the first few minutes of the game, you'll find that prices start going down at tip-off.

For the hard-core basketball fan, the research and haggling and dollars are a small price to pay for a chance to be present at an ACC game. There's nothing like watching your favorite team warm up, or seeing Crazy Towel Guy do his thing at Cameron Indoor Stadium, or being in the same room, albeit a large one, with 10,000 other people who know all the words to your team's fight song.

snag good standing-room spots in the courtside student section of the arena. If you're on campus in season, take a look at their tent city, known as Krzyzewskiville. (Beware, it's not for the Carolina-blue-at-heart. There are as many anti–Tar Heel banners in Krzyzewskiville as there are textbooks.) If you're lucky enough to get into a game, you'll have the treat—or trauma, depending on your loyalties—of seeing the "Cameron Crazies" in the flesh. These Duke fans, often half-naked and painted blue like Picts, are known far and wide for their creative, funny, and sometimes edgy chants and heckles.

The **Durham Bulls** (ballpark at 409 Blackwell St., 919/956-2855, www.durham bulls.com)—yes, of "Bull Durham" fame—are one of the nation's most recognizable minor-league baseball teams. They are the Triple-A farm team for the Tampa Bay Devil Rays, so you're likely to see big-league players here who are rehabbing from injury and rookies on the brink of making it big. The ballpark, designed by the architect who built Baltimore's Camden Yards, is comfortable and fun. A big wooden bull peers down from the end of the third-base line, and when a Bull hits a homer, the bull's eyes light up red, his tail flaps, and smoke billows from his nostrils.

ACCOMMODATIONS

The poshest place to stay in Durham is the **Washington Duke Inn and Golf Club** (3001 Cameron Blvd., 800/443-3853, www .washingtondukeinn.com, from $130). Located on the grounds of the Duke University Golf Course, on the Duke campus, the rooms and suites are sunny and plush, with the option of bunk beds for families traveling with kids. Babysitting services can be arranged by the concierge. Also convenient to the Duke campus, the **University Inn** (502 Elf St., 919/286-4421 or 800/313-3585, www.univer-sityinnduke.com, from $70) is a basic motel, a good value in a good location.

Durham's most celebrated bed-and-breakfast is the **C Arrowhead Inn** (106 Mason Rd., 800/528-2207, http://arrowheadinn.com, from $135), a AAA Four-Diamond awardee on

a Revolutionary-era plantation about 15 minutes from downtown. All of the very luxurious rooms have their own fireplaces, and several have two-person whirlpools. On the inn's grounds are a garden cottage, with a whirlpool and two-person steam shower, and a rather fabulous log cabin with a sleeping loft and spa-like bath appointments.

The **Old North Durham Inn** (922 N. Mangum St., 919/683-1885, www.bbonline .com/nc/oldnorth, from $110) is a pretty house on one of the old primary roads in the city. It's been cited by the Durham Historic Preservation Society for its excellent renovation. Guests receive free tickets to Durham Bulls games, and can look out their bedroom windows across the street at the home where much of *Bull Durham* was filmed. Also downtown is the **Morehead Manor** (914 Vickers Ave., 888/437-6333, www.moreheadmanor.com, from $135), a late-20th century house built for a tobacco executive, in easy walking distance from many downtown attractions.

FOOD
Eclectic American

The **C Cosmic Cantina** (1920 Perry St., 919/286-1875, noon–4 A.M. Mon., 11 A.M.–3 A.M. Tues.–Fri., noon–4 A.M. Sat., noon–midnight Sun., under $10) a casual take-out-or-seat-yourself joint in the middle of the Ninth Street neighborhood by the Duke campus, serves the best burritos you'll find just about anywhere. The friend who introduced me to it preaches that a first visit to the Cantina is a life-changing experience.

The award-winning restaurant **Nana's** (2514 University Dr., 919/493-8545, www.nanas durham.com, 5:30–10 P.M. Mon.–Sat., $18–30) is presided over by chef Scott Howell, a North Carolina native. The fare is hearty but elegant, and the wine list has won *Wine Spectator's* Award of Excellence. Vegetarian pickings are a little slim, but carnivores will be well satisfied.

The **Magnolia Grill's** (1002 Ninth St., 919/286-3609, 6–9:30 P.M. Tues.–Thurs., 5:30–10 P.M. Fri.–Sat., under $20) fine menu based on fresh local ingredients has won the restaurant acclaim far beyond Durham. Twice listed in *Gourmet* magazine's "Top 50 Restaurants" feature, the Magnolia Grill has also been nominated for the James Beard Foundation's Outstanding Restaurant in America award. Needless to say, this is a popular spot, so make reservations or be prepared to wait.

Asian

The **Thai Café** (2501 University Dr., 919/493-9794, www.thaicafenc.com, $10–20) is the sort of restaurant whose regulars might visit a dozen times before they'll try a second item on the menu—because whatever they tried on that first visit was so good they've been craving it ever since. The Thai Café serves all of the classic Thai restaurant dishes, like pad thai, tom yum, and pad prik—all delicious— but the real masterpieces here are the curries. You can choose from yellow and green curries, panang, and massaman, with meat, seafood, tofu, or vegetables. One warning: "not spicy" at Thai Café means incredibly spicy. If you want mild food, you'll need to make a special point of it to the server.

On Ninth Street, convenient to Duke, is an Indian restaurant with the rather unlikely name of **Dale's** (811 Ninth St., 919/286-1760). Dale's has a delicious à la carte menu, but most customers opt for the quick buffet, which includes delicious dal, masalas, and palak paneer, among other items. The sticky-sweet rice pudding, also served at the buffet, is absolutely addictive.

Mexican

Durham is busting out with wonderful Mexican restaurants and taco stands, more every year as the number of Mexican immigrants in the area swells. A local favorite is **La Vaquita** (2700 Chapel Hill Rd., 919/402-0209, $5–10), a little building with an outdoor walk-up counter and a huge fiberglass cow on the roof. (In the Christmas season, the cow wears a Santa hat.) La Vaquita has a huge menu for a place with such limited kitchen space. It's very authentic Mexican

rooftop cow at La Vaquita

cuisine, with many kinds of tacos, stews, tamales, ribs, barbacoa, and lots more. Just a few blocks away is the **Azteca Grill** (1929 Chapel Hill Rd., 919/403-2527), where the food is also just great. Its highest recommendation comes from the clientele: At the lunch hour, the dining room fills with Mexican working men, clearly happy to find a taste of home in North Carolina.

Wildly popular in hot weather, **Loco Pops** (2600 Hillsborough Rd., 919/286-3500, ilovelocopops.com) has several locations in the Triangle from which it vends *paletas,* Mexican-style popsicles. They come in crazy flavors—ginger cantaloupe, mango chili, cucumber chili, tamarind—as well as a few more familiar choices. At just a couple bucks each, the *paletas* are a favorite after-class and after-work treat, and the line at Loco Pops often stretches out the door.

INFORMATION AND SERVICES

Duke University Medical Center (2301 Erwin Rd., 919/416-3853) is the main hospital in Durham. **Durham Regional Hospital** (3643 N. Roxboro Rd., 919/470-4000) is also operated by Duke Health Systems. **Walgreens** (6405 Fayetteville St., 919/544-6430) has a 24-hour pharmacy.

Information for travelers is available from the **Durham Convention and Visitors Bureau** (101 E. Morgan St., 800/446-8604, www.durham-nc.com). The *Durham Herald-Sun* is the primary Durham-specific newspaper here, though many people also read the Raleigh *News & Observer.* The *Independent* is a popular weekly cultural newspaper, available free throughout the region.

GETTING THERE AND AROUND

Plans are in the works in Durham for a regional rail system that would link the city with Raleigh-Durham International Airport (RDU), Raleigh, and the Raleigh suburbs. The projected date of completion of the first phase is 2009, with stations opening at the Duke Medical Center, the Alston Road neighborhood, downtown, and Ninth Street on the Duke campus. In the meantime, information about the Triangle's extensive network of **buses and shuttles** can be found at www.ridetta.org. RDU is 10–20 minutes from Durham, reachable by an easy cab or shuttle ride. **Amtrak** (400 W. Chapel Hill St., 800/872-7245, www.amtrak.com, 7 A.M.–9 P.M. daily) has direct service to Durham on the Carolinian line, pulling in to the station in the heart of downtown.

Chapel Hill, Carrboro, and Vicinity

The third corner of the Triangle is occupied by Chapel Hill and Carrboro. By my lights this is holy ground, but having been raised in a household where, during close Carolina basketball games, we had to turn off the TV so that the family elders wouldn't suffer suspense-induced strokes—no exaggeration—perhaps I'm biased. The University of North Carolina is the heart of the town, but the approximately 50,000 permanent residents, many of them former UNC students who grew so attached to Chapel Hill that they decided to stay, maintain a stimulating community in which the arts thrive. Singer James Taylor, blues guitarist Elizabeth Cotten, and the Squirrel Nut Zippers are among the many Chapel Hill/Carrboro natives who have gone on to much wider fame in the musical world. Music is as ubiquitous here as pine pollen in May or sky-blue shirts on campus, and on a tour of the clubs on any given weekend you may well hear a future legend.

UNIVERSITY OF NORTH CAROLINA

The University of North Carolina campus is made up of a beautiful couple of quads (surrounded by many outlying complexes) that date to 1789—the oldest state university in the country. Massive poplar trees on the quads make the campus an indulgently shady

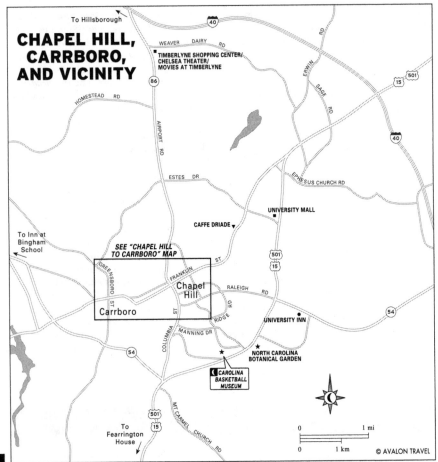

CHAPEL HILL, CARRBORO, AND VICINITY

hideaway during the hundred-degree weather of a central Carolina summer. Elegantly unpretentious federal-style buildings were dorms and classrooms for 18th- and 19th-century scholars, and they're home to undergraduates today. Guided tours of the historic sites on campus depart from the UNC **Visitors' Center** (250 East Franklin St., 919/962-1630, www.unc .edu/depts/visitor) at 1:30 P.M. on weekdays. You can also pick up a brochure and walk through campus at your own pace.

The 1851 Old Playmakers Theater, at East Cameron Avenue in the middle of campus,

was built by Alexander Jackson Davis, originally intended as a library and ballroom. In the 1920s, the University converted the building to a theater.

At **Kenan Football Stadium** (Bell Tower Dr., off of South Rd., 919/966-2575, www.tarheelblue.com), the **Charlie Justice Hall of Honors** chronicles the doughty deeds of UNC's football program. It's open 8 A.M.–5 P.M. Monday–Friday, and for three hours on home-game days until half an hour before kickoff.

The **Ackland Art Museum** (919/966-5736, www.ackland.org, 10 A.M.–5 P.M. Wed.–Sat.,

1–5 P.M. Sun., free), at the heart of the UNC campus near the intersection of Franklin and Columbia, has a very special collection of European sculpture and painting spanning centuries, and an acclaimed collection of Asian art. The **North Carolina Collection Gallery** (919/962-1172, 9 A.M.–5 P.M. Mon.–Fri., 9 A.M.–1 P.M. Sat. 1–5 P.M. Sun.), on the ground floor of Wilson Library, is a cozy museum that will capture the fancy of any Southern history enthusiast.

SIGHTS
C Carolina Basketball Museum
While on campus, visit the Carolina Basketball Museum (Ernie Williamson Athletic Center, 450 Skipper Bowles Dr., www.tarheelblue.com, 10 A.M.–4 P.M. Mon.–Fri., closes 1 hour before weekday games, opens 3.5 hours before and closes 1 hour before weekend games, free), a new addition to the roster of campus attractions. This multimillion-dollar, 8,000-square-foot hagiological shrine holds mementos from a century of Carolina basketball. On a

reproduction of the Heels' court, footprints and even players' actual shoes mark the spots from which some of the program's most memorable baskets were launched. There's a lot of video and interactive content, but the item most likely to please the Tar Heel faithful, and inspire hoots of derision, is a letter from Duke coach Mike Krzyzewski to a high school player from Wilmington, expressing his regret that the young man had chosen to attend UNC rather than Duke. The addressee was, of course, Michael Jordan.

Other Museums
Across Franklin Street from the main quad is **Kidzu** (105 E. Franklin St., 919/933-1455, www.kidzuchildrensmuseum.org, 10 A.M.–5 P.M. Tues.–Sat., 1–5 P.M. Sun.), a children's museum that features imaginative interactive exhibits for kids to explore, as well as a fun gift shop. The **Chapel Hill Museum** (523 E. Franklin St., 919/967-1400, www.chapel hillmuseum.org, 10 A.M.–4 P.M. Wed.–Sat., 1–4 P.M. Sun., free), just down the hill from

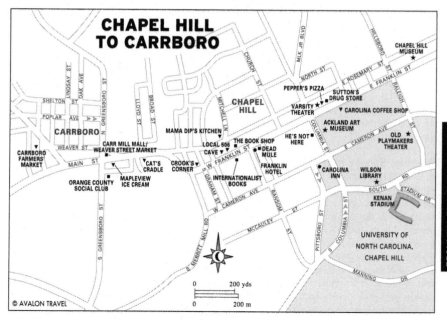

RALEIGH AND THE TRIANGLE

campus, is a small museum that documents the town's heritage and hosts exhibits by local artists. It has a good selection of North Carolina pottery on display, and the gift shop carries the work of local authors and artists.

Nostalgic College Spots

Every college town has a few emblematic hangouts—joints that would seem like no great shakes to the uninitiated, but that to generations of alumni are charged with nostalgia. At UNC, these icons are the **Carolina Coffee Shop** (138 E. Franklin St., 919/942-6875) and **Sutton's Drug Store** (159 E. Franklin St., 919/942-5161). The Carolina Coffee Shop, a dark, soporific re-treat, has been the site of thousands of first dates over the last 90 years. It's a place to have an afternoon breakfast if you've been up studying all night, or to inhale a sandwich be-fore heading across Franklin to a movie at the Carolina Theater. At night, the liquor license kicks in and it becomes a busy bar. Across the street is Sutton's Drug Store, a good place to catch a glimpse of members of the basketball team, who often stop here between classes. An old-time, small-town drugstore, Sutton's has a greasy-spoon burger-and-fries lunch counter, and a tiny prescription window at the back manned by a benevolent druggist who knows everyone's name (and knew their parents too). All along the walls you'll see snapshots of cus-tomers eating at the counter or posing under the front awning. Look close, and you'll find some sports legends.

Weaver Street Market

Weaver Street Market (101 E. Weaver St., 919/929-0010, www.weaverstreetmarket.coop, 7:30 A.M.–9 P.M., Mon.–Fri., 8 A.M.–9 P.M. Sat. and Sun.) is the community hub of the po-litically liberal, artistically active, and often quite eccentric residents of Carrboro. WSM is an organic foods co-op with a small eating area—it's too plain to be called a café—inside and on the front lawn. On a pretty day, the lawn is jam-packed with families and college students eating locally grown food (in nearby Pittsboro and Hillsborough, there's an organic farm or creamery wherever there's an open patch of land) and listening to local bluegrass, old-time mountain, punk, or perhaps Hare Krishna musicians. You'll probably see some tai chi or hula-hooping going on too. One look at Weaver Street Market on a crowded day, and one has a pretty good idea of what a peculiar and congenial community this is.

ENTERTAINMENT AND EVENTS
Movies

Like a good college town should, Chapel Hill has a couple of several movie theaters, including small theaters that show indepen-dent films. The **Varsity Theater** (123 E. Franklin St., 919/967-8665) is on the edge of campus, and the **Chelsea** (1129 Weaver Dairy Rd., 919/968-3005) and the **Movies at Timberlyne** (120 Banks Dr., 919/933-8600) are in the Timberlyne shopping center, up Highway 86 (Columbia Rd./Martin Luther King Jr. Dr.). The **Lumina Theater** (620 Market St., 919/932-9000, www.thelu-mina.com) is located in Southern Village, a development south of Chapel Hill on U.S. 15/501. The Lumina screens movies outdoors on summer evenings.

Nightlife
LIVE MUSIC

Chapel Hill/Carrboro is one of the best places in the Southeast to hear live music, and several small, top-notch clubs here are legendary ven-ues where major artists not only get their starts but return to again and again. The best known is probably the **Cat's Cradle** (300 E. Main St., Carrboro, 919/967-9053, www.catscradle.com). Cat's Cradle is serious about good music; the venue consists of a big, dark room with a stage at the front, a few benches, lots of standing/dancing room, and a small room in the back with a pool table and beer counter. The art-ists who play the Cat's Cradle are leading lights in rock-and-roll, Americana, alt.coun-try, and world music, and the audience comes to hear the music, not to play pool and shoot

Sutton's Drug Store

the breeze. Shows sell out quickly, so keep a sharp eye on the website. **Local 506** (506 W. Franklin St., Chapel Hill, 919/942-5506, www.local506.com) and the **Cave** (452½ W. Franklin St, Chapel Hill, 919/968-9308, http://caverntavern.com, no advance tickets) are also important local venues, tending more towards pop and rock and punk. Note that to attend shows at Local 506, you must first join the club. Membership is only $3, but it has to be arranged at least three days in advance.

PRIVATE CLUBS

Bars and pubs here tend to fall into one of two categories: beer and wine bars, and private clubs. They're not being mean—it has to do with the liquor license. In order for a joint to serve liquor, if it doesn't make more than 30 percent of its revenue from food, it must——like Local 506—be a members-only club that charges annual dues. The three-day rule applies to most such watering holes. Favorite members-only bars include the **Dead Mule** (303 W. Franklin St., Chapel Hill, 919/969-7659, 4 P.M.–2 A.M. daily, $25 membership first year, $5/year renewal), a

hangout for grad students and literary types, in a little house set back from the road on Franklin, and the **Orange County Social Club** (108 E. Main St., Carrboro, 919/933-0669, www .orangecountysocialclub.com, 4 P.M.–2 A.M. daily) in Carrboro, a hip and noisy bar frequented by students.

BEER AND WINE BARS

You have other options if you want to go out for a drink but haven't planned your barhopping three days in advance. The **West End Wine Bar** (450 W. Franklin St., Chapel Hill, 919/967-7599, www.westendwinebar.com, 5 P.M.–2 A.M. daily) has a great rooftop patio, over 100 by-the-glass wines, and lots of "boutique beers." **He's Not Here** (112½ W. Franklin St., Chapel Hill, 919/942-7939, 1 P.M.–2 A.M. daily) has been a hotspot since 1975. There's good live rock and roll, with a low cover charge. **Caffe Driade** (1215-A E. Franklin St., Chapel Hill, 919/942-2333, www.caffedriade.com, 7 A.M.–11 P.M. Mon.–Thurs., 7 A.M.–midnight Fri. and Sat., 7:30 A.M.–11 P.M. Sun.), an elegant little coffee shop in the woods off of East

Franklin Street, serves wine and beer as well as caffeine and pastries, and in the warm months they have live outdoor music on Wednesday, Friday, and Saturday evenings.

SHOPPING
Malls and Shopping Districts
University Mall, on Estes Drive between Franklin and Fordham Boulevard/U.S. 15-501, is gradually changing from being a small 1970s-style mall to a collection of fancy boutiques and commercial art galleries. There are still a few fast-food counters and a discount shoe outlet or two, but these shops are being replaced by upscale jewelry and lingerie stores. Stop in at **Cameron's** (919/942-5554, www.cameronsgallery.com) for pretty one-of-a-kind jewelry and funky stationary, as well as sushi-shaped wind-up toys, librarian action figures, and other comical doodads. University Mall is anchored at its southern terminus by **A Southern Season** (800/253-3663, www.southernseason.com, 10 A.M.–9 P.M. Mon.–Fri., 11 A.M.–6 P.M. Sun.), probably the region's most famous specialty foods seller. With a strong emphasis on local and regional delicacies, Southern Season has a spectacular variety of gourmet foods and fine cookware. Check out the hot sauce and chocolate sections in particular. Southern Season operates a small and very good café, popular for weekend brunches.

Carr Mill Mall (corner of Weaver and Greensboro St., Carrboro behind Weaver Street Market, 919/942-8669, http://carrmillmall.com) in Carrboro is an early example of what has become an important entrepreneurial movement in North Carolina, the transformation of obsolete but historic industrial buildings, particularly old textile mills, into stylish retail space. This 1898 cotton mill building houses some small and very special shops. North Carolina company **Mehera Shaw** (919/929-9133, www.meherashaw.com) has only two retail stores in the world, and unless you're planning a trip to Jaipur, India, now is your chance to browse their lines of handmade but affordable women's clothing, made of gorgeous Indian cotton and silk. **Ali Cat**

(919/932-3954) is an especially nice children's toy store, specializing in high-quality educational games. **Wootini** (919/933-6061), at the other end, is a toy store for grownups. No, not that kind of toys. Wootini is a "purveyor of three-dimensional art." Specializing in plush and wind-up art toys and the work of offbeat cartoonists and pop-artists, the store's concept doesn't translate easily into words—but, like Carrboro, it's strange and charming.

Two fairly recent residential developments, Meadowmont and Southern Village, both planned communities, feature "Main Street" commons dotted with nice stores and cafés. The shops at **Meadowmont,** on Highway 54 (Raleigh Rd.) south of the UNC campus, are a good place to find handmade jewelry, fancy apparel, and luxury cosmetics. On Market Street in **Southern Village,** on U.S. 15-501 south of Chapel Hill, you'll find some lovely garden and home accessory shops, a satellite branch of Weaver Street Market, a pet-friendly bookstore, and, on Thursday evenings in warm-weather months, a farmers market.

Books
Along Franklin Street, which becomes Carrboro's Main Street a few blocks west of campus, you'll find the usual college-town mix of textbook-exchanges, all-night convenience stores, and purveyors of sustainably crafted fair-trade bongs. There are also a handful of chichi women's clothing shops, trendy vintage-wear boutiques, and some great bookstores. Among the best in this last category are **The Book Shop** (400 W. Franklin St., 919/942-5178, www.bookshopinc.com, 11 A.M.–9 P.M. Mon.–Fri., 11 A.M.–6 P.M. Sat., 1–5 P.M. Sun.), a wonderful used and rare book dealer, where you can find a $5 paperback classic or a $1,000 rare first edition. **Internationalist Books** (405 W. Franklin St., 919/942-1740, www.internationalistbooks.org, 11 A.M.–8 P.M. Mon.–Sat., 11 A.M.–6 P.M. Sun.) is the area's best-known source for far-left-of-center political and philosophical literature, and a hangout for progressive activists. **Nice Price Books** (100 Boyd St., Carrboro, 919/929-6222) sells good

NORTH CAROLINA FICTION

Chapel Hill has long been one of the literary capitals of the South, the heart of a state that has produced as many great writers as any in the union. Following is a selection of some of the best fiction by North Carolina writers and/or about North Carolina, past and present.

- Sheila Adams: *My Old True Love; Come and Go With Me*

- Doris Betts: *Souls Raised from the Dead; Beasts of the Southern Wilds; Heading West; The Gentle Insurrection*

- Fred Chappell: *I Am One of You Forever; Brighten the Corner Where You Are; Look Back All the Green Valley; Farewell, I'm Bound to Leave You*

- Charles W. Chestnut: *Stories, Novels, and Essays; The Conjure Woman*

- Clyde Edgerton: *Raney; Walking Across Egypt*

- Charles Frazier: *Cold Mountain; Thirteen Moons*

- Kaye Gibbons: *Ellen Foster; A Virtuous Woman; Charms for the Easy Life; Divining Women*

- Alan Gurganus: *The Oldest Living Confederate Widow Tells All; White People; Plays Well with Others*

- Josephine Humphries: *Nowhere Else on Earth*

- Randall Kenan: *Let the Dead Bury Their Dead; A Visitation of Spirits*

- Margaret Maron: *Uncommon Clay; Bloody Kin*

- Jill McCorkle: *The Cheer Leader; Final Vinyl Days; Crash Diet; Tending to Virginia*

- Robert Morgan: *Gap Creek; The Truest Pleasure; This Rock*

- Reynolds Price: *A Long and Happy Life; Kate Vaiden; Blue Calhoun*

- Lee Smith: *On Agate Hill; Devil's Dream; Oral History; Me and My Baby View the Eclipse*

- Max Steele: *The Hat of My Mother; The Cat and the Coffee Drinkers; Where She Brushed Her Hair; The Goblins Must Go Barefoot*

- Thomas Wolfe: *You Can't Go Home Again; Look Homeward, Angel; Of Time and the River*

secondhand books and music, including a good selection of used vinyl.

SPORTS AND RECREATION
Botanical Gardens

UNC's **North Carolina Botanical Garden** (Old Mason Farm Rd. off of U.S. 15-501/54, 919/962-0522, www.ncbg.unc.edu, 8 A.M.–5 P.M. Mon.–Fri., 9 A.M.–5 P.M. Sat., 1–5 P.M. Sun.) is the Southeast's largest botanical garden. The 800 acres contain beautiful hiking trails, and an herb garden, aquatic plant area, and a carnivorous plant garden. Back on campus, **Coker Arboretum** (corner of E. Cameron St. and Raleigh St., dawn–dusk daily) is much smaller, but it's also a beautiful retreat. The

five landscaped acres are most beautiful in the springtime, when students will make detours on their way to class just to pass through the amazing 300-foot-long arbor of purple wisteria.

Spectator Sports

Tar Heel athletics (www.tarheelblue.com) is the great love of our collective life here in Chapel Hill. The pinnacle of UNC sports is the men's basketball team—five-time NCAA Champions, coached for many years by the legendary Dean Smith and now by fellow Hall of Famer Roy Williams, and college home court to Michael Jordan, James Worthy, Lennie Rosenbluth, and a dizzying number of other all-time great basketball players. The men play at the Dean E. Smith Center on Skipper Bowles Road, a great glowing dome that seats more than 20,000. Carolina women's basketball too is of the highest caliber. Coached by Sylvia Hatchell, a member of the Women's Basketball Hall of Fame, the Tar Heel women play at historic Carmichael Auditorium in the heart of campus. (When the women play Duke at home, their biggest game of the year, they move over to the much larger Smith Center.) Coach Butch Davis leads the football team, whose home field is the 1927 Kenan Stadium. The baseball team plays at Boshamer Stadium which, like the Smith Center and Kenan Stadium, is off of Manning Drive in the southern part of campus, in the area of the Medical School. UNC excels in many other sports too—soccer (Mia Hamm is an alumna), golf (Davis Love III is an alumnus), track (ditto Marion Jones), and more.

Acquiring tickets to UNC athletic events ranges from well nigh impossible to quite easy, with men's basketball tickets at the most precious end of the spectrum, followed by football and women's basketball. Tips on snagging men's basketball tickets can be found in the *Scoring ACC Basketball Tickets* sidebar. For all other tickets, try your luck with the main ticket office (800/722-4335, www.tarheelblue.com). Craigslist (www.craigslist.org) and eBay (www.ebay.com) are pretty reliable sources too.

ACCOMMODATIONS

One of the favorite inns in the entire state, the **C Carolina Inn** (211 Pittsboro St., 800/962-8519, www.carolinainn.com, from approx. $180) has been a landmark on the UNC campus since it first opened in 1924. It's the place where visiting dignitaries are hosted, where the most important faculty functions take place, where very lucky couples get married, and where old alumni couples celebrate their milestone anniversaries. The Carolina Inn is located at the center of the UNC campus, between the original quads and the modern medical school complexes, and not far from the Dean Smith Center. Any special occasion related to the University will book the Carolina Inn far in advance—homecoming weekends, for example, and big basketball and football games. The Inn's restaurant, **Carolina**

© SARAH BRYAN

Carolina Inn

CrossRoads (919/918-2735, $20–30), serves three elegant meals a day, created by chef Jimmy Reale, a believer in creative cuisine from local ingredients. Afternoon tea (3 P.M. Mon.–Sat. except holidays, $18–28) at the Carolina Inn is a popular treat in Chapel Hill; reservations are recommended.

The **Franklin Hotel** (311 W. Franklin St., 866/831-5999, www.franklinhotelnc.com, from approx. $200) is a new boutique hotel, with a great location on Franklin Street near where Chapel Hill and Carrboro blend together. The furnishings are elegant and the beds extremely comfortable. Rooms have great modern touches like flat-screen LCD HDTVs and iPod docks.

The **◖ Inn at Bingham School** (Hwy. 54 and Mebane Oaks Rd., near Saxapahaw, 800/566-5583, www.chapel-hill-inn.com, rooms $150, cottage $195) is a 200-year-old home, originally the residence of the headmaster of the preparatory academy that operated here in the 18th and 19th centuries. The house sits in a region of sweeping countryside, near the little town of Saxapahaw, about 20 minutes outside Chapel Hill. Innkeepers Francois and Christina Deprez are renowned hosts and chefs whose talents shine in this beautiful setting.

Chapel Hill also has a handful of motels where rooms usually run in the $80–100 range. The **Days Inn** (1312 N. Fordham Blvd./U.S. 15-501, 919/929-3090, www.daysinn.com), **Holiday Inn** (1301 N. Fordham Blvd./U.S. 15-501, 919/929-2171, www.hichapelhill.com), and **Hampton Inn** (6121 Farrington Rd., 919/403-8700, www.hamptoninn.com) are all in convenient and safe neighborhoods. None is within walking distance of campus, but campus is only a very brief ride away by car or bus (remember, they're free here!).

FOOD
Southern and Soul
◖ Crook's Corner (610 W. Franklin St., 919/929-7643, dinner 5:30 P.M. Tues.–Sun., brunch 10:30 A.M.–2 P.M. Sun.), is one of the most influential restaurants in the South. It was the late Bill Eliot, its first chef, who put this restaurant on the culinary map with, among other brilliant creations, his now world-famous shrimp and grits recipe. Now led by chef Bill Smith, a native Tar Heel whose simple yet exquisite recipes—including watermelon and tomato salad, honeysuckle sorbet, and some of the best fried green tomatoes you'll ever find—Crook's Corner continues to be a great innovator in Southern cuisine.

Just a few blocks from Crook's Corner is another legendary Carolina chef's restaurant, **Mama Dip's Kitchen** (408 W. Rosemary St., 919/942-5837, www.mamadips.com, 8 A.M.–9:30 P.M. Mon.–Sat., 8 A.M.–9 P.M. Sun.). Proprietress Mildred Council, Mama Dip herself, has been cooking since she was nine years old, and if you grew up in the South, you'll recognize at first bite the comfort-food recipes of a Southern matriarch. Dip's is known for its good fried chicken and for its vegetables. In soul food, the vegetable sides are not an afterthought, but an art in their own right. Vegetarians, be sure to ask your server which vegetable dishes are truly vegetarian. As is the old-time way, Dip's greens and beans sometimes conceal a zest of fatback.

Mrs. Council learned the cooking and restaurant business from her father, Bill Minor, an early African American businessman in the area and the owner of Chapel Hill's first fast-food style restaurant. The Council family's culinary tradition is now in its fourth generation, with Mama Dip's daughter Bon now being the proprietress of a restaurant, which she operates with her own daughter, Tori. **Bon's Home Cooking** (133 W. Franklin St., Chapel Hill, 919/960-7630, www.bonshomecookin.com, 11 A.M.–9 P.M. Mon.–Fri., 9 A.M.–9 P.M. Sat., 10 A.M.–3 P.M. Sun., under $15) serves barbecue, fried chicken and fried fish, and many other home-style specialties. Vegetarians will find plenty of vegetable dishes.

Eclectic American
The dining facilities at **Weaver Street Market** (101 E. Weaver St., 919/929-0100, www.weaverstreetmarket.coop, 7:30 A.M.–9 P.M. Mon.–Fri., 8 A.M.–9 P.M. Sat. and Sun.) are totally

utilitarian, just chairs and metal tables inside and on the front lawn of this organic foods co-op. Customers serve themselves from a hot bar and pay at the grocery register, and the food is priced unceremoniously by the pound. Now that you're prepared for a non-restaurant environment—it is, after all, a grocery store—don't hesitate to dine at Weaver Street Market. The food is delicious. There's always a healthy assortment of vegetable choices, but meat-eaters will find hearty carnivorous fare too. The best item on the menu is a very simple dish of hot, lightly steamed kale or collards—stay with me, now—in a delicate Asian sesame-soy sauce dressing. It will make a convert of the most devout hater of greens.

Pepper's Pizza (127 E. Franklin St., 919/967-7766) is a jam-packed favorite of Carolina students, but it's well worth braving the crowd and the noise to have a meal here. The choose-your-own-toppings menu has dozens of choices, and even the most eccentric pizza lover will be able to construct his dream. The crust is great, the olive oil seeps through the cheese, and the servings are generous. There is little by way of non-pizza fare, but those items too are delicious. The gazpacho may be the best dish on any menu in town.

Spotted Dog (111 E. Main St., Carrboro, 919/933-1117, www.spotteddog.biz, 11:30 A.M.–midnight Tues.–Sat., under $15) is a boisterous and noisy place, especially on Friday and Saturday nights, when it fills up with students. There is often a wait, but Spotted Dog's location in a wedge-shaped block in the middle of Carrboro is a very pleasant place to hang out on a warm evening. The food is terrific, with great burgers and sandwiches, plenty of creative meat and seafood dishes, and a great selection of artfully crafted vegetarian and vegan creations.

A special treat for Triangle diners is **Sage** (Timberlyne Shopping Center, 1129 Weaver Dairy Rd., Chapel Hill, 919/968-9266, around $20), a vegetarian and vegan restaurant that draws at least as many omnivores as hard-core veggies. The proprietress is originally from Iran, where she learned to cook, and Sage's beautiful dishes are a fusion of classic Persian cooking and modern vegetarian haute cuisine.

Try the pomegranate soup and the appetizer platter in addition to the can't-miss entrées.

Also in the Timberlyne Shopping Center, a few doors down from Sage, is **Margaret's Cantina** (Timberlyne Shopping Center, 1129 Weaver Dairy Rd., 919/942-4745, www.margaretscantina.com, lunch weekdays, dinner Mon.–Sat., under $15). This popular Southwestern café uses as many fresh, local, and organic ingredients as possible, and the results are divine. Don't miss the sweet potato and black bean burrito.

Spice Street (University Mall, 201 S. Estes Dr., 919/928-8200, http://ghgrestaurants.com, lunch 11:30 A.M.–2:30 P.M. Mon.–Sat., dinner 5:30–10 P.M. Sun.–Thurs. and 5:30–10:30 P.M. Fri.–Sat., sushi bar 5:30–10 P.M. Mon.–Thurs., 5:30–10:30 P.M. Fri.–Sat., $15–50) is a dark, stylish café tucked into a side of University Mall. The tremendously eclectic bill of fare draws from American, Mediterranean, and Asian cuisines, and includes a long sushi menu and dim sum offerings. On Monday nights during basketball season, the Tar Heels' celebrity coach Roy Williams hosts his radio show from Spice Street, so if you want to visit on a Monday evening, expect limited availability and unlimited Carolina blue.

Local Fare

The **Carrboro Farmers' Market** (301 W. Main St., http://carrborofarmersmarket.com, 7 A.M.–noon Sat., 3:30 P.M.–6:30 P.M. Wed.) is a bustling, festive scene. The market features local organic produce in abundance, as well as gorgeous cut flowers, artisan cheeses, and charmingly cuckoo lawn art.

The Chapel Hill area is blessed with a local dairy, which supplies residents not only with old-fashioned bottled milk, but with fantastic ice cream. To sample Mapleview Ice Cream, you have two choices beyond the freezer aisle of the grocery store. At the Carrboro **Mapleview store** (100 E. Weaver St., 919/967-6842), you can pick up a cone or cup to eat while you listen to one of the free concerts on the lawn of Weaver Street Market, directly across the street. Alternatively, you might choose to make the scenic drive to the home store (3111

Dairyland Rd., 919/933-3600, www.mapleview farm.com, noon–10 P.M. daily), out in the country towards Hillsborough, where you can linger over your ice cream on the front porch, surrounded by the beautiful farmland of Orange County.

HILLSBOROUGH

The beautiful little town of Hillsborough, today home to a large number of authors and other artists, and overflow Chapel Hillians, figured into many important parts of North Carolina history. Now on the National Register of Historic Places, Hillsborough was the site of an early trading path along the Eno River, used by the Occaneechi Indians and later by white settlers; 1788's Constitutional Convention (in which North Carolinians rejected the Constitution); and, supposedly, Daniel Boone's departure for Kentucky in 1776.

Historic Downtown

The **Alexander Dickson House** (150 E. King St., 919/732-7741, www.historichillsborough .org, 9 A.M.–4 P.M. Mon.–Fri., 10 A.M.–4 P.M. Sat., 1–4 P.M. Sun.) was built in the 1790s, a Quaker-plan house that would be headquarters to General Joseph Johnston during the Civil War. Today it's the Orange County Visitors Center, where you can pick up local information before visiting the medicinal garden and beginning your tour.

The **Burwell School** (319 N. Churton St., 919/732-7451, www.burwellschool.org, 11 A.M.–4 P.M. Wed.–Sat., 1–4 P.M. Sun.) has had several interesting lifetimes. The handsome old building was one of the state's earliest girls' schools for its first 20 years, 1837–1857. During the War Between the States, the Collins family, owners of Somerset Plantation down in Creswell, sheltered here. A young woman named Elizabeth Hobbes Keckly grew up a slave here, but she went on to become Mary Todd Lincoln's dressmaker and author of an insightful book about the first lady. Docent- and self-guided tours are available.

The Old Orange County Courthouse, now the county judicial building, is a pretty 1844 Greek Revival civic building, just what one hopes for from a small Southern courthouse town. At the corner of Cameron and East King Streets, a historical marker identifies the spot where six Regulators were hanged in 1771, after they refused Governor Tryon's insistence that they declare loyalty to the crown.

Just east of downtown, **Ayr Mount Historic Site** (376 St. Mary's Rd., 919/732-6886, tours $6, hours vary by season) preserves an important 1815 home built by a Scottish merchant. Tours begin on the hour, and lead visitors through the very fine federal house. A walking trail called the Poets Walk, which traverses scenic parts of the 265-acre property, is free and open every day.

Shopping

The Shops at Daniel Boone, an old strip mall development off of I-40 (exit 261), is home to a cluster of antique shops. The one simply called **Antique Mall** (919/732-8882) is the largest and has the most compelling selection of goods, but several shops surrounding it are also fun places to visit.

Food

Tupelo's Restaurant (101 N. Churton St., 919/643-7722, www.tupelos.com, lunch 11:30 A.M.–3 P.M. Mon.–Sat., 5–9 P.M. Mon.–Thurs., 5–10 P.M. Fri.–Sat.) serves Cajun and New Orleans–style food at a great location in the middle of town. The **Village Diner** (600 W. King St., 919/732-7032, 6:30 A.M.–8 P.M. Mon.–Fri.) is Hillsborough's longest-operating restaurant, a buffet-style country kitchen that serves barbecue and seafood, and a mean banana pudding. **Tony's Barbecue** (646 N. Churton St., 919/732-3591, 6 A.M.–4 P.M. Mon.–Sat.) also serves homemade BBQ, with country ham and biscuits, milkshakes, and other fattening treats. **Valour's Patisserie & Bistro** serves French treats for breakfast and lunch, from croissants and tarts to quiche and croque monsieur.

FEARRINGTON VILLAGE

Between Chapel Hill and Pittsboro on U.S. 15-501, Fearrington Village is a recently developed planned community, but one that is well worth exploring. Fearrington is built on the grounds of an old dairy farm, and it has adopted as its mascots a herd of belted Galloway cattle—beautiful stout beasts with white-belted black hides. Coming in from U.S. 15-501, if you don't spot the signs for Fearrington, you'll certainly notice the cows.

Events

Adding to the appeal of Fearrington Village is the great deal of activity and events that take place here: readings by prominent authors, concerts and square dances, antique shows, and the popular annual **Folk Art Show** (Feb., www.fearrington.com/village/folkart.asp). The Folk Art Show runs more to outsider or visionary art, technically speaking, than folk art, but it's still an exciting event.

Accommodations and Food

The center of the action is the **◖ Fearrington House** (2000 Fearrington Village Center, 919/542-2121, www.fearrington.com, from $250), an extremely luxurious inn that garners awards and accolades from all quarters. It's the only inn in North Carolina to receive both the Five Diamond Award from AAA and Exxon Mobil's Five Star Award. Impossibly plush rooms feature canopied feather beds, restful colors and lighting, beautiful pine floorboards salvaged from an antique building in England, and vases of fresh flowers. Though the prices are steep, the inn offers several weekend package options that are good bargains, combining luxury rooms, three-course dinners and English teatime, gift cards for the shops, and more.

The **Fearrington House Restaurant** (2000 Fearrington Village Center, 919/542-2121, www.fearrington.com, prix fixe $69 for three-course meal, $79 for four-course meal) is no less exceptional than the inn. The restaurant, which occupies the 1927 farmhouse original to the property, has won major awards and recognitions, having been named one of *Travel + Leisure*'s three best United States restaurants in their World's Best Service Awards, one of National Geographic's 10 Best Destination Restaurants, and *Gourmet*

magazine's Best Farm-to-Table Restaurant for Special Occasions. The prix-fixe menu of three or four courses includes such incredible dishes as "Arctic Char with Orange and Grapefruit Salad, Cucumbers, Blood Orange Sorbet, Keta Caviar and a Vanilla Oil," and "Pan-Fried Veal Sweetbreads with Vegetable Tagliatelle and a Sherry Vinegar Sauce." (There's a vegetarian option in each course, though not vegan.) Among desserts offered are "Vanilla Poached Pineapple with a Coconut Gateaux, Lime Sorbet and a Pistachio Biscotti," and one intriguingly called, "Chocolate Chocolate Chocolate."

PITTSBORO

Pittsboro is half an hour south of Chapel Hill on U.S. 15/501, an easy afternoon's trip if you're staying in the Triangle. This small county seat is laid out like a wheel, with the 1881 courthouse at the hub and its antique shops and cafes radiating out in all directions.

Carnivore Preservation Trust

Founded in 1981 by a geneticist from the University of North Carolina, the Carnivore Preservation Trust (1940 Hanks Chapel Rd., 919/542-4684, www.cptigers.org, tours 10 A.M. and 1 P.M. Sat. and Sun., Sat. evenings at sunset Apr.–Oct., $12 adults, $10 off-season, $7 children, $5 off-season, $22 sunset tours, $3 photo release fee) had as its original mission the breeding of endangered wild cats. It soon became apparent, though, that there was also an overwhelming need to create a safe haven for big cats that were abused or abandoned, were illegal pets or in the entertainment industry, or had lived at zoos that closed. Among the dozens of cats living at CPT today are a pair of tigers who were found as cubs walking along a highway near Charlotte; a tiger seized at a traffic stop (he was the passenger); a tiger rescued from an "owner" who tried to have him declawed and defanged; several other tigers, and many leopards, jaguars, serval cats, ocelots, kinkajous, caracals, and binturongs.

On the tour of the Carnivore Preservation Trust, you'll meet many of the big cats, some from just a few feet away. Visitors to CPT can

© ELIZABETH B. THOMSEN

Chatham County Courthouse, Pittsboro

expect tours to last approximately two hours and to involve a lot of walking, as it's a large property. (The paths are not equipped for strollers or wheelchairs.) You'll see the greatest number of cats during the warm-weather sunset tours, when the animals are likely to be prowling about in the evening shade.

Shopping

The Chatham County Courthouse sits in an island in the center of Pittsboro, and the blocks that radiate out from it form a tiny but very interesting shopping district. At a corner nearest to the courthouse is **Beggars and Choosers** (38 Hillsboro St., 919/542-5884), "outfitters to the funky." The Betty Boop statue standing out front gives you an idea about the great vintage clothes you'll find inside. A couple of blocks up are the offices of the **Chatham Arts Council** (121 Hillsboro St., 919/542-0394, http://chathamarts.org). They have a nice little museum shop in front, which sells art from a variety of disciplines by some of Chatham County's amazingly creative folks.

Food

Pittsboro's **General Store Café** (39 West St., 919/542-2432, www.thegeneralstore cafe.com, 8 A.M.–10 P.M. Mon.–Wed., 8 A.M.–11 P.M. Thurs., 8 A.M.–noon Fri.–Sat., and 9 A.M.–3 P.M. Sun.) is a casual and comfortable place to get a really good breakfast, lunch, or dinner. Among their specialties are huge burritos—try the Mayan burrito, with sweet potatoes and jerk chicken, and the Pittsburrito, with spinach and brown rice. The General Store is also a favorite music venue in the area, and on many weeknights and some Sunday brunch-times you can catch good local old-time, jazz, and other kinds of music, while having a chance to peruse paintings and photography by intriguing local artists.

Sandy Lowlands

Between the Triangle and the beaches lie a band of towns and cities that were once important pulse-points in North Carolina's tobacco economy. Though their roles have changed with the waning of that industry, towns like Wilson and its neighbors continue to be culturally vital, architecturally interesting, and full of good places to browse for antiques and to gobble up barbecue.

WILSON
Sights

A peculiar little stone building on Nash Street East houses an unusual and extremely interesting museum, the **Oliver Nestus Freeman Roundhouse African-American Museum** (1202 Nash St. E., 252/296-3056, 9 A.M.–4 P.M. Tues.–Sat.). The Roundhouse is not a railroad roundhouse, but a three-room circular building made of stones, saplings, and an admixture of strange materials like Coke bottles and marbles—with a dinosaur sculpture out front. The museum celebrates the creativity of the builder, Nestus Freeman, as well as the contributions of generations of African Americans in Wilson.

Entertainment and Events

The **Arts Council of Wilson** (124 Nash St. S.W., 252/291-4329, www.wilsonarts.com) hosts a wonderful annual event, the spring **Theater of the American South** (www.theateroftheamericansouth.org). The heart of each year's festival is two repertory productions by prominent Southern playwrights, but it also hosts demonstrations by celebrity Southern chefs (held in the homes of hospitable Wilson citizens), gospel concerts, garden parties, and more fun. Plays take place at the **Edna Boykin Cultural Center** (108 W. Nash St.), a fantastic restored 1919 vaudeville theater.

Sports and Recreation

Wilson's baseball park, Fleming Stadium, was built in 1939 through the Works Projects Administration. The **Wilson Tobs** (300 Stadium St., 252/291-8627, www.wilsontobs.com, $4 general, $5 box seats, games start at 7:05 P.M. Mon.–Sat., 6:05 P.M. Sun.), a Coastal Plain All Star minor-league baseball team, have been playing at Fleming Stadium since that first year. The stadium is also home of the **North Carolina Baseball Museum** (252/296-3048), which honors North Carolina baseball greats including Negro League star and Rocky Mount native Buck Leonard, Hertford native "Catfish" Hunter, and Roxboro's Enos "Country" Slaughter.

ANGIER

For many years, farmer Marvin Johnson of Angier was famous in these parts for two things: his elderly pet alligator, whom he handfed hotdogs, and his **Gourd Museum** (Hwy. 55 across from Kennebec Airport, 919/639-8571, open daylight hours, free). The alligator was called home many years ago, but the Gourd Museum is still going strong. Mr. Johnson's collection contains hundreds of painted and carved gourds—this is a popular craft in North Carolina—including a great many gourd animals, gourd hats, a gourd that looks like Benjamin Franklin, and a scene of the Last Supper in which all the figures are made out of gourd seeds. Marvin Johnson has passed away, and now his nephew maintains the collection. The museum, housed in a small building on family property, is unlocked in the morning and locked up again at night, so stop by and walk right in.

SELMA

The small town of Selma, located east of Raleigh at the intersection of I-95 and U.S. 70, is packed with antique shops. Among the best and largest is **TWM's Antique Mall** (112 S. Pollock St./Hwy. 301, 919/965-6699, www.twmsantiquemall.com), which is one of those rambling antique shops with seemingly endless rooms, each filled with the booths of many dealers, crammed with furniture and china and books and toys. Another huge emporium is the **Selma Cotton Mills** (1105 W. Anderson St., 919/868-8014, 9 A.M.–5 P.M. Fri.–Sun.), a weekends-only warehouse full of antiques and secondhand items. While in Selma, stop in for a snack at the **Edel Weiss Bakery and Café** (103 S. Raiford St., 919/965-8170, www.edelweissbakery.com, 9:30 A.M.–6 P.M. Mon.–Thurs., 9:30 A.M.–9 P.M. Fri. and Sat.), for bratwurst, wiener schnitzel, goulash, and other German specialties, and a full menu of desserts and baked goods.

WINSTON-SALEM AND CENTRAL CAROLINA

The average visitors to North Carolina spend their time at the beach, in the mountains, or in one of the two major metropolitan areas, Charlotte and the Triangle. Those who skip central North Carolina are missing some of the state's most beautiful countryside, most interesting towns, and best food and wine.

Central North Carolina is bounded at the northeast by Raleigh, and at the southeast by a region known as the Sandhills, a band of deep pineywoods and sandy soil, thought by some geologists to be the remains of primeval sand dunes. Charlotte and its brood of suburbs nest just beyond the southwest corner, expanding every day in every direction. All along the northwestern edge of central North Carolina, rich farmland and hardwood forests form a pedestal for the nearby foothills of the Blue Ridge.

Winston-Salem and Greensboro are the two cities in this region, close kin in geography and origins, but different enough that each deserves its own share of your time. Winston-Salem traces its roots to the Moravians, a sect of Central European religious pilgrims who traveled down the Great Wagon Road in the 18th century from their American home base of Bethlehem, Pennsylvania, through the Shenandoah Valley, and into these Carolina hills. The town they established, Salem, was known far and wide in early North Carolina as the home of men and women of integrity and education, whose skills as craftspeople were unsurpassed in the region. Greensboro too counts among its ancestors an early community of quietist Christians, the Quakers, whose abolitionist and pacifist beliefs made

HIGHLIGHTS

◖ **Old Salem:** Craftspeople and historic interpreters bring this 18th- and 19th-century religious community to life in the beautiful restored Moravian village of Salem (page 156).

◖ **North Carolina Zoo:** Drive through rolling countryside and wander among traditional exhibits to see elephants, alligators, and many more exciting creatures one wouldn't expect to encounter here in the Carolina Piedmont (page 172).

◖ **Liberty Antiques Festival:** Held twice a year, this event is a favorite among antique collectors throughout the Southeast. From the finest of antique Southern furniture to baseball cards, tobacco tags, and other fun doodads, enthusiasts of old stuff will find treasures here (page 173).

◖ **North Carolina Pottery Center:** The tiny town of Seagrove is home to a generations-old tradition of folk pottery. Start your visit at the Pottery Center and then explore the 100-plus studios tucked along the lovely country roads surrounding Seagrove (page 174).

◖ **Uwharrie National Forest:** This hauntingly pretty and ecologically unique outcropping of low mountains is unfamiliar even to most North Carolinians. Hiding under the canopy of forest are many miles of hiking trails and wilderness campsites, as well as mysterious back roads (page 176).

LOOK FOR ◖ TO FIND RECOMMENDED SIGHTS, ACTIVITIES, DINING, AND LODGING.

their life in the 18th- and 19th-century South terribly challenging at times. The Moravian and Quaker faiths are still practiced by many in this part of North Carolina, and their marks on the state's history are indelible.

Winston-Salem and Greensboro today are homes of several distinguished universities and colleges. Wake Forest University in Winston is the most prominent, but North Carolina A&T, Guilford College, and UNC-Greensboro are also excellent, historic schools. Both cities have very active artistic scenes, from classical opera, ballet, and orchestras to

museums of ancient fine arts and contemporary folk arts.

Although located smack-dab in the middle of the state, the Uwharrie Mountains are North Carolina's biggest secret. Seemingly out of nowhere sprouts this beautiful and eerie cluster of high hills, full of hiking trails and camping sites and surprising historical treasures. At the edge of the Uwharries is Seagrove, a tiny town known for its traditional pottery. Within just a few miles of the stoplight that is downtown Seagrove, artists at over 100 individual pottery studios turn out highly prized stoneware in the

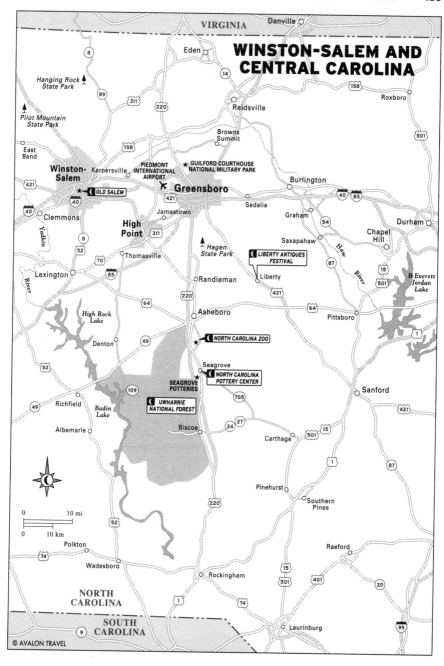

© AVALON TRAVEL

manner passed down to them by the ancestors of the area's great pottery families. Over towards Fayetteville, where the Sandhills unfold into the coastal plain, you'll find Southern Pines and Pinehurst, the location of some of the world's best golf courses. If you watch golf on TV, you're probably very familiar with some of these courses, which have hosted the U.S. Open and other international events.

Ignore those brochures boasting that you can leave Raleigh and be in the mountains or at the beach in two or three hours. The folks who write that kind of promo don't know what's good. Get off of I-40 and I-85 and take a slow road through the small towns.

PLANNING YOUR TIME

As this is a large region with much to see, plan to devote more than one day to central North Carolina. The golf towns of the Sandhills are clustered in the southeast corner of the region, and are an easy drive from Raleigh and Wilmington. The Seagrove potteries and Uwharrie Mountains are most easily accessible from U.S. 220, which will also carry you past the North Carolina Zoo. Winston-Salem and Greensboro are less than a half-hour apart by highway, on a day with light traffic, but both are major cities in their own rights and as such pack a wallop of activities and could easily fill a weekend each.

For the eastern and western thirds of the state, summer is the busiest time and the high season for prices and traffic. July and August weather sends central Carolinians fleeing for the mountains and coast. In the Southern Pines/Pinehurst area, the season peaks in the springtime. Between March and May, temperatures are the nicest for golfing, generally in the 60s–80s. (Come summertime, the heat can make it unpleasant and even unsafe to spend hours on the links.) If you're planning a golf trip to the Sandhills in springtime, make your reservations—for tee times and restaurants, as well as lodging—as far in advance as possible.

GETTING THERE AND AROUND

Winston-Salem and Greensboro are connected to North Carolina's other cities by two of the state's major highways, I-40 and I-85. Southern Pines and the Sandhills are most easily reached by U.S. 1 and U.S. 15/501, and U.S. 220 will carry you into the heart of the region, through Asheboro and Seagrove. There are good **local bus systems** in Winston-Salem (336/727-2648, www.wstransit .com) and Greensboro (336/335-6499, www .greensboro-nc.gov/departments/GDOT), and they are linked to each other and to nearby towns by the Piedmont Area Regional Transit's **Express Bus** (336/662-0002, www.partnc.org). Greensboro is a major air hub, and a stop on **Amtrak's** Piedmont/ Carolinian line (236 E. Washington St., 800/872-7245, station open 24 hours daily).

Winston-Salem

The village of Salem was established in the mid-18th century by the Unitas Fratrum, better known as the Moravians, a community of Protestant pilgrims whose faith led them from Europe to the Americas, and eventually into the hills of North Carolina. Many of the first Carolina Moravians came from the Bethlehem, Pennsylvania, area, and hence some of the Salem area's beautiful architecture and other folk traditions have an appearance that might remind one distinctly of the Pennsylvania Dutch aesthetic. Known for excellent and unostentatious craftsmanship, their strong faith and community bond, and their quiet ways, the Moravians were a unique cultural enclave in early North Carolina. Today more than 20,000 North Carolinians belong to the Unitas Fratrum, keeping alive not only the religion but

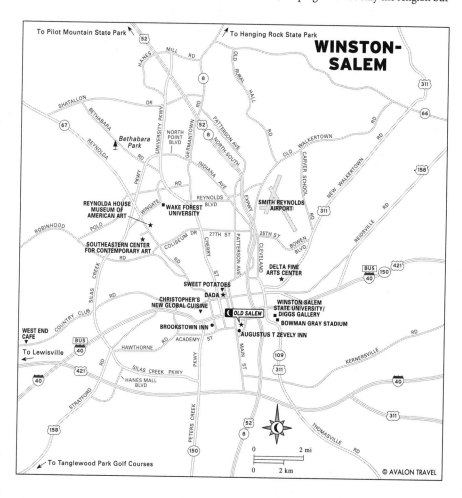

© AVALON TRAVEL

also many Moravian folk traditions, like sacred brass bands, and much-coveted baked goods.

The Winston part of Winston-Salem was founded as Forsyth County's seat, and through the 19th and early 20th century it boomed as an industrial and trading hub, fed by what seemed for generations an endless stream of tobacco and textile money. Though the textile mills are nearly gone in North Carolina, and the cigarette industry sputters along in fits and starts, Winston-Salem is still alive and well as a banking center and the home of Wake Forest University, Winston-Salem State University, and other important educational institutions.

SIGHTS
◖ Old Salem

Though nestled in the center of a modern city, Old Salem (900 Old Salem Rd., 888/653-7253, www.oldsalem.org, 9 A.M.–5:30 P.M. Mon.–Sat., 12:30–5:30 P.M. Sun., closed Mon. during Jan. and Feb.) was once a bustling independent village that was home to the industrious Moravians. Throughout the second half of the 18th century and all of the 19th century, the German-speaking Unitas Fratrum produced beautiful and essential ceramics, furniture, tools, and other goods upon which their neighbors in the Carolina backcountry depended. That era is now recreated in the streets and homes of the old village, where costumed interpreters reconstruct the old Moravian ways and continue to make expertly crafted goods prized by fellow Carolinians.

Old Salem is also home to three museums, each a gem, and all housed in the Horton Museum Center. The **Museum of Early Southern Decorative Arts** (924 S. Main St., www.oldsalem.org, 9:30 A.M.–4:30 P.M. Tues.–Sat., 1–5 P.M. Sun., closed Mon. during Jan. and Feb.) recreates 24 period rooms and six galleries to display the furniture, paintings, fabrics, and other distinctive decorative arts of the Old South, representing the years between 1670 and approximately 1850 in the Lowcountry, Chesapeake, and Backcountry regions. The **Old Salem Toy Museum** (924 S. Main St., www.oldsalem.org,

© LARRY DANIEL

T. Bagge: Merchant is a great place to pick up a souvenir of Old Salem.

9:30 A.M.–4:30 P.M. Tues.–Sat., 1–5 P.M. Sun., closed Mon. during Jan. and Feb.) is a charming collection of antique playthings, not only toys that were played with by Moravian children here in Salem, but the treasures of children from almost 2,000 years ago right up into the 20th century. In the **Old Salem Children's Museum** (924 S. Main St., www.oldsalem.org, 9:30 A.M.–4:30 P.M. Tues.–Sat., 1–4:30 P.M. Sun., closed Mon. during Jan. and Feb.), young visitors can learn 18th-century skills and games in an interactive manner that will make them excited to explore the rest of Old Salem.

As you walk through the streets of the old village, you'll pass dozens of historic buildings that house the workshops of many kinds of artisans, and buildings that hold great significance in the history of this religious community. Among these are the **Single Brothers' House** and **Single Sisters' House,** the 18th-century dormitories in which "choirs," groups of young unmarried Moravians men and women, lived and worked. The **Salem Tavern** is an impressive old lodge where George Washington stayed on his 1791 tour of the South. The **Vierling House** (463 Church St. SE), home of the Berlin-trained doctor who came to be Salem's town physician in 1790, is a fascinating repository of early medical and pharmaceutical goods. **Winkler Bakery** (521 S. Main St.) was run by Swiss-born Christian Winkler and his descendants for over 120 years, and their wood-burning ovens are still turning out Moravian delicacies today. Allow yourself plenty of time to visit Old Salem. There's a great deal to see.

Museums

Winston-Salem's multitude of museums represent art of many places and centuries. **The Southeastern Center for Contemporary Art** (750 Marguerite Dr., 336/725-1904, www.secca.org, 10 A.M.–5 P.M. Wed.–Sat., 10 A.M.–8 P.M. first Thurs. of every month, free) hosts changing exhibits of stimulating modern work in a variety of media. The **Reynolda House Museum of American Art** (2250 Reynolda Rd., 888/663-1149, www.reynoldahouse.org, 9:30 A.M.–4:30 P.M. Tues.–Sat., 1:30–4:30 P.M. Sun, no admittance after 4 P.M., $10 adults, $9 over 60 and teachers with ID, $8.50 AAA members, free for students with ID and children under 18) has a distinguished collection of American masterpieces from colonial times through the present day. The **Diggs Gallery** (601 S. Martin Luther King Dr., 336/750-2458, www.wssu.edu, 11 A.M.–5 P.M. Tues.–Sat., free) at Winston-Salem State University has excellent permanent and changing exhibitions of work by African and African American artists, with a particular emphasis on North Carolina and the Southeast. **Delta Fine Arts Center** (2611 New Walkertown Rd., 336/722-2625, www.deltafinearts.org, 10 A.M.–5 P.M. Tues.–Fri., 11 A.M.–3 P.M. Sat., free) also promotes African American arts, both visual and performing.

A very different kind of gallery is the **Winston Cup Museum** (1355 N. Martin Luther King Dr., 336/724-4557, www.winstoncupmuseum.com, 10 A.M.–5 P.M. Tues.–Sat.,

$5 adults, $3 5–12 years old, free for children under 5), which chronicles R. J. Reynolds' 33-year sponsorship of NASCAR. (There can be no more Carolinian combination than cigarettes and stock cars.) Here you'll see cars driven by Dale Senior and Dale Junior (as the Earnhardts are known in these parts), drivers' helmets, winners' checks, and other great racing memorabilia.

Historic Bethabara Park

In northern Winston-Salem, Bethabara Park (2147 Bethabara Rd., 336/924-8191, www.bethabarapark.com, guided tours Apr. 1–Nov., 10:30 A.M.–4:30 P.M. Tues.–Fri., 1:30–4:30 P.M. Sat. and Sun., $2 adults, $1 children) explores an even earlier period of Moravian settlement than that of Salem. Bethabara was the first foothold of the Moravians in North Carolina. In the fall of 1753, a group of 15 Moravian men came down the Great Wagon Road from Pennsylvania, through the Shenandoah Valley of Virginia, and into the North Carolina Piedmont to begin construction of a village at the northwestern edge of the 100,000-acre tract of land that the church had bought and named Wachovia. The 15 original settlers and the other Moravians who would soon join them constructed a sturdy, attractive little village in a very brief span of years.

During its first two decades of existence, Bethabara was a busy place. The Moravians' reputation as craftspeople drew settlers from all through the surrounding hills to buy their wares. The village's location on the Great Wagon Road was also an important asset in its growth. During the French and Indian War in the 1750s, Bethabara became a stockade, an enclosed safe haven not only for the Moravians but for an even greater number of non-Moravian neighbors. It was touched again by war in 1771, when Lord Cornwallis and his men ransacked the town and stole livestock.

By the late 1760s, construction of Salem was underway, and the population of Bethabara began gradually to decline. The village mill and distillery remained in operation for some decades, but by the early 19th century Bethabara had become a small farming community, and Salem, to the south, became the Moravian metropolis.

Körner's Folly

Without a doubt, one of the most unforgettably strange places in North Carolina is Körner's Folly (413 S. Main St., 336/996-7922, www.kornersfolly.org, 10 A.M.–3 P.M. Thurs.–Sat., 1–5 P.M. Sun., $6 adults, $3 ages 5–16, free under 5), located east of Winston-Salem in Kernersville. The seven-level house with 22 rooms of insanely ornate frippery and eccentric architectural contraptions fits all the requirements of the classic "Victorian monstrosity." But it's no monstrosity, as it turns out; the peculiarities make it oddly, somewhat awkwardly, beautiful. In its late-1870s infancy, Körner's Folly was intended not as a home but a display of designer Jule Körner's architectural innovations, a house of showrooms for his clients to tour. Little by little it also became Körner's home. His wife created an exquisite children's theater in the high-ceilinged attic, well worth a visit in its own right.

ENTERTAINMENT AND EVENTS
Performing Arts

The **Piedmont Opera** (336/725-7101, www.piedmontopera.org, tickets $15–70) is a 30-year-old company that presents several operas each season, with a special emphasis on classic Italian opera. Now more than 60 years old, the **Winston-Salem Symphony's** (336/725-1035, www.wssymphony.org, tickets $15–60) performance schedule includes a variety of music, from baroque to pop.

Events

The **1st Friday Gallery Hops** (336/734-1864, www.dadaws.org) take place on the first Friday evening of every month in the DADA (Downtown Arts District Association) neighborhood, along Sixth, Trade, and Liberty Streets. Throughout the district, art galleries, craft studios, and shops are open well into the

night, with neighborhood restaurants and bars staying open for the occasion even later.

Starting at midnight and lasting into the early hours of Easter Sunday every year, **roving brass bands** play throughout the city, in a tradition that the Moravians of Salem practiced 200 years ago and that remains an important part of Easter worship. The bands' rounds, as they're called, always begin with Bach's "Sleepers, Wake," a composition that was brand-new when the first Moravian band was organized in Saxony. Some bands play in Old Salem, but others get on buses and spread throughout the city, waking Winston-Salem to the news of Easter morning.

April brings the **RiverRun Film Festival** (336/724-1502, www.riverrunfilm.com, $7 regular screenings, varying admission costs for panels and workshops, $275 for pass to gain entrance to the whole festival), one of the largest film festivals in the Southeast. The festival is a great opportunity to see the work of both established and emerging filmmakers, and to attend workshops and panels about the art and business of moviemaking.

In June at the **North Carolina Wine Festival** (www.ncwinefestival.com, $20 advance tickets, $25 at the gate, free for children under 12), you can sample prize wines from dozens of vineyards across the state, from the sandy lowlands to steep mountainsides, and from the famously fertile Yadkin Valley, a short drive from Winston-Salem. The festival is held just outside the city in Clemmons, which is southwest of Winston-Salem on I-40.

The end of July and beginning of August is time for the **National Black Theater Festival** (336/723-2266, www.nbtf.org). The six-day gathering includes classic and modern drama, as well as poetry slams and many other events. The *New York Times* reviewed 1989's inaugural festival, attended by 10,000 people, as "one of the most historic and culturally significant events in the history of black theatre and American theatre in general." It now draws 60,000 visitors annually.

November's **Piedmont Craftsmen's Fair**

(Benton Convention Center, 336/725-1516, www.piedmontcraftsman.org, $6 adults, $5 seniors and students, free for children under 12, $10 weekend pass) has been held in Winston-Salem for more than 40 years. This large gathering of artists and art lovers celebrates craft in media such as fiber, clay, metal, and many more, and demonstrates how innovation and tradition are interwoven to make North Carolina one of the world's great craft centers.

Nightlife

The **Garage** (110 W. 7th St, 336/777-1127, www.the-garage.ws) has a knack for identifying future stars in alternative rock and roll, Americana, blues, and alternative country music, and for booking great established acts. Any show you hear at the Garage is bound to be good. The Piedmont has quite a history of jazz innovation, and Winston's **Speakeasy Jazz** (410 W. 4th St., 336/722-6555, www.speakeasy jazz.net, 7 P.M.–midnight Wed.–Thurs., 6 P.M.–1 A.M. Fri., 7 P.M.–1 A.M. Sat., 21 and over only, cover charge for live music Fri. and Sat.) is a fun place for live music, tasty snacks, and a great selection of drinks.

Club Odyssey (4109-A Country Club Rd., 336/774-7071, www.clubodyssey.info, Tues.–Sat. nights, membership $10) is an energetic dance club with a gay and gay-friendly membership. The club has two dance floor areas (one with dance music and one with urban music), and frequent talent contests and drag events. (Guests ages 18–20 will have to wear wristbands inside the club and steer clear of alcohol.)

SHOPPING

The Downtown Arts District, referred to as **DADA** (www.dadaws.org) is a neighborhood of galleries and boutiques located downtown between Fifth, Sixth, and Trade Streets. There are over a dozen commercial galleries, including the **Piedmont Craftsmen** (601 N. Trade St., 336/725-1516, www.piedmontcraftsmen.org, 10:30 A.M.–5 P.M. Tues.–Fri., 10 A.M.–5 P.M. Sat.), which has a beautiful showroom where you'll find the work of hundreds of North Carolina's finest studio potters, fiber artists, jewelry designers, and craftspeople who work in many other media. Several restaurants, bars, and coffee shops are located in DADA.

The **Reynolda Village Shops** (2201 Reynolda Rd., 336/758-5584, www.reynolda village.com), near the historic Reynolda House and museum, is a cluster of specialty stores and boutiques full of unique jewelry, clothing, books, antiques, and more.

For those who like early Americana, **Old Salem** (www.oldsalem.org, most shops open from 9 or 9:30 A.M. and close 5 or 5:30 P.M. Tues.–Sat., and 1–5:30 P.M. Sun.) has fun shops as well as historical sites to visit. **T. Bagge: Merchant** on Main Street is the primary outlet for the work of Old Salem's own craftspeople, where you can buy beautifully made Moravian household wares and toys, as well as great books for adults and children. At the **Winkler Bakery,** bread and the famous Moravian cookies are made in the old-time way. The **Horton Museum Center Store** is also a great place to find Old Salem's wonderful in-house products, and has an extensive selection of books about early Southern arts and crafts, including the work of master furniture makers from North Carolina.

SPORTS AND RECREATION
Spectator Sports

Wake Forest University is the fourth school in the famous Tobacco Road athletic rivalry, and a worthy competitor to its nemeses in the Triangle: Duke, UNC, and NC State. The jewels in the crown of **Demon Deacon athletics** (888/758-3322, www.wfu.edu/athletic) are Wake's ACC Division I football and basketball teams. Football coach Jim Grobe was awarded the ACC and AP Coach of the Year titles after a fantastic 2006 season that sent the Deacs to the Orange Bowl. The basketball program has produced such notables as Billy Packer and the 5'3" Muggsy Bogues, now both famous sports broadcasters, Randolph Childress, and Chris Paul. Following the tragic sudden death of coach Skip Prosser in 2007, the basketball program has embarked on a new era with coach Dino Gaudio at the helm. The women's field hockey team is consistently among the nation's elite, winning three consecutive NCAA championships in the early 2000s, and the golf program is the athletic alma mater of Arnold Palmer, Curtis Strange, Lenny Wadkins, Scott Hoch, and Jay Haas. As is the case at its Tobacco Road counterparts, scoring a ticket to a Wake Forest football or basketball game can be quite difficult.

The Single-A farm team of the Chicago White Sox plays here in the Piedmont. The **Winston-Salem Warthogs** (401 Deacon Ave., 336/759-2233, www.warthogs.com, $9 box seats, $7 general admission) have been whooping up on their Carolina League competition since 1945.

NASCAR

NASCAR racing at **Bowman Gray Stadium** (1250 S. Martin Luther King Dr., 336/723-1819, www.bowmangrayracing.com, gates open at 6 P.M., races begin at 8 P.M., $10 adults, $1 children 6–11, free for children under 6) is not only a classic Carolina experience—weekly races have been run here for 50 years—but is also a less daunting experience than race events at the massive stadiums elsewhere in the state. Whereas Lowe's Speedway in Concord can accommodate over 200,000 spectators, Bowman Gray seats a cozy 17,000. It's as inexpensive as a minor-league baseball game too, making this an ideal place for one's first NASCAR event. Weekly races include modified, street stock, sportsman, and stadium stock events.

Sporting Clays

Friendship Sporting Clays (4805 Siloam Rd., 336/699-8694, www.friendshipsporting clays.com, 9 A.M.–6 P.M. Wed.–Sat., 9 A.M.–1 P.M. Sun.–Tues., by appointment only for groups of 8 or more) in East Bend, a little town northwest of Winston-Salem on Route 67, halfway to Elkin, is a "golf with a shotgun" course in a beautiful, rural landscape. If you don't tote a gun, you can rent one here, and can sign up for special one-on-one instruction.

ACCOMMODATIONS

A cotton mill built in the 1830s, the building home to the ◖ **Brookstown Inn** (200 Brookstown Ave, 336/725-1120, www.brooks towninn.com, from $90) has been renovated and transformed into a luxurious hotel, with beautiful exposed brick walls and wooden floors. Guests enjoy wine and cheese in the evenings, and milk and cookies at night. The Brookstown Inn is within walking distance of Old Salem.

◖ **Augustus T. Zevely Inn** (803 South Main St., Old Salem, 800/928-9299, www .winston-salem-inn.com, from $95) is the only inn in Old Salem proper. The beautiful 1830s house is furnished in original and reproduction Moravian furniture, with special features peppered throughout, such as steam baths in some rooms, heated brick tile floors in others, and working cooking fireplaces. Every guest room has a view either of the old village or of the house's period gardens.

Like all of North Carolina's major cities, Winston-Salem has a lot of chain motels to choose from. Three good bets here are **La Quinta** (2020 Griffith Rd., 336/765-8777, www.lq.com, pets allowed, from about $90), the **Holiday Inn** (2008 S. Hawthorne Rd., 336/765-6670, www.choicehotels.com, from about $90), and **Hampton Inn** (1990 Hampton Inn Ct., 336/760-1660, www.hamptoninn .com, from about $110). These three motels are all in the same neighborhood, near Forsyth Medical Center and Hanes Mall, on the southwest side of town.

FOOD
Southern

◖ **Sweet Potatoes** (529 N. Trade St., 336/727-4844, www.sweetpotatoes-arestaurant .com, lunch 11 A.M.–3 P.M. Tues.–Sat., dinner 5–10 P.M. Wed.–Sat., $12–21) a much-acclaimed gourmet Southern-style restaurant, is more formally known as "Sweet Potatoes (Well Shut My Mouth!)—a Restaurant." Here you'll find expertly crafted renditions of many Southern favorites and regional delicacies, like catfish, fried chicken, fried green tomatoes, and Gullah shrimp and crab pilau. Sweet Potatoes' signature desserts and mixed drinks add an extra gourmet flair.

Eclectic American

Christopher's New Global Cuisine (712 Brookstown Ave., 336/724-1395, www.christophersngc.com, 5–9 P.M. Tues.–Thurs., 5–10 P.M. Fri. and Sat., 10 A.M.–2 P.M. Sun., $15–28) is probably best known for its lobster macaroni and cheese, but it has quite a menu of innovative dishes to match it. Try the honey lavender–glazed salmon or the baby portabellas on pumpkin risotto. At brunch you can choose from classic shrimp and grits, several specialty omelets, and pumpkin pancakes, among other treats. Christopher's also makes special martinis and "concept cocktails" ($7.50–12), like the key lime pie martini—a blend of Stolichnaya Vanil vodka, Tuaca, Frangelico, Midori, cream, and lime juice, with the rim of the glass rolled in graham cracker crumbs—or the house martini, a simpler mix of Grey Goose L'Orange vodka, Grand Marnier, and Orangina.

The **West End Cafe** (926 W. Fourth St., 336/723-4774, www.westendcafe.com, 11 A.M.–10 P.M. Mon.–Fri., noon–10 P.M. Sat., $10–20), in Winston's West End neighborhood, has been in business for almost 30 years. The "casual elegant" bistro makes great sandwiches—dozens of hoagies, grinders, stuffed pitas, and burgers. Dinner entrées range from homey burritos and rib eyes to exotic fare, like the orange-ginger–grilled North Carolina ostrich with broccoli lo-mein and the sautéed skate wing.

Bakeries

It seems that everything the early Moravians made, from furniture to music, was lovely. Among the best-loved Moravian arts is that of baking, a tradition that is carried on by, among others, **Dewey's Bakery** (3121 Indiana Ave., 2820 Reynolda Rd., and 262 Stratford Rd., 800/274-2994). At its Winston-Salem locations, and several shops elsewhere in the state, you'll find heavenly Moravian cookies, a thin, spiced wafer that is one of this state's most popular exports around Christmastime. In business since 1930, Dewey's Bakery produces a long list of variations on the basic Moravian cookie, as well as cheese straws—another classic Southern snack—shortbread, and more.

INFORMATION AND SERVICES

Winston-Salem's main emergency hospital is **Wake Forest University Baptist Medical Center** (Medical Center Blvd., 336/716-2255, www1.wfubmc.edu), located off of Business I-40 between Cloverdale and Hawthorne. **Carolina Veterinary Specialists** (1600 Hanes Mall Blvd., 336/896-0902, www.carolinavet.com), a 24-hour emergency veterinary hospital, is located off I-40 just west of U.S. 421.

The **Winston-Salem Journal** (www.journalnow.com) is the city's main newspaper. The **Winston-Salem Visitors Center** is located at 200 Brookstown Avenue (866/728-4200). Extensive travel information is available at www.visitwinstonsalem.com.

Greensboro and Vicinity

Greensboro might be more densely packed with colleges and universities than any other city in North Carolina. It's the home of the University of North Carolina at Greensboro and North Carolina A&T, of the small Quaker college, Guilford, and of Bennett, a historically African American women's college known as the "Vassar of the South." And that's just naming a few. Befitting its role as a college town many times over, Greensboro has hopping arts and music scenes, and a very creative, culturally engaged population.

Though hardly the largest city in the state, Greensboro has a somewhat more urban feel than some of its counterparts. This is partly due to its ethnic and national diversity. Significant numbers of Southeast Asian refugees settled here in the 1970s and '80s, making this an important population center in the United States

for members of the Hmong tribe of China, Laos, Vietnam, and other countries, and the Montagnard of Vietnam. There are also many African immigrants here, and, like everywhere in North Carolina, a great many newcomers from Latin America. Mix in the long-established African American population, the Quaker tradition descended from some of the region's early settlers, the Native American population, and a big dose of college students for good measure, and you have a city of unique cultural richness.

SIGHTS
Historic Parks

When one thinks of Revolutionary War battles and campaigns, those that come first to mind are probably in the Mid-Atlantic and New England states. In truth, much of the Revolution was fought in the South, and some

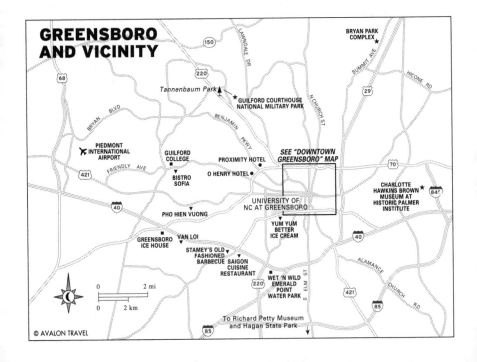

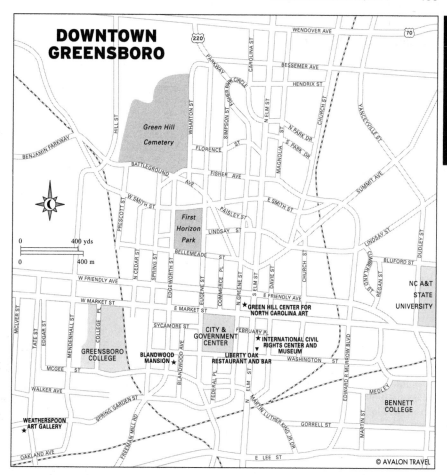

DOWNTOWN GREENSBORO

of the major turning points occurred here in North Carolina. The **Guilford Courthouse National Military Park** (2332 New Garden Rd., 336/288-1776, www.nps.gov/guco, 9 A.M.–5 P.M. daily, free) commemorates the battle of Guilford Courthouse, at which 1,900 British troops led by Lord Cornwallis routed 4,500 Patriots under General Nathaniel Greene. It proved only a pyrrhic victory, however, for Cornwallis' army was severely hobbled by the action. A 2.5-mile self-guided tour, which can be driven, hiked, or biked, stops at the essential spots on the battlefield.

Close by the battlefield is **Tannenbaum Historic Park** (2200 New Garden Rd., 336/545-5315, www.greensboro-nc.gov/ Departments/Parks/facilities/tannenbaum, 9 A.M.–5 P.M. Tues.–Sat. spring and fall, 10 A.M.–4:30 P.M. Tues.–Sat. winter, free), where the Colonial Heritage Center and 18th-century log Hoskins House represent the life of the Carolina yeoman around the time of the Revolution.

African American Historic Sights

Greensboro, the home of North Carolina

CHARLOTTE HAWKINS BROWN

In 1901, an 18-year-old woman named Charlotte Hawkins left Massachusetts, where she had grown up, and returned to her birth state of North Carolina to work as a schoolteacher in Sedalia, near Greensboro. Within a single year of arriving, this African American teenager, whose grandparents had been slaves, raised the capital for, founded, and opened her own school for young African Americans. She named it for her mentor Alice Freeman Palmer, the first woman president of Wellesley College. The Palmer Institute graduated its first class in 1905, and for the next 66 years enjoyed an international reputation for matriculating highly motivated young men and women who went on in remarkable numbers to advanced degrees and prestigious careers.

Charlotte Hawkins Brown (her married name) insisted upon excellence not only in scholarship, but also in the social graces. A proponent of educating students in etiquette, elocution, and all the arts of courtesy usually taught in finishing schools, Brown wrote a 1944 bible of etiquette called *The Correct Thing to Do, to Say, to Wear*. She became a leading figure in African American education, not only as the headmistress of the prestigious academy, but as a speaker who traveled the world and promoted comprehensive preparatory education.

Canary Cottage, the house in which Dr. Brown lived, is one of the many buildings preserved on the campus of the Palmer Memorial Institute in Sedalia, now known as the Charlotte Hawkins Brown Museum.

A&T, a prominent historically black university, has played an important role in African American history. The **International Civil Rights Center and Museum** (www.sitinmovement.org), currently in the planning stages, will be housed in Greensboro's old downtown Woolworth's building, the site of a famous 1960 lunch counter sit-in that lit a fire under North Carolina's civil rights movement. That whites-only counter will be the touchstone for this museum's exploration of the civil rights movement. The four men who staged that sit-in—David Richmond, Franklin McCain, Jibreel Khazan, and Joseph McNeil—are honored on the A&T campus with the **A&T Four Statue** (1601 E. Market St.).

A short ways outside the city, in the crossroads town of Sedalia, is the **Charlotte Hawkins Brown Museum at Historic Palmer Memorial Institute** (U.S. 70 near Rock Creek Dairy Rd., Sedalia, 9 A.M.–5 P.M. Mon.–Sat., 1–5 P.M. Sun. Apr.–Oct., 10 A.M.–4 P.M. Tues.–Sat. and 1–4 P.M. Sun. Nov.–Mar., free). The Palmer Memorial Institute (PMI), founded by Brown, was a prestigious prep school for African Americans from 1902–1971. A walking tour through campus tells of the history of the PMI and its many extant buildings. Canary Cottage, where Charlotte Hawkins Brown lived and hosted salon-like gatherings for her students, has been restored to evoke the era of Brown's residence. In the Carrie Stone Teachers Cottage, visitors will find exhibits about the history of education for African Americans in North Carolina, and can watch a 15-minute film about Charlotte Brown and her legacy.

Art Museums and Exhibits

The **Green Hill Center for North Carolina Art** (200 N. Davie St., 336/333-7460, www.greenhillcenter.org, 10 A.M.–5 P.M. Tues. and Thurs.–Sat., 10 A.M.–7 P.M. Wed., 2–5 P.M. Sun., free, suggested donation $2) presents exhibits of fine artists and artisans who are from or have close ties to North Carolina. Much attention is given to North Carolina's folk art traditions, and deservedly so, but the state is also rich with practitioners of the formal studio arts. Some of the best of those artists are represented in this lovely gallery.

ArtQuest (200 N. Davie St., 336/333-7460, www.greenhillcenter.org/artquest, 12:30–5 P.M. Tues. and Thurs.–Sat., 10 A.M.–7 P.M. Wed., 2–5 P.M. Sun., $5), an interactive children's museum in the Green Hill Center, teaches kids to appreciate the visual arts through hands-on studio experience.

The **Weatherspoon Art Museum** (Spring Garden and Tate Sts., 336/334-5770, http://weatherspoon.uncg.edu, 10 A.M.–5 P.M. Tues., Wed., and Fri., 10 A.M.–9 P.M. Thurs., 1–5 P.M. Sat. and Sun., free), on the campus of UNC-Greensboro, has been dedicated to modern art since the early 1940s, and has assembled a collection that includes work by de Kooning, Warhol, Cindy Sherman, and many other masters of 20th-century art. Theirs is the best collection of modern art in North Carolina, and one of the very best in the Southeast.

Blandwood Mansion

Blandwood Mansion (447 W. Washington St., 336/272-5003, www.blandwood.org, 11 A.M.–2 P.M. Tues.–Sat., 2–5 P.M. Sun., closed in Jan., $5 adults, $2 children under 12) was built in 1790 as a farmhouse, before the city itself was born. In the 1840s, its famous resident was Governor John Motley Morehead, the "Father of Modern North Carolina," whose efforts to institute humane treatment towards the mentally ill, prisoners, and children with disabilities, and to modernize the state's schools and transportation infrastructure, made him one of the most important governors in this state's history. In 1844, Morehead engaged Alexander Jackson Davis, the architect largely responsible for America's gothic revival, to redo Blandwood. The result was the Italianate villa that stands today.

ENTERTAINMENT AND EVENTS
Nightlife

Greensboro is a college town several times over, so there's a lot of late-night mischief to enjoy. Popular pubs include the **Rhinoceros Club** (315 S. Greene St., 336/272-9305, www.rhinoclub.com, membership $2), **Natty Greene's Pub** (345 S. Elm St., 336/274-1373, www.bigdraft.com/pub.html, 11 A.M.–2 A.M. Mon.–Sat., noon–midnight Sun.), and the cigar and drinks bar **Churchill's on Elm** (213 S. Elm St., 336/275-6367, www.churchillsonelm.com).

Warehouse 29 (1011 Arnold St., 336/333-9333, www.w29.com, membership $2) is a rather spectacular place, a hot spot for gay nightlife in this region for more than 15 years. In addition to great dancing, drinks, and shows—"from pageants and contests, to fan dances and go-go boys"—Warehouse 29 has a huge outdoor patio that features a sand volleyball court. A more low-key gay bar is **Club Q** (708 W. Market St., 336/272-2587, www.theqlounge.com, opens 4 P.M. Mon.–Fri., 9 P.M. Sat., 7 P.M. Sun.). It has a more traditional neighborhood-pub ambience, and is a good place to catch up with friends over martinis.

Performing Arts

The **Greensboro Symphony Orchestra** (multiple venues, 336/335-5456 ext. 223, www.greensboro.symphony.org) was born in the 1920s as a student orchestra at Greensboro Women's College (now University of North Carolina at Greensboro). It grew to be a beloved institution in the wider community of the city, and into a highly successful regional orchestra. Today's incarnation is conducted by Azerbaijani violinist Dmitry Sitkovetsky. The **Greensboro Opera** (multiple venues, 336/273-9472, www.greensboroopera.org) has been turning out wonderful performances of classical and modern opera for more than 25 years. Special productions have included guest appearances by such stars as Kathleen Battle. The **Greensboro Ballet** (multiple venues, 336/333-7480, www.greensboroballet.org) presents several major productions each season, starring both long-time professional dancers and up-and-coming, highly talented students. The School of the Greensboro Ballet, an affiliated institution, is one of only a handful of non-profit ballet schools in the country, and mints wonderful dancers from childhood on.

SHOPPING

Featured in a memorable early scene in the 2006 movie *Junebug*, **Replacements, Ltd.** (1089 Knox Rd., just off exit 132 from I-85 between Greensboro and Burlington, 800/737-5223, www.replacements.com, 8 A.M.–10 P.M. daily) is an incredible place to shop as well as simply to gawk. Replacements is five football fields' worth of retail and behind-the-scenes space dedicated to what is surely the world's largest collection of tableware and flatware. This is much more than a plate outlet. What began in the 1970s as a small china collection in a North Carolina state auditor's attic has grown so much that, today it comprises an 11-million-piece inventory featuring 250,000 patterns. If you want to replace your great-grandmother's 1865 baby spoon that you accidentally mangled in the garbage disposal, Replacements is at your service. If you cracked your mom's Fiestaware creamer last time you visited, and are praying she hasn't noticed yet, you can probably find its twin here before she suspects. And of course, if you want to buy a beautiful silver service for a bride, or some brand-new designer stoneware for your own home, you've found the right place. Even if you don't want to weigh down your suitcases, you'll enjoy a visit to Replacements' museum and showroom.

SPORTS AND RECREATION
Spectator Sports

The **Greensboro Grasshoppers** (408 Bellemeade St., 336/268-2255, www.gsohoppers .com, $9 premium seats, $6 lawn, discount of $2 for children and seniors), a Single-A affiliate of the Florida Marlins, plays at First Horizon Park, a field that has been graced by all-star pitcher Dontrelle Willis and catcher Paul LoDuca.

Just north of Greensboro, in the town of Browns Summit, is the home field of the **Carolina Dynamo** (Bryan Park, 6105 Townsend, Browns Summit, 336/316-1266, www.carolinadynamo.com, $10 premium seats, $7 general admission), a professional team in the Premier Development League of the United Soccer League. League champions twice in the 1990s, and first-place regular-season finishers several times in the last decade, the Dynamo are a training ground for soccer's rising stars.

For more than 50 years, central Carolinians have been enjoying the roar and burnt rubber fumes of the race track experience at the **Piedmont Dragway** (6750 Holts Store Road, Julian, six miles from I-85's exit 132, 336/449-7411, http://piedmontdragway.com, ticket prices vary), located between Greensboro and Burlington. All manner of wheeled motor vehicles tear around this 0.1-mile track, and you can catch an event most any time of year.

Recreation

Greensboro's **Wet 'N Wild Emerald Point Water Park** (3910 S. Holden Rd., 336/852-9721, www.emeraldpointe.com, open May–Sept., hours vary, $28.99 general admission, $19.99 under 48" tall, $15.99 over 55 years old) offers more water rides than one could try in a full weekend. In addition to the central attraction, the two-million-gallon Thunder Bay wave pool, which features 48-foot tsunami waves, there are five-story slides and riptide pools for the most intrepid swimmers, lazy rivers and shallow pools for those who prefer to relax, and many adventures in between. The polar opposite of Emerald Point is the Piedmont's only year-round ice rink, the **Greensboro Ice House** (6119 Landmark Ctr. Blvd., 336/852-1515, www.icehouserinks.com/gboro, prices and hours vary). Here you can ice skate at a leisurely glide, practice figure skating, and even play pick-up hockey. If you're the only non-penguin in your party, you can settle in with the Ice House's free Wi-Fi.

ACCOMMODATIONS

The **Proximity Hotel** (704 Green Valley Rd., 336/379-8200, www.proximityhotel.com, from $159), opened in late 2007, is a remarkable venture. The designers of this high-style luxury boutique hotel have set out to create an example of green architectural practices, and are winning awards and high praise for their accomplishments, including the highest rating of "Eco-Getaways" in *Outside* magazine. Solar panels on the roof, huge windows (that really open, miracle of miracles!) in each guestroom, recycled building materials, and many other green features mean that the Proximity reduces energy and water use by almost half over what would be expected of a comparable hotel. It's accomplished with no sacrifice in comfort or style. The hotel's interior is beautiful and chic, and the guestrooms are comfortable, brightly lit with natural light, and full of modern amenities.

The ◖ **O.Henry Hotel** (624 Green Valley Rd., 336/854-2000, www.ohenryhotel.com, from $239), named for the Greensboro-born author of "Gift of the Magi," is a 1920s-style luxury hotel. The oversized guest rooms feature nine-foot ceilings, neighbor-silencing double walls, comfy beds, terrazzo showers and huge bathtubs, and, like the Proximity, windows that open. The O.Henry's own checkered cab will carry you to and from the airport free of charge.

There are plenty of motels in and around Greensboro. One particularly good deal is the **Red Roof Inn** (615 Regional Rd. S., 336/271-2636, www.redroof.com, from $40). Though the low price might cause one to suspect otherwise, the service and facilities are just fine, at a third of the cost of many other area lodging choices.

Camping

Southeast of Greensboro in the town of Pleasant Garden, **Hagan-Stone Park** (5920 Hagan-Stone Park, Pleasant Garden, 336/674-0472, www.greensboro-nc.gov/Departments/Parks/facilities/regionalparks/haganstone, $15/night tent camping for up to five people, $20/night RV camping for up to five people, each additional person $3) offers pleasant campsites for both tents and RVs. Individual camp sites each have a tent pad, campstone/fire ring, lantern pole, and picnic table. Restrooms and showers are nearby. Each RV site (which can also be rented by tent campers who need an electric hookup) has a picnic table and a 30- and 50-amp electrical connection, and shares water with the neighboring site. There are no sewer connections. Trails, a public pool, a pond, and a historic one-room schoolhouse are all within the park's boundaries. No reservations are taken—just arrive and start setting up, and a park staffer will drop by to register you.

FOOD
Southern

Stamey's Old Fashioned Barbecue (2206 High Point Rd., 336/299-9888, 10 A.M.–9 P.M. Mon.–Sat., and 2812 Battleground Ave./US 220, 336/288-9275, 11 A.M.–9 P.M. Mon.–Sat., www.stameys.com, under $10) has been around in one form or another for almost 70 years. The Lexington-style 'Q is pit-fired over hickory wood for as much as 10 hours, old-time quality that's kept customers coming back for generations.

Eclectic American

The ◖ **Liberty Oak Restaurant and Bar** (100-D W. Washington St., 336/273-7057, www.libertyoakrestaurant.com, 11 A.M.– 10 P.M. Mon.–Thurs., 11 A.M.–11 P.M. Fri.–Sat., 10 A.M.–10 P.M. Sun., $10–27) is credited with having started a culinary revolution in Greensboro, a fad for casual restaurants serving New American gourmet cuisine. Specialties here include many seafood creations, duck confit, quail stuffed with andouille, and homemade red pepper and goat cheese ravioli. Originally a wine shop, Liberty Oak has a wine list a mile long, with some nice single-malt scotches and special-blend martinis thrown in for good measure.

Chef Beth Kizhnerman of **Bistro Sofia** (616 Dolley Madison Rd., 336/855-1313, www.bistro sofia.com, 5–10 P.M. Tues.–Sun., $16–36), who comes to Greensboro via Brittany and the New England Culinary Institute, has created a spectacular American-French fusion menu, featuring such dishes as buttermilk-fried rabbit, lobster croquettes, and sautéed frog legs persillade. Bistro Sofia's wine list is one of the best in the state, with over 300 selections, ranging from an Italian chardonnay at $6 a glass to a $1,295 1987 Napa red.

Asian

Greensboro has a long-established Vietnamese community and a wealth of Vietnamese restaurants. A favorite of local diners is **Saigon Cuisine Restaurant** (4205 High Point Rd., 336/294-9286), where some of the best

WINSTON-SALEM

dishes are the grilled pork over vermicelli and the flounder in basil sauce. Try also **Pho Hien Vuong** (4109-A Spring Garden Rd., 336/294-5551, www.phohienvuongrestaurant .com, 11 A.M.–9:30 P.M. daily), for both Vietnamese and Thai food. Nearby, **Van Loi** (3829-D High Point Rd., 336/855-5688, 10 A.M.–10 P.M. Wed.–Mon.) serves good *pho* and Vietnamese sandwiches.

Snacks
Yum Yum Better Ice Cream (1219 Spring Garden St., 336/272-8284, 10 A.M.–5:30 P.M. Mon. and Sat., 10 A.M.–10 P.M. Tues.–Fri., under $5) began in 1906 as a pushcart operation, when a young man named Wisdom Aydelette, who had been working to support his family since he was in the third grade, started peddling ice cream. "W. B." gradually expanded his operations, first graduating from pushcart to mule and wagon, and eventually becoming a full-fledged brick-and-mortar ice cream shop. He also began selling hot dogs, which quickly matched ice cream in popularity. Today, Aydelette's grandson runs Yum Yum, but they still sell ice cream and hot dogs that draw crowds.

INFORMATION AND SERVICES
The **Greensboro Visitors Center** (317 S. Greene St., 800/344-2282, www.greens boronc.org, 8:30 A.M.–5:30 P.M. Mon.–Fri., 9 A.M.–4 P.M. Sat., and 1–4 P.M. Sun.), downtown, across form the Carolina Theater, is open seven days a week. Greensboro has several hospitals, the largest of which is **Moses H. Cone Memorial Hospital** (1200 North Elm Street, 336/832-7000). Should your pet have an emergency, you can go to the **After Hours Veterinary Emergency Clinic** (5505 West Friendly Avenue, 336/851-1990).

NORTH OF GREENSBORO
Well off the proverbial beaten path, the countryside north of Greensboro is a very attractive part of North Carolina, one that is not often explored by visitors. Here you'll find pretty landscape, interesting history, and great river activities.

Eden
Well north of Greensboro is the small town of Eden, near the Virginia border. This is the home of **Three Rivers Outfitters** (413-B Church Street, Eden, 336/627-6215, www .3-r-o.com, store hours 10 A.M.–6 P.M. Wed.– Sat., 1–5 P.M. Sun., call for dates and times of guided trips), a full-service river outfitter that provides both rentals and guided trips along the beautiful Mayo, Dan, and Smith Rivers nearby. Not limited to canoes and kayaks, Three Rivers is the only river guide service in the United States that offers tours by batteau, a flat-bottomed boat that was the workhorse of America's rivers in the 19th century, and which has all but disappeared today. Batteaux are propelled by several crewmen who push against the river bottom with poles, much like gondoliers or punters. It's a leisurely way to enjoy the river, and an experience you won't find anywhere else.

Eden's most famous resident was the banjo player Charlie Poole, a leading light in the earliest years of recorded country music whose playing is still idolized and emulated. Poole lived fast and died young in 1931, and is buried here in Eden. Every June the town hosts the **Charlie Poole Music Festival** (Eden Fairgrounds, www.charlie-poole.com), a weekend of concerts and contests showcasing the traditional music of the North Carolina Piedmont, with special emphasis on the legacy of Poole and his band, the North Carolina Ramblers. It's a great opportunity to hear some of the region's greatest old-time bands, in a less intense setting than MerleFest or the other area mega-festivals.

Milton
Northeast of Yanceyville, hard by the Virginia border, the tiny town of Milton preserves much of the historic architecture of its circa-1800 heyday. In the 1820s and '30s, Milton was home to cabinetmaker Thomas Day, a free African American craftsman whose furniture can be seen in museums throughout the region. His workshop at Yellow/Union Tavern is undergoing renovation, eventually to be opened to the public. Day's woodwork is seen in the beautiful pews of **Milton Presbyterian Church** (66 Broad St.,

webpages.charter.net/ljeffress/MPCweb.htm), which is open to visitors. It is said that Day donated his work to the church with the understanding that he and his wife Acquilla would be permitted to sit in a pew in the main chapel, rather than in the slave gallery above.

BURLINGTON AND ALAMANCE COUNTY

One of North Carolina's early railroad towns, Burlington was an economic center in the Piedmont through much of the 19th and 20th centuries. The much smaller town of Graham, a little ways southeast of Burlington, is the seat of a largely rural Alamance County. The county is crossed from east to west by the not-at-all-pretty I-85, but crossed roughly north to south by the lovely Haw River, a rocky channel that's an area favorite for canoeing, kayaking, and tubing.

Sights

Alamance Battleground (5803 S. Hwy. 62, 336/227-4785, www.alamancebattleground .nchistoricsites.org, 9 A.M.–5 P.M. Mon.–Sat.,

free), south of Burlington, marks the spot where the War of the Regulation ended. On this battleground in 1771, Governor Tryon's colonial militia squashed an uprising by a band of backcountry settlers, the Regulators, who had banded together in protest of corruption in the colonial administration. On the grounds, a visitors center presents the history of the uprising, and a log house connected to the family of one of the Regulators is restored to period condition.

Haw River Wine Trail

The Haw River Wine Trail (www.hawriver winetrail.com) is a lovely day's excursion for the oenophile. Tracing 50 miles along the Haw River, the trail will guide you to four wineries in the graceful hills of the northern Piedmont. **Creek Side Winery** (3515 Stoney Creek Church Rd., Elon College, 336/584-4117, www.creek sidewinery.com) in Elon (pronounced "EE-lahn") produces a range of dry red, sweet white, and fruit wines, and has a large tasting room. **Grove Winery** (7360 Brooks Bridge Rd.,

Haw River at Saxapahaw

© ANDREA SCHWARTZ

Gibsonville, 336/584-4060, http://grovewinery .com, noon–5 P.M. Mon.–Sat., 1–5 P.M. Sun.) in Gibsonville produces over a dozen award-winning wines, and in season, they allow volunteers to help crush grapes on Saturdays. **Glen Marie Winery** (1838 Johnson Rd., Burlington, 336/578-3938, www.glen mariewinery.com, noon–6 P.M. Thurs.– Sun.) is located on Mebane-Graham Lake in Burlington, and has an extensive list of lovely and prize-winning wines. **Iron Gate Vineyards** (2540 Lynch Store Rd., Mebane, 919/304-9463, irongatevineyards.com, 10 A.M.–7 P.M. Mon.–Fri., 10 A.M.–6 P.M. Sat., 1–6 P.M. Sun.) has won a great many awards, including gold medals in the Mid-Atlantic Southeastern Wine Competition for its chambourcin and Dixie Dawn wines.

Sports and Recreation

North Carolina is one of the major hubs for that great Southern entertainment: professional wrestling. For those who are too polite to suggest that pro wrestling is fake, the handy euphemism "sports entertainment" has been coined. To paraphrase wrestling icon Rowdy Roddy Piper (who lived and wrestled in Charlotte in the early 1980s), it's one thing to think that wrestling isn't real, but don't ever doubt that the wrestlers are. Watch one card (match) in the little warehouse bay in Burlington that grandly calls itself the **Carolina Wrestling Federation** (www.cwfmidatlantic.com), sit six feet from the ring as 300-pounders slam each other headfirst into the mat, and you'll know what the rowdy one meant. These guys may be acting out a heavily scripted pantomime of good and evil, after which they'll go out for a beer with their erstwhile enemies, but it takes a real athlete to make a living in the "squared circle."

No Carolina textile town would be complete without a serious baseball team, and Burlington is home to the **Burlington Royals** (1450 Graham St., 336/222-0223, $6 reserved, $5 general admission, $3 children and seniors), a rookie-level affiliate of the Kansas City Royals. They play at Burlington Athletic Stadium, convenient to I-40/I-85.

The Haw River runs through Alamance County, a great river for flat-water canoeing, rafting, wafting, and tubing. The **Haw River Trail** (www.hawrivertrail.org) designates river access areas all along the river. Among the outfitters who run the Haw is the **Haw River Canoe and Kayak Company** (Saxapahaw, 336/260-6465, www.hawriver canoe.com), which leads half-day and full-day paddles along different stretches in the Triangle and Triad regions and also rent canoes and kayaks.

HIGH POINT

North Carolina has contributed a surprising number of greats to the world of jazz—most famously John Coltrane from here in High Point, Thelonious Monk from Rocky Mount, and Maceo Parker from Kinston. A **statue of Coltrane,** with his horn, presides over the intersection of Commerce Avenue and Hamilton Street, near the home where he grew up on Underhill Street.

Also on Hamilton Street you'll find the **World's Largest Chest of Drawers** (508 Hamilton St.). The 40-foot-tall Goddard block-front chest, a tribute to the city's furniture industry, has huge socks dangling out one of the drawers in deference to the local hosiery mills. It was built in 1926 by the High Point Chamber of Commerce, which was unable to resist the temptation to designate the chest of drawers the High Point Bureau of Information. Of all the nerve, a furniture mall in nearby Jamestown constructed an 80-foot highboy. It's built into the side of the mall rather than freestanding, like the Hamilton Street bureau, but if you want to be really technical about it, it's actually the larger chest of drawers. To maintain primacy as well as accuracy, High Point's bureau is sometimes referred to as the World's Largest Goddard Block-Front Chest. While you're at it you might want to make a side trip to see Thomasville's World's Largest Duncan Phyfe Chair, or the World's Largest Coffee Pot in Winston-Salem. One can only assume that all these home furnishings belong to the enormous pioneer who stands on top of a

© SCOTT SOEHLIG

High Point's bureau

truck stop in Lexington, glaring over I-85. One wonders why the Lexington Big Man is glaring at the eastern horizon rather than scanning the west; maybe he's waiting for his furniture to be delivered.

Apparently a city of extremes, High Point is also home to the **Angela Peterson Doll and Miniature Museum** (101 W. Green Dr., 336/885-3655, 10 A.M.–4 P.M. Mon.–Fri., 9 A.M.–4 P.M. Sat., 1–4 P.M. Sun., closed winter Mondays), the amassed treasure of one lady's lifetime, a collection of 2,700 dolls, dollhouses, and doll-sized accoutrements. Ms. Peterson's sub-specialty was Shirley Temple dolls, of which she had no fewer than 130, all on display here.

High Point is on I-85, southwest of Greensboro and a roughly equal distance southeast of Winston-Salem.

Accommodations

The **J. H. Adams Inn** (1108 N. Main St., 888/256-1289, www.jhadamsinn.com, from $140), a 1918 Italianate villa listed on the National Register of Historic Places, operates as a small luxury hotel. Seven guest rooms are located in the main inn, the house itself, while the rest of the bedrooms and suites are located in a modern addition. Though the Adams Inn is a hotel rather than a bed-and-breakfast, the attentive staff and special touches like an evening glass of wine combine the best of both lodging styles.

Food

Kepley's Pit-Cooked Barbecue (1304 N. Main St., 336/884-1021, www.kepleysbarbecue.com, 8:30 A.M.–8:30 P.M. Mon.–Sat., BBQ $7.50/lb.) is the oldest restaurant in High Point still operating in the same spot. The Burleson family, proprietors, make the barbecue themselves (in more of an eastern-Carolina style than that typical of nearby Lexington), as well as the slaw, hushpuppies, and chili. It's a classic barbecue joint, the kind that uses paper placemats printed with block ads for local funeral homes and laundries. If you're coming at the lunch hour, expect a crowd.

JAMESTOWN

There are many sites in this part of the state (as well as in the northeastern area) important to the history of Southern Quakers. **Mendenhall Plantation** (603 W. Main St., 336/454-3819, www.mendenhallplantation.org, open Mar.–Dec. 11 A.M.–3 P.M. Tues.–Fri., 1–4 P.M. Sat., 2–4 P.M. most Sun., and in Jan. and Feb. 11 A.M.–3 P.M. Fri., 1–4 P.M. Sat., 2–4 P.M. most Sun., $2 adults, $1 children, students, and seniors), built in 1811, is a beautiful plantation house located in what is now the center of Jamestown, southwest of Greensboro and about two-thirds of the way to High Point. The plantation is a significant example of the folk architecture of early German-Americans, both in the simple Quaker aesthetic of the house, and in its "bank barn," a traditional German livestock barn built into a hillside. The Mendenhalls were abolitionists, which was common among Quakers, of course, but rare in the South. On the estate is one of only a very few surviving false-bottomed wagons, in which slaves were hidden during their journey on the Underground Railroad.

The Sandhills

Far from most of North Carolina's major highways, the region known as the Sandhills, an exceptionally beautiful part of the state, is often forgotten by travelers and travel writers. These roads less traveled will carry you through placid countryside, to a tiny town that seems inhabited almost entirely by artists, to savannas traversed by elephants and zebras, and into some mysterious hidden, haunted mountains—and into towns called Whynot and Climax. The centerpiece of the Sandhills—indeed, the very center of North Carolina—is the tiny town of Seagrove (population approximately 250), where a distinctive style of folk pottery is approaching its third century of tradition and innovation. The Uwharrie Mountains are nearby, an outcropping of deep hills and dark forests. Asheboro, the largest town in the Sandhills, with 20,000 residents, is home to the wild animals of the North Carolina Zoo, and to one of North Carolina's greatest achievements, Cheerwine.

INFORMATION AND SERVICES

Asheboro is the population center of Randolph County, where you'll find plenty of affordable chain motels and a fast food jungle clustered along U.S. 64. This is also a center for area medical services. The **Asheboro/Randolph County Chamber of Commerce** (317 E. Dixie Dr., 336/626-2626, http://chamber.asheboro.com) can fix you up with all the logistical information you need as you venture into the Sandhills.

GETTING THERE AND AROUND

U.S. 220, which runs from Greensboro almost to the South Carolina border, is the only major artery in this region, which is served by no major airports or rail lines. (The Charlotte, Greensboro, and Raleigh-Durham airports are all within an hour's drive.)

ASHEBORO AND VICINITY
◖ North Carolina Zoo

The North Carolina Zoo (Zoo Parkway, 800/488-0444, www.nczoo.org, 9 A.M.–4 P.M. daily Apr. 1–Oct. 30, 9 A.M.–5 P.M. daily Nov. 1–Mar. 31, $10 adults, $8 college students with ID and seniors over 62, $6 children 2–12) sprawls over more than 500 acres of Purgatory Mountain, at the edge of the Uwharries. Animals—from elephants and zebras to polar bears to alligators, and many, many more in between—live on large expanses of land planted and landscaped so as to approximate their native habitats. Over five miles of hiking trails, with a parking lot at each end of the zoo, are the best way to see the animals. Trails are wheelchair-accessible, and for those who don't wish to walk long distances, buses and trams run from exhibit to exhibit within

COURTESY OF ONCLE BERNARD ON FLICKR.COM

elephants at the North Carolina Zoo

the park. (One must still leave the vehicle to see the animals.) This acclaimed zoo is operated by the state of North Carolina.

Other Sights and Activities

At the **North Carolina Aviation Museum** (2222-G Pilots View Rd., 336/625-0170, www .ncairmuseum.org, 10 A.M.–5 P.M. Mon.– Sat., 1–5 P.M. Sun., $5 adults, $3 students, free for children under 6), World War II through Vietnam-era fighter aircraft gleam in restored splendor. After touring the two hangars where the airplanes and other military memorabilia are housed, check out the gift shop, which is a model plane lover's dream.

The **Asheboro Copperheads** (McCrary Stadium, Southway Rd. off of McCrary St., 336/460-7018, www.teamcopperhead.com) part of the Coastal Plain League, are a summer team of college players from schools in North Carolina and throughout the South, whose alumni include at least two current big-league pitchers.

◖ Liberty Antiques Festival

Liberty, located between Asheboro and I-85, hosts a twice-yearly antiques fair that draws crowds from all over the Southeast. At the Liberty Antiques Festival (2855 Pike Farm Rd., in Staley, just outside Liberty, 336/622-3040, www.libertyantiquesfestival .com, $5), usually held over a three-day weekend in late April and again in late September, hundreds of vendors set up shop in a farm field, creating a huge outdoor antiques mall that offers many happy hours of browsing. (Since it's in the open air, come prepared for bad weather and/or mud.) There's a huge variety among the dealers' wares, but overall the theme leans towards the rustic Southern (including some really fine early Southern furniture, museum-quality folk pottery, and other highly sought-after folk art collectibles), with a good balance between items that cost a dollar and items that cost as much as a car, and everything in between.

SEAGROVE

The Carolina Sandhills are home to a generations-old pottery industry, known as the Seagrove tradition, which is more alive today than ever. The little crossroads town of Seagrove is built over beds of clay that perfectly suited the needs of 18th- and 19th-century Carolina potters. Several families of potters settled in this region and, drawing from the excellent red and gray clays so readily available here, were soon supplying much of the rest of the state with jugs, crocks, plates, and other utilitarian wares. The pottery that their descendants make today is much more decorative than those early wares, combining beauty and function in a most charming balance. Within just a few miles of Seagrove's downtown, reaching into little nearby communities like Whynot and Westmoore, are the shops and studios of over 100 potters. Many of these potters are members of families that have been right here for generations—the Luck, Teague, Owen, Owens, Craven, and Chriscoe clans, to name just a few—and learned their art directly from family elders. Other potters here have been drawn to the region precisely because of the pottery tradition, and have learned the techniques of the old local masters. The pottery made by all of these Seagrove artists is among the most collectible of Southern folk art.

◀ North Carolina Pottery Center

The North Carolina Pottery Center (233 East Ave., 336/873-8430, www.ncpotterycenter.com, 10 A.M.–4 P.M. Tues.–Sat., $2 adults, $1 high school students) is the ideal place to start your tour of Seagrove. Though the primary focus of the Pottery Center is to preserve and present the work of Seagrove-area potters, you'll also see representative work from the state's several other highly distinctive pottery traditions. The permanent exhibit and rotating shows introduce visitors to such late master artists as M. L. Owens, A. R. Cole, and Dorothy and Walter Auman, all in a beautiful, airy building designed to echo the lines of a barn. There's also a very nice little gift shop. On your way out the door, pick up a map of area

on the Montgomery-Randolph County line

© SARAH BRYAN

potteries. There are dozens and dozens, each uniquely appealing, each representing a different facet of the tradition, and you'll need a map to help you choose which ones to sample.

Pottery Studios

Ben Owen Pottery (2199 Hwy. 705, 910/464-2261, www.benowenpottery.com), three miles south of the Pottery Center on Highway 705, "The Pottery Highway," is the studio and showroom of one of Seagrove's finest young potters. Ben Owen III learned the art from his grandfather, who was also a renowned area potter. Incorporating elements of Asian ceramics into his native Seagrove tradition, Owen has made a name for himself in the fine arts world. Much of his work is positively monumental, massive vases and jars, many glazed in the brilliant red for which the family is famous. A small museum attached to the shop shows some of his father and grandfather's beautiful work.

David and Mary Farrell of **Westmoore Pottery** (4622 Busbee Rd., Westmoore, 910/464-3700, www.westmoorepottery.com, 9 A.M.–5 P.M. Mon.–Sat.) were attracted to Seagrove by its pottery tradition, and after many years of living and working in the community are now very much a part of it. The Farrells specialize in recreating historical ceramics, primarily of North Carolina styles. Their work is so accurate that it appears in historic houses throughout the United States, at Old Salem and Colonial Williamsburg, and has been featured in many movies, including *Amistad* and *Cold Mountain*.

Luck's Ware (1606 Adams Rd., Seagrove, 336/879-3261, 9 A.M.–5 P.M. Mon.–Fri.) is the workshop of Sid Luck and his sons Matt and Jason, today's representatives of a generations-old family tradition. Sid fires (bakes) his pots in a groundhog kiln—an old-timey Carolina form, a long, arched brick tunnel, part of which is usually subterranean. Some of the bricks with which the Lucks built their groundhog kiln came from Sid's great-grandfather's own kiln.

Shopping

It's hard to imagine, but there is one shop in Seagrove with wares that rival the gleaming pottery in beauty. **Seagrove Orchids** (3451 Brower Mill Rd., 336/879-6677, www.seagrove orchids.com, 10 A.M.–5 P.M. Tues.–Sun. and by appointment) is a wonderful place to visit even if your hobbies don't include exotic horticulture. There are over 220 kinds of orchids in the greenhouses here, from rare plants to affordable species good for the beginner. Seagrove Orchids even propagates new hybrid varieties of its own.

Accommodations

The **Duck Smith House** (465 N. Broad St., 888/869-9018, www.ducksmithhouse.com, $125), a farmhouse built in 1914, is the classic Southern bed-and-breakfast, with a large wraparound porch and a hearty country breakfast. The location is perfect for a weekend of pottery-shopping.

UWHARRIE MOUNTAINS

The Uwharrie Mountains are strange and beautiful, a range of hills covered in deep, rocky woods and dotted with small, quiet towns with names like Ether and Troy. Peaks of this range, one

© HARRY HOOVER

kayaking in the Uwharrie Mountains

of the oldest in North America, once soared to 20,000 feet, but the millennia have worn them down until the highest mountain now stands at just over 1,000 feet. Lakes, hiking trails, and history are hidden in these mountains.

◖ Uwharrie National Forest

The trail system of the Uwharrie Forest has been compared to a "mini-Appalachian Trail," a description that's pretty apt. Although the Uwharrie Mountains are significantly lower than the Blue Ridge Mountains and Smokies, they do shelter delicate mountain ecosystems closely related to those of the Appalachians. Two major trails run through the park, the Uwharrie National Recreational Trail and the Dutchman's Creek Trail. Both begin 10 miles west of Troy, with parking at Highway 24/27. The 10-mile Dutchman's Creek trail loops with the 20-mile Uwharrie Trail, which ends two miles east of Ophir at State Route 1306. The hikes are somewhat strenuous—these are mountains, after all, though low ones—and they travel through pretty and kind of spooky terrain, rocky woods with old homesites and graveyards, with some abandoned gold mines nearby.

Two large campgrounds are located near Badin Lake, at the western edge of the park. **Arrowhead Campground** (Forest Road 597B off of Mullinix Rd./1154, 910/576-6391, reservations 877/833-6777, www.cs.unca.edu /nfsnc/recreation/uwharrie/index.htm, with electricity $15/night, without electricity $12/ night) has 50 sites with picnic tables and tent pads, 33 of which have electrical hookups. There are spigots for drinking water, and a bathhouse with hot showers, flush-toilets, and a laundry sink. The Arrowhead Campground is a half-mile from Badin Lake. **The Badin Lake Campground** (Forest Road 576, off of 109, 910/576-6391, reservations 877/444-6777, $8/night), which has 34 sites, is directly on the lake. Each site has a picnic table, grill, and tent pad. Water spigots and chemical toilets are nearby. Several smaller sites throughout the park are accessible for tent camping, and one, Canebrake Horse Camp near Badin Lake, is for folks traveling with their horses.

Morrow Mountain State Park

Located catty-corner to Badin and Albemarle, Morrow Mountain State Park (49104 Morrow Mountain Rd., Albemarle, 704/982-4402, www.ncparks.gov/Visit/parks/momo/main .php) preserves one of the Uwharries' highest peaks, the 936-foot Morrow Mountain. Within the park, visitors can go boating on Lake Tillery or on the Pee Dee River, with rowboat and canoe rentals available in the spring and summer. More than 15 miles of trails snake up and down the mountains. Cabins are available for rental, at $400 per week in the summertime and $80 per night (with a two-night minimum) in the off-season. There are also over 100 campsites ($9–15/night) with water, restrooms, and showers nearby, but no electricity. Visitors can also check out the exhibit hall (10 A.M.–5 P.M. daily) to learn about the ecology and Native American heritage of the region, and visit the restored 1870s home and infirmary of the first physician to venture into these parts.

Denton

The annual **Southeast Old Threshers' Reunion** (Denton Farm Park, 336/859-2755, www.threshers.com) takes place in Denton, southwest of Asheboro and just to the north of the Uhwarries. The gathering, usually held around the Fourth of July, celebrates the old ways of farming that were replaced by tractors and motorized combines. At the Reunion, farmers who have kept the traditional methods alive gather to show off the strength of their draft horses in pulling competitions, horsepowered equipment demonstrations, and other feats of strength and skill. There's also plenty of music and food.

If you'd like a taste of Lexington-style barbecue, a good bet here is **Troutman's BBQ** (18466 S. Hwy. 109, 336/859-2206), a local landmark for many years.

Mount Gilead

The **Town Creek Indian Mound** (509 Town Creek Mound Rd., Mt. Gilead, 910/439-6802, www.ah.dcr.state.nc.us/sections/hs/town/town

.htm, 10 A.M.–4 P.M. Tues.–Sat., 1–4 P.M. Sun., free) is an extraordinary archaeological site, the remains and reconstruction of a center of ancient Pee Dee Indian culture. The mound itself was the location of three successive structures, including an earth lodge and a temple. Over 500 people were buried at this site, and the remains of a mortuary were excavated nearby. Today, in addition to the mound, visitors can see reconstructions of two temples and the mortuary. The visitors center includes displays of artifacts and interpretive exhibits about the site's history.

Southern Pines and Pinehurst

Flip through the old postcards at any antique shop in the Carolinas, and you're likely to come across turn-of-the-century images of the Southern Pines region of the North Carolina Sandhills. The area's development kicked into high gear in the 1890s, when Bostonian James Tufts constructed the Pinehurst Resort with money gleaned in the soda fountain industry. He commissioned Frederick Law Olmstead to design a village, which he named Pinehurst. The first hotel opened in 1895, followed by the Pinehurst golf course (now called Pinehurst No. 1) in 1898, and the Pinehurst No. 2 course in 1907. The area quickly became a haven for northern snowbirds. Postcards from that early era are clearly geared to a Yankee audience, portraying the early spring blossoms that cover the Sandhills while New York and Chicago and Milwaukee are still buried in snow, or showing rustic cabins and rural African Americans driving ox-carts or playing the banjo—holdovers from the stereotypical Victorian notions of the Old South, very much appealing to urbanites in search of a change of pace. The origin of early visitors is also evident on streets signs in Southern Pines, where many of the roads are named for northeastern and upper Midwestern states.

Today, this whole section of Moore County, anchored by the two picturesque towns of Pinehurst and Southern Pines, is a sea of golf courses, and still a magnet for snowbirds and halfbacks (northerners who retired to Florida, found it too hot, and came halfway back to North Carolina). Primarily known for golf, the Pinehurst area has hosted the U.S. Open, the U.S. Women's Open, and the USGA National Championship. The spring months here are exceptionally pretty, and the weather is usually warm but not dangerously hot (as it will be in a few months), so between March and May hotels and restaurants fill to the gills, and golf courses can book solid. The key to having a good golf vacation in the springtime is planning well in advance. The golf package is the coin of the realm here; by bundling lodging and greens fees, you can save cash and hassle.

SPORTS AND RECREATION
Golf

One of the most famous golf centers in the world, there are more than 40 major courses in the Southern Pines/Pinehurst/Aberdeen area. The **Pinehurst Resort** (1 Carolina Vista Dr., Pinehurst, 800/487-4653, www.pinehurst.com) is comprised of eight major courses (called Pinehurst No. 1, 2, etc.), designed by some of the great golf course architects of the last century: Donald Ross, Ellis Maples, George and Tom Fazio, and Rees Jones. **Pine Needles** (Midland Rd., Southern Pines, 910/692-7111, www.pineneedles-midpines.com, $135–235 greens fees) incorporates the Pine Needles (18 holes, par 71) and Mid-Pines (18 holes, par 72) courses, both Donald Ross creations. The **Talamore** (48 Talamore Dr., Southern Pines, 800/552-6292, www.talamoregolfresort.com, 18 holes, par 71, $60–130 greens fees) was designed by Rees Jones. If you visit at the right time, you might be treated to the able caddying services of the Talamore llamas.

Other courses in the area were designed by Jack Nicklaus, Jack Nicklaus II, Dan Maples, Gary Player, and other leading lights of golf course architecture. Information about all of them can be found at www.homeofgolf.com.

Hiking and Walking

Weymouth Woods-Sandhills Nature Preserve (1024 Fort Bragg Rd., Southern Pines, 910/692-2167, http://ncparks.gov/Visit/parks/wewo/main.php, 8 A.M.–6 P.M. daily Nov.–Feb., 8 A.M.–8 P.M. daily Mar.–Oct.) is comprised of nearly 900 acres, home of red-cockaded woodpeckers, fox squirrels, and other natives of the longleaf pine barrens. Most of the preserve is a limited-use area, and subject to periodic prescribed burning, but several trails, most of a mile or less, let visitors explore the woods and swamps.

Another nice spot for walking is the **Horticultural Garden** (3395 Airport Rd., Pinehurst, 910/695-3882, www.sandhills.cc .nc.us/lsg/hort.html, dawn–dusk daily) at Sandhills Community College. A full acre of the property is dedicated to a formal English garden, while other areas show off plants of the woodlands and wetlands, and collections of roses, holly, and conifers.

ACCOMMODATIONS
【 Pinehurst Resort

A separate entity from the town of Pinehurst, the Pinehurst Resort (Village of Pinehurst, 800/487-4653, www.pinehurst.com), opened in 1895, is the world's second-largest golf resort. The resort is built around eight golf courses, including the famed Pinehurst Numbers 1, 2, 3, and 4, designed by Donald Ross. There are three inns to choose from. The **Carolina** (from $250), built in 1901 and listed in the National Register of Historic Places, is a grand hotel in the Edwardian style, with long piazzas and lush lawns. The 1895 **Holly Inn** (from $230) was the first hotel built at the resort, and is a smaller and more cozy, club-like inn. The third inn, the **Manor** (from $150), is the smallest and most laid-back of the accommodations here.

For beginning golfers, as well as experienced players, the **Pinehurst Golf Academy** (from $1,329) gives weekend- and week-long classes, taught on Pinehurst 1, 3, and 5, with

a stay at the Carolina included in the course fee. Also on the grounds is a four-star **Spa at Pinehurst**, with a long menu of skin and body care therapies. The **Pinehurst Tennis Club** is regarded as a top tennis resort nationally, with a high quality pro shop and adult tennis camps. Golf, spa, and tennis packages can significantly reduce the overall costs of a stay at the Pinehurst, though surcharges for amenities might still apply.

Inns

The **Pine Crest Inn** (Dogwood Rd., Pinehurst, 800/371-2545, www.pinecrestinnpinehurst .com, $70–120 plus 15 percent service charge) was owned for many years by Donald Ross, the golf course designer who helped make the Pinehurst Resort famous. Operated for the last 40 years by the Barrett family, the Pine Crest is a favorite for golfers and vacationers, and for local diners who come to the Pine Crest Inn Restaurant and Mr. B's Lounge.

The **Magnolia Inn** (corner of Magnolia and Chinquapin, Pinehurst, 800/526-5562, www.themagnoliainn.com, $75–190), built in 1896, sits in a great downtown location. Guests are just steps from local shopping and restaurants, and very close to the best area golfing.

The 【 **Knollwood House** (1495 W. Connecticut Ave., Southern Pines, 910/692-9390, from $140) is one of the most popular inns in the area, a bed-and-breakfast located on the 15th green of the Mid Pines golf course. The elegant house, built in 1927 as a Philadelphia family's vacation home, has a beautiful sunroom and front porch overlooking the azalea-spangled yard.

FOOD

Some of the best places to dine in this area are at the Pinehurst Resort (800/487-4653). The **Carolina Dining Room** (Carolina Inn, Pinehurst, $36–37, dinner jacket required) is the resort's most formal dining room, serving fine chops and steak, and presented with the chef's suggestions for wine accompaniment. At the **1895 Restaurant** (Holly Inn, Pinehurst, $24–35), specialties feature savory grilled veal and steak, filet of grouper served over oyster risotto, and the signature cider-brined grilled pork chop with apple-pecan chutney. The **Tavern** (The Manor, Pinehurst, $16–27) serves a lighter café fare, with entrée soups and sandwiches, as well as an array of pasta dishes. Seven other restaurants, cafés, and tea shops are scattered throughout the Pinehurst.

At the **Magnolia Inn** (Magnolia and Chinaquapin, Pinehurst, 800/526-5562, www .themagnoliainn.com, dining room $15–35, pub $6–12), the main dining room serves three-course meals with such specialties as lobster chimichanga, pork napoleon, fire-roasted pepper over grits, and the inn's special tomato bisque. At the pub, several of these specialties are served, along with sandwiches like the corned beef reuben panini, barbecue pork sandwich, and pub burger, with the works.

CHARLOTTE AND RACING COUNTRY

To old-time Carolinians, Cousin Charlotte's behavior has always been inexplicable. She's the type who would wear natty white shoes after Labor Day, or sit in church on Sunday with her legs crossed at the knee instead of the ankle. But if you look close, her roots are showing. More than the weather gives this city a Southern ambience. You might have to pay big-city prices at an Uptown parking garage, but in what other metropolis would the garage cashier, whom you've only known long enough to hand him your money, implore you to "Come on back and see me soon, darling!"?

Charlotte is one of the most diverse cities in the Southeast, a magnet for newcomers from around the world and from all over the United States. In a single year recently, the number of people who moved to Charlotte was equal to the entire population of Asheville. Tens of thousands of immigrants from Latin America, Africa, Southeast Asia, and other faraway places have brought new languages, cuisines, holidays, and religions, making this a city of dazzling cultural richness. Driving out Central Avenue or South Boulevard, it's almost easy to lose track of what country you're in. All of North Carolina's cities are sophisticated and complex, but Charlotte possesses a worldliness that is unique.

The epicenter of North Carolina's auto racing industry and culture is just north and northeast of Charlotte, in the area around Mooresville, Concord, and Kannapolis. In addition to NASCAR's huge presence, this area offers unique local food and a window into a rapidly diminishing world of textile mills.

© BRIAN LEON

HIGHLIGHTS

◖ Levine Museum of the New South:
This important museum tells the complicated and sometimes painful story of the post-Civil War South, and Charlotte in particular, in ways that are both respectful and courageous (page 187).

◖ U.S. National Whitewater Center:
Home to the U.S. Olympic canoe and kayak teams, this innovative facility is also designed for first-time paddlers, as well as hikers, climbers, and other adventure sports enthusiasts (page 190).

◖ Lowe's Motor Speedway: This Concord stadium seats well over 150,000 fans around a 1.5-mile track. It's a spectacular sight, whether there's a race on or not (page 195).

◖ Mill Village Museum: One of the best small museums in North Carolina, Cooleemee's Mill Village Museum celebrates the incredibly rich heritage of Southern textile workers' "mill hill" communities (page 197).

LOOK FOR ◖ TO FIND RECOMMENDED SIGHTS, ACTIVITIES, DINING, AND LODGING.

CHARLOTTE

PLANNING YOUR TIME

To get a good feel for Charlotte, I recommend spending at least a long weekend here—if not years. Lodging is plentiful, though more expensive than much of the rest of North Carolina. Uptown hotels are in easy walking distance or short cab rides away from many of the major museums, sports complexes, and performance venues. Inns in the Myers Park, Dilworth, and Plaza-Milwood neighborhoods are a quick hop away from Uptown, but have a less urban pace. There's a great deal to do in the Plaza-Milwood area—good cafés, fun shopping, and easy access to NoDa (the North Davidson neighborhood). Motels along I-85 to the north of Charlotte, particularly in the Concord Mills

area, are not far from the city and are also convenient to the destinations in Kannapolis, Mooresville, Salisbury, and Spencer.

Charlotte sprawls, but it's fairly easy to get from place to place in a short amount of time—if you're not on the road in rush hour. When traveling to the city, though, it's a good idea to check ahead of time if there will be any major sporting events during your visit. The Bobcats' and Panthers' stadiums are both downtown, so expect heavier traffic right before and right after games. Lowe's Motor Speedway, a few miles north of the city in Concord, can hold more than 200,000 people, so you can imagine the state of traffic and hotel availability around race days. Other events that sell out area hotels

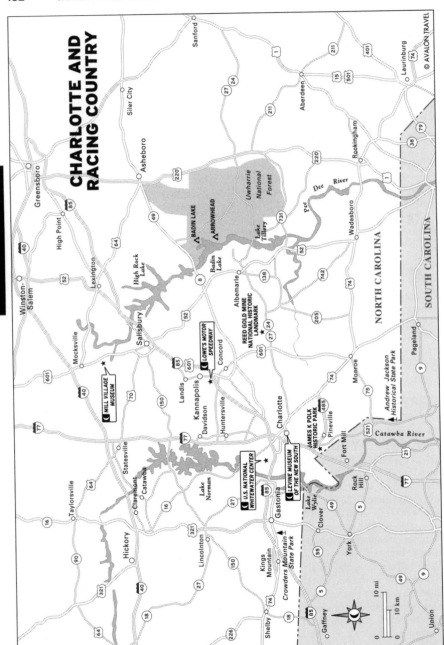

are the CAA and ACC basketball tournaments, in February and March. (CAA has been held in Charlotte for the last several years, and the ACC tourney comes through every few years.)

INFORMATION AND SERVICES

Two Uptown (Charlotte's name for downtown) locations serve as Charlotte **visitors centers**: one at 330 South Tryon Street (704/331-2700, www.crva.com, 8:30 A.M.–5 P.M. Mon.–Fri., 9 A.M.–3 P.M. Sat.), and the other in the lobby of the Levine Museum of the New South at 200 East 7th Street (704/331-2753, 10 A.M.–5 P.M. Mon.–Sat., noon–5 P.M. Sun.). The Charlotte *Observer* publishes an excellent annual guide to the region, geared towards new residents as well as tourists, called "Living Here." You can pick it up at many major destinations, or read it at www.charlotteobserver.com/images/livinghere/livinghere.html. Another comprehensive resource is www.visitcharlotte.com.

Carolinas Medical Center (1000 Blythe Boulevard, 704/355-2000, www.carolinasmedicalcenter.org), is one of the largest hospitals in the Carolinas. Emergency vet clinics include **Carolina Veterinary Specialists** (2225 Township Rd., 704/588-7015 or 704/504-9608, www.carolinavet.com) and **Emergency Veterinary Clinic** (2440 Plantation Ctr. Dr., Matthews, 704/844-6440).

GETTING THERE AND AROUND

Charlotte-Douglas International Airport (5501 Josh Birmingham Pkwy., 704/359-4013, www.charmeck.org) is the 10th-largest hub in the United States, with nonstop flights to and from over 120 worldwide destinations. Nearly 30 million passengers come through CLT each year. Charlotte's **Amtrak** station is on Tryon Street (1914 N. Tryon St., 704/376-4416, www.amtrak.com), a short cab ride from major Uptown hotels and attractions.

Charlotte's extensive and ever-expanding **public transportation** system provides affordable jaunts from place to place throughout the city. Some routes around the Center City/Uptown area are free. The city has inaugurated an ambitious light rail system, **LYNX,** which will eventually give rapid access to and from Charlotte's many far-flung neighborhoods and suburbs. Routes and rates are posted at www.charmeck.org/Departments/Home.htm, or call 704/336-7433.

Charlotte

There has only been one brief period, in Charlotte's earliest days, when it was not a boom town. In the late 18th century it was a mid-sized county seat, hardly distinguishable from Salisbury or Hillsborough. But 1799 brought a taste of things to come when a child's creekside discovery of a 17-pound lump of gold—which his family, not recognizing the material, would employ for several years as a doorstop—sparked a minor gold rush.

When the railroad came to the Carolina backcountry, Charlotte was first in line to get her ticket punched. Concerted courtship of the railroad companies brought several important early lines through town, and soon Charlotte was a giant in the regional economy. Cotton farmers throughout the Carolina Piedmont carried their crop to Charlotte, and brokers funneled the raw cotton down the line to the port of Charleston, from which it was shipped to the mills of New England and old England. These early ties to South Carolina could arguably be the origin of the subtle but pervasive sense that Charlotte is only technically part of North Carolina.

Economically adventurous, Charlotte rebounded quickly after the War Between the States, encouraging Northern and foreign investment and businessmen —again drawing the disapprobation of other North Carolinians, but laying the groundwork for greater and greater prosperity. Textile mill money enriched

CHARLOTTE

Charlotte skyline

the city throughout the early 20th century. Today, Charlotte is the second-largest banking center of the United States, after New York City. Bank of America, Wachovia, and other locally based giants continue to bring waves of newcomers to the Queen City.

SIGHTS
Art Museums and Installations
The **Mint Museum of Art** (2730 Randolph Rd., 704/337-2000, www.mintmuseum.org, 10 A.M.–10 P.M. Tues., 10 A.M.–5 P.M. Wed.–Sat., noon–5 P.M. Sun., $6 adults, $5 seniors and college students, $3 ages 6–17), and the **Mint Museum of Craft + Design** (220 N. Tryon St., 704/337-2000, www.mintmuseum .org, 10 A.M.–5 P.M. Tues.–Sat., until 8 P.M. third Thurs. of the month, noon–5 P.M. Sun., $6 adults, $5 seniors and college students, $3 ages 6–17), are two of the state's premier art galleries. The Mint Museum of Art occupies an 1836 building that originally served as a branch of the federal mint. Its collections include an array of art from many lands and eras. The Mint Museum of Craft + Design focuses

on studio craft, with special attention to North Carolina artists, but also with a global sweep.

The **Light Factory** (345 N. College St.,704/333-9755, www.lightfactory.org, 9 A.M.–6 P.M. Mon.–Sat., 1–6 P.M. Sun, free) is a gallery of modern photography and film. It hosts traveling exhibitions and offers classes and workshops.

Public art installations are scattered throughout Uptown. A walking tour brochure is available from the Arts and Science Council (www.artsandscience.org). Among the most notable North Carolinian artists whose work is here are Charlotte-born Harlem Renaissance painter Romare Bearden (whose 1989 mural "Before Dawn" is at the main public library at 310 N. Tryon) and celebrated fresco artist Ben Long (whose frescoes include those at the Bank of America Corporate Center at 100 N. Tryon, and the Charlotte-Mecklenburg Police Headquarters at 601 E. Trade St.).

History Museums and Sites
The **Charlotte Museum of History** (3500 Shamrock Dr., 704/568-1774,

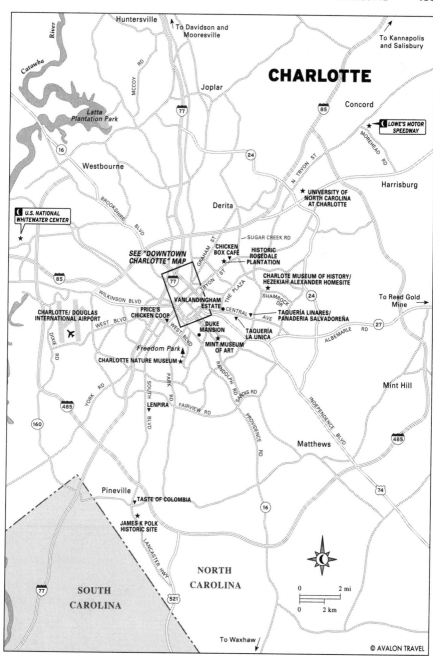

Huntersville

To Davidson and
Mooresville

To Kannapolis
and Salisbury

Catawba River

MCCOY RD

Joplar

CHARLOTTE

Concord

Latta
Plantation Park

77

85

LOWE'S MOTOR
SPEEDWAY

16

24

MOREHEAD RD

Westbourne

BROOKSHIRE BLVD

Harrisburg

N. TRYON ST

U.S. NATIONAL
WHITEWATER CENTER

Derita

UNIVERSITY OF
NORTH CAROLINA
AT CHARLOTTE

SUGAR CREEK RD

GRAHAM ST

CHICKEN
BOX CAFE

SEE "DOWNTOWN
CHARLOTTE" MAP

HISTORIC
ROSEDALE
PLANTATION

TRYON ST

CHARLOTE MUSEUM OF HISTORY/
HEZEKIAH ALEXANDER HOMESITE

85

77

WILKINSON BLVD

VANLANDINGHAM
ESTATE

THE PLAZA

SHAMROCK DR

CENTRAL AVE

24

To Reed Gold
Mine

CHARLOTTE/
DOUGLAS
INTERNATIONAL AIRPORT

PRICE'S
CHICKEN COOP

WEST BLVD

WEST BEND

TAQUERÍA LINARES/
PANADERIA SALVADOREÑA

27

DIXIE RD

DUKE
MANSION

TAQUERIA
LA UNICA

ALBEMARLE RD

Freedom Park

MINT MUSEUM
OF ART

CHARLOTTE NATURE MUSEUM

RANDOLPH RD

SARDIS RD

Mint Hill

YORK RD

SOUTH BLVD

PARK RD

LENPIRA

FAIRVIEW RD

PROVIDENCE RD

INDEPENDENCE BLVD

485

160

Matthews

485

Pineville

74

TASTE OF COLOMBIA

16

JAMES K POLK
HISTORIC SITE

LANCASTER HWY

**NORTH
CAROLINA**

77

**SOUTH
CAROLINA**

521

0   2 mi

0   2 km

To Waxhaw

© AVALON TRAVEL

CHARLOTTE

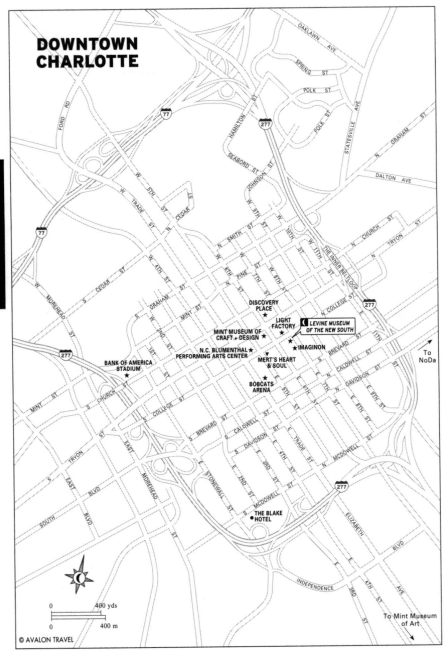

DOWNTOWN CHARLOTTE

DISCOVERY PLACE ★

LIGHT FACTORY ★

MINT MUSEUM OF CRAFT + DESIGN ★

★ LEVINE MUSEUM OF THE NEW SOUTH

N.C. BLUMENTHAL ★ PERFORMING ARTS CENTER

★ IMAGINON

★ MERT'S HEART & SOUL

BANK OF AMERICA STADIUM ★

BOBCATS ARENA ★

THE BLAKE ● HOTEL

To NoDa

To Mint Museum of Art

0   400 yds

0   400 m

© AVALON TRAVEL

www.charlottemuseum.org, 10 A.M.–5 P.M. Tues.–Sat., and Mon. between Memorial Day and Labor Day, 1–5 P.M. Sun., $6 adults, $5 students and seniors, $3 children) chronicles the origins of Charlotte in entertaining exhibits geared towards all ages, and the 1774 **Hezekiah Alexander Homesite,** on the museum grounds, is the oldest structure in Mecklenburg County.

On a busy block of North Tryon Street just outside of Uptown is **Historic Rosedale Plantation** (3427 N. Tryon, 704/335-0325, www.historicrosedale.org., 1:30–3 P.M. Thurs.–Sat.), a graceful 1830s house. Twenty slaves worked the surrounding 911 acres, most of which are now hidden under strip malls and parking lots. Early plantation life is also represented at **Historic Latta Plantation** (5225 Sample Rd., Huntersville, 704/875-2312, www.lattaplantation.org, 10 A.M.–5 P.M. Tues.–Sat., 1–5 P.M. Sun., house tours on the hour, $6 adults, $5 students and seniors over 62, free for children under 5), a circa-1800 cotton farm, which presents living history events year-round to teach about life in the late 18th century and early to mid-19th century. It also sits alongside a 1,300-acre nature preserve, an important haven for migratory birds and the home of the Carolina Raptor Center. A farm of a similar era is recreated at the **James K. Polk Historic Site** (12031 Lancaster Hwy., Pineville, 704/889-7145, www.nchistoric sites.org/polk/polk.html, 9 A.M.–5 P.M. Tues.–Sat., free), where the 11th president was born. Visitors can tour log buildings that date to the era of his childhood (though are not original to the site), and can learn about Polk and the often-overlooked significance of his presidency at the visitors center.

Levine Museum of the New South

The Levine Museum of the New South (200 E. 7th St., 704/333-1887, www.museumofthe newsouth.org, 10 A.M.–5 P.M. Mon.–Sat., noon–5 P.M. Sun., $6 adults, $5 children, $17 family) tells the story—in its permanent exhibit called "Cotton Fields to Skyscrapers"—of the

South's emergence from the devastation of the Civil War and the rancor of Reconstruction, through the post-war reign of King Cotton, and the lives of the tobacco and textile industries that for so long were the staples of North Carolina's economy. Interwoven are the stories of segregation and the civil rights movement, and the waves of globalization and immigration that are defining today's new New South. Changing exhibits address head-on, often in daring ways, community, race, nationality, stereotyping, religion, and other fascinating and extremely complex issues of Southern life, past and present, in presentations that are engaging and thought-provoking. The Museum of the New South has a busy programming schedule, including the "Global Dish" series—which presents new regional foodways brought by Charlotte's tremendous waves of immigration—and walking tours and historical lectures having to do with the culture and future of Charlotte.

If you happen to be a new resident of Charlotte, or simply curious about the Charlottean culture (that's pronounced "Sharla-TEE-an," by the way), you'll enjoy the Levine Museum's **New South for the New Southerner** series ($4, reservations required). Led by museum historian Tom Hanchett, with guest speakers including local politicians, writers, religious leaders, and other community experts, the evening salon will teach you the quirks and charms of Charlotte in a fun social setting, while you sample local wine and hors d'oeuvres.

Kids' Museums and Activity Centers

Discovery Place (301 N. Tryon, 704/372-6261, www.discoveryplace.org, 9 A.M.–5 P.M. Mon.–Fri., 10 A.M.–6 P.M. Sat., 12:30–5 P.M. Sun., $8.50 adults, $7.50 children and seniors) is an interactive museum with an indoor rain forest, an IMAX theater, preserved human body parts, and much more. Discovery Place also operates the **Charlotte Nature Museum** (1658 Sterling Rd., 704/372-6261) next to Freedom Park, which is home to live animals and a walk-through butterfly pavilion. **ImaginOn** (300 E. 7th St., 704/973-2780, www.imaginon.org,

CHARLOTTE

9 A.M.–9 P.M. Mon.–Thurs., 9 A.M.–6 P.M. Fri. and Sat., 1–6 P.M. Sun.) is a major Uptown arts complex for children and teens. It has theaters, libraries, a story lab, and a teen center.

ENTERTAINMENT AND EVENTS
Performing Arts

Among the city's several excellent theater companies are **Theatre Charlotte** (501 Queens Rd., 704/376-3777, www.theatrecharlotte.org), which has been in business since the 1920s; the **Actor's Theatre of Charlotte** (650 E. Stonewall St., 704/342-2251, www.actorstheatrecharlotte.org), a company specializing in contemporary drama; the **Carolina Actors Studio Theatre** (1118 Clement Ave., 704/455-8542, www.nccast.com) for "experiential" art; and the **Children's Theatre of Charlotte** (www.ctcharlotte.org, 704/973-2800), which has its home at ImaginOn.

The **Blumenthal Performing Arts Center** (130 North. Tryon St., 704/372-1000, www.blumenthalcenter.org) in Uptown is the home theater of the **Charlotte Symphony** (www.charlottesymphony.org), which has been in existence for nearly 80 years. These days, under the direction of Christof Perick and conductor Alan Yamamoto, it puts together seasons of baroque, romantic, and modern classical music, as well as a series of pops-style concerts with guest artists. Almost 40 years old, the **North Carolina Dance Theater** (www.ncdance.org) is another venerable institution in Charlotte's arts scene. They dance full-length classical ballets and modern works, and tour widely. **Opera Carolina** (www.operacarolina.org), at 60 years old, is the leading opera company in the Carolinas. They produce four major operas each year, as well as an annual run of *Amahl and the Night Visitors* at Christmastime. The **Carolinas Concert Association** (www.carolinasconcert.org) has been bringing artists of international renown to the people of Charlotte for generations, from the 1930s, when the likes of Nelson Eddy and Jose Iturbi performed here, to recent years when Joshua Bell and the Russian National Ballet, among many others, have appeared. Each year's concert schedule is spectacular.

BEYOND BANKTOWN

Charlotteans and outsiders alike often refer to the Queen City as Banktown, a name meant to conjure images of spotless sidewalks and shining office towers, a nine-to-five corporate culture with little room for the arts or nonconformity. But there's a lot more to Charlotte than the Bank of America tower (sometimes called the Taj McColl, for former CEO Hugh McColl).

I happen to think that Uptown, with its sparkly skyscrapers and stampeding suits, is kind of cool – a little bit of Washington's K Street in a more tropical clime. But we do a disservice to Charlotte and to ourselves as travelers if we overlook the beautiful variety of people who live here. In addition to the suggestions you'll find in this chapter, explore these websites and pick up these publications while you're in Banktown to find out what's happening outside the tower's shadow.

· *Creative Loafing* (http://charlotte.creativeloafing.com), a free weekly that you can find all over the city, does a bang-up job of covering the arts, food, politics, and everything else that makes Charlotte hum. The website is as good a resource as the print edition.

· *Banktown U$A* (www.banktownusa.com), a print quarterly, takes direct aim at Charlotte's bland rep and highlights creative people and singular doings.

· **Weird Charlotte** (www.weirdcharlotte.com) – motto "Keep Charlotte weird? Make Charlotte weird!" – is an online compendium of "Current weirdness," "historic weirdness," "random acts of weirdness," and "weirdos" in this fine city.

© SARAH BRYAN

Charlotte is home to a multitude of international communities.

Festivals

Each May, race fans take over several blocks of Uptown for **Speed Street** (www.600festival.com). For three days, entertainers, race drivers, and thousands of enthusiasts celebrate the area's auto racing industry. Autograph sessions throughout the festival bring participants in close contact with racing royalty.

September's **Charlotte Shout** (www.charlotteshout.com) is a month-long, city-wide festival of the arts—music, dance, visual arts, and especially culinary arts. It includes dozens of events, many of which are major festivals in their own right. There are film festivals, gospel extravaganzas, cook-offs, ethnic festivals, gallery crawls, and a great deal more.

Charlotte is an incredible city for foodies, and one way to learn the culinary ropes here in a short time is to come to the early-June **Taste of Charlotte** (www.tasteofcharlotte.com). Dozens of area restaurants make samples of their art available, from haute European masterpieces to soul food favorites, plus plenty of international flavors from this wonderfully diverse community.

Charlotte's rapidly expanding population of immigrants has filled the city's entertainment calendar with dozens of festivals and holidays from around the world. June's Annual **Asian Festival** (704/588-4288) features dragon boat races on Ramsey Creek in Cornelius. Early September brings the **Yiasou Greek Festival** (704/334-4771, www.yiasoufestival.org), which celebrates one of the South's long-established Greek communities. October's **Latin American Festival** (www.latinamericancoalition.org) celebrates the South's largest immigrant group.

Nightlife

The **Milestone** (3400 Tuckaseegee Rd., www.themilestoneclub.com) has been hosting underground and up-and-coming bands since 1969, and was a major landmark for punk music in the South in the '80s. Artists who've made appearances in the club's history run the gamut from R.E.M. to Hasil Adkins to Fugazi. Today's lineups are just as inspired.

A popular Latin dance club, **Skandalo's** (5317 E. Independence Blvd., 704/535-3080) has great salsa, reggaeton, and other tropical music, and gives salsa dancing lessons. **Coyote Joe's** (4621 Wilkinson Blvd., 704/399-4946, www.coyote-joes.com) is a huge country dance hall and honky-tonk, which hosts top Nashville artists. **Puckett's Farm Equipment** (2740 W. Sugar Creek Rd., 704/597-8230, www.pucketts farm.com) is a smaller country juke joint, with regular bluegrass and rockabilly shows.

There are several significant rock-and-roll clubs in Charlotte as well. The **Double Door Inn** (1218 Charlottetown Ave./Independence Blvd., 704/376-1446, http://double-doorinn.com) calls itself "Charlotte's home of the blues." They've brought the glitterati of blues, roots, and roots-rock music to Charlotte for nearly four decades. The **Neighborhood Theatre** (511 E. 36th St., 704/358-9298, www.neighborhoodtheatre.com, all ages admitted) in the NoDa (North Davidson) neighborhood is a place where artists already high on the charts, or new artists starting to make the climb to stardom, appear when they're in Charlotte. Visitors of all ages are admitted to most shows. **Amos' Southend** (1423 S. Tryon St., 704/377-6874, www.amossouthend.com) also attracts some prestigious acts to play in its cool warehouse-style space.

SPORTS AND RECREATION
Spectator Sports
The Carolinas' only NBA franchise, the **Charlotte Bobcats** (333 E. Trade St., 704/262-2287, www.bobcatsbasketball.com), play in the massive Bobcats Arena in Uptown. The Bobcats attract a statewide following by recruiting talent from the ranks of UNC Tar Heel basketball alums. The current roster includes two of the stars of the Heels' 2005 NCAA championship team, Raymond Felton and Sean May, and Carolina legends Phil Ford and Buzz Peterson are part of the team's administration.

Charlotte is also home to the Carolinas' only NFL team, the **Carolina Panthers** (9800 S. Mint St., 704/358-7800, www.panthers.com), who play at the Bank of America Stadium at the edge of Uptown. Fans, twirling their growl-towels, cheered them on to NFC titles in 2003 and 1996.

The Boston White Sox Triple-A affiliate is the **Charlotte Knights** (704/357-8071, www.charlotteknights.com), whose home field is just over the state line in Fort Mill, South Carolina. As with any AAA team, there's a good chance at any given game of seeing a major-leaguer rehabbing from injury or brushing up on his skills, or a young turk about to break into a big-league career.

Professional ECHL hockey team the **Charlotte Checkers** play at the Bobcats Arena. Ticket and schedule information are available from www.gocheckers.com and 704/342-4423.

◖ U.S. National Whitewater Center
The U.S. National Whitewater Center (820 Hawfield Rd., 704/391-3900, www.usnwc.org), which opened in 2007, features "the world's only multi-channel recirculating whitewater river"—that is, a complex of artificial rapids—designed for training athletes at the Olympic level (it is the home of the U.S. Olympic canoe/kayak team), as well as first-time thrill-seekers. The center's 300 acres also feature mountain biking trails, a climbing center, and more.

ACCOMMODATIONS
When it comes to the languid elegance of the Old South, ◖ **The Duke Mansion** (400 Hermitage Rd., 704/714-4400, www.duke-mansion.com, from $179) is close kin to heaven. The circa-1915 mansion in Charlotte's lovely Myers Park neighborhood was home to North Carolina royalty, the Duke family, including the young Doris Duke. The downstairs foyer and gallery were clearly designed for entertaining high society, but the bedrooms—most restored to reflect the Duke family's tastes of around 1930—are simple and comfortable, and some of the en suite bathrooms still have their original tubs and tiles. In a wonderful Southern tradition, most rooms open

onto sleeping porches, which themselves are worth more than the price of the rooms. You'll receive first-rate service from all of the staff, and the culinary team will present you with a splendid breakfast. Bring a book to read in the gardens, and keep an eye out for two friendly black cats. If you visit while the magnolias are blooming, you'll never want to leave.

The ☾ **VanLandingham Estate** (2010 The Plaza, 704/334-8909 or 888/524-2020, www.vanlandinghamestate.com, from $140), built in 1913, provides a glimpse of the affluent infancy of the neighborhood known as Plaza-Midwood. A streetcar ran down the middle of The Plaza, and wealthy families established five- and six-acre estates in what was then a bucolic suburb. Plaza-Midwood now feels very close to the center of the city, and the lots have long since been subdivided, but it is still a charming enclave of early 20th-century Craftsman-style bungalows. The VanLandingham is an architectural marriage of the best arts-and-crafts design elements and aesthetics individually tailored to the tastes of the builders, early textile magnates Ralph and Susie Harwood VanLandingham. The staff take good care of guests, the grounds are beautiful, and Uptown is only a few short minutes away.

The Blake Hotel (555 S. McDowell St., 704/372-4100, www.theblakehotel.net, from $129) is a work in progress. The building shows its age, and the garage is dark and spooky. That said, there is much to recommend this hotel. The snack bar is open 24 hours and the all-night shuttle will carry you safely to and from Uptown nightspots. The decor is 1960s mod, and how. When you open the door to your room, you'll half expect to find Felix Leiter sitting on the bed, waiting to check in about your latest mission.

About 20 minutes from downtown Charlotte, the **Davidson Village Inn** (117 Depot St., Davidson, 800/892-0796, www.davidsoninn.com, from $110) is tucked away on a cozy side street in this tiny college town. The rooms are very nicely appointed, the staff helpful, the breakfast bountiful. This is a pleasant alternative to staying in the city.

By North Carolina standards, lodging is pretty expensive in Charlotte. It's pretty hard to find a good place to stay for under a hundred bucks, and extremely difficult to find a decent low-cost room within striking distance of Uptown. However, there are more choices as you head out of town. The **Microtel Inn and Suites** (1111 W. Sugar Creek Rd., 704/598-2882, www.microtelinn.com, from about $40) is located out to the northeast part of the city, near the UNC-Charlotte campus. On the opposite side of town, the **Best Western Sterling Hotel and Suites** (242 E. Woodlawn Rd., 704/525-5454, http://book.bestwestern.com, from about $60) is not too far from the airport.

FOOD

Charlotte is the eatingest place. There are so many good new restaurants opening every week that it's hard to keep up, but for reviews of the newest restaurants (with lots of interesting cultural observation), check out Tricia Childress' column in *Creative Loafing* (free at many area businesses, http://charlotte.creativeloafing.com), and Helen Schwab's and Kathleen Purvis' food writing in the *Charlotte Observer* (www.charlotteobserver.com/restaurants).

Southern and Soul

Price's Chicken Coop (1614 Camden Rd., 704/333-9866, www.priceschickencoop.com, 10 A.M.–6 P.M. Tues.–Sat., under $10) is one of Charlotte's favorite chicken places, a take-out counter where you can buy a box of deep-fried chicken, perch, shrimp, or liver and gizzards. Another venerable fried chicken laboratory is the **Chicken Box Café** (3726 N. Tryon St., 704/332-2636, 11 A.M.–9 P.M. daily, under $10). **Mert's Heart & Soul** (214 N. College St., 704/342-4222, www.mertsuptown.com, 11 A.M.–9:30 P.M. weekdays, brunch 9 A.M.–3 P.M. and dinner until 11:30 P.M. Sat. and Sun., under $10) serves Lowcountry- and Gullah-inspired soul food, with special home-style fried chicken, cornbread, shrimp and grits, greens, and other country delicacies.

CAROLINA BREADS

The following catalog of Tar Heel taste in baked goods appeared in the 1955 *North Carolina Guide.*

Outside of baker's bread, Tar Heels like (in an ascending scale from plain to fancy) cornbread, ashcakes, hoecakes, Johnny cakes, cracklin' bread, potato bread, soda biscuits, buttermilk biscuits, rolls, muffins, popovers that pop, buckwheat cakes, eggbread or batterbread (called "spoonbread" in Virginia), bland Sally Lunn and flaky beaten biscuits; the last two are company bread.

It's significant that the list begins with cornbread, for that is the food that filled our ancestors' bellies for generations; all other foods are just side dishes, really. Once at a family reunion, I was rounding the buffet table with an elderly cousin from the most rural side of my family, filling our plates with Sunday dinner. As if to assure herself that living in a nest of depravity like Chapel Hill hadn't caused my blood to flow backwards, she asked me in a grave voice, "You do like cornbread, don't you?" I responded that of course I did, how could I not? (She might as well have asked if I have a head, or if I sometimes sleep.) Relieved, she petted my arm, and said with a gravity that indicated she was speaking the wisdom of the ages, "We're cornbread people."

We're still cornbread people, but the 1955 list should be updated for the 21st century's multiethnic and multinational culinary culture in North Carolina to include tortillas (there are dozens of *tortillerías* around the state), *papadum, roti,* chappati, naan, baguettes, madeleines, biscotti, pita, bagels, challah, matzo, and *banh mi.*

Pizza

Among the many kinds of exotic foreigners arriving in Charlotte by the thousands every year, few have so difficult a time adjusting to the culture of the Southern United States as do Yankees. They have to become accustomed to a new language, a new climate, a new structure of social mores, and a new cuisine. Like so many immigrants, Northerners in Charlotte spend a lot of time trying to recreate aspects of their home culture in their new surroundings, often starting with native foodways. Based upon close ethnographic field observation, I have deduced that the natives of Northeastern North America who migrate to North Carolina share a singular obsession with pizza. Endless arguments rage in online forums as to where in Charlotte one can find the best and most authentic New York pizza. (Parallel conversations track the respective merits of Philly and Chicago pizza, but the Tri-State natives seem to approach the issue with a more violent passion than other Northerners.) I have to confess to being a hick when it comes to pizza connoisseurship.

To me, authentic handmade New York/New Jersey pizza, frozen Lean Cuisine, and Pizza Hut pizza all taste the same—really good. But based upon a consensus of opinions gathered from real, live, actual Yankees, I've assembled the following recommendations for authentic New York–style pizza in Charlotte.

Everyone seems to like **Brooklyn South Pizza** (19400 Jetton Rd., Cornelius, 704/896-2928, www.lakenorman.com, 11 A.M.–9 P.M. Mon.–Wed., 11 A.M.–10 P.M. Thurs. –Sat., noon–9 P.M. Sun.) in Cornelius, north of the city. With two locations in the city and several more elsewhere in the state, **Tony's Pizza** (14027 Conlan Circle, 704/541-8225, and 1530 Overland Park, 704/688-6880, http://tonyspizza.org, 11 A.M.–9:30 P.M. Mon.–Fri., noon–8 P.M. Sun., $5–25), founded by two Italian-born, Brooklyn-raised friends, is another favorite. Also loudly lauded are **Anzi Pizza-n-Pasta** (7308 E. Independence Blvd., 704/531-1119, www.anzispizza.com, 11 A.M.–8:45 P.M. Mon.–Thurs., 11 A.M.–9 P.M. Fri., noon–8:45 P.M. Sat., noon–7 P.M. Sun.,

$5–30), and **Hawthorne's Pizza** (1701 E. 7th St., 704/358-9339; 5814 Prosperity Church Rd., 704/875-8502; 4100 Carmel Rd., Suite A, 704/544-0299; 11 A.M.–midnight Sun.–Thurs., 11 A.M.–2 A.M. Fri. and Sat., http://hawthornespizza.com).

There are other kinds of top-notch pizza around Charlotte too. **Luisa's Brick Oven** (1730 Abbey Pl., 704/522-8782, 11:30 A.M.–9 P.M. Mon.–Fri., 5–9 P.M. Sat. and Sun., under $20) has, among other extremely tempting choices of topping, a muffuletta pie. You won't drive far in Charlotte without passing a **◖ Fuel Pizza** (14145 Rivergate Pkwy., 704/588-5333; 500 S. College St., 704/370-2755; 214 N. Tryon St., 704/350-1680; 1801 South Blvd., 704/335-7375; 1501 Central Ave., 704/376-3835; 4267 Park Rd., 704/525-3220; also with locations in Davidson, Cornelius, and Rock Hill, South Carolina; www.fuel pizza.com, hours vary, under $20). This regional chain was founded in Charlotte by New Yorkers, and has grown to include nine locations on both sides of the Carolinas' state line.

Latin American

Charlotte has a large Latino population, comprised of people from many countries, and their imprint on the culinary landscape of the city adds a most welcome dimension to the diversity of restaurants here. Most immediately noticeable are the wealth of small, home-style Mexican taquerias. Many of them can be found along Central Avenue. Try **Taquería Linares** (4918 Central Ave., 704/535-6716), **Taquería las Delicias** (5111 Central Ave., 704/537-5156), and **Taquería la Única** (2801 Central Ave., 704/347-5115). **Lenpira** (5906 South Blvd., 704/552-1515) is an especially good Central American restaurant on South Boulevard. Delicious Latin American bakeries also are popping up all over, like **Panadería Salvadoreña** (4800 Central Ave., 704/568-9161) and **Taste of Colombia** (212 N. Polk St., Pineville, 704/889-5328).

Brazas Brazilian Grill (4508 E. Independence Blvd., 704/566-1009, www.braz-ascharlotte.com, lunch 11 A.M.–2:30 P.M. Tues.–Fri. and noon 3 P.M. Sat. and Sun., dinner 5:30–10 P.M. Tues.–Fri. and 3–10 P.M. Sat. and Sun., lunch $15, dinner $25) declares that their goal is to "present you with choice cuts of the finest meats until you say 'Stop.'" This meat-o-rama is a carnivore's dream, with an endless buffet of beef, chicken, rabbit, ostrich, and quail brought to your table for carving.

European

The Plaza-Midwood neighborhood has lots of appealing eateries, and among the most popular is **Lulu's** (1911 Central Ave., 704/376-2242, www.luludinewine.com, 11 A.M.–10 P.M. Mon.–Thurs., 11 A.M.–11 P.M. Fri., brunch 10 A.M.–3 P.M. Sun., dinner 5–9 P.M. Sun., under $30). The American and pan-European fare ranges from burgers and reuben sandwiches to *choucroute* (garlic sausage) and wild boar ragout.

Another special place is **Fiamma** (2418 Park Rd., 704/333-4363, 11:30 A.M.–3:30 P.M. and 5–11 P.M. every day, under $30), an Italian restaurant in the Dilworth neighborhood. For their spectacular menu, Fiamma has fresh fish flown in every day from Italy, and they make their pasta and pizza crust dough twice every day from scratch. Such dedication to quality can be tasted at first bite.

Indian

◖ Woodlands (7128-A Albemarle Rd., 704/569-9193, 11:30 A.M.–3 P.M. and 5–9:30 P.M. Mon.–Fri., and 11:30 A.M.–10 P.M. Sat. and Sun., $7–15) serves absolutely wonderful vegetarian southern Indian cuisine, offering nearly 20 different curries, *utthapam* (rice and lentil pancakes), Chinese-influenced rice and noodle dishes, and dozens of other components with which to assemble one of the best Indian meals you'll find in North Carolina.

A newcomer to the scene here is the great Indian fast-food restaurant **Chaat 'n' Chai** (9609 N. Tryon St., Suite 1, 704/503-4748, www .chaat-n-chai.com, lunch 11:30 A.M.–2:30 P.M.

weekdays, 11:30 A.M.–3 P.M. weekends, dinner 5–9:30 P.M. Sun.–Thurs., 5 P.M.–10:30 P.M. Fri. and Sat., under $10). They serve northern and southern Indian and Indo-Chinese cuisine, all the pakoras and samosas and curries you can carry. Their motto is "We love cooking more than you love eating," which sounds like a challenge to me.

Vicinity of Charlotte

The number of NASCAR-related attractions and sites of interest to racing enthusiasts in general are too many by far to name, but you'll find a selection of the best listed among the attractions here. This region's love of stock cars feeds into a generalized devotion to things with wheels. Within an easy drive of Charlotte you'll find a museum honoring a tribe of red trucks, an old roundhouse that shelters a fleet of beautiful restored locomotives, and even a paddlewheel steamboat.

Several of the state's special food traditions intersect here. The fumes of Lexington barbecue waft over the entire Piedmont, causing an irresistible urge to mix catsup into one's barbecue sauce. Serious aficionados of fried fish don't drive all the way to the coast to get their fix, but instead scout out inland fish camps on the back roads of Gaston and neighboring counties. Folks in country kitchens radiating out from Shelby and down from the foothills know that the best thing to do with those spare pig heads and organs lying around is to mash them up with cornmeal and serve them up as livermush. You'll see livermush sandwiches on the menu of many a little café in this region.

The rocky rivers that cross what's now the I-85 corridor once powered hundreds of textile mills, brick fortresses around which sprouted little towns with a culture all their own. In the wake of NAFTA, the last generation of these mill villages are vanishing, scattering their people to the wind and leaving unwieldy but sometimes quite beautiful structures to puzzle the developers tasked with demolishing or repurposing them. In this region in transition, North Carolina's textile mill culture is a laboratory of globalization.

MOORESVILLE AND LAKE NORMAN

Downtown Mooresville is an attractive historic area filled with appealing turn-of-the-century small-town commercial architecture. There are several antique shops and galleries, and the **Mooresville Ice Cream Company** (172 N. Broad St., 704/664-5456), which has been in operation since 1924.

Racing Sights

Mooresville is home to some of the state's—and the nation's—most important racing facilities and attractions, as well as the home bases of more than 60 individual teams. There are several racing museums here, including the **North Carolina Auto Racing Hall of Fame** (Mooresville Visitor Center, 119 Knob Hill Rd., 704/663-5331, www.ncarhof.com, 10 A.M.–5 P.M. Mon.–Fri., and 10 A.M.–3 P.M. Sat. and Sun., $5 adults, $3 children and seniors). The **Memory Lane Motorsports Museum** (769 River Hwy., 704/662-3673, www.memorylaneautomuseum.com, 9 A.M.–6 P.M. daily during race weeks, $8 adults, $6 children 6–12, free for children under 6) features the largest private collection of retired NASCAR automobiles and the world's largest collection of Go-Karts.

Major teams and racing companies are based here, and some operate facilities that are open to the public. **Dale Earnhardt Inc.** (1675 Dale Earnhardt Hwy. 3, 704/334-9663, www.daleearnhardtinc.com, 9 A.M.–5 P.M. Mon.–Fri. and 10 A.M.–4 P.M. Sat.) has a showroom and a museum about the career of Dale, Sr., a figure of legend here. Teams' complexes are scattered throughout the area, including Dale Earnhardt, Jr.'s **JR Motorsports** (349 Cayuga

Dr., 704/799-4800, www.jrmotorsport.com), **Penske Racing** (200 Penske Way, 704/664-2300, www.penskeracing.com), and **Robert Yates Racing** (112 Byers Creek Rd., 704/662-9625, www.robertyatesracing.com).

Racing Schools

Not to be missed either are the **NASCAR Technical Institute** (220 Byers Creek Rd., 704/658-1950, www.uti.edu/NascarTech), a formal training school for motorsports automotive technology, and **PIT Instruction and Training, LLC** (156 Byers Creek Rd., 866/563-3566, www.5orr5on.com), a pit crew training school.

Entertainment

Queens Landing (1459 River Hwy., 704/663-2628, www.queenslanding.com) is a huge lakeside entertainment complex that offers sightseeing and dinner cruises on the paddleboat *Catawba Queen* and the yacht *Lady of the Lake*. There is also a lakeside restaurant, two bars, a water park, bumper boats, and miniature golf.

Sports and Recreation

If it's too hot to be around all that asphalt, there's plenty to do on the water. **Lake Norman State Park** (159 Inland Sea Ln., Troutman, 704/528-6350, www.ncparks.gov/Visit/parks/lano/main.php) shelters the state's largest artificial lake, with boating, swimming, and camping, and more than six miles of biking and hiking trails.

CONCORD AND KANNAPOLIS

Cabarrus County, which wraps around the northeastern corner of Charlotte, is one of the phonetic zones that give newcomers and longtime North Carolinians alike the fits. The place names tend not to be pronounced as the standard rules of Carolinian speech would dictate. The county's name is accented on the middle syllable, breaking one of the cardinal Carolinian rules, that of front-loading multisyllabic words. Banish from your mind all thoughts of three-headed dogs and celebrated jumping frogs: it's "Cuh-BA-russ," and the 'a' is pronounced as in "hat." Kannapolis rhymes with the capital of Maryland. Even more vexing are the two-syllable town names. The emphasis in Concord and Midland is weighted equally between the two syllables—"Con. Cord." and "Mid. Land."—as if the area was settled by errant Newfoundlanders.

◀ Lowe's Motor Speedway

Lowe's Motor Speedway (800/455-3267, www.lowesmotorspeedway.com, tours on non-event days 9:30 A.M., 10:30 A.M., 11:30 A.M., 1:30 P.M., 2:30 P.M., 3:30 P.M. Mon.–Sat., 1:30 P.M., 3:30 P.M. Sun., $5), on Highway 29 South, is Concord's best-known attraction. The 167,000-seat arena with a 1.5-mile track hosts the NASCAR NEXTEL Cup, as well as other NASCAR, Busch, and Craftsman Truck Series events. The Speedway is also home to the **Richard Petty Driving Experience,** where you can ride—or even drive—a 600-horsepower stock car at speeds up to 165 mph, as well as the **Xtreme Measures Teen Driving School,** where teenage drivers can spend two days learning safe driving skills in an exhilarating environment. Oddly enough, the Speedway's Smith Tower, on the second floor, hosts the **Carolinas Boxing Hall of Fame** (704/455-3200).

Racing Sights and Racing Schools

Not to be outdone by its neighbor Concord, Kannapolis honors racing and the life of its hometown star Dale Earnhardt, Sr., with the **Dale Trail.** "Dale Sr." died at the age of 50 in a famous last-lap crash at the 2001 Daytona 500, one of the tragedies in racing history that have most starkly illustrated the great danger to which drivers subject themselves. Dale Sr. is honored by a nine-foot bronze statue, fan-financed granite monument, and huge murals, all at the **Dale Earnhardt Tribute** at Main and B. Streets in the middle of Cannon Village, a historic shopping district in Kannapolis. The Dale Trail also goes by **Mike Curb's Motorsports Museum** (600 Dale Earnhardt Blvd., 704/938-6121, www.mikecurb.com),

CHARLOTTE

which displays 21 race cars driven by Curb Motorsports drivers, a star roster that includes Richard Petty, Dale Jarrett, and many others.

The **Jeff Gordon Racing School** (6025 Victory Ln., Concord, 877/7223-5277, www.4jeff24.com) is based in Concord, and the **Backing Up Classics Museum** (4545 Concord Pkwy., 704/788-9500, www.backingupclassics .com, 9 A.M.–6 P.M. Mon.–Fri., 9 A.M.–5 P.M. Sat., and 10 A.M.–5 P.M. Sun.) is just north of the Speedway.

Historic Sights

In all the racing excitement, don't miss the sights of downtown Concord. The **Union Street Historic District** preserves some of the area's most spectacular homes built with turn-of-the-century textile dollars. Also along Union Street you'll find the **Cabarrus Creamery** (21 Union St. S.), an old-time ice cream shop, and the historic **George Washington Book Store & Tavern** (16 Union St. S.).

The heart of Kannapolis is the former **Cannon Mills** textile complex, now transformed into the **Cannon Village** shopping district (200 West Ave., 704/938-3200, www.cannonvillage.com, 9 A.M.–5 P.M. Mon.–Sat.). Among the boutiques in this restored historic complex, you'll find the **Fieldcrest Cannon Textile Museum & Exhibit** (Cannon Village Visitors Center, 704/938-3200, 9 A.M.–5 P.M. Mon.–Sat., 1–6 P.M. Sun.). In a self-guided tour you can find out about this industrial giant of the Carolinas that once employed 25,000 people, and you can also see the world's largest towel.

While in Cabarrus County, pay a visit to the **Reed Gold Mine National Historic Landmark** (9621 Reed Mine Rd., 704/721-4653, www.reedmine.com, 9 A.M.–4 P.M. Tues.–Sat. Apr.–Oct., 10 A.M.–4 P.M. Tues.–Sat. Nov.–Mar., free) in Midland, to find out about a bonanza that hit this area long before the heyday of the textile mills and before stock cars were even imagined. In 1799, a local 12-year-old discovered—but didn't recognize the value of—a 17-pound gold nugget. Three years later, a sharp-eyed visitor noticed the huge lump of gold that the family was using as a doorstop,

and bought it for $3.50. This was the beginning of the first gold rush in the United States.

SALISBURY AND POINTS NORTH

Well north of Charlotte, and well worth a day trip, are the Salisbury and Mocksville areas. This is another area of peculiar place names that take the newcomer some getting used to. Salisbury is easy enough—just remember that the first syllable rhymes with "Paul." It's "SAWLS-bree." Odder, though, is the county of which Salisbury is the seat: Rowan. In the Carolinas, Rowan, whether as a place name or a person's name, is pronounced with the emphasis on the second syllable, which sounds like the girl's name. "Row-ANN." The first syllable is as in rowing a boat, not arguing. Oddest of all is Cooleemee, a tiny mill village in Davie County. This town's name is pronounced "COOL-uh-mee."

Sights

Salisbury has a very pretty downtown, girded all around by attractive historic residential and commercial neighborhoods. The **Confederate monument** at West Innes and Church, which was dedicated in a 1909 ceremony attended by Stonewall Jackson's widow, is surely one of the South's most beautiful war memorial statues. There are many historically significant buildings downtown, including the **Kluttz Drug Store** building (101 Main St.), which was the tallest commercial building in North Carolina at the time of its construction in 1858; **The Plaza,** an early seven-story "skyscraper" directly across the street; the 1819 **Utzman-Chambers House** (116 S. Jackson); the 1820 **Josephus Hall House;** and literally hundreds more. Many of these places are open to the public, and a walking tour brochure can be picked up at the local **visitors bureau** (204 East Innes).

In Spencer, just north of Salisbury, the **North Carolina Transportation Museum** (Spencer Shops, 704/636-2889, http://nctrans.org, 9 A.M.–5 P.M. Mon.–Sat., 1–5 P.M. Sun. Apr. 1–Oct. 31, 10 A.M.–4 P.M. Tues.–Sat.,

Confederate monument, Salisbury

CHARLOTTE

of this village, but of "mill hill" life throughout the South. Just down the block from Zachary House, which houses the Mill Village Museum, is the Mill Family Life Museum, an authentic mill house restored and furnished to reflect life in Cooleemee around 1934.

Shopping

Downtown Salisbury is home to many restaurants, antique shops, and boutiques. Stop in at the **Literary Book Post** (119 S. Main St., 704/630-9788), a small bookshop with a good array of titles in many genres, including a very well chosen selection of books about North Carolina. The shop is home to three very placid black cats.

Accommodations

Salisbury has a beautiful downtown bed-and-breakfast, **⚫ Rowan Oak House** (208 S. Fulton St., 800/786-0437, www.rowanoak bb.com, from $130), an ornate, turreted 1901 house with four plush guestrooms. Breakfast might include such treats as crab grits or an egg and tortilla casserole. Race fans should inquire about the three-night NASCAR packages, a special rate available during some of the top events at Lowe's Motor Speedway.

Food

The **Red Pig** (7136 Hwy. 801 S., Mocksville, 336/284-4650, under $10) is a favorite barbecue place at a little crossroads known locally as Greasy Corner, near Cooleemee. While the barbecue here is great, as are the vegetables and daily specials, try the livermush and egg sandwich with a slice of chocolate pie and a bottle of Cheerwine if you want the full Piedmont Carolina experience.

1–4 P.M. Sun. Nov. 1–Mar. 31, free) occupies the old Spencer Shops, a 100-year-old Southern Railroad complex. The museum includes a restored 1890s passenger station, a mechanic's office, boiler flue repair shop, and 37-bay roundhouse where more than 25 restored locomotives and train cars are on display. Extensive exhibits about railroad history, and a gift shop full of transportation books and ephemera, will be great fun for any train spotter.

⚫ Mill Village Museum

Northwest of Salisbury on Highway 801 is the small town of Cooleemee, home of the Mill Village Museum (Old #14 Church St., 336/284-6040, www.textileheritage.org, 10 A.M.–4 P.M. Wed.–Sat. and by appointment). This very interesting little museum tells the story of the village that was built here at the turn of the century around a large cotton mill on the banks of the Yadkin River. More than 20 years of oral history research have been conducted among Cooleemee's old-timers, resulting in an extremely rich portrait not only

WEST OF CHARLOTTE
Sights

You'll have noticed by now that North Carolinians really like things with wheels, and like to enshrine in museums those that aren't on the road. Cherryville's **C. Grier Beam Truck Museum** (111 N. Mountain St., Cherryville, 704/435-3072, www.beamtruckmuseum.com,

10 A.M.–3 P.M. Thurs., 10 A.M.–5 P.M. Fri., 10 A.M.–3 P.M. Sat., free) houses a fleet of beautiful, cherry-red Carolina Freight Carriers trucks, dating from the 1930s. There's also a great restored 1927 filling station.

The **International Lineman's Museum** (529 Caleb Rd., Shelby, 704/482-7638, www.linemanmuseum.com, 8 A.M.–5 P.M. Mon.–Fri., free) contains thousands of artifacts from the early electrical industry, fascinating historical photos of linemen at work in generations past, and the International Lineman's Hall of Fame.

Recreation

Crowders Mountain State Park (522 Park Office Ln., 704/853-5375, www.ncparks.gov /Visit/parks/crmo/main.php) embraces a small mountain range, where Crowders Mountain and King's Pinnacle tower dramatically over the upper Piedmont landscape. Ten trails, ranging from short and easy to long, steep, and extremely strenuous, scale the ridges and explore the woods below. The high, sheer cliffs are frequented by experienced rock climbers (who must obtain permits and observe a set of strict rules found on the website). Primitive campsites are located about a mile from the visitors center.

Food

One might not expect to find a generations-old seafood tradition up here in the Piedmont, but in fact this region is dotted with old-time eating places called fish camps. Today's fish camps evolved from river- and lakeside shacks, where a day's catch would be fried up and served to local mill workers and neighbors. While most of the fish served in these joints nowadays is not locally caught, the tradition of waterfront fried fish eateries persists. Presentation is often as plain as can be, a heap of fried stuff on a paper plate, but folks don't come to these places for aperitifs and tapas; they just want them some fried fish. Some favorite area fish camps include **Dotson's Fish Fry** (600 E. Henry St., Mount Holly, 704/827-3291), **Twin Tops Fish Camp** (4574 S. New Hope Rd., Gastonia, 704/825-2490), **Graham's Fish Fry** (4539 S. New Hope Rd., Gastonia, 704/825-8391), **Love's Fish Box** (1104 Shelby Rd., Kings Mountain, 704/739-4036, takeout only), and **Shelby Fish Camp** (1025 E. Dixon Blvd., Shelby, 704/482-7391). Fish camp hours are often unpredictable, so call ahead.

Tony's Ice Cream (604 E. Franklin Blvd., Gastonia, 704/853-0018, www.tonysice cream.com, under $5) has been serving homemade ice cream in its present location since 1947, but the business was born a generation earlier, when Carmine Coletta (father of Tony) began selling snacks from a push-cart in 1911. Today it's run by Tony's sons, who serve 25 flavors done up in cones, sundaes, shakes, and splits. You can also choose from a list of diner-style sandwiches.

NORTHERN BLUE RIDGE AND FOOTHILLS

One of the first impressions recorded by a visitor to North Carolina's Blue Ridge Mountains came in 1752, when Bishop Augustus Spangenberg came down from Pennsylvania in search of a prospective Southern home for the Moravian Church. He eventually found a welcoming spot near present-day Winston-Salem, but it's a wonder he didn't turn back when he first saw the Blue Ridge, a sight that filled him with dread. Upon cresting a ridge, this man who had crossed the Atlantic and tramped all over the colonial frontier wrote in his diary, "We have reached here after a hard journey over very high, terrible mountains and cliffs… When we reached the top we saw mountains to the right, to the left, before and behind us, rising like great waves in a storm."

Until the 20th century, the farthest northwestern counties of North Carolina were so remote, and so cut off from the rest of the state, that they were known as the Lost Provinces. Gradually, improved roads and the construction of the Blue Ridge Parkway brought curious flatlanders up into the clouds, and the region evolved into a popular destination for vacationers. Today, the mountains around Boone feel subtly different from the ranges closer to Asheville, and from the Smokies farther south. The northern Blue Ridge is no less beautiful, but the peaks seem perhaps a little less craggy, and the wilderness a little less wild. There are plenty of bears and April snowfalls, but overall these mountains are more the realm of summer camp-goers and front-porch breeze-takers than fugitives and woodsmen.

© KEITH M. MORGAN

HIGHLIGHTS

(Grandfather Mountain: Grandfather Mountain is smaller than Mount Mitchell, but still fully a mile high, and no less beautiful (page 212).

(Penland School of Crafts: One of the venerable old centers of art in the mountains, Penland offers residential classes in dozens of media. The innovative studio creations of many of these artists are exhibited and sold in the elegant gallery (page 213).

(Mount Mitchell: You'd have to travel west until you hit the Black Hills of South Dakota before you could find a higher mountain. The East's tallest peak was the subject of a scholarly feud in the mid-1800s, and one of the feuders, Mitchell himself, is buried at the summit (page 213).

(Brown Mountain Lights: The mysterious lights that hover over Brown Mountain have been seen by Carolinians since at least the 1770s. Whether they're vapors, reflections, or ghosts has never been settled. If you're in the right place at the right time, you may see them for yourself (page 214).

(MerleFest: For one long weekend in April, many of the best artists in American roots music are in North Wilkesboro, along with thousands of their fans (page 216).

(The Merry Go-Round Show: Mount Airy is blessed with a rich musical tradition and a great small-town radio station, WPAQ. The weekly Merry Go-Round show is broadcast in front of a live audience from the old movie theater downtown (page 219).

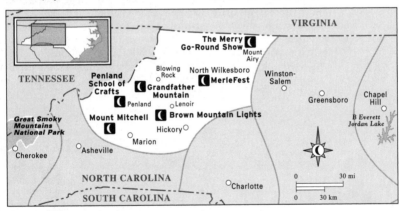

LOOK FOR **(** TO FIND RECOMMENDED SIGHTS, ACTIVITIES, DINING, AND LODGING.

That's not to say that there isn't plenty of wild country left to explore. Stands of virgin forest are still hidden in remote coves, and places like the Linville Gorge dare the most accomplished outdoors enthusiasts. It's easy to get lost in the tangles of tiny mountain roads, especially along the Tennessee border. There are some back roads that only feel the sun at high noon, and where the mossy trees are

gnarled from centuries of their gasping, grasping existence between boulders and the wind. On these mountain tracks, approaching rattling, one-lane plank bridges over thundering streams, you'll almost expect a troll to jump out and demand that you answer his riddles.

Much of the meaty Appalachian folklore collected and popularized in the last hundred years has come out of this section of North

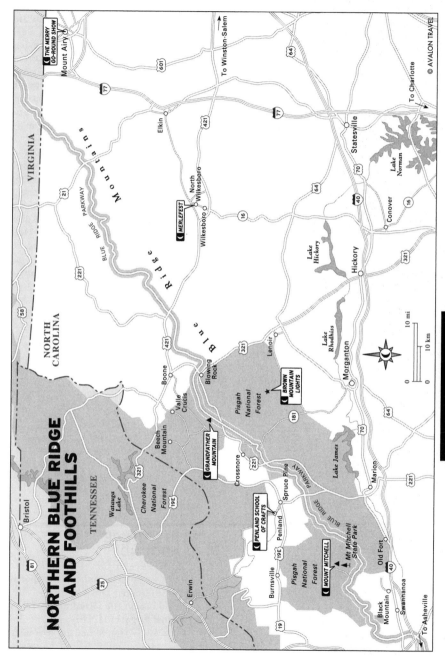

NORTHERN BLUE RIDGE AND FOOTHILLS

© AVALON TRAVEL

NORTHERN BLUE RIDGE

Carolina. It was here that young Confederate veteran "Tom Dooley"—a real person, whose crime is still hotly debated in these parts—killed his unfortunate girlfriend, Laurie Foster. In Wilkesboro, you can visit the very jail cell where he stewed before being taken down to the Statesville gallows. Another ghastly local crime immortalized in folktale and song is the 1831 murder of 19-year-old Charlie Silver, apparently in self-defense, by his young wife Frankie. She too was carried down the mountain to hang, and died in Morganton. The region's folklore isn't all horrid, though. Many of the Jack Tales that so epitomize Appalachian storytelling were recorded around Beech Mountain, told by the Harmon and Hicks families for generations. On any given weekend in Mount Airy, and in many other mountain and foothills towns, you can hear the old-time string band music that is as popular here today as it was in the days before the radio.

During your visit to the northern Blue Ridge, check out the studios of area potters and weavers. Have dinner at a barbecue joint with live bluegrass music. Buy some hoop cheese and blackberry jam to take home with you. Even if you've come to the mountains to ski or to eat at the gourmet restaurants in Boone and Blowing Rock, be sure to set aside a little time for the back roads.

PLANNING YOUR TIME

Weather is a major concern when driving in the mountains here, not only snow and ice in the winter (and fall and spring), but frequent dense fog throughout the year. Conditions can be completely different from one moment to the next, and from one mountain to the next. Use extreme caution when driving in adverse weather. Take it slow, and leave plenty of room between your car and the next. Don't hesitate to pull over and wait out a fog. They often lift and dissipate quickly.

If you're planning on spending most of your time roaming in the deep mountains, around Mount Mitchell and Grandfather Mountain, the Linville area, and the Banner Elk and Beech Mountain areas, Boone is a fairly convenient place to stay. Most of these destinations are within half an hour to an hour's drive of Boone if you take the numbered highways; travel on the Blue Ridge Parkway, though scenic and often more direct, is generally much slower. If you're not pressed for time, it's the easiest way to get around. Wilkesboro and Mount Airy are both at the edge of the mountains, and easily accessible to the junction of I-77 and U.S. 421 that's a jumping-off point to most any foothills location.

If you're planning on hitting several of the major attractions while you're in the mountains, the **Go Blue Ridge Card** (800/887-9103, www.goblueridgecard.com) might be a money-saver for you. Among the attractions in this chapter that the Go Blue Ridge Card will give you access to are Grandfather Mountain, the Orchard at Altapass, and Linville Caverns. It costs between $50 and $160, depending on where you go and how many days you want to use it. At participating attractions that charge admission, the card gets you in without having to buy tickets. At many shops and restaurants throughout the region, it'll get you a good discount.

INFORMATION AND SERVICES

The state Department of Transportation operates a real-time road conditions map at http://apps.dot.state.nc.us/tims. For current conditions along the Blue Ridge Parkway, you can check the recorded message at 828/298-0398.

Hospitals are located in most of the major towns in this region, but in case of an emergency, help might be delayed by weather, road conditions, or distance. In many areas—not just deep in the woods, but in populated areas as well—there may be no cell phone signal.

GETTING THERE AND AROUND

There are no major airports in this region, but two are reasonably close: **Asheville Regional Airport** (61 Terminal Drive, 828/684-2226, www.flyavl.com) and **Piedmont Triad International Airport** (6415 Bryan Blvd., 336/665-5600, www.flyfrompti.com) in Greensboro. There is one major highway, I-77, in this region, and it runs north–south along the edge of the mountains west of Mount Airy. Two other major interstate highways run along or just beyond the boundaries of the northern mountains: I-40 to the east and south, running between Winston-Salem and Asheville, and I-26 to the south and west, between Asheville and Johnson City, Tennessee. U.S. 321 and 421 are the main roads here, and U.S. 19 winds through the southwest edge of the area covered in this chapter.

The Blue Ridge Parkway follows some of its most beautiful miles in the northern mountains and connects several important towns. While it's probably the most fun and scenic route, it is not the most efficient if you're trying to cover a lot of ground fast. The maximum speed limit is 45, and because of weather, traffic, and twists and turns, you can figure on driving slower than that most of the time.

Watauga County, which includes the towns of Blowing Rock, Boone, Deep Gap, and Zionville, is covered by **AppalCart bus routes** (828/264-2278, www.appalcart.com). Riders must make reservations to ride, and the service is only available on weekdays, but the fares, which vary by route, are much cheaper than the gas it takes to get from place to place. AppalCart also runs routes to Charlotte, Winston-Salem, Hickory, Lenoir, and Wilkesboro, with fares ranging $10–50 round-trip. Another way to get to and from the area is via the **Mountaineer Express bus** (336/662-0002 or 800/588-7787, www.partnc.org), which runs between Greensboro, Winston-Salem, Yadkinville, Wilkesboro, and Boone. The highest-price one-way trip (Greensboro–Boone) is only $10, and the fare is half-price for students, wheelchair users, and passengers over age 60.

Deep Mountains

There's something exciting about the ascent into the High Country--glimpses of a shadowy mountain range on the horizon; cows grazing in steep, rocky fields; hairpin turns in the road around dynamited stone faces, and the popping sound in your ears as you reach the first mountain. Most travelers experience this part of North Carolina by winding along the Blue Ridge Parkway (BRP), making side-trips deeper into the mountains, and peering down from the crest to the Piedmont below. These miles are widely regarded as the most beautiful section of the Parkway, a ribbon of road that's a destination in itself, not just a way to get from Asheville to the Virginia line. The Blue Ridge Parkway connects the bluffs and coves along the Virginia border to the canoe launches and Christmas tree farms around Jefferson and Glendale Springs, and the college town of Boone and old resort of Blowing Rock with the natural wonders found in the Linville Gorge wilderness.

Boone is a fun and hip little city, the home of Appalachian State University, good antique shops and organic markets, and a rambunctious green counterculture. Blowing Rock and Linville were tony summertime roosts for wealthy folks early in the 20th century, and much of that elegance remains, both in the stylish bungalows left behind and in the modern spas and resorts found here today.

Venturing off the Parkway and into the deep mountains, visit the little settlements of Penland and Crossnore, as well as Bakersville and other towns in the Toe River Valley. Here you'll find a thriving colony of artists. Many of them came to this area to be part of the folk school at Penland, which in its quiet way has exerted a great deal of influence on modern American craft movements. If you like folk and studio pottery and glasswork, hand-wrought ironwork, delicately crafted jewelry, and innovative textile art, you'll find few communities in the United States where you can see and buy as much fine craft as here in the North Carolina mountains.

BLOWING ROCK

The town of Blowing Rock, named for the nearby geological oddity, is an old rocking chair

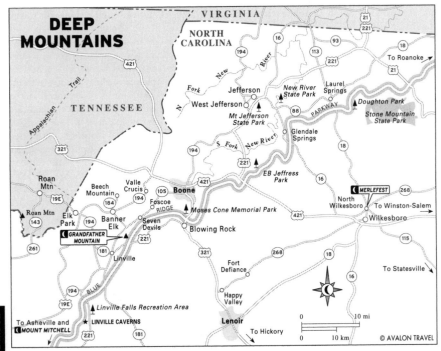

resort, graced by stately old houses that were built long ago by early 20th-century captains of industry. Cafés and galleries make this a very pleasant place to stroll, and the Blue Ridge Parkway gives easy access to the Moses Cone Manor and other notable local landmarks.

Sights

Many of western North Carolina's best-known tourist attractions are geological ones: Chimney Rock, Linville Caverns, Mount Mitchell, and lumpy-headed old Grandfather Mountain. The **Blowing Rock** (U.S. 321 S., 828/295-7111, www.theblowingrock.com, hours vary by season) is a strange rock outcropping purported (by *Ripley's Believe It or Not)* to be the only place in the world where snow falls upward. Indeed, light objects (think handkerchiefs, leaves, hats) thrown off of Blowing Rock—not allowed, by the way, else the valley should fill up with too-heavy litter—do tend to come floating back

up. The rock was the scene of an early vacation trauma in my childhood, when a family member (mentioning no names, not even my mother's) in an impish mood suggested that my constant companion, a stuffed cat named Sabrina, might enjoy being tossed over the edge and carried back to me on a gust of wind. She was kidding, of course, and Sabrina stayed safe in my white-knuckled grip, but just the thought of Blowing Rock gave me nightmares for years to come. Childhood terrors aside, the view from the rock is quite lovely.

The **Moses Cone Manor** (BRP milepost 294, 828/295-7938, 9 A.M.–5 P.M. daily Mar. 15–Nov. 30) is a huge white mountain palace, the 1901 country home of North Carolina textile baron Moses Cone. After making his fortune, Cone became a leading philanthropist, and as you drive around the state, particularly in the northern Piedmont, you'll notice that his name still graces quite a few institutions. Flat Top

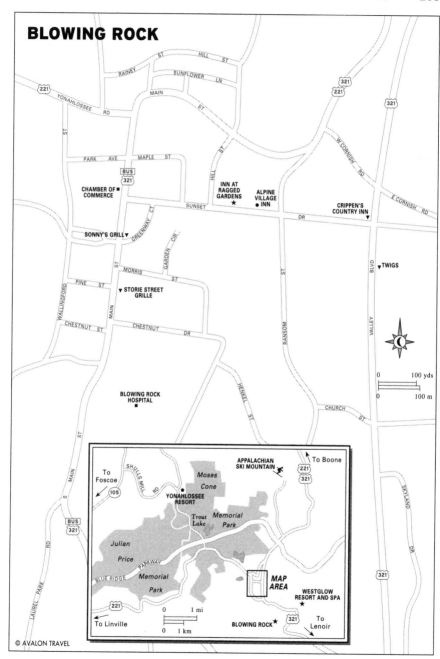

BLOWING ROCK

NORTHERN BLUE RIDGE

COURTESY OF ONCLE BERNARD ON FLICKR.COM

Moses Cone Manor

Manor, as the mansion on the Parkway was called, is a wonderfully crafted house, white and ornate like a wedding cake. Appropriately, it is home to one of the **Southern Highland Craft Guild** (www.southernhighlandguild.org) stores, a place to buy beautiful textiles, pottery, jewelry, furniture, dolls, and much more, handmade by some of the best craftspeople of the Appalachian mountains. There are also extensive hiking and riding trails on the estate.

Accommodations

The lavish 1916 Greek Revival mansion of painter Elliott Daingerfield is now home to the **C Westglow Resort and Spa** (224 Westglow Cr., 828/295-4463 or 800/562-0807, www.westglow.com, from $250, spa packages from $450). In addition to the cushy rooms, many of which have whirlpool tubs, private decks, and views of Grandfather Mountain, the menu of spa treatments and health services befits the elegance of the surroundings. All kinds of massage and body therapy are available, as well as fitness classes, cooking and makeup lessons, and a variety of seminars in emotional well-being. Taking advantage of the spa's wonderful location, visitors can also sign up for hiking, biking, snowshoeing, and camping trips.

The **Inn at Ragged Gardens** (203 Sunset Dr., 877/972-4433, www.ragged-gardens.com, from $140) is a handsome, stylish turn-of-the-century vacation home, a stone-walled and chestnut-paneled manor. The plush guestrooms feature goose down bedding, fireplaces, and, in most cases, balconies and whirlpool tubs.

Alpine Village Inn (297 Sunset Dr., 828/295-7206, www.alpine-village-inn.com, from $50) in downtown Blowing Rock has comfortable accommodations at a good price. The rooms are located in a main inn and in a motel-style wing. It's a convenient location for checking out the shops and restaurants in town. Another good value is the **Cliff Dwellers Inn** (116 Lakeview Tr., 800/322-7380, www.cliffdwellers.com, form $70) with clean, simple rooms and a beautiful lakefront view.

CAMPING

The campground at **Julian Price Park** (BRP milepost 297, near Blowing Rock,

877/444-6777, www.recreation.gov, $16) is the largest on the Parkway, with a good selection of standard and tent-only non-electric campsites. Pets are allowed, flush toilets and a telephone are accessible, and there's good hiking and boating nearby (boat rentals available).

Food

C Crippen's Country Inn (239 Sunset Dr., 877/295-3487, www.crippens.com, supper only, days and hours vary by season, $23–40) is one of the famous High Country restaurants, with a kitchen captained by Chef James Welch, who won the 2006 Best Dish in North Carolina contest at the state fair for his watermelon and mozzarella salad on flatbread. If that's not enough to get you up here, consider the fact that George Lindsey, who played Goober on *The Andy Griffith Show,* highly recommends Crippen's. The entrées are splendid—the menu's crown jewel is "bittersweet chocolate infused espresso-crusted grilled beef tenderloin with Irish cream sauce, pistachio-goat cheese au gratin and French beans"—but Welch is most renowned for his talent for creating special soups and sauces. Before proceeding to the espresso-crusted tenderloin or the barbecue-grilled rare tuna, pause for a soup—either the one with potato, goat cheese, and pistachio or the braised beef, pork, white bean, and potato.

Storie Street Grille (1167 Main St., 828/295-7075, www.storiestreetgrille.com, 11 A.M.–3 P.M. and 5–9 P.M. Mon.–Sat., open later in the summer, lunch $6–13, dinner $10–30) has a long lunch menu of sandwiches, quesadillas, and main-course salads. Try the pot-roast melt, or the bacon, brie, and apple panini. For dinner they serve many Italian choices, grilled steak and seafood, and intriguing twists on Southern snacks, like crab hush puppies and pork barbecue spring rolls. **Bistro Roca and Antlers Bar** (143 Wonderland Trail, 828/295-4008, http://bistroroca.com, 11:30 A.M.–10 P.M. Mon., Wed.–Sat., brunch 11 A.M.–2:30 P.M. Sun., bar open until midnight, closed Tues., $20–30) serves hearty and creative dishes like chicken and duck pot pie,

roasted duck pizza, prosciutto and manchego pizza, and crab and crawfish cakes with gouda and grits. Also popular is **Twigs** (U.S. 321 Bypass, Blowing Rock, 828/295-5050, http://twigsbr.com, 5:30–9:30 P.M. Tues.–Thurs. and Sun., 5:30–10 P.M. Fri.–Sat., bar open until 2 A.M., $17–34), which has both a casual bar and a fancier dining room. Popular regional dishes like shrimp and grits and mountain trout appear on the menu alongside more unusual fare like sautéed boar sausage. There are 17 wines available by the glass, and another 133 by the bottle, featuring a wide selection of California wines as well as Australian, European, and Argentine choices.

For a comfy, small-town ambience, visit **Sonny's Grill** (1119 Main St., 828/295-7577), which for more than 50 years has served diners at its tiny lunch counter. It serves breakfast and lunch, of the grits-and-eggs and BLT-and-fries variety, but the most popular dishes are ham biscuits and sweet potato pancakes. If you're up from the Piedmont and feeling homesick, you can get your livermush fix here too.

BOONE

Boone is the quintessential western North Carolina city, a blend of old and new, where proponents of homesteading and holistic living find a congenial habitat in the culture of rural Appalachia. It's also a college town, the home of Appalachian State University, and as such has an invigorating youthful verve.

Shopping

Several antique shops in Boone make the downtown a great place for browsing. **Appalachian Antiques** (631 W. King St., 828/268-9988, www.appalachianantiques.net, 10 A.M.–6 P.M. Mon.–Sat. and 11 A.M.–6 P.M. Sun. during the summer, 10 A.M.–5 P.M. Mon.–Sat. and noon–5 P.M. Sun. during the winter) is one of the best and biggest.

Footsloggers (corner of Depot and Howard St., 828/262-5111, www.footsloggers.com) has been selling gear for climbing, hiking, and camping for almost 40 years. At their Boone location (there's also a store in Blowing Rock)

COURTESY OF ONCLE BERNARD ON FLICKR.COM

Appalachian State University, Boone

they have a 40-foot climbing tower that simulates many conditions you might find climbing real rock faces.

There are several branches of the **Mast General Store** in the Carolina High Country, but the original is in Valle Crucis (Hwy. 194, 828/963-6511, www.mastgeneralstore.com, 7 A.M.–6:30 P.M. Mon.–Sat., noon–6 P.M. Sun., hours vary in the winter), about 20 minutes west of Boone. Though it's been a tourist attraction for more than 20 years now, its history as a community institution goes back generations, to the 1880s and before. When the Mast family owned it, the store had the reputation of carrying everything "from cradles to caskets," and today it still has an awfully varied inventory, with specialties in outdoor wear (Carhartt, Columbia, Teva, etc.), camping gear, and ever so much candy.

Sports and Recreation
ROCK CLIMBING
Rock Dimensions (131 Depot St., 828/265-3544, www.rockdimensions.com) is a guide service that leads rock climbs at gorgeous locations throughout western North Carolina

and to parts of Tennessee and Virginia. Guides teach proper multi-pitch, top rope anchoring, and rappelling techniques, and lead caving expeditions over the state lines.

SKIING
The Banner Elk area has some of the state's best ski slopes. **Sugar Mountain** (800/784-2768, www.skisugar.com) is North Carolina's largest winter resort, with 115 acres of ski slopes and 20 trails. In addition to skiing, activities on the 5,300-foot-high mountain include snow-tubing, skating, snowshoeing, and, in the summertime, the Showdown at Sugar National Mountain Bike Series. They offer lessons in skiing and snowboarding for adults and children. Nearby **Ski Beech Mountain Resort** (1007 Beech Mountain Parkway, Beech Mountain, 800/438-2093, www.skibeech.com) peaks at a good 300 feet higher than Sugar Mountain, and has 15 slopes and 10 lifts, as well as skating and snowboarding areas. **Hawksnest** (2058 Skyland Dr., Seven Devils, 800/822-4295, www.hawksnest-resort.com) is on a 4,800-foot mountain in Seven Devils. It has 12 slopes,

COURTESY OF ONCLE BERNARD ON FLICKR.COM

Ski Beech

many geared for beginners and intermediate skiers.

HIKING, RAFTING, AND CAVE TRIPS

Down the road from the Mast General Store in Valle Crucis, **River and Earth Adventures** (3618 Broadstone Rd., 866/411-7238, www.raftcavehike.com) leads all sorts of exciting trips on the water, in the woods, and in the area's deep caves. Rafting expeditions ($65–85 adults, $55–65 children) ride the Lower Nolichucky (Class II–III), French Broad (Class III–IV), and Watauga (Class II–III) Rivers. Cave trips ($75/person, daily year-round) meet at the Valle Crucis shop, from which you'll proceed to Elizabethton, Tennessee, about an hour away, for a day's spelunking in Worley's Cave. Guided hiking trips are available too, including all-day kids-only hikes (with adult guides, of course) to free up parents who'd like a day on their own.

High Mountain Expeditions (1380 Hwy. 105 S., Banner Elk, 800/262-9036, www.highmountainexpeditions.com), which also has a Boone location, leads rafting trips on the Watauga River (Class I–III) and the much more challenging Nolichucky River (Class III–IV). They also lead caving expeditions for adults and children, for which no experience is necessary.

Accommodations

The **Lovill House Inn** (404 Old Bristol Rd., 800/849-9466, www.lovillhouseinn.com, $139–209) is close to the Appalachian State campus, and it was in the parlor of this 1875 farmhouse that the papers were drawn up that led to the founding of the university. The inn sits on 11 evergreen-shaded acres, and is a lovely place to relax and read. The **Smoketree Lodge** (11914 Hwy. 105 S., 800/422-1880, www.smoketree-lodge.com, from $75 in-season, from $55 out of season) is another good choice; it's a large hotel with basic but comfortable rooms and efficiencies, a large rustic lobby, and a nice indoor pool and saunas.

The **Yonahlossee Resort** (Shulls Mill Rd., 800/962-1986, www.yonahlossee.com, from $109) between Boone and Blowing Rock, is a former girls' camp built in the 1920s. The resort has a big stone inn and studio cottages, a fitness center and sauna, tennis courts with a pro shop, and a 75-foot indoor heated pool.

Food

The menu at **Our Daily Bread** (627 W. King St., 828/264-0173, 11 A.M.–6 P.M. Mon.–Sat., noon–5 P.M. Sun.) includes no fewer than 30 specialty sandwiches, from their bestselling Jamaican Turkey Sub ($6.50) to the Elvis Prezz ($4.95, bananas and peanut butter, the King's favorite). Try their Tempeh Reuben ($6.25), a daring mixture of flavors that features marinated tempeh, sauerkraut, Swiss cheese, and mustard on rye. Sounds outrageous, but it works. Our Daily Bread also makes a variety of fresh soups and chili (meat and veggie) every day.

Melanie's Food Fantasy (664 W. King St., 828/263-0300, www.melaniesfoodfantasy.com, 8 A.M.–3 P.M. Tues.–Sat., 9 A.M.–3 P.M. Sun.) is worth a special trip to Boone. The breakfast menu is nothing short of spectacular, with its variety of wholegrain waffles, pancakes, and French toast ($4.25–7.95), all sorts of fancy omelets (try the spinach-garlic-provolone-Swiss, $5.95), and enough options to keep both carnivores and vegetarians full. Lunch at Melanie's is every bit as good.

The **Dan'l Boone Inn** (130 Hardin St., 828/264-8657, http://danlbooneinn.com, hours vary by season and on holidays) serves old-time country food family-style. Despite the complicated pricing system (dinner: $14.95 adults, $8.95 children 9–11, $6.95 children 6–8, $4.95 children 4–5, free for children under 3; breakfast: $8.95 adults, $5.95 children 9–11, $4.95 6–8, $3.95 children 4–5, free for children under 3), the food is straightforward good. At breakfast, you can feast on country ham and red-eye gravy, stewed apples, grits, and much more; at dinner, there's fried chicken, country-style steak, ham biscuits, and lots of vegetable sides.

The **Gamekeeper Restaurant and Bar** (3005 Shull's Mill Rd., 828/963-7400, www.gamekeeper-nc.com, bar opens at 5 P.M. daily, with dinner service beginning at 6 P.M.

Sun.–Fri., 5:30 P.M. Sat. May–Oct., $17–50) is tucked away between Boone and Blowing Rock at the Yonahlossee Resort. This restaurant is making a stir as an innovator in high Southern fusion cuisine, with a menu that features appetizers like fried green tomatoes and fried okra, and entrées that include mountain trout, ostrich, wapiti, and buffalo. Don't miss the bourbon pudding and white Russian cheesecake—or the seemingly endless wine list ($20–215/bottle).

NORTH OF BOONE
Sports and Recreation

Mount Jefferson State Natural Area (SR 1152, Jefferson, 336/246-9653, www.ncparks.gov/visit/parks/moje/main.php) preserves a peak that was known long ago as Panther Mountain, as well as a couple of less savory names. Mount Jefferson has a forbidding countenance, with outcroppings of black volcanic rock, and on the north slope a stunted forest of wind-daunted aspen and maple. Hiking trails, ranging from gentle to strenuous, wend along the crests and up to the peak, and through laurel thickets and virgin red oak forests.

New River State Park (park office on Wagoner Access Rd./SR 1590, east of Jefferson, 336/982-2587, www.ncparks.gov/Visit/parks/neri/main.php) threads along what is, despite the name, believed to be one of the oldest rivers in North America. The beautiful New is a very popular canoeing river, a gentle ride through some stunning countryside. Water is highest in May and June, lowest in August and September. Access points are located all along the river. There are also many campsites, both canoe-in and drive-to; some have access to hot showers, while others have no facilities. Fees range from $9 per night for the primitive sites to $20 per night for drive-to/walk-in sites with showers and restrooms.

New River Outfitters (10725 U.S. 221 N., Jefferson, 800/982-9190, www.canoethenew.com) offers canoe runs, ranging from one hour to six days, and tubing trips along the New. They operate from the old New River General Store, where you can buy mountain

© JOHN RICHBURG

On the other side of the Blue Ridge Parkway from New River State Park sits Stone Mountain, a 600-foot granite dome.

honey and hoop cheese and local crafts. **Zaloo's Canoes** (3874 Hwy. 16 S., Jefferson, 800/535-4027, www.zaloos.com) is another long-established area outfitter, and also offers canoe and raft trips.

Accommodations

West Jefferson's **Dog House Resort** (Daniel Pierce Rd., West Jefferson, 336/977-3582, www.dog-house-resort.com, from $149) is as pet-friendly as a bed-and-breakfast can be. Not only will your dog find his or her own plumped-up dog bed in your guestroom, but when you amble off to the resort's spa room for a massage, your dog can come along and get a dog massage. Dogs must be gentle and housetrained, of course, and must be on-leash when outside the guestrooms, but the innkeepers provide a fenced dog-park area on the property for rowdy play.

◖ **Bluffs Lodge** (Blue Ridge Parkway Milepost 241, 336/372-4499, Apr. 28–Nov. 5, from $85) is as peaceful a place to stay as any you'll find in North Carolina. The accommodations are extremely simple, an old stone motel-style lodge, in which the rooms have only the most basic amenities (bed, bathroom with shower and tub, air conditioner, a chair or two). It's the old Park Service aesthetic, just a step more luxurious than summer camp, and an acquired taste. If, like me, you have a fondness for that style of lodging, you will find your stay here blissfully relaxing. The view and the silence are what make Bluffs Lodge so special. Half of the rooms and a large guest patio (with outdoor fireplace) overlook a long expanse of misty hills and farmland, and in the foreground, pastures where a herd of beautiful black and white cows will eye you sulkily as they graze around the boulders. The only noise you're likely to hear is the cows' lowing. It's the perfect place for reading and sleeping.

If you're a writer, you may find this to be an ideal location for uninterrupted contemplation. On the other hand, if you're a technophile, or have a job that requires you to be available by phone or email at all times, you may prefer to stay somewhere down off the mountain. The guest rooms at Bluffs Lodge have no telephones (the one public phone is in the office), nor even TVs. You're unlikely to pick up a cell phone signal, and forget about finding a wireless connection for your laptop. There's no choice but to relax and tune out the world. Next Monday, back in front of the computer in your office, you'll be daydreaming about Bluff Mountain.

SOUTH OF BOONE
◖ Grandfather Mountain

Grandfather Mountain (U.S. 221, two miles north of Linville, 800/468-7325, www.grandfather.com, $14 adults, $12 seniors over 60, $6 children under 12, 8 A.M.–7 P.M. summer, 8 A.M.–6 P.M. spring and fall, 8 A.M.–5 P.M. winter, open year-round weather permitting), at a lofty 5,964 feet, is not the very highest mountain in North Carolina, but it is one of the most beautiful. The highest peak in the Blue Ridge Mountains (Mount Mitchell is in the Black Mountains), Grandfather is a United Nations–designated International Biosphere Reserve. Privately owned for decades, though open to the public, Grandfather Mountain has remained a great expanse of deep forests and wildlife, with many hiking trails. The main attraction is the summit, and the **Mile High Swinging Bridge.** (It's quite safe, but it is indeed a mile high and it swings in the breeze.) The view from Grandfather Mountain is stunning, and the peak is easily accessible by the beautiful road that traces the skyward mile.

Linville Gorge

The deepest gorge in the United States, Linville Gorge is located near Blue Ridge Parkway Milepost 316 in a 12,000-acre federally designated Wilderness Area. It's genuine wilderness, and some of the hollers in this preserve are so remote that they still shelter virgin forests—a rarity even in these wild mountains. **Linville Falls** (BRP Milepost 316) is one of the most photographed places in North Carolina, a spectacular series of cataracts that fall crashing into the gorge. It can be seen from several short trails that depart from the **Linville Falls Visitors Center** (Milepost 316, 9 A.M.–5 P.M.

Linville Gorge

daily Apr. 25–Nov. 2 and weekends in Apr.). The National Park Service operates the **Linville Falls Campground** (828/765-7818, www.recreation.gov, $14/night) near the falls at BRP Milepost 316.3. Tent and RV sites are mixed together, and water and flush-toilets are available between May and October.

Linville Gorge is girded with some great climbing spots. They range in difficulty from Table Rock, parts of which are popular with beginning climbers (and other parts of which should only be attempted by experts) to the extremely strenuous Hawksbill cliff face and Sitting Bear rock pillar. Speak to the folks at the visitors center or at **Fox Mountain Guides** (3228 Asheville Hwy., Pisgah Forest, 888/284-8433, www.foxmountainguides), a Hendersonville-area service that leads climbs in the gorge, to determine which of Linville Gorge's many climbing faces would be best suited to your skill level.

Orchard at Altapass

At Milepost 328 on the Blue Ridge Parkway, the

Orchard at Altapass (888/765-9531, www.altapassorchard.com, 10 A.M.–6 P.M. Mon., Wed.–Sat., noon–6 P.M. Sun., closed Tues.) is much more than an orchard, although it does produce apples in abundance. The land on which the orchard grows has been settled since the 1790s, when Charlie "Cove" McKinney and his large family lived here. McKinney had four wives—at the same time—who bore him 30 sons and a dozen daughters. An early chronicler of local history wrote that the four wives "never had no words bout his havin so many womin. If it ware these times thar would be har pulled." Many of the McKinneys are buried on the mountain. Around the turn of the 20th century, the land became an orchard, and in its best years produced 125,000 bushels of apples. (To get a sense of how many apples that would have been, consider that today's standard for a bushel of apples is 48 pounds.)

Today the Orchard at Altapass continues to turn out wonderful apples. It is also a favorite music venue in this region. On weekends, country, bluegrass, old-time, and gospel musicians, and artists of a variety of other styles, perform at the Orchard. There is a staggering amount of musical talent in these mountains, and the Orchard at Altapass is a showcase of local treasures.

◖ Penland School of Crafts

In the 1920s, Lucy Morgan, a teacher at a local Episcopal school, and her brother embarked on a mission to help the women of the North Carolina mountains gain some hand in their own economic wellbeing. Equipping several households in the Penland area with looms, they touched off a local cottage industry in weaving, which quickly centralized and grew into the Penland School, a center for craft instruction and production. Several "folk schools" sprouted in the Southern Appalachians in this era, most of them the projects of idealistic Northerners wanting to aid the benighted mountaineers. The Penland School, however, has the distinction of being one of the few such institutions that was truly home-grown, as Miss Lucy was herself a child of the rural Carolina

highlands. Today, the Penland School of Crafts (off Penland Rd., Penland, 828/765-2359, www.penland.org) is an arts instruction center of international fame. More than 1,000 people, from beginners to professionals, enroll in Penland's one-, two-, and eight-week courses every year, to learn about craft in many different media. While the studios are not open to the general public, tours are given on Tuesdays and Thursdays, except between January and March. (Advance reservations are required.) The school operates a beautiful shop, the **Penland Gallery** (Conley Ridge Rd., 828/765-6211, www.penland.org/gallery/gallery.html, 10 A.M.–5 P.M. Tues.–Sat., noon–5 P.M. Sun.), where the work of many of the school's instructors and students can be purchased.

◖ Mount Mitchell

At 6,684 feet, Mount Mitchell (accessible from BRP Milepost 355, near Burnsville, 828/675-4611, www.ils.unc.edu/parkproject/visit/momi/home.html) is the highest mountain east of South Dakota. It is the pinnacle of the Black Mountain range, a 15-mile-long, J-shaped ridge that was formerly considered to be one mountain. Now that the various peaks are designated as separate mountains, six of them are among the 10 highest in the eastern United States. Poor Elisha Mitchell, for whom the mountain is named, is buried at the summit. He was one of North Carolina's first great scholars, a geologist and botanist who taught at the University of North Carolina in Chapel Hill. His skill as a scientist is demonstrated by his 1830s calculation of the height of the peak that now bears his name; using the technology of the day, the height that he estimated was within 12 feet of today's consensus measurement. But in the 1850s he became embroiled in a controversy when Senator Thomas Clingman, one of his former students, disputed the calculation. On a return trip to re-measure Mount Mitchell, Elisha Mitchell fell from the top of a waterfall (now Mitchell Falls) and drowned in the water below. The rivalry calls to mind the climactic moment in the Sherlock Holmes mysteries when Holmes and his nemesis Dr.

© JOHN RICHBURG

the high peaks of the Black Mountain range

Moriarty fall to their deaths from the top of a waterfall—although in this case, only one of the rivals suffered that scary fate, while the other, Senator Clingman, went on to live another 40 years. He too has a mountain named for him. Clingman's Dome, a mere 41 feet shorter, glares up at Mount Mitchell from the Tennessee border.

Mount Mitchell State Park (www.ncparks .gov/Visit/parks/momi/main.php) is not only a place to catch an amazing, panoramic view—up to 85 miles in clear weather—but it also has an education center, restaurant, gift shop, and nine campsites. Camping is $15 per night ($10 for senior citizens) in season (late Apr.–late Oct.), and $9 per night off-season.

◖ Brown Mountain Lights

One of North Carolina's most enduring mysteries is that of the Brown Mountain Lights, the appearance of glowing orbs that float in the air some evenings around Brown Mountain, at the Burke/Caldwell County line. According to the U.S. Geological Survey, one of the many official agencies that have studied the phenomenon, the orbs may be a reflection of cars' and trains' headlights in the valley below. This theory would seem to ignore the fact that the lights have been seen since at least 1833, long before the first headlights shone in this valley. The Brown Mountain Lights are widely believed to be of supernatural origin, and no scientific explanation has yet been proffered that satisfactorily clears up the mystery. Ghost fanciers will be delighted to know that the Brown Mountain Lights can be observed by visitors from the Lost Cove overlook on the southeast side of the road near Milepost 310 on the Blue Ridge Parkway. Try a clear evening in the summer, right around dusk, and you might see them.

Other Sights

Since the early 1920s, the master weavers of the **Crossnore Weaving Room** (100 D.A.R. Dr., Crossnore School, Crossnore, 828/733-4305, www.crossnoreweavers.org) have produced beautiful textiles—afghans, rugs and runners, baby blankets, scarves, and more—which they've sold for the benefit of the Crossnore

School. Founded in the 1910s for orphaned and disadvantaged children, the Crossnore School is today an actively operating children's home for western North Carolina kids who have no guardians—and for some local children who live with their families, but whose educational needs are best served by the structure offered here. The fame of the weaving room is much more than a fund-raising program. The skills of the Crossnore Weavers are highly regarded among craftspeople throughout this region, and the sales gallery is an essential stop for the visitor interested in seeing some of North Carolina's finest crafts.

The **Mountain Gateway Museum** (102 Water St., Old Fort, 828/668-9259, http://ncmuseumofhistory.org/osm/mgw.html, noon–5 P.M. Mon., 9 A.M.–5 P.M. Tues.–Sat., 2–5 P.M. Sat.) presents the cultural history of the North Carolina mountains, from its earliest days, to the time before the Revolution when Old Fort was the wild frontier, to the present day. The museum hosts wonderful events throughout the year, showcasing all manner of traditional arts from this region. During the Summerfest series, some of western North Carolina's best old-time, bluegrass, and gospel bands give performances at the museum's lovely outdoor amphitheater. If you're in the area on a Summerfest concert night, it's a treat not to be missed.

You just can't visit the Blue Ridge Mountains without visiting a caverns. **Linville Caverns** (Hwy. 221 between Linville and Marion, south of BRP Milepost 317, 800/419-0540, www.linvillecaverns.com, 9 A.M.–4:30 P.M. daily Mar. and Nov., 9 A.M.–5 P.M. daily Apr., May, Sept., Oct., 9 A.M.–6 P.M. daily June–Aug., 9 A.M.–4:30 P.M. weekends Dec.–Feb., $6 adults, $4.50 seniors age 62 and over, $4 ages 5–12) is one of the venerable underground tourist attractions of the Southern mountains. The natural limestone caverns feature all sorts of strange rock formations, underground trout streams and, of course, a gift shop.

Sports and Recreation

Lake James State Park (NC 126, 5 mi. northeast of Marion, 828/652-5047, www.ncparks .gov/Visit/parks/laja/main.php) is comprised of a 6,500-acre lake and its 150 miles of shoreline. Lake James is artificial, created around 1920, but the graceful mountain setting among hemlocks and rhododendrons makes this a favorite natural area. The park rents canoes for $5 per hour. Campsites are open between March 15 and November 30 for $15 per night. Restrooms, showers, and drinking water are available nearby.

Accommodations

Linville's **Eseeola Lodge** (175 Linville Ave., 800/742-6717, www.eseeola.com, from $400) has been in the business of luxury mountain vacations for more than 100 years. The first lodge was built in the 1890s, along with a nine-hole golf course. The original lodge burned and was succeeded by the present lodge, and, in 1924, Donald Ross was engaged to build the championship golf course now known as the Linville Golf Club. Eseeola Lodge offers a complex but splendid array of lodging packages, with breakfast and dinner at the Lodge's restaurant included and, depending on your predilections, tee times at the Linville Golf Club, spa services, and even croquet lessons. Greens fees for non-guests are $115 for the first round, $57.50 for same-day second rounds.

Scattered about a 92-acre private nature preserve in Marion, the six **Cottages at Spring House Farm** (219 Haynes Rd., Marion, 877/738-9798, www.springhousefarm.com, from $245) are quiet hideaways with eco-conscious comforts. The proprietors, who live in a historic farmhouse on the property, stock the cabin kitchens with fresh bread and eggs and local honey. Each cottage has an outdoor hot tub and access to pond-side gazebos and hiking trails.

Food

◀ **Famous Louise's Rockhouse Restaurant** (23175 Rockhouse Ln., Linville Falls, near BRP Milepost 321, 828/765-2702, 6 A.M.–8 P.M. daily), built in 1936 with stones taken from the Linville River, is not a large restaurant, but the dining room is spread out over three counties. The lines of Burke, McDowell, and Avery Counties meet on this exact spot, and customers, for reasons of loyalty or legality, often have preferences about where to take their repast. Famous Louise's is owned by a mother and daughter, and Louise, the mom, is a cook of some renown. The fare is traditional and homemade—the pimento cheese is mixed here, the cornbread and biscuits are whipped up from scratch, the pot roast stewed at a leisurely simmer. On your way out, pick up a jar or two of Louise's homemade berry jams, probably the best $3 souvenirs to be found in the mountains. You'll find them in Avery County.

In the Shadow of the Blue Ridge

The foothills are like the rich topsoil from which the natural and cultural heritage of the mountains grow. The Yadkin Valley and surrounding hills are some of North Carolina's most beautiful countryside. Dotted with homes and forts from a time when this was the colonial frontier, the region is a gateway to mountain culture today, much as it was in the 18th century, when pioneers looked west and wondered what lay behind the veil of mountains.

This is an incredibly energetic area for what we think of as "mountain music." Several major festivals are held here in the spring and summer, most famously North Wilkesboro's annual MerleFest. MerleFest has become one of this country's most important music festivals, drawing major bluegrass, country, old-time, and Americana artists for a weekend of outdoor performances. Mount Airy is a community of many charms, but it is best known for two things: music, and *The Andy Griffith Show*. Since the dawn of recorded country music in the 1920s, the old-time and, later, bluegrass musicians of the area between Mount Airy and Galax, Virginia, have been known as some of the greatest string band artists in the South. One familiar with the regional cadences of Appalachian music can recognize a Mount Airy fiddler or banjo player almost at first note. The area's musical tradition is noteworthy not only for the masterful playing of its practitioners and the depth of its repertoire and stylistic variations, but also for the passionate interest that people of all ages in this region continue to feel in the music that their ancestors loved. There are perhaps as many twenty-something old-time musicians in and around Mount Airy as musicians in their seventies, and in the realm of regional folk traditions, that's a truly extraordinary distinction.

Mount Airy is also a friendly, comfortable town, and its annual Fiddlers' Convention is one of the best events in the old-time music summer festival circuit. To the south in the town of Union Grove, another important fiddlers' convention, known as Fiddlers Grove, happens every year a week or two before the Mount Airy festival.

Hanging Rock State Park near Danbury is one of the state's favorite climbing spots, and down near Morganton, South Mountains State Park is a jagged range of tough backcountry trails. For outdoor adventurers, the foothills conceal environments as wild and challenging as any you'll find in the deep mountains.

WILKESBORO AND NORTH WILKESBORO
MerleFest

It began as a small folk festival more than 20 years ago, but MerleFest (www.merlefest.com, usually the last weekend in Apr.) has grown into one of the premier roots music events in the country. It was founded in honor of Merle Watson, the son of legendary guitarist Doc Watson. Merle, who was also a guitarist, passed away unexpectedly in 1985 in a tractor accident, cutting short what promised to be (and, indeed, already was) an influential career. Doc Watson, who grew up in the nearby community of Deep Gap, continues to be the festival's ceremonial host, and nowadays he is joined by Merle's son Richard, who has also grown up to be an expert guitarist. MerleFest draws thousands of visitors every year and many of the top-name performers in folk, country, and bluegrass music. Recent years' headliners include Ralph Stanley, Gillian Welch, and Emmylou Harris. With multiple stages and dozens of artists, there's a great deal of musical variety to sample. It's quite expensive: $35–50 a day for general admission, and $130–250 for multi-day packages. Springtime in the mountains can be changeful; some years it's boiling hot and sunny at MerleFest, other times as damp and raw as winter, and sometimes it's both by turns. If traveling through the northern mountains during MerleFest, keep in mind too that all the motels within an hour's drive of North Wilkesboro, and probably farther, will be booked solid, so be sure to put dibs on a room well in advance. Tenting and RV camping are available on the festival grounds.

Entertainment and Events

Follow Highway 901 southeast out of Wilkesboro, and you'll come to the little town of Union Grove. This is the home of two great local music institutions—one a year-round venue, and one an annual festival. The **Cook Shack** (Hwy. 901, two miles west of I-77, Union Grove, 704/539-4353, http://uniongrovemusic.site.voila.fr) is a little country store and grill that has been hosting live bluegrass, old-time, and country music for more than 40 years. Owners Myles and Pal Ireland open the Cook Shack early Saturday morning for a community jam session that begins at 8 A.M.—and for musicians to get up that early on a Saturday, you know this place has to be special. There are also concerts throughout the year at the Cook Shack, including on evenings in the middle of the week, so this is a great place to catch touring bands between stops in Asheville and the Triangle. Come to listen or to play, and have a burger or a liver-mush sandwich between tunes.

Union Grove is also one of the most important festival sites on both the old-time and bluegrass summer festival circuit. The **Fiddler's Grove Ole Time Fiddlers and**

Bluegrass Convention (late May, Fiddlers Grove Campground, Union Grove, 828/478-3735, www.fiddlersgrove.com, tickets $10–50 depending on when you buy them and when you plan to attend) has taken place every year since 1924. Hundreds of musicians and fans come every year, camping at the festival itself or staying nearby, to jam with friends and hear some of the best old-time and bluegrass music you'll find anywhere.

Food

North Wilkesboro's **Brushy Mountain Smokehouse and Creamery** (201 Wilkesboro Blvd., 336/667-9464, www.brushymtnsmokehouseandcreamery.com) is famous for its pulled pork barbecue and country sides (biscuits, fried okra, baked apples), but it's also a great ice cream shop. The ice cream is made there, and they bake their own waffle cones, so it's as fresh as it can be. Fried apple pie, cobbler, and ice cream pie are all available by the slice as well as whole-hog.

MOUNT AIRY AND VICINITY
Sights

In downtown Mount Airy, you'll notice 1960s police squad cars, business names that may seem oddly familiar, and cardboard cutouts of Barney Fife peering out from shop windows. Mount Airy is the hometown of Andy Griffith, and the mecca for fans of *The Andy Griffith Show.* As I can attest personally, people who grew up in small towns in the Carolinas—and probably, in fact, in small towns anywhere in the United States—recognize their families and neighbors in the fictional residents of Mayberry. The show's inspired writing and acting are a deep well of nostalgia, and its fans legion. TAGSRWC (www.mayberry.com) is an intentionally obtuse acronym for The Andy Griffith Show Rerun Watchers Club, the show's international fan club whose hundreds of chapters have in-reference names like "Her First Husband Got Runned Over by a Team of Hogs" (Texas) and "Anxiety Magnifies Fearsome Objects" (Alabama). The Surry Arts Council hosts the citywide **Mayberry**

NORTHERN BLUE RIDGE

© JOHN RICHBURG

Hanging Rock

Days, an annual fall festival entering its second decade, in which TAGSRWC members, other fans, cast members, and impersonators of Mayberry characters come to town and have a big time getting haircuts at Floyd's Barbershop, riding in squad cars, and arresting each other.

For a one-of-a-kind view of Mount Airy, hop into a Mayberry squad car to tour all the major sights in town. **Mayberry Squad Car Tours** (625 S. Main St., 336/789-6743, www.tour mayberry.com) leave from "Wally's Service Station," and cost "$25 for a carload."

Finally, two roadside oddities in Mount Airy are not to be missed. At 594 North Andy Griffith Parkway/U.S. 52 stands the **Giant Milk Carton.** This 12-foot-tall metal milk carton now advertises Pet Milk, but since its creation in the 1940s it has also stood as an advertisement for Coble Dairy and Flavo-Rich Milk. At the intersection of U.S. 52 and Starlite Drive stands a **great big man,** a very tall, metal, friendly service station attendant. He is an old friend to out-of-towners who come to Mount Airy for the fiddlers' convention every year, who remember to turn off the highway to get to Veterans Park when they see "the Big Man."

A little more than 20 miles away in Pinnacle is **Horne Creek Living Historical Farm** (308 Horne Creek Farm Rd., Pinnacle, 336/325-2298, www.ah.dcr.state.nc.us/sections/hs/horne/horne.htm, 10 A.M.–4 P.M. Tues.–Sat.). The farm life of the Hauser family—an ancient clan in this area—is re-created as Thomas and Charlotte Hauser, and their one daughter and 11 sons, would have experienced it around 1900. Costumed interpreters demonstrate the old ways of farm work, while livestock of historic breeds go about their own work, probably not realizing that they're museum docents. The Hausers had an orchard, of which only a single superannuated pear tree remains, but today a new orchard has taken its place. The Southern Heritage Apple Orchard preserves old Southern heirloom species, trees grown from seeds that have been passed down in families for generations.

CHANG AND ENG

Andy Griffith may be Mount Airy's most famous living son, but in the middle of the 19th century, two of the most famous men in the world lived on a quiet farm in rural Surry County, just outside Mount Airy. Chang and Eng were born in Siam (now Thailand) in 1811, joined at the sternum by a cartilaginous band of flesh. Had they been born today, it probably would have been an easy operation to separate the brothers, but in 1811 they were lucky not to have been killed at birth. Beginning when they were teenagers, Chang and Eng toured the world, eventually becoming top draws at P. T. Barnum's shows.

During their travels through the United States, they took a shine to North Carolina, and when they burned out on show business, around the age of 30, they decided to settle in Wilkesboro. In North Carolina they adopted the last name of Bunker. Chang fell in love with a local girl named Addie Yates, and soon Eng took to courting her older sister Sally. The four married and moved in together, and raised a very large family – Eng and Sally had 11 children, and Chang and Addie had 10. Many of their descendants live in the area today.

In some ways Chang and Eng seemed like one person. When they first learned English, they referred to themselves as "I," and they were rarely observed to speak to each other, as if it was unnecessary. In one of countless medical experiments they underwent, the examining doctor tickled one brother, resulting in the other brother becoming angry. Yet in other ways they were very different, and inevitably this caused them great unhappiness. Chang was temperamental and vivid; Eng was reticent and contemplative. More dangerously, Chang liked to drink and Eng liked to gamble. Sometimes they had bitter arguments and, on a couple of occasions, fistfights. Perhaps it's best not to dwell upon the Bunkers' conjugal relations overmuch, but their domestic arrangements required plenty of compromise. They divided their time between Chang and Addie's and Eng and Sally's houses, each brother being the other's houseguest half of the time.

In spite of the limitations that biology placed upon them, the Bunkers became fairly conventional upper-middle class farmers, owning slaves and sending two sons to fight in the Confederate Army. The War left them in dire financial straits, though, and in 1870 they sailed for Europe for another tour. On the voyage home, Chang had a severe stroke, from which he never fully recovered. He began to drink heavily, and his health declined. One January night in 1874, Eng awoke to find that Chang was dead. Within a few hours, Eng, who was in excellent health, was also dead. An autopsy showed that Chang had died of a cerebral hemorrhage, but Eng's cause of death is still unknown. It's thought that he may have died of fright.

Chang and Eng Bunker, to whom we owe the existence of the phrase "Siamese twins," are buried at White Plains Baptist Church, at 506 Old Highway 601, south of Mount Airy.

◖ The Merry Go-Round Show

Teamed up with WPAQ 740, the Surry Arts Council hosts "The Merry Go-Round," the country's third-longest-running live bluegrass/old-time music radio show. Come to the **Downtown Cinema Theater** (142 N. Main St., Mount Airy, 800/286-6193, www.surryarts.org) for the 11 A.M.–1:30 P.M. Saturday show, or show up as early as 9 A.M. toting an instrument if you'd like to join in the pre-show jam session. It's one of the state's great small-town treats.

Entertainment and Events

When you visit Mount Airy or pass within close enough range, tune in to **WPAQ** (AM 740, also streaming online at www.wpaq740.com). For over 60 years, WPAQ has provided a venue for live, local talent to perform old-time, bluegrass, and gospel music. To get a really good idea of this community's life, tune in for the live Saturday-morning The Merry Go-Round show, or any other day of the week, when you'll hear local call-in shows, old-style country preaching, and more music. Along with WPAQ, another local institution that has a great deal to do with the vitality of Mount Airy's musical traditions is the **Bluegrass and Old-Time Fiddlers Convention** (631 W. Lebanon St., 800/286-6193, www.mtairyfiddlersconvention.com), held for almost 40 years during the first full weekend in June at Veterans Memorial Park. Thousands of people come to the festival from around the world to play old-time and bluegrass music with their friends and compete in what is a very prestigious competition in this genre of music. The heart of the action takes place at the hundreds of individual campsites that spring up all over the park, in the informal jam sessions among old and new friends. It's some of the best old-time music to be heard anywhere.

The Brightleaf Drive-In (Hwy. 52/ Andy Griffith Pkwy. N., 336/786-5494, www.thebrightleaf.com), built in 1955, is everything you could wish of an old-fashioned drive-in movie theater. It's cheap (children under 10 are free, and everyone else gets into the double-feature for $5), you can choose between the original hang-on-the-window speakers or tuning your radio to 89.5 for "theater sound," and the concession stand boasts the "best dogs in town." Shows start at dusk, winter and summer, but call ahead or check the website for more exact times. The ticket booth opens one hour before the show in winter, and two hours before in summer.

The **Surry Arts Council** is one of the hubs of artistic activity in the Mount Airy/Surry County area. Located at the **Andy Griffith Theater** (218 Rockford St., 800/286-6193, www.surryarts.org), they sponsor and host many events throughout the year that showcase local talent in drama, visual arts, and especially, music. On third Saturdays, local and regional old-time and bluegrass bands perform in the **Voice of the Blue Ridge Series** ($10 adults, free for children under 6).

Sports and Recreation

Mount Airy and its neighbors are foothills towns, and you have to drive a little ways farther west before you start to climb the Blue Ridge. This is why the geographical anomaly of Pilot Mountain is so startling. The 1,400-foot mountain, with a prominent rocky knob at the top, kind of looks like a giant dog's head, or the UHF knob of an old TV set that you could use to turn on *The Andy Griffith Show*. The surrounding **Pilot Mountain State Park** (792 Pilot Knob Park Rd., Pinnacle, 336/325-2355, www.ils.unc.edu/parkproject/visit/pimo/home.html) is a beautiful place for hiking, swimming, rock climbing and rappelling (in designated areas), canoeing on the Yadkin River, and camping (Mar. 15–Nov. 30). Camping at one of the 49 designated tent and trailer sites costs $15 per day, or $10 per day for campers 62 and older. Each site has a tent pad, picnic table, and grill, and access to drinking water and hot showers.

A series of 400-foot rock faces, extending for two miles, are the most striking feature of **Hanging Rock State Park** (SR 2015, four miles NW of Danbury, 336/593-8480, www.ils.unc.edu/parkproject/visit/haro/home.html, 8 A.M.–6 P.M. Nov.–Feb., 8 A.M.–7 P.M. Mar. and Oct., 8 A.M.–8 P.M. Apr., May, Sept., 8 A.M.–9 P.M. June–Aug.). It's of course a great place for rock climbing and rappelling (which requires a permit and registration with park staff, as well as a schedule that allows climbers to be finished and out of the park by closing time). You can also hike to waterfalls and beautiful overlooks, and swim in a nearby lake. Hanging Rock State Park has 73 tent and trailer campsites, one of which is wheelchair-accessible. Each site has a tent pad, a picnic table, a grill, access to drinking water and, from mid-March through November, access to a wash house with hot showers and laundry sinks. There are also two-bedroom/four-bed vacation cabins available for rent, by the week ($400) during the summer and for a minimum of two days ($80/day) off-season. Registration is best arranged at least a month in advance; contact the park office for application details.

Yadkin River Adventures (104 Old Rockford Rd., Rockford, 336/374-5318, www.yadkinriveradventures.com) offers rentals of canoes, kayaks, and sit-on-tops, and shuttle service for full- and half-day paddling adventures. The Class I Yadkin River is great for paddlers of all ages and experience levels, and it has some beautiful views of Pilot Mountain.

Balloon pilots Tony and Claire Colburn lead tours of the Yadkin Valley by hot air balloon, any time of year, weather permitting. **Yadkin Valley Hot Air Balloon Adventures** (336/922-7207, www.balloonadventure.net) requires special arrangements—contact the Colburns for fees and availability—but is an amazing way to see the Carolina foothills.

Accommodations

Pilot Knob Inn Bed and Breakfast (361 New Pilot Knob Ln., Pinnacle, 336/325-2502, www.pilotknobinn.com, $129–249) is an unusual B&B in that guests can stay not only in suites in the main lodge, but in one of several restored, century-old tobacco barns on the property. Each one-bedroom barn-turned-cabin is well equipped with modern conveniences, including two-person hot tubs, as well as stone wood-burning fireplaces. No children are allowed, and no pets are allowed other than your horse, who can occupy a stall on the property for an additional $50 per night.

The Rockford Bed and Breakfast (4872 Rockford Rd., Dobson, 800/561-6652, www.rockfordbedandbreakfast.com, $100–120) is a beautiful mid-19th century farmhouse, south of Mount Airy in Dobson, convenient to many of the Yadkin Valley wineries.

Food

The Snappy Lunch (125 N. Main St., 336/786-4931, www.thesnappylunch.com) is most famous for having been mentioned in *The Andy Griffith Show*. But having seated its first customer in 1923, the Snappy Lunch is much older than the show, and a little older than Andy himself. Pack your cholesterol drugs when you go to Mount Airy, so you can enjoy the Snappy's signature pork chop sandwich.

There are at least two sources for good, strong coffee in Mount Airy. My favorites are the **Good Life Café** (corner of Main and Oak downtown in the Main-Oak Emporium, 336/789-2404,

www.mainoakemporium.com/goodlife.html, 10 A.M.–6 P.M. Mon.–Sat., 1–5 P.M. Sun., open until 8 P.M. Fri. Labor Day–Christmas) and **Moby's Coffee** (2123 Rockford St./Hwy. 601, Suite 200, 336/786-1222, 7 A.M.–10 P.M. Mon.–Thurs., 7 A.M.–1 P.M. Fri. and Sat., closed Sun.).

South of Mount Airy in the town of Dobson is **Strudel's** (3095 Rockford Rd., Dobson, 336/374-3022, www.strudelsbakery.com, 8 A.M.–6 P.M. Fri. and Sat.), a little European bakery. It's only open on Fridays and Saturdays, but if you can arrange your travel plans accordingly, you'll be wowed by the menu of cakes, cookies, muffins, pies, tarts, breads, petit fours, ruggelah, and, of course, strudels.

SOUTH ALONG U.S. 321
Sights

Traditions Pottery (4443 Bolick Rd., 3 miles south of Blowing Rock, 828/295-5099, www.traditionspottery.com) is a hotbed of Piedmont and Appalachian folk traditions. The Owen-Bolick-Calhoun families trace their roots as potters back through six generations in the sandhills community of Seagrove, and here in Caldwell County. They have also become renowned old-time musicians and storytellers. Traditions Pottery is not only a place to buy beautiful ceramics with an impeccable folk pedigree, but also the location of the Jack Tales Festival in August (Glenn Bolick learned his storytelling from the great Ray Hicks of Beech Mountain, a National Heritage Award winner), as well as numerous music jams and kiln openings throughout the year.

A serious collector is a rare sort of a person, someone who spends hours driving around the countryside or scanning the Internet in search of his quarry, and who sees the beloved objects—be they records, bottle caps, baseball cards—dancing behind his eyelids when he tries to sleep at night. Such an affliction can lead to spectacular collections of delightfully unexpected objects, and just such a collection is located in Granite Falls. The **Antique Vending Company Museum** (30 S. Main St., Granite Falls, 828/962-9783, www.antiquevending.com, call for tour hours) is a collection of more than 1,000 early soda machines (which North Carolinians are more likely to identify as "coke machines," regardless of the brand of soft drink contained therein). The machines go back to the earliest days of automated cold-drink-dispensing, and include the only known 1925 Icy-O Coca-Cola machine left in the world.

The county seat of Caldwell County, Lenoir (pronounced "Luh-NORE," not "Len-war"), was named for General William Lenoir, a Revolutionary War hero and chronicler of the Battle of King's Mountain. **Fort Defiance** (1792 Fort Defiance Dr./Hwy. 268, Happy Valley, 828/758-1671, www.fortdefiancenc.org,

10 A.M.–5 P.M. Thurs.–Sat. and 1–5 P.M. Sun. Apr.–Oct., weekends only and by appointment Nov.–Mar.), his 1792 plantation house in Happy Valley, is beautifully restored and open to the public. Among its unusual charms are a 200-year-old oriental chestnut tree, an English boxwood garden of the same vintage, and the largest beech tree in the state.

The **Hickory Museum of Art** (243 3rd Ave. NE, Hickory, 828/327-8576, www.hickorymuseumofart.com, 10 A.M.–4 P.M. Tues.–Sat., 1–4 P.M. Sun., free) was established in the early 1950s, and was the first major museum of American art in the Southeast. Its early partnership with the National Academy of Design in New York gained it the nickname of the

THE REAL TOM DOOLEY

What is probably North Carolina's most famous murder case, the 1867 murder of a young Wilkes County woman named Laura Foster by her lover Tom Dula, is known around the world because of a 1950s recording by the Kingston Trio. "The Ballad of Tom Dooley," as it has come to be known, was sung in the North Carolina mountains long before its emergence as a Folk Revival standard. Most notably, the Watauga County banjo player and ballad singer Frank Profitt kept the story alive through song. Even today, almost a century and a half later, the intricacies of the Dula case are debated in this area by descendants of the principal players, and by neighbors who have grown up with the legend.

The story is a sordid one. Tom Dula was 18 years old when he enlisted in the Confederate Army, and by that time he had already been involved for several years in a romantic relationship with a woman named Ann Melton. Following the Civil War, much of which he spent as a prisoner at the notoriously ghastly Point Lookout prison in Maryland, Dula came home to Wilkes County, older but apparently no wiser. He picked up where he left off with Ann Melton, by then married to another man, while at the same time he commenced to living with another local girl, Laura Foster. (In one version

of the story, he was seeing yet a third woman too, another Melton girl.)

The subtleties of the motives and means that led to Laura Foster's death are still subjects of hot debate, but the facts are as follows. On May 25, 1866, Laura Foster set off from home riding her father's horse. The next day, the horse returned without her. After searchers had combed the woods and riverbanks for nearly a month, Laura Foster's body was finally discovered. She had been stabbed to death, and buried in a shallow grave. When news got out that the body was found, Dula disappeared.

He was caught a few weeks later in Tennessee. Back in Wilkes County, Tom Dula and Ann Melton were indicted for murder. Officials moved the trial down the mountain to nearby Iredell County, where a jury found Dula guilty. (Ann Melton was acquitted.) After a series of appeals and an eventual overturning of the verdict by the state Supreme Court, a new trial was convened, and Dula was again convicted. He was hanged on May 1, 1868, in Statesville. Historians write that even before the hanging was carried out, people in the area were singing a song with the verse, "Hang your head, Tom Dula/Hang your head and cry/You killed poor Laura Foster/And now you're bound to die."

"Southern Outpost of the National Academy." The museum has an impressive permanent collection, with special emphases on American painting, outsider and folk art, North Carolina folk pottery, and American studio pottery and glass.

Festivals

Every Labor Day weekend, Caldwell County is home to the **Historic Happy Valley Old-Time Fiddlers' Convention** (828/726-0616, www.happyvalleyfiddlers.com), a laid-back event in a gorgeous location, the Jones Farm. The festival includes music competitions and concerts, drawing some great traditional artists from all over the hills. There are also a rubber duck race, demonstrations by instrument makers, tours of Fort Defiance, and visits to the grave of Laura Foster, the 1867 victim of North Carolina's most famous murderer, Tom "Dooley"—who happened to be a fiddler. Participants and visitors can camp along the Yadkin River on the Jones Farm during the festival for $10 per night. No alcohol is allowed; pets are permitted as long as they're leashed.

The Catawba Valley is one of the important pockets of North Carolina folk pottery, with a tradition all its own dating back to the early 19th-century potter Daniel Seagle, and exemplified in modern times by the late Burlon Craig (one of the giants of Southern folk art) and contemporary master Kim Ellington. Hickory's annual **Catawba Valley Pottery and Antiques Festival** (Hickory Convention Center, late March, $6 adults, $2 children) brings together more than 100 potters and dealers in pottery and antiques. It's a great introduction to Southern folk pottery, and a

danger zone if you're on a budget, because the wares sold here are most covetable.

Sports and Recreation

The **Hickory Crawdads** (2500 Clement Blvd. NW, Hickory, 828/322-3000, www.hickory crawdads.com) are a Single-A affiliate of the Pittsburgh Pirates. The 2002 and 2004 South Atlantic League Champions play at the modern Frans Stadium, where you may meet the mascot, Conrad—yes, Conrad—the Crawdad.

South of Morganton, **South Mountains State Park** (3001 South Mountains State Park Ave., Connelly Springs, 828/433-4772, www.ncparks.gov/Visit/parks/somo/main.php) is located in a low but rugged mountain range of 1,000–3,000 feet. The Jacob's Fork River threads through the park, tumbling 80 feet at the beautiful High Shoals Falls. Primitive and equestrian campsites are located in several sections of the park, including along Jacob's Fork, for $9 per night.

Food

If you're traveling between Lenoir and Hickory on a weekend, take a detour to the little community of Dudley Shoals, where you'll find **Sims Country BBQ** (6160 Petra Mill Rd., Dudley Shoals, 828/396-5811, www.scc.clog dancing.com/BBQ.html, 5–9 P.M. Fri. and Sat., all-you-can-eat buffet $11). Sims is known not only for its all-you-can-eat Texas-style barbecue, which they pit-cook all day, but for live bluegrass music and clogging. It also hosts the annual Molasses Festival on the second Saturday in October, with bluegrass, dancing, and harvest-time activities.

ASHEVILLE AND THE SOUTHERN BLUE RIDGE

Like countless others, you may have made reference to the Asheville area many times without realizing it. Asheville is the seat of Buncombe County, (pronounced "bunkum"). It was in 1820 that Felix Walker, congressman from this district, brought debate over the important Missouri question to a standstill with a long-winded, elaborately hyperbolic speech. When an attempt was made to halt this seemingly interminable production, he answered that he would not stop, as he was speaking not so much for the benefit of his colleagues assembled in the House, but for his constituents—he was, he said, "speaking for Buncombe." "Speaking for Buncombe," and ultimately the words "bunkum" and "bunk," came to mean hollow political grandstanding. Push that bit of trivia to the corner of your mind, because the Asheville area is, in fact, a volcanically rich cultural zone.

For over a century, Asheville has been a peculiar little hive of progressive cosmopolitanism: the "Paris of the South." Its location at the confluence of the Swannanoa (pronounced "swan-uh-NO-uh") and French Broad (better get your snickering out of the way now, because you'll be seeing this name a lot) Rivers, and on over-mountain stagecoach routes, brought commerce to the settlement in the 18th and early 19th centuries. The boom hit in the latter years of the 19th century, when the railway lines began to bring tens of thousands of vacationers every year. The small town underwent rapid expansion between 1880 and 1930, until it became, by any standards, a small city.

The mountains around Asheville are home

© SARAH BRYAN

HIGHLIGHTS

(Downtown Architecture: In the late 19th and early 20th centuries, wealthy summer vacationers and industrialist investors left their mark in Asheville's downtown, a district packed with art deco and Beaux-Arts masterpieces (page 228).

(Biltmore Estate: Asheville's most popular attraction is not only an awe-inspiring palace of America's gilded age, but a collection of great little restaurants and shops, a winery, equestrian activities, and much more, all in a beautiful riverside setting (page 228).

(Folk Art Center: This Blue Ridge Parkway treasure is a store and gallery where you can learn about the master craftspeople of the Southern Appalachians and purchase gorgeous handmade items, from unique jewelry to traditional weaving and woodcarving to fine-art furniture (page 232).

(Bluegrass at the Fiddlin' Pig: This is the place to hear nationally renowned bluegrass bands who happen to live around Asheville. It's a barbecue restaurant with a dance floor for clogging, a full bar, and a great atmosphere for all ages (page 232).

(Pisgah Ranger District: This 150,000-plus-acre section of the Pisgah Forest encompasses the Cradle of Forestry Museum, Shining Rock Wilderness, Sliding Rock, Cold Mountain, and many other favorite outdoor destinations (page 244).

LOOK FOR **(** TO FIND RECOMMENDED SIGHTS, ACTIVITIES, DINING, AND LODGING.

(Chimney Rock: A strange natural tower of stone growing out of a mountainside like a rhino's horn, Chimney Rock is the centerpiece of a large park with amazing hiking trails (page 247).

to deep traditions of folk art and music, dating to long before the first folklorist came around with a microphone. Old-time Appalachian string band music thrives here, not only among those people who are descendants of the region's early settlers, but also due in a large part to hundreds of fiddlers, guitarists, banjo players, and other musicians who have come from all corners of the earth to be part of the music scene here. Asheville is one of the best places in the world to hear old-time and bluegrass music,

as well as a more obscure local specialty known as mountain swing. More than 80 years ago, Bascom Lamar Lunsford, a banjo-playing folklorist and Buncombe County native, founded the Mountain Dance and Folk Festival. This annual downtown event is now the longest-running folk festival in the United States.

One of the epicenters of the visual arts in the Southeast, the Asheville area draws upon its centuries-old traditions of folk carving, weaving, and other arts, and merges those

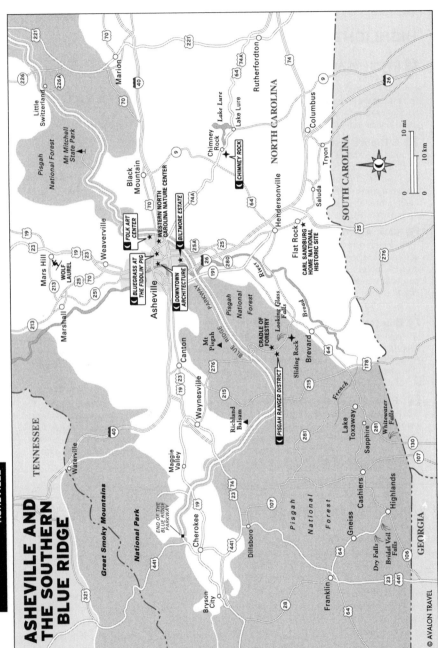

ASHEVILLE

ASHEVILLE AND THE SOUTHERN BLUE RIDGE

© AVALON TRAVEL

with exponents of modern craft movements of the last hundred years, to form a pressure cooker of studios and galleries. A regional infrastructure of arts organizations like the Southern Highland Craft Guild (www.southerhighlandguild.org), and the dozens, perhaps hundreds, of local galleries and studios, make Asheville an exciting place for the lover of fine art and craft.

Asheville is Haight-Asbury, Woodstock, and the Grand Ole Opry rolled into one, and its denizens are works of art in their own right. Despite its name having become associated with empty claptrap, Buncombe County is a deeply complicated community, a place where the old-time Appalachian and the global avant-garde meet and merge.

PLANNING YOUR TIME

Many mountain towns shut down for tourists after the leaf season ends, but Asheville is awake all year. Visiting Asheville in the winter is less expensive than when thousands of tourists are competing for hotel rooms. Restaurants and shops are open and the live music for which the city is famous doesn't slow down. Driving up into the mountains around Asheville, winter weather is more likely to be an issue than it is in the city, though between winter ice and snow and year-round fog, the weather in the highlands always calls for caution. (This is

apparently where Subaru all-wheel-drive station wagons go to die; count them sometime when you're stopped at a red light.) The summer is, of course, a great time to be up in the cool air, when it's boiling hot down in the flatlands. It's also the time when the most festivals and special events are held, and when the shades of blue and green of the Blue Ridge are most vivid. The fall colors appear at slightly different times each year, depending on factors like temperature and rainfall. Trees at the ridgeline usually start to turn around mid-September, petering out in the valleys by early November, though in recent years hot weather has extended leaf season nearly to Thanksgiving.

The Biltmore House, Chimney Rock, and several other attractions listed in this chapter are participants in the **Go Blue Ridge Card** (800/887-9103, www.goblueridgecard.com) discount program. The card costs $50–160, depending on where and for how many days you want to use it. It's a good deal, especially if you're touring through the whole mountain region and hitting a lot of the top sites.

The website of the **Blue Ridge National Heritage Area** (www.blueridgeheritage.com) is a great place to plan your trip. It lists outdoor recreation spots, arts events, historical sites, and many more destinations, with a great deal of information about the environment and culture of the North Carolina mountains.

ASHEVILLE

Asheville

SIGHTS
◖ Downtown Architecture

One of Asheville's chief charms is its striking architecture, which dates largely to the 1920s. Most famously, Biltmore Estate and the surrounding developments brought together the illustrious minds of landscape architect Frederick Law Olmstead and architect Richard Morris Hunt, who were in their day two of the leading lights in American design, to create a palace and estate for George Washington Vanderbilt. The Montford neighborhood, contemporary to Biltmore, is a striking mixture of ornate Queen Anne houses and Craftsman-style bungalows. The Grove Park Inn was constructed in 1913, a huge, luxurious hotel fitted with rustic architectural devices to make vacationing New York nabobs feel like they were roughing it. Asheville's downtown features the second-greatest concentration of art deco buildings in the United States, second only to Miami Beach. The **Buncombe County Courthouse** (60 Court Plaza, dating from 1927–1929), the **Jackson Building** (22 S. Pack Square, dating from 1923–1924), **First Baptist Church** (Oak and Woodfin Streets, dating from 1925), the **S&W Cafeteria** (56 Patton Ave., dating from 1929), the **Public Service Building** (89–93 Patton Ave., dating from 1929), and the **Grove Arcade** (37 Battery Park Ave., dating from 1926–1929) are just a few of the 1920s masterpieces in a city overflowing with important early 20th-century architecture.

◖ Biltmore Estate

The largest home in America, and still privately owned by the Vanderbilt family, Biltmore Estate (1 Approach Rd., 800/411-3812, www.biltmore.com, 9 A.M.–5:30 P.M. Jan. 1, 9:30 A.M.–4:30 P.M. Jan. 2–Mar. 25, except open at 9 A.M. on Feb. 9–10, 9 A.M.–5:30 P.M. Mar. 26–Nov. 2, 8:30 A.M.–5:30 P.M. Nov. 3–Dec. 31) is the realized dream of George Washington Vanderbilt. Grandson of Gilded Age magnate Cornelius Vanderbilt, G. W. Vanderbilt, like

Grove Arcade

© SARAH BRYAN

many wealthy Northerners of his day, was first introduced to the North Carolina mountains when he came to Asheville for his health. So impressed was he with the beauty and the climate of this area that he amassed a 125,000-acre tract of land south of Asheville on which to build his "country home." He engaged celebrity architect Richard Morris Hunt to build the mansion itself, and because the estate reminded them both of the Loire Valley, Hunt and Vanderbilt agreed that the house should be built in the style of a 16th-century château. No less illustrious was Vanderbilt's choice of landscape architect for Biltmore. The grounds would be designed by Frederick Law Olmstead, creator of New York City's Central Park. It's hard to imagine that Olmstead could find a grander commission than that of designing Central Park, but in the Biltmore Estate, he was given a canvas that was fully nine times larger than that dinky lot in Manhattan. While Biltmore

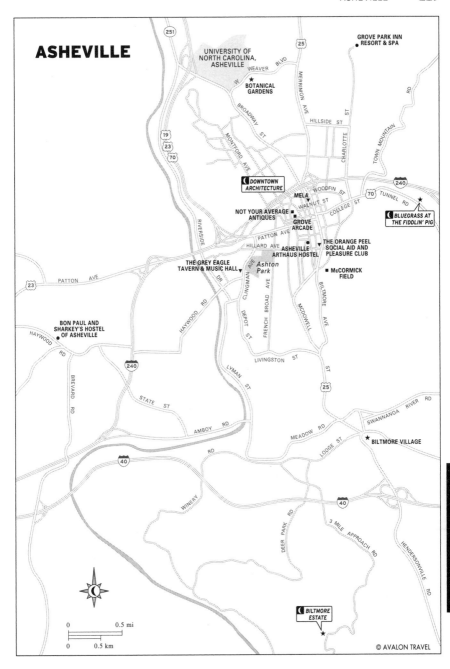

ASHEVILLE

UNIVERSITY OF
NORTH CAROLINA,
ASHEVILLE

★ BOTANICAL
GARDENS

GROVE PARK INN
RESORT & SPA

WEAVER BLVD

MERRIMON AVE

BROADWAY ST

HILLSIDE ST

CHARLOTTE ST

TOWN MOUNTAIN RD

MONTFORD AVE

RIVERSIDE

☾ DOWNTOWN
ARCHITECTURE

MELA
▼
WALNUT ST

WOODFIN ST

COLLEGE ST

NOT YOUR AVERAGE ■
ANTIQUES

GROVE
ARCADE

PATTON AVE

HILLARD AVE

ASHEVILLE
ARTHAUS HOSTEL

THE ORANGE PEEL
SOCIAL AID AND
PLEASURE CLUB

THE GREY EAGLE
TAVERN & MUSIC HALL ▼

Ashton
Park

■ McCORMICK
FIELD

TUNNEL RD

☾ BLUEGRASS AT
THE FIDDLIN' PIG

70

240

PATTON AVE

CLINGMAN AVE

DEPOT ST

FRENCH BROAD AVE

McDOWELL

BILTMORE AVE

HAYWOOD RD

BON PAUL AND
SHARKEY'S HOSTEL
OF ASHEVILLE

HAYWOOD RD

BREVARD RD

240

STATE ST

LYMAN ST

LIVINGSTON ST

ST

25

AMBOY RD

40

WINERY RD

RD

DEER PARK RD

MEADOW RD

LODGE ST

SWANNANOA RIVER RD

★ BILTMORE VILLAGE

40

3 MILE APPROACH RD

HENDERSONVILLE RD

☾ BILTMORE
ESTATE
★

0   0.5 mi

0   0.5 km

© AVALON TRAVEL

ASHEVILLE

THOMAS WOLFE

A native son of Asheville, author Thomas Wolfe (*You Can't Go Home Again, Look Homeward, Angel*) grew up here in a boardinghouse that his mother ran, and which is operated today as the **Thomas Wolfe Memorial** (52 N. Market St., Asheville, 828/253-8304, www.wolfememorial.com, 9 A.M.-5 P.M. Tues.-Sat. and 1-5 P.M. Sun. Apr.-Oct., 10 A.M.-4 P.M. Tues.-Sat. and 1-4 P.M. Sun. Nov.-Mar., $1, $0.50 students). He described the town of "Altamont" (Asheville) and its people so vividly in *Look Homeward, Angel* that the Asheville library refused to own it, and Wolfe himself avoided the town for almost eight years.

In this passage from *Look Homeward, Angel*, Wolfe describes the excitement of approaching Asheville as a traveler.

The next morning he resumed his journey by coach. His destination was the little town of Altamont, twenty-four miles away beyond the rim of the great outer wall of the hills. As the horses strained slowly up the mountain road Oliver's spirit lifted a little. It was a gray-golden day in late October, bright and windy. There was a sharp bite and sparkle in the mountain air: the range soared above him, close, immense, clean, and barren. The trees rose gaunt and stark: they were almost leafless. The sky was full of windy white rags of cloud; a thick blade of mist washed slowly around the rampart of a mountain.

Below him a mountain stream foamed down its rocky bed, and he could see little dots of men laying the track that would coil across the hill toward Altamont. Then the sweating team lipped the gulch of the mountain, and, among soaring and lordly ranges that melted away in purple mist, they began the slow descent toward the high plateau on which the town of Altamont was built.

In the haunting eternity of these mountains, rimmed in their enormous cup, he found sprawled out on its hundred hills and hollows a town of four thousand people.

There were lands. His heart lifted.

Estate's original 125,000 acres are now greatly diminished—though a large part of that tract was fortunately donated to the federal government, and has become part of Pisgah National Forest—the gorgeously landscaped core of the property remains.

The mansion, constructed between 1888 and 1895, has over 250 rooms—three acres of floor space!—most of which are open to the public for gawking. The wonders inside the house are too numerous to list, but they include paintings by Renoir, Whistler, and Sargent; an amazing collection of European antiques, among them Napoleon's chess set; and room after room that show, in every inch of paneling, tiles, woodwork, and stonework, the work of the best craftsmen of the 1890s.

Technologically, the house was a wonder in its day. It had electricity, central heat, elevators, and hot water. The bowling alley and basement swimming pool are reminiscent of Rich Manor, home of Richie Rich, and as it happens, the 1994 movie *Richie Rich* was indeed filmed here.

G. W. Vanderbilt found the concept of the self-sustaining estate appealing, and attempted to create just that in the Biltmore Estate. Much more than a working farm, Biltmore was a manorial village. The Asheville neighborhood known as **Biltmore Village** was part of this mountain empire.

Vanderbilt would be pleased to know that today the estate runs like clockwork, just as he had envisioned. Each cog and spring is an attraction in itself. There is more than enough to do and see here to occupy a full weekend. The inn and restaurants are only the beginning. The **Biltmore Winery** operates in what was once the estate's dairy. Daily tours and tastings allow visitors to sample the award-winning wines. **River Bend Farm** recreates the working farm that supported the estate and its many workers. Blacksmiths, woodworkers, and other artisans work in the River Bend barn. The kitchen garden is— backyard gardeners, just imagine this—four square acres.

The **Equestrian Center** gives lessons, and if you happen to travel with your own horse, the two of you can explore 80 miles of equestrian trails. Your horse can even have his or her own stall and board like a Vanderbilt steed. Visitors without the equestrian urge can also tour the estate by carriage, bike, raft, canoe, Segway, or, of course, on foot. Last but not least, you can zip around in a Land Rover, after receiving expert training from Biltmore's own **Land Rover Experience Driving School.**

Admission to Biltmore varies by season: $38–44 for adults, $19–22 for ages 10–16, with discounts for buying tickets in advance online. Children ages 9 and under are admitted for free. There is no charge for parking. Your ticket gets you in to the mansion itself, the gardens, the winery, and the farm. Some of the other features carry additional fees.

North Carolina Arboretum

The enormous North Carolina Arboretum (100 Frederick Law Olmstead Way, 818/665-2492, www.ncarboretum.org, 8 A.M.–9 P.M. daily Apr.–Oct., 8 A.M.–7 P.M. daily Nov.–Mar., greenhouse 8 A.M.–2 P.M. Mon.–Sat., parking $6) is considered by many to be one of the most beautiful such institutions in the country. The 434 natural and landscaped acres back into the Pisgah National Forest, just off Blue Ridge Parkway Milepost 393. Major collections include the National Native Azalea Repository, where you can see almost every species of azalea native to the United States, as well as several hybrids, and the very special Bonsai Collection,

where staff horticulturists care for over 200 bonsais, many of their own creation. Bicycles and leashed dogs are permitted on many of the trails. Walking areas range from easy to fairly rugged. For an unusual approach, sign up for one of the Arboretum's twice-daily **Segway Tours** (828/665-2492, 10 A.M. and 2 P.M. Mon.–Sat., $45 weekdays, $55 weekends, riders must be over the age of 14 and between 80 and 250 pounds). The price may seem steep, but there's a lot packed into these tours. First, you'll get 45 minutes of training on how to drive a Segway. Then for the next 2–2.5 hours, you'll glide all around the Arboretum, stopping in beautiful spots throughout for photos and learning. The Arboretum also has a very nice café, the **Savory Thyme Café** (10 A.M.–4 P.M. Mon.–Sat., noon–5 P.M. Sun.) and gift shop, the **Garden Trellis** (10 A.M.–5 P.M. Mon.–Sat., noon–5 P.M. Sun.).

Botanical Gardens

The Botanical Gardens (151 W. T. Weaver Blvd., adjacent to UNC-Asheville campus, 828/252-5190, www.ashevillebotanicalgardens .org, open during daylight hours year-round, free) is a 10-acre preserve for the region's increasingly threatened native plants. Laid out in 1960 for this purpose by landscape architect Doan Ogden, the Gardens are an ecological haven. The many "rooms" are planted to reflect different environments of the mountains—the Wildflower Trail, the Heath Cove, the Fern and Moss Trail, and others. Spring blooms peak in mid-April, but the Gardens are an absolutely lovely, visually rich place to visit any time of year. Because of its serious mission of plant preservation, neither dogs nor bikes are allowed. Admission is free, but as the Gardens are entirely supported by donations, your contribution will have a real impact. On the first Saturday in May, the **Day in the Gardens** brings food and music to this normally placid park, and garden and nature enthusiasts from all around come to tour and to buy native plants for their home gardens. The gift shop is open noon–4 P.M. daily mid-March–December.

Western North Carolina Nature Center

Asheville—and western North Carolina generally—is very ecologically conscious. This concern is reflected in the Western North Carolina Nature Center (75 Gashes Creek Rd., 828/298-5600, www.wildwnc.org, 10 A.M.–5 P.M. daily, $7, $6 senior, $3 ages 3–15, $5 and $4 Asheville residents, under 16 must be accompanied by an adult). On the grounds of an old zoo—don't worry, it's not depressing—wild animals who are for various reasons unable to survive in the wild (they were injured, for example, or raised as pets and abandoned) live in wooded habitats where the public can see them. This is the place to see some of the mountains' rarest species, animals that most lifetime mountain residents have never seen: cougars, wolves, coyotes, bobcats, and even the incredibly elusive hellbender. What's a hellbender, you ask? Come to the Nature Center and find out.

Black Mountain College

Considering the history of Black Mountain College from a purely numerical standpoint, one might get the false impression that this little institution's brief, odd life was a flash in the pan. In its 23 years of operation, Black Mountain College had only 1,200 students, 55 of whom actually completed their degrees. But in fact, between 1933 and 1956, the unconventional school fired a shot heard round the world as an innovative model of education and community life.

The educational program was almost devoid of structure. Students had no set course schedule or requirements. They lived and farmed with the faculty, and no sense of hierarchy was permitted to separate students and teachers. Most distinguished as a school of arts, Black Mountain College hired Josef Albers as its first art director, when the Bauhaus icon fled Nazi Germany. Willem de Kooning taught here for a time, as did Buckminster Fuller, who began his design of the geodesic dome while he was in residence. Albert Einstein and William Carlos Williams were among the roster of guest lecturers.

Black Mountain College closed in 1956, due in part to the prevailing anti-leftist climate of that decade. The **Black Mountain College Museum and Arts Center** (56 Broadway, 828/350-8484, www.blackmountaincollege .org, noon–4 P.M. Wed.–Sat.) is located not in the town of Black Mountain, but in downtown Asheville. It's both an exhibition space and a resource center dedicated to the history and spirit of the college.

◖ Folk Art Center

An essential sight near Asheville is the Folk Art Center (BRP Milepost 382, 828/298-7928, 9 A.M.–5 P.M. daily Jan.–Mar., 9 A.M.–6 P.M. daily Apr.–Dec.). At this beautiful gallery, coupled with the oldest continuously operating craft shop in the United States, **Allanstand Craft Shop,** you'll find the work of members of the prestigious Southern Highland Craft Guild, a juried-membership organization that brings together many of the best artists in Appalachia. Though the folk arts are well represented here in the forms of beautiful pottery, baskets, weaving, and quilts, you'll also find the work of contemporary studio artists in an array of media, including gorgeous handcrafted furniture, clothing, jewelry, and toys. Bring your Christmas shopping list, even if it's April.

ENTERTAINMENT AND EVENTS

There is no shortage of live music venues here, and no shortage of great music. In this freakishly creative environment, there are so many bands, and they're so very good, that big-name out-of-town groups face stiff local competition for gigs. Everywhere you turn in this city, you'll stumble upon musicians—on street corners, in cafés, on front porches. There are also formal music venues where, on any given weekend and many weeknights, you can hear rock, bluegrass, Appalachian, "Afrolachian," blues, honky-tonk, country, and mountain swing.

◖ Bluegrass at the Fiddlin' Pig

The Fiddlin' Pig (28 Tunnel Rd., 828/251-1979, www.thefiddlinpig.com), a popular barbecue joint on U.S. 70, has live bluegrass music six

BABE RUTH IN ASHEVILLE

One day in 1925, the New York Yankees were on their way to Asheville to play an exhibition game at **McCormick Field** (30 Buchanan Pl., 828/258-0428). Babe Ruth was on the train, and he didn't feel well – a touch of flu, perhaps, or indigestion, but the bumpity rails of western North Carolina did him no good. Stepping off the train at Asheville, greeted by a rush of fans, he fainted and fell. Luckily, Ruth passed out next to the catcher, Steve O'Neill, who did his job and caught his bulky teammate before the famous mug hit the station's marble floor. Ruth was rushed off to the Battery Park Hotel, where apparently he made a full recovery. The newspapers failed to note that fact, though, and it was briefly reported that Ruth had died in Asheville – a story that caused no small consternation. All was well a few years later when, on April 8, 1931, Ruth returned to Asheville, and both he and Lou Gehrig hit homeruns here at McCormick Field. This august ground is now the home field of the **Asheville Tourists** (30 Buchanan Pl., 828/258-0428, www.theashevilletourists.com), the Class A farm team of the Colorado Rockies.

nights a week. The host bands, the Whitewater Bluegrass Company and Balsam Range, are all-star locals whose fame spreads far beyond Asheville. The Pig has a good small dance floor, shared by clogging teams and dancing customers. There's also a full bar, but the restaurant remains a very child-friendly environment.

Nightlife

A leading host of roots music is the **Grey Eagle Tavern and Music Hall** (185 Clingman Ave., 828/232-5800, www.thegreyeagle.com). A listening room–style venue rather than a bar or club—that is, folks come here when they want to hear music, not bar-hop—the Grey Eagle does provide good Louisiana-style eats at its **Twin Cousins Kitchen,** and plenty of good beers and wines. The **Orange Peel Social Aid and Pleasure Club** (101 Biltmore Ave., 828/225-5851, www.theorangepeel.net) is another fabulous nightspot. Billed as "the nation's premiere live music hall and concert venue," they can back up that claim by boasting of performances by Bob Dylan, Sonic Youth, Smashing Pumpkins, Blondie, and many other artists of that caliber—as well as some of the best up-and-coming acts from Asheville and the Southeast. There's a great dance floor and a cool bar.

Asheville is home to some excellent microbreweries, and to visit them in the company of enthusiastic experts, try the **Asheville Brews Cruise** (828/545-5181, www.brewscruise.com, $37/individual, $70/couple). Mark and Trish Lyons, founders of the Cruise, will take you all around town in the Brews Cruise van to sample some home-grown beers. You'll visit the **Asheville Pizza and Brewing Company** (675 Merrimon Ave., 828/254-1281, www.ashevillepizza.com), where you can start off the evening with one of this pizzeria/microbrewery/movie house's tasty IPA beers, and fortify yourself for the evening by filling up on good pizza. The **French Broad Brewing Company** (828/277-0222, www.frenchbroad brewery.com) is another popular local nightspot that's grown up around a first-rate beer-making operation, and here you can choose from a varied menu that includes signature pilsners, lagers, ales, and more, while listening to some good live music. The third destination on the Cruise is the **Highland Brewing Company** (12 Old Charlotte Highway, Suite H, 828/299-3370, www.highlandbrewing.com) Asheville's first microbrewery. They've been making beer and raking in awards for well over a decade, and on first sip you'll understand why they're one of the Southeast's favorite breweries.

Ballet

Asheville's noteworthy ballet company, **Terpsicorps** (2 South Pack Square, 828/257-5530,

ASHEVILLE

http://terpsicorps.org), performs for two brief but brilliant runs in the summer. Under the direction of North Carolinian dancer and choreographer Heather Malloy, Terpsicorps takes advantage of what is normally a slow season for other companies and hires some of the country's best dancers for a brief stint in Asheville. They have two productions each summer, and each usually has only a three-night run, so the tickets sell out fast.

Festivals

Twice yearly, in late July and late October, the Southern Highland Craft Guild hosts the **Craft Fair of the Southern Highlands** (Asheville Civic Center, www.southernhighlandguild.org, 10 A.M.–6 P.M. Thurs.–Sun., $6). Since 1948 this event has brought much-deserved attention to the Guild's more than 900 members, who live and work throughout the Appalachian Mountains. Hundreds of craftspeople participate in the Craft Fair, selling all sorts of gorgeous handmade items.

Asheville's **Mountain Dance and Folk Festival** (www.folkheritage.org, 828/257-4530, $20/day or $54/three days, $10/$24 for children under 12) is the nation's longest-running folk festival, an event founded in the 1920s by musician and folklorist Bascom Lamar Lunsford to celebrate the heritage of his native Carolina mountains. Musicians and dancers from western North Carolina perform at the downtown Diana Wortham Theater at Pack Place for three nights each summer. On Saturday nights at Martin Luther King, Jr., Park, also downtown, many of the same artists can be heard in the city's **Shindig on the Green** concert series.

In October, a series of creepy and offbeat happenings take place in the month-long festival called **Ashtoberfest** (www.myspace.com/horrordan). Among the events are a horror film festival, a summit of horror writers, and—the pinnacle of Ashtoberfest—the Zombie Walk. Ashevillians (and a surprising number of out-of-towners, from as far away as New York and Seattle) prepare for the Zombie Walk a month in advance by burying clothes in their yards. This way, when they dig them back up and don their zombie garb, they'll give off a properly fetid, sepulchral funk. On the appointed date, the zombies, in their grubby duds and nasty makeup, gather at a city cemetery, and all at once begin to lurch, in the top-heavy fashion of the zombies in *Night of the Living Dead,* in an undead shamble along the sidewalks of Asheville. The Zombie Walk ends as the ghouls gradually disappear into various pubs and parties downtown. Event dates and locations vary each year, so take a look at Ashtoberfest's MySpace pages for details.

SHOPPING
Antiques and Secondhand Goods

The best store in Asheville—of any kind—is the tiny curiosity shop **Not Your Average Antiques** (21 Page Ave., across from the Grove Arcade, 828/252-1333, www.notyouraverageantiques.com, hours vary). This fine retailer trades almost exclusively in items that were coveted by 10-year-old boys between the years 1900 and 1960, approximately. Included in this bounty: tin robots and spacemen, ray guns, magician and circus posters, carousel animals, and cowboy accoutrements. Interspersed is some wonderful Southern folk art, birds made by area woodcarvers, and pottery from all over the state. It's quite a shop. You probably didn't realize until now that you needed a wind-up Buck Rogers toy from the 1930s—but you do.

It's an unusual sort of a town that has both the supply and demand necessary for a business like **Second Gear** (415-A Haywood Rd., 828/258-0757, www.secondgearwnc.com, 10 A.M.–6 P.M. Mon.–Fri., 10 A.M.–5 P.M. Sat., closed Sun.). This consignment shop deals exclusively in secondhand outdoor equipment and clothes. It's a great place to find canoes and kayaks, tents, climbing gear, men's and women's outdoor clothing and shoes, and many other items at very low prices.

Galleries

One of Asheville's best places to shop is the 1929 **Grove Arcade** (1 Page Ave., 828/252-

7799, www.grovearcade.com). The expansive Tudor revival fortress, ornately filigreed all around, inside and out, in ivory-glazed terra-cotta, was originally meant to be the base of a 14-story building, a skyscraper for that time and place. As it is, the Grove Arcade is rather like an exposition hall at an early World's Fair. There are some great little galleries and boutiques here, including **Mountain Made** (828/350-0307, www.mtnmade.com, 10 A.M.–6 P.M. Mon.–Sat., and noon–5 P.M. Sun.) and the **Grove Arcade ARTS & Heritage Gallery** (828/255/0775, www.grovearcade.com, 10 A.M.–6 P.M. Mon.–Sat. and noon–5 P.M. Sun.), both galleries of local artists' work; **Asheville Home Crafts** (828/350-7556, www.ashevillehomecrafts.com, 10 A.M.–6 P.M. Mon.–Sat. and noon–6 P.M. Sun.), which sells handmade quilts, dolls, afghans, and knit garments; as well as several cafés and a chocolatier.

Books, Toys, and Crafts
One of the social hubs of this city is **Malaprop's Bookstore and Café** (55 Haywood St., 828/254-6734, www.malaprops.com, 8 A.M.–9 P.M. Mon.–Thurs., 8 A.M.–10 P.M. Fri. and Sat., 8 A.M.–7 P.M. Sun.). The very good bookstore—progressive, with a deep selection on many subjects and a particular interest in regional literature—is joined to the requisite coffee bar and wireless café. Malaprop's has, in addition to its appealing inventory, a great atmosphere for hanging out. It's bright and comfortable, and as you sip your strong coffee you can watch the Ashevillians stroll down Haywood Street. The variety of people who live here is striking, and among the young and artistic, there's a great deal of creativity invested in clothes, hairstyles, tattoos, and jewelry.

Dancing Bear Toys (144 Tunnel Rd., 800/659-8697, www.dancingbeartoys.com, 10 A.M.–7 P.M. Mon.–Sat., noon–5 P.M. Sun.) is located among the motels and chain restaurants out on U.S. 70 (Tunnel Road), but inside it has the ambience of a cozy village toyshop. Dancing Bear, which also has a location in Hendersonville, has toys for everyone from babies to silly grownups—a fabulous selection of Playmobil figures and accessories, Lego, Brio, and other favorite lines of European toys; beautiful stuffed animals of all sizes; all sorts of educational kits and games; and comical doodads that would be a welcome find in an adult's or a child's stocking.

There are a lot of bead shops in North Carolina, but my two favorites are Carrboro's Original Ornament, and Asheville's **Chevron Trading Post & Bead Company** (40 N. Lexington Ave., 828/236-2323, www.chevronbeads.com, 10 A.M.–6 P.M. Mon.–Sat.). The millions of beads, in bowls and tubes and strands on every surface in the shop, are so irresistibly twinkly and colorful that even if you're not crafty you'll want to buy them by the basket just to hoard like a magpie.

River Arts District
Along the Swannanoa River in Asheville, old warehouses and industrial buildings are gradually being reborn as studio space in an area that has come to be known as the River Arts District (www.riverartsdistrict.com). These are working studios, and as such, most are open to the public only sporadically. (Others do have regular shop hours.) Twice a year, however, they open for two days for the **Studio Stroll**, during the first weekends of June and November. The **240 Clingman and Odyssey studios** are housed in adjoining circa-1940 warehouses at 240 Clingman Road. Odyssey is full of sculptors—ceramic and mixed-media artists whose work runs more towards the figural than the functional—and other kinds of artists, too. At the 1910 **Cotton Mill**, at the corner of Riverside and West Haywood, several painters work alongside potters and even a flute maker. **Riverview Station**, a circa-1896 building at 191 Lyman, houses the studios of a wonderful array of jewelers, ceramicists, furniture designers, painters, and photographers. This is just a sampling of what's happening in the River Arts District. Visit the River Arts website for detailed listings of the artists and their studios.

ACCOMMODATIONS
Under $50

Bon Paul and Sharky's Hostel of Asheville (816 Haywood Rd., 828/350-9929, www.bon-paulandsharkys.com) is a pleasant old white house with a porch and porch swing, high-speed Internet access, and dorm-style bunks (in a shared room, women only or coed) for $22 per night. You can camp in the yard for $13, or rent the private room with a TV and queen-size bed for $65. Dogs must stay in the outdoor kennels. The hostel offers pick-up service for $8 from the bus station or $15 from the airport. Bon Paul and Sharky, by the way, were goldfish.

$50-150

The **Asheville ArtHaus Hostel** (16 Ravenscroft Dr., 828/225-3278, http://aahostel.com) is a private room-only hostel. The two-person rooms (one with a queen bed and one with two twins) are $50 per night, the three-person room (one queen and one twin) is $60, and the family room (one queen and two twins) is $70. Pets are not permitted. The website has a handy text-only page (linked from the main page) with walking directions and contact information for mobile browsers.

In the days before motels became the norm for budget lodging, the motor court or cottage court was a favorite overnight option for middle-class travelers. In perhaps the greatest road trip movie ever, *It Happened One Night,* unmarried, feuding Clark Gable and Claudette Colbert erect a "Wall of Jericho" between their beds—a rope and a blanket—to keep themselves in check while staying in a wonderful cottage court somewhere between Miami and New York. This style of lodging is almost a thing of the past, and the buildings themselves are disappearing steadily, but there are still some very cool examples scattered through the North Carolina mountains. At least two in the Asheville area are still in business and in good repair, providing today's travelers with charmingly retro accommodations. **Asheville Log Cabin Motor Court** (330 Weaverville Hwy., 828/645-6546, www.cabinlodging.com,

a classic motel sign in Asheville

© SARAH BRYAN

$55–250, two-night minimum stay, pets allowed with a fee) was constructed around 1930, and appears in the 1958 Robert Mitchum movie *Thunder Road*. The cabins have cable TV and wireless Internet access, but no phones. Some are air conditioned, but that's not usually a necessity at this elevation. Another great cabin court is the **Pines Cottages** (346 Weaverville Hwy., 888/818-6477, http://ashevillepines.com, $45–175 depending on season, up to two pets allowed with $15/pet fee). Billed as "A nice place for nice people," it's also a friendly place for pets.

$150 and Up

The **Grove Park Inn Resort & Spa** (290 Macon Ave., 800/438-5800, www.groveparkinn.com) is the sort of place that Asheville residents will bring their out-of-town houseguests when giving them a grand tour of the city, simply to walk into the lobby and ooh and ah. The massive stone building—constructed by a crew of 400 men who had only mule teams and a single steam shovel to aid them—was erected in 1912 and '13, the project of St. Louis millionaire E. W. Grove. Mr. E. W. was the Grove behind Grove's Tasteless Chill Tonic, a medicinal syrup that outsold Coca-Cola in the 1890s. You may have seen it in antique shops; on the label was a picture of a wincing baby, who looks more like he's just been given a dose of the tonic than that he needs one.

The opening of the Grove Park Inn was cause for such fanfare that William Jennings Bryan addressed the celebratory dinner party. In the coming years, at least eight U.S. presidents would be guests here, as would a glittering parade of early 20th-century big shots: Henry Ford, Thomas Edison, Eleanor Roosevelt, Harry Houdini, F. Scott Fitzgerald, Will Rogers, George Gershwin. Even if you don't stay at the Grove Park while you are visiting Asheville, swing by just to see it. You can drive right up to the front door, and if you tell the valets that you just want to nip in and see the lobby, they'll probably be willing to watch your car for five minutes. (Don't forget to tip.) The lobby is quite amazing, like a cross between a Gilded Age hunting lodge and the great hall of a medieval castle. There are 14-foot fireplaces at each end, and the elevators are, believe it or not, inside the chimneys. It's easy to imagine flappers and foreign dignitaries and mobsters and literati milling about the lobby with their martinis when this hotel was young.

Being a guest at the Grove Park is quite an experience. In addition to the spectacle of the lodge and its multiple restaurants, cafés, bars, and shops, guests have (for an additional charge) access to its world-famous spa. Day passes cost $55 for guests on weekdays, and $65 on weekends. Non-guests can purchase day passes Monday–Thursday. The pass gives access to the lounges, pools, waterfall, steam room, inhalation room, and outdoor whirlpool tub. The indoor pool is a truly nifty pirate's cove of a place, a subterranean stone room with vaulted skylights and tropical plants. For extra fees (ranging $75–500, with most around $200–300), guests can choose from a four-page menu of spa treatments: massage, facials, manicures, aromatherapy, body wraps, the works.

For $60, you can have your aura photographed before and after the treatment, to gauge the depth of your relaxation.

If you've spent the day touring Biltmore House, viewing the incredible splendor in which a baron of the Gilded Age basked, it may be jarring to return to real life unless you're Richard Branson or the Queen of England. But you can soften the transition with a stay at the luxurious **Inn on Biltmore Estate** (800/411-3812, www.biltmore.com, $189–479). It's everything you'd wish for from a hotel in this location. The suites are beautifully furnished, the view is magnificent, and the lobby and dining room and library have the deluxe coziness of a turn-of-the-century lodge. On the other hand, if you do happen to be Richard Branson or the Queen of England, and simply need a mountain getaway, consider the Inn's **Cottage on Biltmore Estate.** This historic two-room cottage was designed by Richard Howland Hunt, the son of the mansion's designer, Richard Morris Hunt. Your own personal butler and chef come with the digs. (Call to inquire about rates.)

FOOD
Eclectic American

Though only a few years old, **C Early Girl Eatery** (8 Wall St., 828/259-9292, www.early girleatery.com, 7:30 A.M.–3 P.M. Mon.–Fri., 5–9 P.M. Tues.–Thurs., 5–10 P.M. Sat. and Sun., brunch 9 A.M.–3 P.M. Sat. and Sun., $10–15) has caused a stir among area locavores. More than half of the vegetables, meat, and fish that go into Early Girl was raised or caught within 20 miles of the restaurant. The menu is very accommodating of Asheville's large vegetarian and vegan contingent, but non-veg diners can feast on pan-fried trout with green tomato–blackberry sauce, squash casserole, and hush puppies, or pan-seared duck with roasted shallots, sweet potato fritters, and sautéed greens—and many other delicious New Southern creations.

Say you've been at the Grey Eagle or the Orange Peel, and the show has just let out. It's the middle of the night. You and your friends are not ready for the night to end, but you've got to refuel with some good food in order to keep going. The lights are on at **Rosetta's Kitchen** (111 Broadway Ave., 828/232-0738, www.rosettaskitchen.com), and the stove is hot. There's so much to recommend this place. First off, the food is good. It's all vegetarian, mostly vegan, and made with local produce in season. It's open late on weekends, 10 P.M.–3 A.M. They compost every scrap of organic material that makes its way back to the kitchen, they recycle hundreds of pounds of trash, and make sure their used vegetable oil goes to power biodiesel cars. It's Asheville all over.

The **Laughing Seed** (40 Wall St., 828/252-3445, www.laughingseed.com, 11:30 A.M.–9 P.M. Mon., Wed., Thurs., 11:30 A.M.–10 P.M. Fri. and Sat., 10 A.M.–9 P.M. Sun., under $20) achieves what vegetarian restaurants always aim for, but are seldom able to achieve—their food is so good, and so widely praised, that a legion of non-vegetarians become loyal fans and customers. The restaurant describes its style as "international vegetarian cuisine," and it draws upon Latin American, Thai, Indian, and other cuisines of the world to create hearty and addictively flavorful dishes. The Laughing Seed also has a great cocktail menu, and local vegetarians will gladly compromise their principles just long enough to drink a Bloody Mary.

BILTMORE VILLAGE AND ESTATE

In one of the historic cottages of Biltmore Village is the **Corner Kitchen** (3 Boston Way, 828/274-2439, www.thecornerkitchen.com, breakfast 7:30 A.M.–11 A.M. Mon.–Sat., brunch 9 A.M.–3 P.M. Sun., lunch 11:30 A.M.–3 P.M. Mon.–Sat., supper at 5 P.M. daily). Head chef Joe Scully, first in his class at the Culinary Institute of America, counts among his illustrious former gigs the Waldorf Astoria and the United Nations (where he served as executive chef). He is joined in the Corner Kitchen by Josh Weeks, a young Carolina-born chef with an impressive resume and expertise in Southern, French, and Pacific cuisines. Chefs Joe and Josh have put together an elegant

menu that combines home-style and haute most harmoniously. It includes heavenly appetizers (most around $9) like almond-fried brie, served over a bed of greens (in the winter) with pear and apple conserve and a red-wine reduction; and entrées like the blackberry ketchup pork chop, which comes with sweet potatoes and fried green tomatoes ($21); and sweet potato salad with chow-chow (a Southern specialty relish) and a fried green tomato napoleon ($18). For lunch you can choose from a nice selection of classic sandwiches, or order the Ploughman's Lunch ($9)—a cup of soup, a small salad, two cheeses, and either country-style terrine or roasted portabella mushroom. Also tempting at lunch are the fried-oyster salad, apple-poached salmon, and sesame catfish ($9 and $10). The long wine list features many Napa Valley, French, and Italian wines, including several fine champagnes and sparkling whites and rosés. Prices range $9–120 by the bottle, and the wines under $20 per bottle are available for $6 by the glass. The cozy, cheerful dining room of this Victorian cottage opens into the kitchen, where guests can see every step of their meal's preparation while chatting with the staff.

There are no fewer than nine places to eat on the Biltmore Estate (800/411-3812, www.biltmore.com, estate admission required to visit restaurants). The **Dining Room** (5:30–9:30 P.M. daily, reservations required) is an elegant restaurant, led by Chef Richard Boyer, featuring Estate-raised Angus beef, mountain trout, and Biltmore wines. Evening dress and reservations are suggested. At the **Biltmore Bistro** (11 A.M.–9 P.M. daily), Chef Edwin French creates a fabulous gourmet menu from the Biltmore's own kitchen garden, locally raised heirloom crops, meat and seafood delicacies, and artisan cheeses and breads. The dining room of the **Deerpark Restaurant** (10 A.M.–3 P.M. Sat. and Sun. and 5–8 P.M. Fri. Jan. 2–Mar. 14, 11 A.M.–3 P.M. Mon.–Sat. and 10 A.M.–3 P.M. Sun. Mar. 15–Jan. 1, also offers buffet dinner from 5 P.M. Nov. 3–Jan. 1) is a former barn designed by architect Richard Morris Hunt, now renovated to an airy splendor with walls of windows. Here Chef Angela Guiffreda creates hearty and homey meals based on Appalachian cuisine. Like the Deerpark, the **Stable Café** (11 A.M.–4 P.M. daily for lunch and from 5 P.M. for dinner daily) is former livestock housing, and guests can sit in booths that were once horse stalls. This is a meat-eater's paradise, where you can order Estate-raised Angus beef, pork barbecue with Chef Don Spear's famous special sauce, and lots of other tasty dishes. The **Arbor Grill** (noon–7 P.M. Mon.–Thurs., noon–8 P.M. Fri. and Sat.) is an alfresco café next to the winery, featuring live music on weekends. In the stable area near the mansion, both the **Bake Shop** and **Ice Cream Café** serve fresh treats. The **Creamery Grill** is the place for sandwiches and hand-dipped ice cream, and the **Conservatory Café** will keep your children happy with hot dogs and soft drinks.

Indian

◖ Mela (70 Lexington Ave., 828/225-8880, www.melaasheville.com) is one of the best Indian restaurants in North Carolina. The elaborate menu offers dozens of choices, combining cuisines of both Northern and Southern India, with great meat, seafood, and vegetable dishes. The restaurant is dark and elegant, but the prices are surprisingly low. While the entrées are mostly in the $10–15 range, you can put together a great patchwork meal of appetizers, which start at $2, soup, and roti. Don't miss the samosas.

Latin American

Ask an Asheville resident for restaurant recommendations, and chances are **Salsa's** (6 Patton Ave., 828/252-9805, 11:30 A.M.–2:30 P.M. and 5:30–9 P.M. Mon.–Thurs., 11:30 A.M.–2:30 P.M. and 5:30–10 P.M. Fri., noon–3 P.M. and 5:30–10 P.M. Sat., noon–3 P.M. and 5:30–9 P.M. Sun., $10–20) will be one of the first names intoned. Salsa's pan-Latin concoctions, from their famous fish burritos to exquisite cocktails, keep this tiny little café jam-packed with locals and with visitors who drive to Asheville just for a special meal.

BLACK MOUNTAIN
Sights

Black Mountain is a beautiful little town, only a short ways from Asheville. Step into the **Swannanoa Valley Museum** (223 W. State St., 828/669-9566, www.swannanoavalley museum.org, 10 A.M.–5 P.M. Tues.–Sat., 2–5 P.M. Sun., free) to learn about the history of this area, from its prehistory, Cherokee settlement, and early industrialization, through the close of the all-important Beacon Blanket Factory, to today. Asheville is by no means the only interesting and significant part of Buncombe County; a lot has happened up in this neck of the woods too. While you're here, stop in next door at the **Black Mountain Center for the Arts** (225 W. State St., 828/669-0930, www.blackmountainarts .org, 10 A.M.–5 P.M. Mon.–Fri., 1–4 P.M. Sat.), to get a feel for what some of this region's many artists are up to.

Entertainment and Events

Twice yearly, in the spring and fall, Black Mountain is the scene of the **Lake Eden Arts Festival** (377 Lake Eden Rd., 828-686-8742, www.theleaf.com), better known as LEAF. Though based around the roots music of the world—and there are some amazing performers here every year—LEAF is also a festival of visual arts, poetry, food, and even the healing arts. It's an amazing scene, and it takes place, appropriately, at Camp Rockmont, which was once the campus of Black Mountain College.

Shopping

Black Mountain Books (103 Cherry St., 828/669-8149, 11 A.M.–5 P.M. Mon.–Sat., 11 A.M.–3 P.M. Sun.) specializes in rare and out-of-print titles, and is a great place to find unusual volumes on "North Carolina, Black Mountain College, the Southern Appalachians, Nature, Religion, [and] 18th- and 19th-century England and Scotland."

Down the road, stop in at **Chocolate Gems** (106 W. State St., 828/669-9105, www.chocgems .com) to see works of art of an entirely different flavor. This chocolatier makes all sorts of truffles and barks, and even chocolate sculptures, right on the premises.

Accommodations

The **Monte Vista Hotel** (308 W. State St., 888/804-8438, www.montevistahotel.com, $42–117, depending on season and day of the week) is a charming old hotel first opened in 1919. For such an appealing, historic inn, the prices are extremely affordable. The **Inn Around the Corner** (109 Church St., 800/393-6005, www.innaroundthecorner.com, no credit cards accepted) is a classic bed-and-breakfast in a lovely 1915 wooden house with a big front porch.

Food

Over on Church Street you'll find the **Black Mountain Bakery** (102 Church St., 828/669-1626, www.blackmountainbakery.com, 8 A.M.–4 P.M. Tues.–Sat.), a little café where you can order a quick soup and sandwich as well as a dessert or cookie for the road.

WEAVERVILLE
Shopping

There are a lot of great potters in western North Carolina, but Rob and Beth Mangum of **Mangum Pottery** (16 N. Main St., Weaverville, 828/645-4929, www.mangumpottery.com, 9 A.M.–5 P.M. Mon.–Fri., 10 A.M.–4 P.M. Sat.) are two of the most innovative. They make earthy-colored dinnerware and mugs (all beautiful) to satisfy the practical side of life, but then they build the most unexpected things out of pottery—ceramic clocks, ceramic furniture, ceramic musical instruments that really play—all in the most Dr. Seussian shapes and colors. If Salvador Dali and the Cat in the Hat were on vacation together in the mountains, Mangum Pottery would be their first stop, and even they would be knocked out by how cool this stuff is.

Food

A few doors down from Mangum Pottery, you'll find **Well Bred Bakery & Café** (26 N. Main St., Weaverville, 828/645-9300, www.well-bred bakery.com, 7 A.M.–8 P.M. Tues.–Thurs.,

7 A.M.–10 P.M. Fri., 8 A.M.–10 P.M. Sat., 8 A.M.–8 P.M. Sun.), which sells elegant soups, sandwiches, quiche, and salads, as well as a dazzling array of artisan breads and elaborate desserts. They promise "karma-free coffee" (I think that means fair-trade), and even sell the *New York Times*.

In a 1910 gristmill on Reems Creek, the **Weaverville Milling Company** (1 Old Mill Ln., Weaverville, 828/645-4700, www.weaver villemilling.com, 11:30 A.M.–3 P.M. and 5–9 P.M. Mon.–Sat., 10:30 A.M.–3 P.M. Sun.) has been a restaurant for more than 35 years. They specialize in filling comfort food—pork tenderloin with apple nut stuffing and plum sauce, beef stroganoff, pan-fried chicken livers. Favorite dishes sell out quickly, and lines can be long, so reservations are a good idea here.

MADISON COUNTY

North of Asheville, Madison County is a world unto itself, wild mountain terrain with a handful of small, peculiar towns whose reputation in the rest of the state is that of tough independence. Madison is revered by lovers of traditional balladry because a group of families—including Chandlers, Wallins, Nortons, and their kin—have committed to disc and tape over the course of the last half-century some of the finest and most powerful renditions of the ancient ballads brought to the mountains by its first English and Celtic settlers. These ballads are not archaic oddities here, survivals from an otherwise forgotten past, but are lovingly cared for and taught by family elders to their children and grandchildren. A new generation of singers is emerging today, with a core group of young women reared in the tradition who have inherited the remarkable voices, memories, and sense of stewardship for which their ancestors are honored.

Entertainment and Events

Mars Hill, a tiny college town, is a center of mountain culture thanks to Mars Hill College. The **Bascom Lamar Lunsford "Minstrel of the Appalachians" Festival** (usually early September, 828/689-1262, www.mhc.edu /regional/lunsford_festival.asp, $10 adults, $5 children) is a nearly half-century-old annual gathering of some of the best mountain musicians, dancers, and craftspeople from this hotbed of folk traditions. Mars Hill College is also the home of the **Southern Appalachian Repertory Theatre** (Owen Theatre, 44 College St., 828/689-1239, www.sartheatre.com), a highly regarded ensemble presenting a range of contemporary drama, musicals, and family productions. SART's stage is in the Owen Theater, a great-looking old Baptist Church on the Mars Hill campus.

Sports and Recreation

On a 4,700-foot mountaintop above Mars Hill, the **Wolf Ski Resort** (578 Valley View Circle, 800/817-4111, www.skiwolfridge.com) has more than 80 acres of prime skiing and snowboarding slopes. It is also the home of the Snow Sports School, which offers private and group lessons for all ages of beginning and intermediate winter sports enthusiasts. There are multiple lifts, two lodges for relaxing, and multiple hearty dining options. The attached **Scenic Wolf Resort** offers year-round cabin accommodations ($240–290), a huge indoor heated pool, and numerous recreational activities.

Sandy Bottom Trail Rides (1459 Caney Fork Rd., Marshall, 800/959-3513, www.sandybottomtrailrides.net, rides depart at 10 A.M., noon, 2 P.M., and 4 P.M.), based at a hundred-year-old family farm, leads horseback treks deep into the forest, on one- to four-hour expeditions to an early 19th-century garnet mine. They'll also carry you in style in a horse-drawn buggy, if you prefer.

There are plenty of whitewater rafting opportunities up here, and several guide companies to choose from. **Huck Finn River Adventures** (158 Bridge St., Hot Springs, 877/520-4658, www.huckfinnrafting.com) runs guided and unguided whitewater rafting and float trips and overnight paddles. **Rock 'N' Water** (60 Wolf Laurel Rd., Mars Hill, 828/689-3354, www.yearroundadventures.com) leads rafting, hiking, biking, and horseback expeditions into the mountains. **French Broad Rafting Expeditions** (U.S. 25/70, Marshall,

828/273-7238, www.frenchbroadrafting.com) can get you equipped and ready for a guided or unguided rafting trip on the French Broad River, which has both whitewater and calm sections to choose from.

Accommodations and Food

Defying that worn-out stereotype of mountain isolation, Madison County has for centuries been a destination for vacationers because of its natural hot springs. Going back at least to the mid-18th century—and, according to tradition, long before the first white settlers arrived—the springs have had a reputation for curative powers. A succession of grand hotels operated at Hot Springs, all long since burned down. In one of the area's odder historical moments, the resort served as an internment camp for German prisoners during World War I, mainly commercial sailors and members of an orchestra who had the misfortune of being in the United States when the war broke out. This in itself was not an uncommon arrangement, but the oddity of the camp at Hot Springs is that the prisoners constructed for themselves a miniature German village, an almost Disneyesque collection of tiny picturesque fachwerk cottages, alpine lodges, and rustic churches. The village is long gone, but you can see pictures of the internees' astonishing project at www.ibiblio.org/ww1gd/Index.html.

Modern visitors can still take the waters. **Hot Springs Resort and Spa** (U.S. 25/70 at the entrance to the town of Hot Springs, 828/622-7676, www.nchotsprings.com, suites $150–200, cabins $50–150, camping $50–60) is a much simpler affair than the old hotels here, not a luxury destination but a place where you can lodge or camp for the night and soak in the famous 100° water.

The **Mountain Magnolia Inn** (204 Lawson St., Mars Hill, 828/622-3543 or 800/914-9306, www.mountainmagnoliainn.com, $95–268) provides lodging in an ornate 1868 home and in nearby creekside cabins. The inn's dining room is a nice gourmet restaurant that features locally raised organic produce, meats, cheeses, and wines.

INFORMATION AND SERVICES

The **Asheville Visitors Center** (36 Montford Ave., Exit 4C off of I-240, 828/258-6129), can set you up with all the maps, brochures, and recommendations you could need. Other sources are www.exploreasheville.com and www.ashevillechamber.org.

Mission Hospital (509 Biltmore Ave. and 428 Biltmore Ave., 828/213-1948, 828/213-4063, www.missionhospitals.org) in Asheville has two campuses and two emergency departments.

GETTING THERE AND AROUND

Asheville lies spread-eagle at the crossroads of I-40, North Carolina's primary east–west highway, and I-26, a roughly north–south artery through the Southern highlands. Splitting the difference, U.S. 19 runs at a diagonal, deep into the Smokies in one direction and into the northern Blue Ridge in the other.

Asheville has an extensive public bus system, connecting most major points in the metropolitan area, including the airport, with downtown. Buses run 6 A.M.–11:30 P.M. Mon.–Sat, and cost $1 ($0.50 seniors). Visit www.ashevillenc.gov for routes and schedules.

Asheville Regional Airport (61 Terminal Dr., 828/684-2226, www.flyavl.com) is a bit of a jog from the city, located to the south in Fletcher. It's an easy 20-minute drive, though, connected by I-26.

Southern Blue Ridge and Foothills

The mountains of Polk, Rutherford, and Henderson Counties, south of Asheville, have an air of enchantment to them, by which I mean not that they are an enchanting place to visit—though they certainly are that—but rather that the area gives the impalpable sense of having had a spell cast on it. No doubt a parapsychologist could assign a name to this atmosphere; it has a weird energy, in which it seems as likely that one will encounter a fairy or spaceman as the mailman.

There are some quantifiable symptoms of this peculiarity. For one, Polk County has its own climate. Called the Thermal Belt, the meteorological pocket formed on this sheltered slope of the Blue Ridge has distinctly milder summers and winters than the surrounding areas. In the 19th century it became a favorite summering spot for the Charleston elite and other Southerners of the plantation class. Some pretty old houses and inns remain as vestiges of this genteel past.

In January 1874, Bald Mountain, which sits to the north of Chimney Rock, began to give off low rumbles. Its grumbling and groaning grew louder and louder until, by the spring of that year, the mountain shook with such force that windows and crockery in valley homes fell and shattered. A smoking, hissing crack opened in the side of the mountain, causing residents to fear a volcanic eruption. Many moved away or got baptized.

The shaking and rumbling eventually settled down. A crew of spelunkers a generation later concluded that the mountain was hollow, and that enormous boulders sometimes became dislodged in the belly of the mountain, showering onto the caves below and causing enormous, reverberating booms. Perhaps.

Chimney Rock itself was the scene of bizarre phenomena in the first decade or so of the 1800s. Locals and visitors began to report witnessing spectral gatherings, crowds of people gathered on top of the rock and rising together into the sky. In the fall of 1811, multiple witnesses saw, on different occasions, two armed cavalries mounted on winged horses battling in the air over Chimney Rock, their gleaming swords clashing audibly. Whichever phantom cavalry triumphed in that battle, the rock is now maintained by the state of North Carolina, and climbed daily by hundreds of tourists.

ASHEVILLE

BREVARD

Brevard is the pleasant seat of the improbably named Transylvania County. As you might expect, Halloween is a big deal in this town. Brevard is also known for sheltering a population of rather startling white squirrels. The local legend about their origin goes that their ancestors escaped from an overturned circus truck in Florida in 1940, and made their way to Brevard as pets. More likely, say researchers, is that they came from an exotic pet breeder in Florida, and were acquired by a Brevard area family that way. In any case, the white squirrels escaped into the wild of Transylvania County, and you'll probably see their descendants in the area when you visit.

Entertainment and Events

The **Brevard Music Center** (349 Andante Ln., 828/862-2105, www.brevardmusic.org) has attracted highest-caliber young musicians for more than 70 years for intensive summer-long classical music instruction. Throughout the summer, Brevard Music Center students, as well as visiting soloists of international fame, put on a world-class concert series in the summer, performing works from Tchaikovsky to Gilbert and Sullivan.

Shopping

A center for a very different sort of music is **Celestial Mountain Music** (16 W. Main St., 828/884-3575, www.celestialmtnmusic.com). This nice little shop carries, among the usual wares of a good music store, two lines of very special locally made instruments. Cedar Mountain Banjos, of the open-backed, old-time variety, are beautifully crafted and ring clear and pretty. The work of local fiddle builder Lyle Reedy is also sold at Celestial Mountain Music. His violins are handmade of a variety of fine woods and have a deep, biting sound loved by fiddlers. Musicians and woodworkers alike will enjoy a stop at this Main Street shop.

Sports and Recreation

About 10 miles south of Brevard, **Dupont State Forest** (U.S. 276, 828/877-6527,

© TIM PERRY

Looking Glass Rock, near Brevard

ASHEVILLE

www.dupontforest.com) has more than 90 miles of hiking trails covering 10,000 acres. Some of Transylvania County's beautiful waterfalls are located within the forest and accessible by foot (most trails in the forest are moderate or strenuous) or, with special permits and advance reservation for people with disabilities only, by vehicle. Visitors should use caution, wear brightly colored clothing, and leave their bearskin capes at home from September through the end of the year, when hikers share the woods with hunters.

PISGAH RANGER DISTRICT

Just to the north of Brevard in the town of Pisgah Forest is the main entrance to the Pisgah Ranger District (off U.S. 276, 828/877-3265, www.cs.unca.edu/nfsnc) of the Pisgah National Forest. The forest covers half a million acres, a large swath of western North Carolina, but this 157,000-acre ranger district encompasses many of the forest's favorite attractions. A good topographical map of the ranger district is available from National Geographic (Map 780, $9.95, sold at Cradle of Forestry store and online, www.cradleofforestry.com). In the ranger district are more than 275 miles of hiking trails and several campgrounds, the most easily accessible of which is **Davidson River Campground,** a mile and a half from the Brevard entrance ($10/night, year-round, 877/444-6777, www.recreation.gov, showers and toilets).

The Shining Rock Wilderness, and the Middle Prong Wilderness, which joins Shining Rock at the southwest, are a rugged terrain that rises from 3,200 feet at its lowest point, along the West Pigeon River, to a towering 6,400 feet at Richmond Balsam. Cold Mountain, made famous by the book and movie of the same name, is a real peak located within the Shining Rock Wilderness. These mountains are steep and the forests dense, and what trails there are have no signage. This is a popular area among experienced backwoods trekkers, but is not recommended for casual visiting as it is exceedingly easy to get lost here. It's recommended that, at a minimum, one should be adept at

Art Loeb Trail in Pisgah Ranger District

© JOHN RICHBURG

using both a compass and a topo map before venturing into these wilderness areas.

Not to be confused with Shining Rock, Sliding Rock is an easily accessible waterfall and swimming spot with a parking lot, bathhouse, and lifeguards between Memorial Day and Labor Day (on duty 10 A.M.–6 P.M.). You can actually ride down the 60-foot waterfall, a smooth rock face (not so smooth that you shouldn't wear sturdy britches) over which 11,000 gallons of water rush every minute into the chilly swimming hole below.

The **Cradle of Forestry** (U.S. 276, Pisgah Forest, 828/877-3130, www.cradleofforestry .com, 9 A.M.–5 P.M. mid-Apr.–early Nov., $5 adults, free for 15 and under) is a museum and activity complex commemorating the rise of the forestry profession in the United States, which originated here at a turn-of-the-century training school in the forests once owned by George Washington Vanderbilt, master of Biltmore. Plow days and living history days throughout the year give an interesting glimpse into this region's old-time methods of farming and frontier living. Self-guided trails lead through the woods to many interesting locations of this campus of America's first school of forestry.

HENDERSONVILLE

An easy drive from Asheville, Hendersonville is a comfortable small city with a walkable downtown filled with boutiques and cafés. It's also the heart of North Carolina's apple industry. Hundreds of orchards cover the hillsides of Henderson County, and all along the highway long packinghouses bustle in the late summer as they process more than three million tons of apples. There are also many shops and produce stands run by members of old orchard-owning families, where you can buy apples singly or by the bushel, along with cider, preserves, and many other apple products.

Sights

One of North Carolina's cool small transportation museums is located at the Hendersonville Airport. The **Western North Carolina Air Museum** (Hendersonville Airport, off of U.S. 176/Spartanburg Hwy., 828/698-2482, www.wncairmuseum.com, 10 A.M.–5 P.M. Sat., noon–5 P.M. Sun. and Wed. Apr.–Oct., noon–5 P.M. Sat., Sun., and Wed. Nov.–Mar., free) houses a collection of more than a dozen historic small aircraft, both originals and reproductions. Most are from the 1930s and 1940s, though some are even older, but they're all wonderfully fun contraptions to visit.

Shopping

Hendersonville's downtown **Curb Market** (221 N. Church St. at 2nd Ave., 828/692-8012, www.curbmarket.com, 8 A.M.–2 P.M. Tues., Thurs., and Sat. Apr.–Dec., 8 A.M.–2 P.M. Tues. and Sat. Jan.–Mar.) has been in operation since 1924. Here you can buy fresh, locally grown fruits, vegetables, and flowers; fresh-baked cakes, pies, and breads; jams, jellies, and pickles made in local home kitchens; and the work of local woodcarvers, weavers, and other craftspeople.

While in the Hendersonville area—or, for that matter, in any gourmet food store in North Carolina—keep an eye out for brightly colored, folk painting–adorned packages of **Immaculate Baking Company** (www .immaculatebaking.com) cookies. Besides making totally delicious cookies, this Hendersonville-based company helps support the work of visionary "outsider" artists throughout the South. They're "cookies with a cause."

FLAT ROCK
Sights

Just south of Hendersonville is the historic village of Flat Rock. Founded in the early 19th century as a vacation spot for the Charleston, South Carolina, plantation gentry, Flat Rock retains a delicate, cultured ambiance created so many years ago. Many artists and writers have lived in this area, most famously Carl Sandburg, whose house, Connemara, is preserved as the **Carl Sandburg Home National Historic Site** (81 Carl Sandburg Ln., Flat Rock, 828/693-4178, www.nps.gov/carl, 9 A.M.–5 P.M. daily, house

ASHEVILLE

tour $5 adults, $3 seniors ages 62 and over, free for under 16). Here Sandburg and his family lived for more than 20 years, during which time he wrote, won the Pulitzer Prize for "Complete Poems," and no doubt observed bemusedly as his wife and daughters raised champion dairy goats. (A herd of goats lives on the grounds today.) Half-hour tours take visitors through the house to see many of the Sandburgs' own belongings. There is a bookstore in the house, and more than five miles of trails through the property.

Entertainment and Events

Another literary landmark in the village is the **Flat Rock Playhouse** (2661 Greenville Hwy., Flat Rock, 866/732-8008, www.flatrockplay house.org). Now the state theater of North Carolina, the Flat Rock Playhouse's history dates to 1940, when a roving theater company called the Vagabonds wandered down from New York and converted an old gristmill here in the village into a stage. They returned every summer for the next few years, entertaining the locals with plays held in a succession of locations, from the old mill to a circus tent, eventually constructing their permanent theater. They now have a 10-month season, drawing more than 90,000 patrons yearly.

Shopping

You'll find quite a few nice galleries and studios in Flat Rock. One of the best is **Hand in Hand Gallery** (2720 Greenville Hwy., Flat Rock, 828/697-7719 or 877/697-7719, www.hand-inhandgallery.com, 10 A.M.–5 P.M. Mon.–Sat., 1–5 P.M. Sun. in the summer). The proprietors are ceramicist David Voorhees and jeweler Molly Sharp, whose exquisite porcelain and beautiful hand-wrought jewelry are sold here, alongside the work of more than 100 other artists from Flat Rock and nearby.

SALUDA AND VICINITY

Just east and south of Hendersonville, bordering South Carolina, Polk County is home to several interesting little towns, most notably Tryon and Saluda, and a lot of beautiful mountain countryside. In Saluda you'll find a tiny downtown, laid out along the old Norfolk Southern railroad tracks. The tracks at Saluda are the top of the steepest standard gauge mainline railroad grade in the United States. This county's history abounds with exciting stories of runaway trains that derailed at spots like the "Slaughterhouse Curve," and more than two dozen railroad men were killed on this grade.

Entertainment and Events

For one weekend every July, Saluda busts at the seams with visitors to the **Coon Dog Day Festival** (800/440-7848, www.saluda.com/events). Hundreds of beautifully trained dogs from all over the region come to town to show off in a parade and trials, while the humans have a street fair and 5K race.

Shopping

Six miles southeast of Columbus, potters Claude and Elaine Graves have been making distinctive pottery for 35 years at **Little Mountain Pottery** (6372 Peniel Rd., www.crowsounds.com). The Graves' work draws on North Carolina's folk traditions in ceramics, but it's quite different from much of the pottery made in this area in that it also draws inspiration from the ceramics of North Africa and the Canary Islands, and Spain and Mexico. The tones of Little Mountain's glazes reflect the many colors, by turns earthy and airy, of the North Carolina mountains. A showroom and sales shop is attached to the kiln, and the pottery is surprisingly affordable. Don't miss Claude's wonderful portraits of influential North Carolina potters, arranged in an outdoor gallery along the walls of his barns and kiln.

Sports and Recreation

The equestrian life plays a growing role in Polk and the surrounding counties of North Carolina's southern mountains. The **Foothills Equestrian Nature Center** (3381 Hunting Country Rd., Tryon, 828/859-9021, www.fence.org), known as FENCE, occupies 380 beautiful acres along the border with

South Carolina. The equestrian center has stables for 200 horses, and two lighted show rings. FENCE hosts cross-country, three-day, A-rated hunter/jumper, dressage, and many other equestrian events throughout the year. The annual Block House Steeplechase has been held in Tryon for 60 years, and FENCE has hosted the event for 20 of those years. FENCE also offers regular hikes and bird-watching excursions on its beautiful property.

Food

For such a tiny town, there are an awful lot of eating places in Saluda. Just stand in the middle of Main Street and look around; there are several choices, and you won't go wrong at any of them. The **Whistlestop Café** (173 Main St., 828/749-3310, 11 A.M.–5 P.M. Thurs.–Mon.) serves good hearty meals and strong coffee in its tiny dining room. The apple poundcake is perfect. **Wildflour Bakery** (173 E. Main, 828/749-9224, www.saluda.com/wildflour, 8 A.M.–3 P.M. Wed.–Sat., 10 A.M.–2 P.M. Sun.) stone grinds wheat every single morning, with which it makes absolutely delicious breads. Breakfast and lunch are served here, making this a great place to fill up before a day of kayaking or hiking.

CHIMNEY ROCK AND LAKE LURE
C Chimney Rock

Chimney Rock Park (Hwy. 64/74A, Chimney Rock, 800/277-9611, www.chimneyrock park.com, ticket plaza open 8:30 A.M.–4:30 P.M. or 8:30 A.M.–5:30 P.M. during daylight savings time, park is open an hour later, $14 adults, $6 ages 6–15) is home to some amazing rock formations. The star of the show, of course, is the Chimney Rock itself. Whether you climb the long series of steps to the top of this 315-foot tower of rock or take the elevator, you'll get there just the same, and the view is great. Also dazzling are the "Needle's Eye," the "Opera Box," and many more formations that visitors can explore.

The 400-foot **Hickory Nut Falls** can be reached by the Hickory Nut Falls trail, a fairly leisurely 0.75-mile walk. An easy walk for children, the 0.6-mile Woodland Walk is dotted with animal sculptures and "journal entries" by Grady the Groundhog. The Skyline-Cliff Trail Loop is a good deal more strenuous, but this two-hour hike will carry you to some spectacular sights. (You may also recognize it from the 1992 film *The Last of the Mohicans*.) Chimney Rock's website (www.chimneyrockpark.com) has a nifty interactive trail map that will show you the lay of the land.

Needless to say, Chimney Rock Park is a mighty desirable location for rock climbing. By all means, give it a go—but remember that in this park, you must arrange your climb with **Fox Mountain Guides** (www.foxmountain guides.com, 888/284-8433). They offer all sorts of instruction and guide services for climbers of all levels.

Sports and Recreation

Lake Lure, a 720-acre highland lake, was created in the 1920s. Several local outfitters will guide you on or get you all prepared for a day on the lake or on area rivers. For a relaxed sightseeing tour on the lake, try **Lake Lure Tours** (next to Lake Lure Town Marina, 828/625-0077, www.lakelure.com, 9 A.M.–6 P.M. daily, twilight cruises 6–9 P.M., dinner cruises 6 P.M. and 7 P.M., $10–40 adults, $6–16 under 12), which offers dinner and sunset cruises as well as daytime jaunts.

Accommodations

The 1927 **Lake Lure Inn and Spa** (2771 Memorial Hwy., 888/434-4870, www.lake lure.com, from $109) is a grand old hotel that was one of the fashionable Southern resorts in its day. Franklin Roosevelt and Calvin Coolidge stayed here, and so did F. Scott Fitzgerald. The lobby is full of strange antiques that are the picture of obsolete opulence—such as a Baccarat chandelier much older than the hotel and a collection of upright disc music boxes (up to eight feet tall) that were all the rage before the invention of the phonograph. The Lake Lure Inn has been restored beautifully and equipped with two restaurants, a bar, and a spa.

ASHEVILLE

HIGHLANDS AND VICINITY
Waterfalls

This country is blessed with some beautiful waterfalls, some of which are easily visited. **Whitewater Falls** (NC 281 on the state line, south of Highlands, $2/vehicle), at over 400 feet, is reported to be the highest waterfall east of the Rockies. An upper-level viewing spot is located at the end of a wheelchair-accessible paved trail, while a flight of more than 150 steps leads to the base of the falls. The falls are a fabulous sight, but remember to stay on the trails; several visitors have fallen to their deaths when they left the trail for a different perspective. A much smaller but still very beautiful waterfall is **Silver Run Falls** (NC 107, 4 miles south of Cashiers), reached by a roadside pull-off. **Bridal Veil Falls** (U.S. 64, 2.5 miles west of Highlands) flows over a little track of road, right off of U.S. 64. You'll see a sign from the main road where you can turn off and actually drive behind the waterfall, or park and walk behind it. Another falls that you can walk through is **Dry Falls** (U.S. 64, between Highlands and Franklin, $2/car), reached by a small trail off the highway, curving right into and behind the 75-foot waterfall.

Sports and Recreation

North Carolina's newest state park, **Gorges State Park** (NC 281 S., Sapphire, 828/966-9099, www.ncparks.gov/Visit/parks/gorg /main.php) is a lush mountain rainforest, receiving 80 inches of rain a year. The steep terrain rises 2,000 feet in four miles, creating a series of rocky waterfalls and challenging trails. The park is so new that facilities are still under development, but currently primitive camping is permitted for $9 per night in designated areas.

Accommodations and Food

The 3,500-foot-high town of Cashiers ("CASH-ers") is home to the **High Hampton Inn and Country Club** (1525 Hwy. 107 S., 800/334-2551, www.highhampton inn.com, from $100, three-night minimum), a popular resort for generations of North Carolinians. This was originally the home of Confederate General Wade Hampton, the dashing Charlestonian cavalryman. The lodge, a big old 1930s wooden chalet with huge, cozy fireplaces in the lobby, is surrounded by 1,400 acres of lakeside woodlands, with an 18-hole golf course, a good restaurant that serves buffet-style (dinner jacket requested in the evening), clay tennis courts, and a fitness center that features a climbing tower.

INFORMATION AND SERVICES

In addition to Asheville's **Mission Hospital** (509 Biltmore Ave. and 428 Biltmore Ave., 828/213-1948, 828/213-4063, www.mission hospitals.org), there are several regional hospitals with emergency or urgent care departments. **Park Ridge Hospital** (77 Airport Rd., Arden, 828/651-0098, www.parkridge hospital.org), located between Asheville and Hendersonville, has urgent care that is open 8 A.M.–7 P.M. Mon. –Fri. and 11 A.M.–6 P.M. Sat. and Sun. Hendersonville also has **Pardee Hospital** (800 N. Justice St., 828/696-4270, www.pardeehospital.org). In Brevard, the main hospital is **Transylvania Community Hospital** (90 Hospital Dr., Brevard, 828/883-5243, www.tchospital.org), and in Rutherfordton is **Rutherford Hospital** (288 S. Ridgecrest Ave., Rutherfordton, 828/286-5000, www.rutherford hosp.org).

Maps and guides are available at the **Hendersonville and Flat Rock Visitors Information Center** (201 S. Main St., Hendersonville, 800/828-4244, www.historic hendersonville.com), and at the **Transylvania County Tourism Development Authority** (35 W. Main St., Brevard, 800/648-4523, www.visitwaterfalls.com).

GETTING THERE AND AROUND

The Hendersonville/Brevard area is an easy drive from Asheville, with Hendersonville less than half an hour down I-26, and Brevard a short jog west from there on U.S. 64. **Asheville Regional Airport** (61 Terminal Dr., Fletcher, 828/684-2226, www.flyavl.com), south of Asheville, is very convenient to this region.

GREAT SMOKY MOUNTAINS

If you began your exploration of North Carolina on the Outer Banks and have experienced the diversity of life and environments encompassed within our state's vast wingspan, you now understand why the phrase "from Murphy to Manteo" is used here to signify an almost impossibly long journey, one that might as well be from the earth to the moon. Starting in Asheville, you can drive southwest for more than a hundred mountain miles, a journey of two or three hours, and still be in North Carolina. In fact, the town of Murphy, which snuggles in the toe of the state, is actually a few miles closer to Atlanta than it is to Asheville. There's a certain cultural kinship between residents of the deep mountains and the Outer Banks, born of the remoteness of their respective homes.

When the Olympic Park bomber, Eric Rudolph, was on the lam in the Smokies several years ago, there was a commonly held opinion among western North Carolinians that he would never be found. No doubt people watching the news from living rooms around the country were mystified that a man couldn't be tracked down in this relatively small geographical area, a few sparsely populated counties largely made up of federal lands. But after driving a little ways into the high country south and west of Asheville, one can easily imagine that hundreds of people could hide in this wilderness and that the outside world wouldn't notice so much as a rustling leaf.

In fact, exactly that occurred in the 1830s, though under very different circumstances, when President Van Buren gave the final

© JOE MILLER, ONEONTA, AL

GREAT SMOKY MOUNTAINS

HIGHLIGHTS

(**Cades Cove:** The most visited spot in the Great Smoky Mountains National Park is a formerly bustling mountain village that is witness to the depth of history in the Southern highlands (page 257).

(**Clingmans Dome:** From this third-highest peak in the eastern United States, set in a dramatic alpine environment, you'll find an astounding view of up to 100 miles on a clear day (page 258).

(**Museum of the Cherokee Indian:** The Cherokee people have lived in the Smoky Mountains for thousands of years, and this excellent museum tells unforgettable tales of their history (page 263).

(**Qualla Arts and Crafts Mutual:** Ancient craft traditions still thrive among Cherokee artists in western North Carolina, and at the Qualla Mutual, visitors to the tribal seat can learn about and purchase the work of today's masters (page 264).

(**Nantahala River Gorge:** So steep that in some places the water is only brushed by sunlight at high noon, this gorge is an unbeatable place for whitewater rafting (page 265).

(**John C. Campbell Folk School:** For nearly a century, the Folk School has been a leading light in promoting American craft heritage, nurturing new generations of artists, and securing the future of Appalachian artistic traditions (page 273).

LOOK FOR (TO FIND RECOMMENDED SIGHTS, ACTIVITIES, DINING, AND LODGING.

go-ahead to start the removal of the Cherokee people on the Trail of Tears. Several extended Cherokee families took to the deep mountains, and these resisters who refused to leave their homeland—choosing instead to brave months of living in fear, exposed to the elements—are the ancestors of many of today's Eastern Band of the Cherokee.

The ancient Cherokee culture has been rooted in the Smokies for thousands of years, from the early days described in tribal mythology, when the Ani-gituhwa-gi shared these mountains with witches and fairies, and birds and leeches as big as bears. The darkest hour came in the 19th century, when the tribe was rent apart by forced exile to Oklahoma. But between those who stayed and hid out in the mountains, and those who walked home from Okalahoma to rebuild their lives in the ancestral home, the Cherokee people regained strength—and today the seat of the Eastern Band is here in far western North Carolina on the tribal land known as the Qualla Boundary.

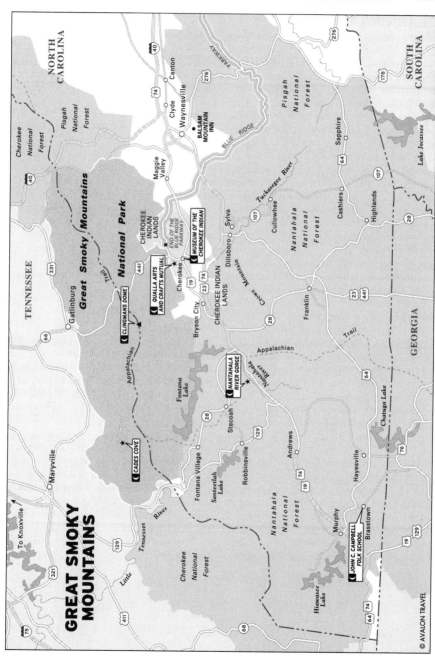

© AVALON TRAVEL

PLANNING YOUR TIME

Many people plan their visits to the Smokies to coincide with what's blooming or blazing on the mountainsides. Spring wildflowers begin to bloom in late March, and peak in mid- to late April. Azalea, mountain laurel, and rhododendron are the showiest blooms of the summer, and they begin to bloom at the lower elevations first, of course, and then high up in the mountains. Flame azalea peaks in different areas between April and July, mountain laurel in May and June, and rhododendron in June and July. The fall colors appear in the opposite sequence, appearing first at the peaks in early October, and gradually moving down the mountains until, in mid- to late October and early November, trees in the lower elevations change. Factors including summer heat and rainfall, or lack thereof, can throw these schedules off a bit, but if you call Great Smoky Mountains National Park or check regional websites, you can find out how the season is progressing.

The Newfound Gap Road bisects the national park across the middle, from Cherokee in the southeast, where it meets the southern end of the Blue Ridge Parkway, to Gatlinburg at the northwest. For a brief visit to the park, Gatlinburg is the entry point that gives easiest access to short loop roads. For a longer visit, Gatlinburg and Cherokee are good places to find a motel, and the Elkmont and Smokemont campsites are centrally located frontcountry camping areas, where you can sleep in the woods but have your car with you for daytime driving. While you can certainly cross the park in an afternoon and see some sights, the more time you can devote to your visit the better. Many visitors spend a week or more at a time in the Great Smoky Mountain National Park. Campground stays are limited to one week at a time May 15–October 31, and two weeks November 1–May 14.

INFORMATION AND SERVICES

The national park's official website is www.nps.gov/grsm. Much tourist information can be found to help you plan your trip at the websites of Smoky Mountain Host (www.visit smokies.org) and the Blue Ridge National Heritage Area (www.blueridgeheritage.com). Detailed touring suggestions for sites associated with Cherokee history and heritage can be found at the websites of Cherokee Heritage Trails (www.cherokeeheritagetrails.org) and the North Carolina Folklife Institute (www.ncfolk.org), and in *Cherokee Heritage Trails,* an excellent guidebook that can be purchased at either website.

Area hospitals include those in Bryson City, Sylva, and Clyde, as well as a little farther afield in Asheville and in Knoxville and Maryville, Tennessee.

GETTING THERE AND AROUND

The closest commercial airports to the Smokies are **Asheville Regional Airport** (61 Terminal Dr., 828/684-2226, www.flyavl.com) in Fletcher, and the **Gatlinburg-Pigeon Forge Airport** (1255 Airport Rd., Sevierville, 865/453-6136) over the state line in Tennessee. Amtrak doesn't run anywhere in this area, but the closest stations, both hours away, are in Gastonia, near Charlotte, and in Spartanburg, South Carolina. Unless you're hiking through on the Appalachian Trail, the best way to get around the Smokies is by car. U.S. 19 and 23 stretch down from Asheville to the Georgia line, while U.S. 64, which literally stretches from Murphy to Manteo, snakes along the southern edge of the Smokies. Cresting the northern edge is I-40, running between Asheville and Knoxville.

Great Smoky Mountains National Park

An environment like no other, the Great Smoky Mountains National Park (GSMNP) comprises over 800 square miles of high, cloud-ringed peaks and genuine rainforests. Tens of thousands of species of plants and animals live in the national park—80 different kinds of reptiles and amphibians alone (the park is sometimes called the Salamander Capital of the World), 200 species of birds, and more than 50 mammals, from mice to mountain lions. The organization Discover Life in America (www.dlia.org) has for several years been conducting an All Taxa Biodiversity Inventory—that is, a census of all non-microbial life forms—in the GSMNP, and as of August 2007, had discovered nearly 900 species of plants and animals hitherto unknown to science. The deep wilderness of the Great Smoky Mountains National Park is also a wonderful refuge for today's outdoors enthusiast, while the easy accessibility of ravishing scenery makes this the most visited national park in the United States.

© JOE MILLER, ONEONTA, AL

Roaring Fork near Gatlinburg

VISITING THE PARK
Weather Considerations

To get a sense of the variability of the weather in the GSMNP, keep in mind that elevation here ranges from under 1,000 feet to over 6,600. A low-lying area like that around Gatlinburg, Tennessee, is not a whole lot cooler than Raleigh in the summertime, with an average high of 88°F in July. For only three months of the year (Dec.–Feb.) does Gatlinburg have average lows under freezing, and then only by a few degrees. The opposite extreme is illustrated by Clingmans Dome, the highest elevation in the park. There the average high temperature is only 65°F in July—and only in June, July, and August can you be sure that it won't snow. If ever there were a place for layered clothing, this is it. No matter what season the calendar tells you it is, be on the safe side and pack clothing for the other three as well. Keep these extremes in mind, too, in terms of safety; a snowstorm can bring two feet of snow to high elevations,

and it's not at all unusual that the weather will be balmy at the foot of the mountain and icy at the top. At times, the temperature here has fallen to -20°F. Roads can be closed in the winter if the weather gets bad or restricted to vehicles with snow chains or four-wheel drive. Drive super-slowly when it's icy. Leave plenty of room between yourself and the next car, and shift to a lower gear when going down slippery slopes. You can find out current conditions by calling 865/436-1200, extension 630.

Seasonal Considerations

The most crowded times in the park are from mid-June to mid-August, and all of October. Traffic is most likely to be heavy on the Cades Cove Loop Road and Newfound Gap Road. Several roads in the park are closed in the wintertime, though the dates vary. Among these are Balsam Mountain, Clingmans Dome, Little

GREAT SMOKY MOUNTAINS

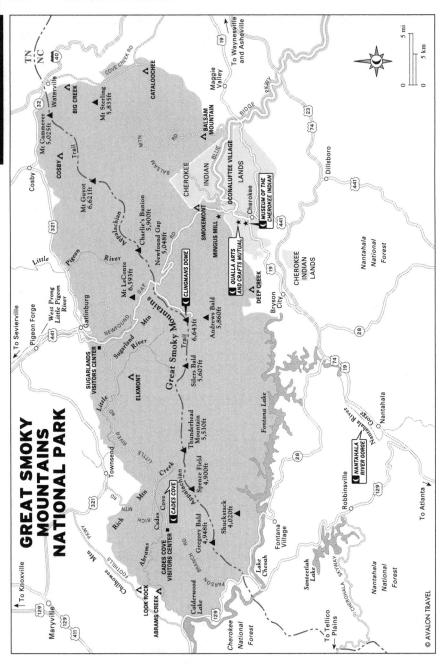

© AVALON TRAVEL

Greenbrier, Rich Mountain, and Round Bottom Roads, and Roaring Fork Motor Nature Trail.

Safety

Sometimes even the most experienced outdoorsmen and women have emergencies. Whether going into the backcountry by yourself or with others, make sure that someone you trust knows where you're going, what your likely route is, and when to expect you back. The Park Service recommends leaving this number with someone at home, to call if you're not back when expected: 865/436-1230.

Some of the basic safety rules may seem obvious, but it's good to review them. Climbing on rocks and waterfalls is always dangerous, and crossing a deep or flooded stream can be treacherous as well. If you have to cross a stream that's more than ankle-deep, it's recommended that you unbuckle the waist strap on your backpack (so you don't get pinned underwater if you fall), that you use a hiking stick to steady yourself, and that you wear non-slippery shoes.

Cold is a concern, even in the summer. Wear layers, pack additional warm duds (warmer than you think you'll need), and try to stay dry. It may be shorts-and-t-shirt weather when you set out, but even in the summer it can be very cold here at night. Plan well, double-check before setting out that you have everything you could possibly need on your trek, and, says the Park Service, "eat before you're hungry and rest before you're tired." Water from streams must be boiled or filtered before it's potable.

Wildlife can pose hazards here. Despite assurances to the contrary, there are still panthers (mountain lions) in these mountains. Ignore what the officials say in this (and only this) regard; locals see and hear them throughout Appalachia. But panthers are rare and reclusive, as are coyotes, wild hogs, and other resident tough-guys.

On a very grim note, in recent years there was a series of terrible murders of hikers in the highlands of North Carolina and Georgia. The apparent perpetrator of some, and possibly all, of the cases is behind bars. It bears remembering, though, that one is very vulnerable out

in the woods. You might know how to protect yourself from wild animals and the elements, but sometimes the greatest danger is other people. It's always better to hike or camp with at least one companion. A sturdy walking stick can be a lifesaver, and pepper spray, readily available and cheap in many different kinds of stores, should always be within easy reach when you're in the woods.

Permits and Regulations

Permits are required for camping in the national park, but are quite easy to obtain. You can register at any of the more than a dozen visitors centers and ranger stations. This must be done in person, though, not online or over the phone. Fishing requires permits as well, which can be bought at outfitters and bait shops in nearby towns. Strict rules governing how, when, where, and what one can fish also apply, and can be read on the park website. Other rules apply to interaction with wildlife. Don't feed animals, and make sure to seal up your foodstuffs to discourage night visitors. Firearms are forbidden in the park as, of course, is hunting.

Your dog is welcome in the park, but only in certain areas. To prevent transmission of diseases to or from the wildlife, and to avoid disrupting or frightening the resident fauna, as well as for their own safety, dogs are not permitted on hiking trails. They are, however, allowed to accompany you at campgrounds and picnic sites.

WILDLIFE IN THE PARK

The largest animals in the park are also the most recently arrived. In the spring of 2001, the National Park Service experimentally reintroduced **elk** to the Great Smoky Mountains, a species that used to live here but was hunted to regional extinction in the 18th century. In the years since their re-introduction to the park, the herd has reproduced steadily, boding well for a successful future. If you hear a strange bellowing in the early autumn, it may be a male elk showing off for his beloved. One of the best places to see the elk is in the Cataloochee

ruffed grouse on the Blue Ridge Parkway

Valley, particularly in fields at dawn and dusk. Be sure to keep your distance; these animals can weigh up to 700 pounds, and the males have some formidable headgear.

An estimated 1,600 **black bears** live in the GSMNP—two per square mile—so it's quite possible that you'll encounter one. Though they are a wonder to see, bears, which in this park weigh 100–400 pounds as adults, do pose a real risk to humans—and we to them—so it's important to be very aware of how we interact with them. It is illegal to come within 50 yards (150 feet) of a bear or elk, and those who knowingly get closer can be arrested. It sounds like a cliché, but the recommended procedure is this: If you see a bear, back away slowly. The Park Service recommends that if the bear follows, you should stand your ground. If he keeps coming towards you persistently and looks menacing (and how could a bear persistently coming towards you not look menacing?), make yourself big and scary. Stand on a rock to look taller, or close to anyone else present, to show the bear that he's outnumbered. If he keeps coming closer, make a lot of noise and chuck things at him. (Rocks or sticks, that is; a bag of marshmallows or the fish you were just grilling would scarcely be deterrents.) Should a bear actually attack you, the Park Service recommends that you "fight back aggressively with any available object."

The best course of action is simply to avoid them and hope that any sightings you have will be from a safe distance. When camping, lock your food in the trunk of your car, if possible—or hoist it into a tree too high off the ground for a bear to reach it on his hind legs, and at a long enough length of rope from the nearest branch that one can't reach it by climbing the tree. Bears may approach in picnic areas. For goodness sake, don't feed them, no matter how winsome they look! "Habitual panhandler bears" (this is a real term) have been proven to die sooner than those afraid of humans, as they are more likely to be hit by cars, swallow indigestible food packaging, become easy targets for hunters, or even, if they are too problematic, be captured and euthanized.

Bears are hardly the only huge, ferocious animals in the park. Believe it or not, there are hundreds of snorting, tusky **wild hogs** here, descendants of a herd that escaped from a hunting preserve in Murphy in the 1910s. There are **coyotes, wolves,** and **bobcats,** and, though extremely rare, there are **mountain lions** (often called panthers or painters in this region) as well.

Of the many natural miracles in this park, one of the most astonishing is the light show put on for a couple of weeks each year by synchronous **fireflies.** Of the park's 14 species of fireflies, only one, the *Photinus carolinus,* flashes in this manner. While the average back yard's worth of fireflies twinkles like Christmas lights, synchronous fireflies, as their name implies, are capable of flashing in unison, by the hundreds or thousands. The sight is so amazing that, during the peak flashing period (usually in June), the park organizes nighttime expeditions to the best viewing spots.

If you go hiking in the backcountry, you might well see a **snake.** It's unlikely that you'll encounter a poisonous one, as there are only two kinds of vipers here—rattlesnakes and copperheads—that pose a danger to humans. There has never been a death from snakebite in the park, as far as anyone knows, but to be on the safe side, please watch where you step or put your hands; it wouldn't do to be first on that list. But snakes are shy souls, so don't worry overmuch.

SIGHTS
Mountain Farm Museum
The area that is now the Great Smoky Mountains National Park was once dotted with towns and farms, communities that were displaced by the federal government for the establishment of the park. The Mountain Farm Museum (U.S. 441, 2 miles north of Cherokee, 828/497-1900), next to the Oconaluftee Visitors Center, re-creates a mountain fastness of the late 19th and early 20th century. On the site of what was the Enloe family's farm, on the banks of the Oconaluftee River, a collection of historic buildings are preserved, some original to the site and others moved from elsewhere in the

Smokies. The Davis House, a circa-1900 log house, is remarkable in that it is constructed from enormous chestnut timbers, a wood not available in this region for several generations (since the chestnut blight of the 1930s). A large cantilevered barn is constructed to allow wagons to be driven straight through, with stalls and haylofts to the sides. A variety of other dependencies—a meathouse, chicken house, apple house, corncrib, gear shed, blacksmith shop, and springhouse—give a notion of what a plethora of homesteading skills were necessary for a mountain farm like this to prosper. Demonstrations are held here throughout the year, as well as two festivals, one a harvest festival and the other a commemoration of women's work in mountain farm life.

🄲 Cades Cove
On the Tennessee side of the park, an 11-mile, one-way loop road traverses Cades Cove, a historic settlement dating to the late 18th century. Originally part of the Cherokee Nation, the land was ceded to the United States in 1819. The population grew throughout the 19th century until it was a busy town of several hundred souls. The village is preserved today as it appeared around 1900, with homes, churches, barns, and a working gristmill, but minus the people—a mountain counterpart to Cape Lookout National Seashore's Portsmouth Village. Because of the cove's scenic beauty and abundance of wildlife, this is the most popular part of the nation's most visited national park. The loop road through Cades Cove takes about an hour to drive when visitors are sparse. On crowded days—in the peak summer and fall seasons, and most weekends—it can take several hours to cover the 11 miles.

The **Cades Cove Visitors Center** (9 A.M.–4:30 P.M. Dec. and Jan., 9 A.M.–5 P.M. Feb. and Nov., 9 A.M.–6 P.M. Mar., Sept. and Oct., and 9 A.M.–7 P.M. Apr.–Aug.) is located at about the halfway point on the Cades Cove Loop. It has a bookstore, exhibits on Southern mountain culture, and seasonal ranger programs. At the southwestern side of the park, Cades Cove is most easily reached from the

© JOE MILLER, ONEONTA, AL

Gregg-Cable House at Cades Cove

Laurel Creek Road inside the park, which links up to Route 73 near Townsend, Tennessee. Cades Cove Loop road begins and ends at Laurel Creek Road, but there are two outlets towards the western end—Forge Creek Road and Rich Mountain Road—which both lead out of the park, one-way, and are closed in wintertime.

Cataloochee

Cataloochee in North Carolina was an even larger village than Cades Cove. Several important historic buildings from this extremely remote apple-growing town are standing and can be toured, including Palmer Chapel, the settlement's only church house, which was served by once-monthly visits by circuit riding Methodist preachers. Cataloochee is also a prime spot for watching the park's elk, reintroduced in 2001 and prospering. Look for them in the open fields around sunrise and twilight. The Cataloochee area is at the far northeastern edge of the park, and a reasonably direct drive from I-40 via the Cove Creek Road. The

Park Service recommends a more adventurous route as well for those with plenty of time and immunity to car sickness (it's a twisty road): Route 32 from Cosby, Tennessee. Whichever way you go, part of the route will be on a gravel road. The park sells an auto tour booklet at the visitors centers, which will help guide you through Cataloochee. Several houses, a school, churches, and barns are open to the public.

◖ Clingmans Dome

At 6,643 feet, Clingmans Dome is the third-highest mountain in the eastern United States, and the highest in the Great Smoky Mountains. A flying saucer–like observation tower at the end of a long, steep walkway, gives 360-degree views of the surrounding mountains, and on a clear day, that view can be as far as a hundred miles. More often, though, it's misty up here in the clouds, and Clingmans Dome receives so much precipitation that its woods are actually a coniferous rainforest. The road to the summit is closed December 1–March 31, but the observation tower remains open for those willing to make the hike. To get to Clingmans Dome, turn off Newfound Gap Road 0.1 mile south of Newfound Gap, and then take Clingmans Dome Road (closed in the winter), which leads seven miles to the parking lot. The peak is right near the center of the park, due north as the crow flies (though not directly accessible) from Bryson City.

Fontana Dam

At the southeastern edge of the park, Fontana Dam, 11,000 acres of water, is an artificial impoundment of the Little Tennessee River. This largest dam east of the Rockies was built in the 1940s, a stupendous wall of concrete the height of a 50-story skyscraper. It caused the river to flood back through little mountain towns, vestiges of which can be seen every five years when the water level is lowered for dam inspection. The **visitors center** (Hwy. 28, Fontana Dam, 828/498-2234 or 800/467-1388, 9 A.M.–7 P.M. May–Nov., free) is well worth a visit, and the Appalachian Trail goes right along the top of the dam.

SPORTS AND RECREATION

The Great Smoky Mountains National Park covers over half a million acres, and within that expanse are more than 800 miles of hiking trails, ranging from easy walks around major attractions to strenuous wilderness paths suited to the most experienced backpackers. A section of the Appalachian Trail goes through the park, crossing the Fontana Dam. There are dozens of books available about hiking in the Smokies, available at bookstores and outfitters throughout the region, as well as online. The park staffs a **Backcountry Information Office** (865/436-1297, every morning 9 A.M.–noon), and the knowledgeable folks who work there are a good first resource when planning a hiking trip. The park website (www.nps.gov/grsm) has some downloadable maps to give you a general sense of the lay of the land. The Great Smoky Mountains Association website (www.smokiesinformation.org) has a good online bookstore where you can find many books about hiking in the park.

Hiking to Waterfalls

As if the mountains and valleys, flora and fauna, and close-enough-to-touch clouds weren't wonder enough, the GSMNP has literally hundreds of waterfalls. Several of the most popular and most beautiful are accessible from major trails.

Close to Bryson City, 25-foot **Indian Creek Falls** is a moderately difficult hike of less than two miles round-trip, and it's a two-for-one deal, as the path also goes by Tom Branch Falls. Crossing Deep Creek on bridges and logs and going by old homesites, this is an especially interesting hike. The Deep Creek/Indian Creek Trailhead is at the end of Deep Creek Road in Bryson City. It gets very crowded in nice weather, particularly because this is a popular area for tubing, and this makes parking quite difficult. Restrooms are available at the picnic area. Also accessible from the Indian Creek Trailhead is the path to 90-foot **Juney Whank Falls.** The hike to Juney Whank Falls is shorter but more difficult than that to Indian Creek Falls. Since it shares the same trailhead, you can expect to find the same crowds and parking difficulties as for the trail to Indian Creek Falls.

Mingo Falls, a beautiful 120-foot plume, is just outside the park, on the Qualla Boundary (Cherokee tribal land). It can be seen from the Pigeon Creek Trail, which begins in the Mingo Falls Campground, off of Big Cove Road south of Cherokee. The hike is very short, less than half a mile round-trip, but is fairly strenuous.

Some longer hikes on the Tennessee side of the line lead to equally beautiful falls. **Rainbow Falls** is 80 feet high, and is as much a cloud of mist—so much so that, when the sun hits it just right, you can see a rainbow—as it is a cataract. In the winter, it sometimes freezes solid—an amazing sight. The Rainbow Falls Trail near Gatlinburg is difficult, and is almost 5.5 miles round-trip. It ascends about 1,500 feet, and is very rocky most of the way, but it gives some great views, both of the falls and of Gatlinburg. Parking is available on Cherokee Orchard Road in Gatlinburg, but it fills up pretty quickly, and you may need to pay to park a little farther from the trailhead.

The tallest waterfall, 100-foot **Ramsey Cascades,** is also the most difficult to reach. Those able to make a strenuous eight-mile round-trip hike are richly rewarded with a journey through old-growth hardwood forests and along fast-moving rivers. The pool at the bottom of the falls is a great place to glimpse some of the creatures that make GSMNP the "Salamander Capital of the World."

It is never safe to climb on waterfalls, and quite a few people in the park have died trying, so please admire cascading water from the trails. This is a particularly important warning on this trail, because numerous hikers have died falling from the ledges around Ramsey Cascades. The parking area for the Ramsey Cascades Trail is off of Greenbrier Road, a few miles southeast of Gatlinburg. The nearest port-a-johns are at the picnic area on Greenbrier Road.

Maps and guides to the waterfalls are available at many locations in the park.

Horseback Riding

Three commercial stables in the park offer "rental" horses on a by-the-hour basis (average $20/hour). Smokemont is located in North Carolina near Cherokee (828/497-2373). Two are in Tennessee: Smoky Mountain (865/436-5634, www.smokymountainridingstables.com) and at Cades Cove (10018 Campground Dr., Townsend, 865/448-6286, http://discovercadescove.com/_horsbac/cchrofs.htm).

Bike Rentals

The Cades Cove store (near Cades Cove Campground, 865/448-9034) rents bicycles in the summer and fall. From the second week in May to the second-to-last Saturday in September, the park closes off the loop road through Caves Cove on Wednesday and Saturday mornings, from sun-up until 10 A.M., so that bikers and hikers can enjoy the cove without having to worry about vehicular traffic.

Field Schools

Two Tennessee-based organizations affiliated with the GSMNP offer ways to get to know the park even better. The **Smoky Mountain Field School** (www.ce.utk.edu/Smoky/, registration through the University of Tennessee-Knoxville) teaches workshops and leads excursions to educate participants in a wide array of fields related to the Smokies. One-day classes focus on the history and cultural heritage of the park, the lives of some of the park's most interesting animals, folk medicine and cooking of the southern Appalachians, and much more. Instructors also lead one-day and overnight hikes into the heart of the park.

The **Great Smoky Mountains Institute at Tremont** (9275 Tremont Road, Townsend, TN, 865/448-6709, www.gsmit.org) teaches students of all ages about the ecology of the region, wilderness rescue and survival skills, and even nature photography. Many of the classes and guided trips are part of Elderhostels, kids' camps, or teacher training institutes; however, there are also rich opportunities for unaffiliated learners.

ACCOMMODATIONS

There is only one inn in the entire half-million acre park, and it's a highly unusual one. **LeConte Lodge** (865/429-5704, www.lecontelodge.com, cabin beds $64/night adults, $53 children, lodges $512–768/night, meals $33 adults, $23.50 children, cash or check only, no pets), built in the 1920s, is at an elevation of nearly 6,600 feet, and is accessible only on foot after a hike of several hours. The lodge is supplied by thrice-weekly llama train. There are flush toilets, but no showers. Nor is there electricity at the lodge, and though kerosene heaters will keep you toasty at night, remember that even in the summertime, temperatures can fall into the 30s at night. It's an amazing place, and enough people are willing and able to make the necessary trek to stay here that reservations are often required very far in advance.

Luckily for those who don't wish to camp or to hike to a rustic lodge, there are countless motels just outside the GSMNP. Reservations are always a good idea, especially in the summer and in leaf season, but you'll not want for choices in Cherokee, Maggie Valley, Bryson City, Pigeon Forge, Gatlinburg, Sevierville, and other neighboring communities. In addition to the many chain motels, affordable mom-and-pop motels also dot this landscape in abundance. Two homey choices in Gatlinburg are the **River House Motor Lodge** (610 River Rd., Gatlinburg, 865/436-7821, www.riverhouse motels.com, from $120 in season, from $59 out of season), and **Johnson's Inn** (242 Bishop Ln., Gatlinburg, 800/842-1930, www.johnsonsinn.com, $49–104 depending on season).

Camping

The GSMNP has many locations for camping, fees for which range $14–23 per night. Campers can stay up to three nights at campsites, but only one night at a time in shelters. There are 10 frontcountry (car-accessible) campgrounds, each of which has cold running water and flush toilets in the bathrooms, but no showers or power and water hookups. Most of these sites are first-come-first-served, but between May 15 and October 15, sites at the Elkmont, Smokemont, Cades Cove, and Cosby campgrounds can be reserved online or by calling 877/444-6777.

The highest campground in the park, Balsam Mountain Campground, sits at a lofty 5,300 feet, and is a short drive from the terminus of the Blue Ridge Parkway. It's open only mid-May through late September, and is less likely to be crowded than many of the other campgrounds here. Another particularly nice site is the Big Creek Campground, at the northeastern corner of the park near I-40. This walk-in, tenting-only campsite features the beautifully soporific sound of rushing water from the nearby creek. If you plan to do any boating on Fontana Lake, Cable Cove Campground, a half-mile from a boat ramp, is a nice, quiet option.

Backcountry camping is abundant. It is only permitted at designated sites and shelters, and a permit is required, but the permits are free and can be obtained at any of 15 different visitor centers and campground offices throughout the park. There are also five drive-in horse camps ($20–25/night) and seven group campgrounds ($35–65/night). A map of the available campsites is downloadable at www.nps.gov/grsm/planyourvisit. Before camping at the GSMNP, be sure to familiarize yourself with the park's backcountry regulations and etiquette, available online and at locations in the park.

FOOD

Unless you're staying at the LeConte Lodge, or have packed a picnic or provisions, you'll have to leave the park for meals. The easiest way is simply to drive into Bryson City or Gatlinburg, Tennessee, both of which are right on the edge of the park. You'll find recommendations for restaurants in Bryson City and nearby towns later in this chapter. In Gatlinburg, try the **Smoky Mountain Brewery** (1004 Parkway, Suite 501, 865/436-4200, www.smoky-mtn-brewery.com, under $20), a popular brewpub and restaurant. The **Wild Plum Tea Room** (555 Buckhorn Rd., 865/436-3808, under $10) is a nice spot for soup and sandwiches, homemade desserts, and the signature wild plum muffins served with every entrée. The formal restaurant of the **Buckhorn Inn** (2140 Tudor Mountain Rd., 866/941-0460, www.buckhorninn.com, $30 prix fixe, reservations required) has a different beautiful, multi-course set menu every day of the week. Vegetarian meals can be prepared with advance notice.

Maggie Valley

Maggie Valley is a family vacation town from the era of the nuclear family in their wood-paneled station wagon, the kids in the back seat eating Lik-M-Aid and wearing plastic Indian headdresses. Coming down the mountain towards Maggie Valley, you'll pass an overlook, which, on a morning when the mountains around Soco Gap are looped with fog, is surely one of the most beautiful vistas in the state. Drink in your fill, because you're headed into a different world. You'll know it when you pass the hand-lettered sign that says, "Have your picture made with a real moonshine still and a real moonshiner and his truck for a donation of $3.00 use your own camera."

SIGHTS AND ENTERTAINMENT

The most famous attraction in Maggie Valley is **Ghost Town in the Sky** (May 25–Sept. 3, 9 A.M.–7 P.M., Fri.–Sun. 10 A.M.–6 P.M. Sept. and Oct., Nov. 10 A.M.–5 P.M. Fri.–Sun., weather permitting), an Old West theme park where the good guys and bad guys shoot it out daily for your viewing pleasure. That's in addition to the rides—which include a 98-foot free fall tower and a mountainside roller coaster—and bluegrass and gospel concerts.

Bluegrass music and clogging are a big deal in this town. The great bluegrass banjo player Raymond Fairchild is a Maggie native, and after his 50-year touring and recording career, he and his wife Shirley are now the hosts of the **Maggie Valley Opry House** (3605 Soco Rd., 828/648-7941, www.raymondfairchild.com, 8 P.M. nightly May–Oct.). In season, you can find bluegrass and country music concerts and clogging exhibitions every night.

In a state with countless attractions for automotive enthusiasts, Maggie Valley's **Wheels Through Time Museum** (62 Vintage Ln., 828/926-6266, www.wheelsthroughtime .com, 9 A.M.–5 P.M. daily Apr. 1–Oct. 31, 10 A.M.–4 P.M. daily Nov. 1–Mar. 31, $12 adults, $10 seniors over age 65, $6 ages 5–12, free under 4) stands out as one of the most fun. A dazzling collection of nearly 300 vintage motorcycles are on display here, ranging from a 1908 Indian and 1914 Harley Davidson, to military motorcycles from both World Wars, through some gorgeous post-war machines. This collection, which dates mostly to before 1950, is maintained in working order—almost every one of the bikes is revved up from time to time, and the museum's founder has been known to take a spin on one of the treasures.

SPORTS AND RECREATION

Maggie Valley's **Cataloochee Ski Area** (1080 Ski Lodge Rd., off U.S. 19, 800/768-0285, slopes report 800/768-3588, www.cataloochee .com, lift tickets $20–60, equipment rentals $15–30) has slopes geared to every level of skier and snowboarder. Classes and private lessons are taught for all ages. At the nearby **Tube World** (U.S. 19, next to Ski Area, 800/768-0285, www.tubemaggievalley.com, $25/session, must be over 42 inches tall, "Wee Bowl" area for smaller visitors $5/session, call ahead for Wee Bowl, Thanksgiving–mid-March), you can zip down the mountain on inner tubes.

ACCOMMODATIONS

The main drag through Maggie Valley (Soco Road/U.S. 19) is lined with motels, including some of the familiar national brands. Among the pleasant private motels are the **Valley Inn** (236 Soco Rd., 800/948-6880, www.thevalley inn.com, from $39 out of season, in-season rates vary depending on demand, call for specifics during your target dates), and **Jonathan Creek Inn and Villas** (4324 Soco Rd., 800/577-7812, www.jonothancreekinn.com, from about $90). The latter has creekside rooms with screen porches.

FOOD

J. Arthurs Restaurant (2843 Soco Rd., 828/926-1817, www.jarthurs.com, $15–25) is a popular spot locally for steaks, which are the house specialty. The restaurant also has a variety of seafood and pasta dishes, but very little by way of vegetarian meals. Visit their website for a printable coupon. The **Mountaineer**

Restaurant (6490 Soco Rd., 828/926-1730, www.firesidecottages.net, $10–20) is a typical mountain café, serving barbeque, steaks, and country cooking specialties three meals a day.

Cherokee and the Qualla Boundary

The town of Cherokee is a mixture of seemingly contradictory forces: tradition and commerce, nature and development. Cherokee is the civic center of the Eastern Band of the Cherokee, a people who have lived in these mountains for many centuries and whose history, art, government, and language are very much alive. It is the seat of the Qualla (pronounced "KWA-lah," like the marsupial but with just two syllables) Boundary, which is not precisely a reservation, but a large tract of land owned and governed by the tribe. Institutions like the Museum of the Cherokee Indian and the Qualla Arts and Crafts Mutual provide a rock-solid foundation for the Eastern Band of the Cherokee's cultural life. Take a look at the road signs as you drive around here. That beautiful, Asiatic-looking lettering below the English road names is the Cherokee language, in the written form famously created by Sequoyah. That language, once dying away with the Cherokee elders, is now taught to the tribe's youth. (There are even plans for a Cherokee-language immersion school on the Qualla Boundary.)

On the other hand, much of Cherokee's main drag is a classic old-timey tourist district. Here you'll find the "Indian" souvenirs—factory-made moccasins, plastic tomahawks, the works—so familiar to gift shop-goers across the country. In its own retro way, this side of Cherokee can actually be kind of charming, if you have a soft spot for the mid-20th century family vacation aesthetic, the world of fudge counters and garish motel signs. (There are some incredible examples of the latter in Cherokee. Keep an eye out for the Princess, Warrior, and Chief Motels, each featuring a larger-than-life figure from the imaginary world of Hollywood and comic book Indians.)

Enjoy this facet of Cherokee for what it's worth, but dig deeper—don't take this for the real Cherokee. The tribe are a people with thousands of years of history, much of which you can learn about here.

SIGHTS
◖ Museum of the Cherokee Indian
Make a visit to the Museum of the Cherokee Indian (589 Tsali Blvd., 888/665-7249, www.cherokeemuseum.org, 9 A.M.–7 P.M. Mon.–Sat. and 9 A.M.–5 P.M. Sun. June–Aug., 9 A.M.–5 P.M. daily Sept.–May, $9, $6 ages 6–13, free for children under 6). Founded in 1948 and originally housed in a log cabin, this is now a widely acclaimed modern museum and community cultural locus. In the exhibits that trace the tribe's long, sometimes tragic history, you may notice the disconcertingly realistic mannequins. Local members of the tribe volunteered to be models for these mannequins, allowing casts to be made of their faces and bodies so that the figures would not reflect an outsider's notion of what an Indian should look like, but rather the real people whose ancestors this museum honors. The Museum of the Cherokee Indian traces their history from the Paleo period, when the ancestral Cherokees were hunter-gatherers, through the ancient days of the people's civilization, into historic times. A great deal of this exhibit area focuses on the 18th and 19th centuries, times when many tragedies befell the Cherokee as a result of the European invasion of their homeland. It was also a time of great cultural advancement, which included the development of Sequoyah's syllabary. The terrible Trail of Tears began near here, along the North Carolina/Georgia border. A small contingent

of Cherokees remained in the Smokies at the time of the Trail of Tears, successfully eluding, and then negotiating with, the U.S. military, who were trying to send all of the tribe to Oklahoma. Those who lay out in the woods, along with other Cherokees who were able to return home from Oklahoma, are the ancestors of today's Eastern Band, and their history is truly remarkable.

◖ Qualla Arts and Crafts Mutual

Catty-corner to the museum is the Qualla Arts and Crafts Mutual (645 Tsali Blvd., 828/497-3103, www.cherokee-nc.com, 9 A.M.–5 P.M. Mon.–Fri.), a community arts co-op. Local artists sell their work here, and the gallery's high standards and, of course, the tribe's thousands of years of artistry, make for a collection of very special pottery, baskets, masks, and other traditional Cherokee art. As hard as it is to survive as an artist in Manhattan, artists in such rural areas as this have an exponentially more difficult go of it, trying to support themselves through the sale of their art, while at the same time maintaining the integrity of their vision and creativity. The Qualla co-op does a great service to this community in providing a year-round market for

the work of traditional Cherokee artists, whose stewardship of and innovation in the tribal arts are so important.

ENTERTAINMENT AND EVENTS

Of the several outdoor dramas for which North Carolina is known, among the longest running is Cherokee's **Unto These Hills** (Mountainside Theater, 441 N., 866/554-4557, www.cherokee-nc.com, 8 P.M. Mon.–Sat. in the summer). For 60 summers, Cherokee actors have told the story of their tribe's history, from ancient times through the Trail of Tears. Recently updated by Kiowa playwright Hanay Geiogomah, in consultation with the Cherokee tribe, the drama is now called *Unto These Hills: A Retelling*.

ACCOMMODATIONS

The Eastern Band of the Cherokee operates **Harrah's Cherokee Casino and Hotel** (777 Casino Dr., 828/497-7777, www.harrahs.com, from $60). This full-bore Vegas-style casino with two towers of guest rooms has more than 3,000 games, mostly digital slots, with some digital table games run by croupiers. There's also a 1,500-seat theater that hosts major country artists throughout the year.

Bryson City and the Nantahala Forest

Mossy gorges, misty riverbanks, and cloud-ringed mountain peaks make the Nantahala region feel like a setting for fairy tales and conjuration. Cherokee mythology tells of a witch, Spearfinger, known to have frequented the Nantahala Gorge, which was also the abode of a monstrous snake and, of all things, an inchworm so large that it could span the top of the gorge and block out the light of the sun. Today the Nantahala River, running through the narrow gorge, has become a favorite whitewater rafting run.

Nearby Bryson City is an aqua-centric river town, one whose proximity to great whitewater rapids makes it a favorite haunt for rafters and

kayakers and their ilk. If you approach Bryson City from the north on U.S. 19, you're in for a strange sight: The banks of the Tuckasegee River are shored up with crushed cars. Look close, and you may recognize the fenders of trusty warhorses of your childhood.

SIGHTS

The **Great Smoky Mountain Railroad** (Bryson City and Dillsboro depts., 800/872-4681, www.gsmr.com, from $30 adults, from $16 children) is one of the best and most fun ways to see the Smokies. On historic trains, the GSMR carries sightseers on excursions, from two to several hours long, through some of the most beautiful scenery in the region. Trips between Dillsboro and Bryson City (with a layover at each end for shopping and dining) follow the banks of the Tuckasegee River, while round-trips from Bryson City follow the Little Tennessee and Nantahala Rivers deep into the Nantahala Gorge, and the Fontana Trestle Excursion crosses over the top of the Fontana Dam just at sunset. Many other excursions are offered, including gourmet dining and wine and beer tasting trips, Thomas the Tank Engine– and Little Engine That Could–themed trips for kids, and runs to and from river rafting outfitters.

SPORTS AND RECREATION
◖ Nantahala River Gorge
The stunningly beautiful Nantahala River Gorge, just outside Bryson City in the Nantahala National Forest, supports scores of river guide companies, many clustered along U.S. 19 West. "Nantahala" is said to mean "Land of the Noonday Sun," and there are indeed parts of this gorge where the sheer rock walls above the river are so steep that sunlight only hits the water at the noon hour. Eight miles of the Nantahala River flow through the gorge, over Class II and III rapids. The nearby Ocoee River is also a favorite of rafters, and the Cheoah River, on the occasions of controlled releases, has some of the South's most famous and difficult Class III and IV runs.

Outfitters and Tours
Endless River Adventures (14157 U.S. 19 W., near Bryson City, 800/224-7238, www.endless riveradventures.com) gives white-water and flat-water kayaking instruction, rentals, and guided trips on the Nantahala, Ocoee, and Cheoah Rivers. They'll be able to suggest a run suited to your skill level. **Carolina Outfitters** (12121 U.S. 19 W., near Bryson City, 800/468-7238, www.carolinaoutfitters.com) has several package outings that combine river trips with horseback riding, bicycling, panning for gems, and riding on the Great Smoky Mountains Railway. In addition to river guide services, **Wildwater Rafting** (10345 U.S. 19 W., 12 miles west of

Bryson City, 800/451-9972, www.wildwater-rafting.com) leads **Wildwater Jeep Tours** ($40–90 adults, $25–70 children), half- and full-day jeep excursions through back roads and wilderness, and to waterfalls and old mountain settlements.

Because some of these rapids can be quite dangerous, be sure to call ahead and speak to a guide if you have any doubts as to your readiness. If rafting with children, check the company's weight and age restrictions beforehand.

ACCOMMODATIONS
The ◖ **Folkestone Inn** (101 Folkestone Rd., 888/812-3385, www.folkestoneinn.com, from $80) is one of the region's outstanding bed-and-breakfasts, a roomy 1920s farmhouse expanded and renovated into a charming and tranquil inn. Each room has a balcony or porch. Baked treats at breakfast include shortcake, kuchen, cobblers, and other delicacies.

An 85-year-old hotel on the National Register of Historic Places, the **Fryemont Inn** (245 Fryemont St., Bryson City, 800/845-4879, www.fryemontinn.com, from $125 including meals, lodge and dining room closed in winter) has a cozy, rustic feel, with chestnut-paneled rooms, and an inviting lobby with an enormous stone fireplace.

Some river outfitters offer lodging, which can be a very cheap way to pass the night if you don't mind roughing it. The **Rolling Thunder River Company** (10160 U.S. 19 W. near Bryson City, 800/408-7238, www.roll-ingthunderriverco.com, no alcohol permitted) operates a large bunkhouse, with beds available for $8–12 per night for its rafting customers. The **Nantahala Motel** at Carolina Outfitters has very simple rooms with private baths, starting at $39.95 per night. Many of the outfitters also offer camping on their properties.

Way back in the forest by Fontana Lake, the **Fontana Village Resort** (Hwy. 28, Fontana Dam, 800/849-2258, www.fontanavillage.com, from $60) was originally built as housing for the men working on the construction of the dam, a massive wartime undertaking that created a whole town out here in the woods. Renovated into a comfortable resort, Fontana Village features a lodge, cabins, camping (from $25/night) and, for the more adventurous lodger, houseboats. Houseboats are a tradition on the lake, and the two that are rented by Fontana Village make for a most memorable vacation.

Camping

For a look at the range of camping options available in the Nantahala Forest, visit www.cs.unca.edu/nfsnc. Among the nicest is **Standing Indian Campground** (90 Sloan Rd., Franklin, 828/524-6441, www.cs.unca .edu/nfsnc, $14), open April–November. Standing Indian has a nice diversity of campsites to choose from, from flat, grassy areas to cozy mountainside nooks. Drinking water, hot showers, flush toilets, and a phone are all available on-site, and leashed pets are permitted. This 3,400-foot-high campground is close to the Appalachian Trail.

Waynesville and Vicinity

Over towards Asheville and the Balsam Range, the town of Waynesville is an artistic community where crafts galleries and studios line the downtown. In nearby Cullowhee, Western Carolina University is one of the mountain region's leading academic institutions, as well as the location of the wonderful Mountain Heritage Center museum and Mountain Heritage Day festival.

WAYNESVILLE

Waynesville's downtown can keep a gallery-hopper or shopper happy for hours. Main Street is packed with studio artists' galleries, cafés and coffee shops, and a variety of boutiques.

Shopping

Blue Ridge Books & News (152 S. Main St., 828/456-6000, www.brbooks-news.com, 8 A.M.–8 P.M. Mon.–Sat., 8 A.M.–5 P.M. Sun.) is a very nice bookstore, with specialties in books of regional interest and cups of good coffee. **Good Ol' Days Cigars** (46 N. Main St./145 Wall St., 828/456-2898, www.goodoldays cigars.com, 10 A.M.–6 P.M. Mon.–Thurs., 10 A.M.–7 P.M. Fri. and Sat.) offers a large selection of fine tobacco and smoking products—cigars, of course, as well as pipes, loose tobacco, rolling papers, and much more—and a TV lounge in which you can enjoy them.

One of the **Mast General Store's** (63 N. Main St., 828/452-2101, www.mastgeneral store.com, 10 A.M.–6 P.M. Mon.–Sat., noon–5 P.M. Sun., hours vary in the wintertime) several locations is here in Waynesville. While the stores are perhaps best known among vacationers for making children clamor—they carry over 500 varieties of candy, many kept in big wooden barrels, old-time dry-goods-store style—they have an even larger selection of merchandise for adults. The specialties are camping gear (such as top-brand tents, cookware, maps) and outdoors-oriented, fairly expensive but very nice clothing and shoes (by Columbia, Teva, Birkenstock, and the like).

Galleries

Waynesville's galleries are many and varied, though the overarching aesthetic is one of studio art with inspiration in the environment and folk arts. **Twigs and Leaves** (98 N. Main St., 828/456-1940, www.twigsandleaves.com, 10 A.M.–5:30 P.M. Mon.–Sat., 1–4 P.M. Sun.) carries splendid art furniture that is both fanciful and functional, pottery of many hand-thrown and hand-built varieties, jewelry, paintings, fabric hangings, mobiles, and many other beautiful and unusual items inspired by nature.

Textures on Main (142 N. Main, 828/452-0058, www.texturesonmain.com, 10 A.M.–6 P.M. Mon.–Sat., noon–5 P.M. Sun.) is a gallery showcasing the work of John and Suzanne Gernandt, furniture and fabric artists, respectively, and several other partners. Suzanne's fabric art is often abstract and features beautiful, deeply saturated colors. John's furniture and that of his fellow designers whose work is carried by Textures cover a stunning array of sensibilities—from Jonathan Adler's hyper-mod pieces to Robin Bruce's gorgeous, understated upholstery, to Gernandt's own dazzling cabinetry, which has the grace of Shaker carpentry and the slightest hint of a Tim Burton–style offbeat aesthetic.

Studio Thirty Three (33 Pidgeon St., 828/456-3443, www.studio33jewelry.com) carries the work of a very small and select group of fine jewelers from western North Carolina. Their retail and custom inventory consists of spectacular handcrafted pieces, in a variety of styles and an array of precious stones and metals. This is a must-see gallery if you are engaged, or have another super-special occasion coming up. The gallery describes its stock as ranging in price from "$65 to $16,000," and most items cost upwards of $2,000. Even if you're not about to mark a major life event or spend that kind of money just for fun, it's worth stopping in to gaze at all that sparkle.

Accommodations

Outside of Waynesville in the community of Balsam, the ◖ **Balsam Mountain Inn** (68 Seven Springs Dr., Balsam, 800/224-9498, www.balsaminn.com, $139–219, dogs and cats permitted with prior approval) has stood watch for a century. It's a haunting, and haunted, location—an imposing old wooden hotel, with huge double porches overlooking, in the foreground, a rather spooky little railroad platform, and, in the background, the beautiful ridges of Jackson and Haywood Counties. The interior is barely changed from the earliest days, paneled in white horizontal bead board throughout, with 10-foot-wide hallways said to have been designed to accommodate steamer trunks. The one telephone is at the front desk, and there are no TVs, so plan to go hiking or to sit on the porch before dining in the downstairs restaurant, and then curl up and read in the library. (There is, paradoxically, fast

Wi-Fi.) Among the inn's ghosts is a lady in a blue dress. She is said to originate in room 205, but comes and goes elsewhere on the second floor. I'm a total wuss about the paranormal, and once stayed on the second floor on a freezing, damp November night straight out of a Victorian ghost story. I fell asleep expecting to be awakened by ghostly footsteps, but heard nothing all night except the cozy hiss of the radiator. In the morning I went downstairs to a breakfast that included the best bowl of grits I've ever eaten in my grits-rich life. This inn has a few rough edges, but an atmosphere to be found nowhere else.

Up on the Blue Ridge Parkway above Waynesville, and quite close to Asheville, is another of my favorite inns in all of North Carolina. The ◖ **Pisgah Inn** (BRP Milepost 410, 828/235-8228, www.pisgahinn.com, open late Mar.–early Nov., from $100) is much like Skyland and Big Meadows on Virginia's Skyline Drive, with motel-style accommodations surrounding an old lodge with a large family-style dining room and a Parkway gift shop. The inn sits on a nearly 5,000-foot-high mountaintop, so the view is sensational. Trails surround the Pisgah like wheel spokes, leading to short pretty strolls and challenging day-long hikes. The restaurant, open for breakfast, lunch, and dinner (7:30 A.M.–10:30 A.M., 11:30 A.M.–4 P.M., 5–9 P.M. daily), has a mesmerizing view and an appetizing and varied menu ($5–25) of both country and fancy meals. The rooms are simple but comfortable, each with its own balcony and rocking chairs overlooking the valley, and with a TV but no telephone. The Pisgah is a perfect spot for resting, reading, and porch-setting.

Waynesville also has quite a selection of luxury inns. The **Andon-Reid Inn** (92 Daisey Ave., 800/293-6190, www.andonreidinn.com, from $115, no pets, guests under 16 not encouraged) is a handsome turn-of-the-century house close to downtown, with five tranquil rooms, each with its own fireplace, and a sumptuous four-course breakfast menu that might include sweet-potato pecan pancakes and pork tenderloin, homemade cornbread with honey butter, and many more treats.

The **Inn at Iris Meadows** (304 Love Ln., 888/466-4747, www.irismeadows.com, from $225, dogs permitted with advance notice, children not encouraged) is another splendid house, on a hillside surrounded by lush trees and gardens. Shepherd-mix Scratch and gray tabby-cat Zephyrus help run the place, and are added attractions themselves. For absolute tip-top luxury, try **The Swag** (2300 Swag Rd., 800/789-7672, www.theswag.com, $430–750). Superb rooms and cabins of rustic wood and stone each have a steam shower, and several have saunas, wet bars, and cathedral ceilings. The inn is at 5,000 feet, at the very edge of the Great Smoky Mountains National Park.

Food

Waynesville's **Lomo Grill** (44 Church St., 828/452-5222, www.lomogrill.com, $16–35) serves a very nice menu of Italian favorites and steaks, with a create-your-own-pasta option that makes things easier for vegetarians. In some seasons Lomo has an early-evening "3-Course Sundown Supper," a prix fixe ($20/person) sampling of some of their best dishes. Another popular spot is **Bogart's** (303 S. Main St., 828/452-1313, $10–20), which is locally famous for its filet mignon. If you're just passing through town and need a jolt of really strong, good coffee, visit **Panacea** (66 Commerce St., 828/452-6200, under $5) in the funky Frog Level neighborhood downhill from downtown.

SYLVA

The small town of Sylva, southwest of Waynesville, is crowned by the pretty Jackson County Courthouse, an Italianate building with an ornate cupola, and kept under wistful watch by the requisite courthouse-square Confederate monument.

Sights

South of Sylva, the mysterious **Judaculla Rock** (off Caney Fork Rd.) has puzzled folks for centuries. The soapstone boulder is covered in petroglyphs, estimated to be at least 500 years old. The figures and symbols and squiggles are clearly manmade and significant, but as of yet not understood. The soft rock is greatly eroded, and the pictures are not as clear as they were in earlier generations, but many of them can still be discerned. To reach the rock, drive south on Highway 107 eight miles past the intersection with Sylva's U.S. Business 23. Make a left on Caney Fork Road/County Road 1737, and drive 2.5 miles to a gravel road. Turn left, and just under half a mile you'll see the rock on the right, and a parking area on the left.

Shopping

Sylva's City Lights Bookstore (3 E. Jackson St., 828/586-9499, www.citylightsnc.com, 9 A.M.–9 P.M. Mon.–Sat.) is hardly a knock-off of the monumental beat establishment in San Francisco with which it shares its name. Instead, it's a first-rate small-town bookstore, with a stock that has the novelty sought by vacationers, and the depth to make regulars of the local patrons. In addition to the sections you'll find in any other good bookstore, at City Lights there is an excellent selection of books of regional interest, including folklore, nature, recreation guides, history, and fiction and poetry by Appalachian and Southern authors.

Food

The North Carolina mountains are blessed with a booming organic foods movement, and you'll find eco-aware eateries throughout the area.

Lulu's Café (612 W. Main St., 828/587-5858, www.lulusonmain.com, 11:30 A.M.–9 P.M. Mon.–Sat. in the summer, and 11:30 A.M.–8 P.M. Mon.–Sat. in the winter) is one of the most acclaimed restaurants of the North Carolina mountains. The menu is American gourmet at its heart, with splashes of Mediterranean and Nuevo Latino specialties. Try the walnut-spinach ravioli, or the raspberry rum pork loin. There are plenty of vegetarian options.

A more casual option is **Nick and Nate's Pizza** (556 W. Main, 828/586-3000, 11:30 A.M.–9 P.M. Mon., Wed.–Sat., and noon–9 P.M. Sun., closed Tues., $6–8 lunch,

$8–15 dinner), where the dough is handmade, the toppings are fresh, and the beer is from fine microbreweries.

Also, try **Annie's Naturally** (506 W. Main., 828/586-9096, www.anniesnaturally bakery.com, open for breakfast, lunch, and snacks 7 A.M.–5 P.M. Tues.–Fri., 8 A.M.–5 P.M. Sat., closed Sun. and Mon.), a bakery and sandwich shop owned by Joe and Annie Ritota. Joe is a fourth-generation professional baker from an old Italian American family known for its skill in the kitchen. The breads, cookies, and pastries are baked on-site in the Ritotas' old-time way. **Soul Infusion** (628 E. Main, between Sylva Tire and UPS, 828/586-1717, www .soulinfusion.com, 11 A.M.–9 P.M. Tues.–Thurs. in the off-season, 11 A.M.–10 P.M. Tues.–Thurs. in warm weather, noon–midnight Fri., 5 P.M.–midnight Sat., closed Sun. and Mon., $5–106) is a cozy hippie-gourmet teahouse in an old house on Main Street. Here you can get very good burritos, sandwiches, pizza, wraps, and choose from several dozen kinds of loose-leaf tea, and even more selections of bottled beer. On weekends and some weeknights, local blues, folk, reggae, and experimental musicians put on a show. Seize the opportunity to hear some of the talent in this incredibly musical region.

DILLSBORO

Next door to Sylva is Dillsboro, a river town of rafters and crafters. **Dogwood Crafters,** in operation for more than thirty years, is a gallery and co-op that represents approximately 100 local artisans. While the shop carries some of the ubiquitous country-whimsical stuff, mixed in is the work of some very traditional Blue Ridge weavers, potters, carvers, and other expert artisans, and the shop is well worth visiting for that reason.

Sports and Recreation

Dillsboro River Company (18 Macktown Rd., across the river from downtown Dillsboro, 866/586-3797, www.dillsbororiver.com, open after May 20, 10:30 A.M.–6 P.M. daily, rentals $10–30, guided trips $20–35) will set you afloat on the Tuckaseegee River, a comparatively

warm river with areas of Class II rapids. (It's pronounced "Tuck-a-SEE-jee," but often simply referred to as the Tuck.) They rent rafts, "ducks," and inflatable and sit-on-top kayaks. If you'd like to hire a river rat, guides will be happy to lead you on tours twice daily, and for an extra fee you can share a boat with the guide. There are minimum weight restrictions for these watercraft, so if you are traveling with children, call ahead and ask if the guides think your young'uns are ready for the Tuckaseegee.

Accommodations

Of the many historic inns in this region, one of the oldest is Dillsboro's **Jarrett House** (100 Haywood St., 800/972-5623, www.jarrett house.com, $80–95, includes breakfast). The 1880s three-story lodge was built to serve passengers on the railway, and today is once again a busy rail stop, now for the Great Smoky Mountains Railroad's excursion trains. The rooms are furnished in old-fashioned furniture, and while they have air conditioning and private bathrooms, the only TV is in the lobby. The Hartbarger family, keepers of this inn for over 30 years, are serious about giving their guests a chance for what they call "honest loafing"—real recuperative peace and quiet.

Food

The ◖ **Jarrett House** is also famous for its dining room (11:30 A.M.–2:30 P.M. and 4:30–7:30 P.M. daily, up to $15), an extravaganza of country cooking based around the staples of country ham and red-eye gravy. You can also order many other mountain specialties, like fried catfish, fried chicken, sweet tea, biscuits, and for dessert the daily cobbler or vinegar pie (it's good). There's not much for vegetarians, but if you like heavy Southern fare you'll think you're in heaven.

CULLOWHEE

The unincorporated village of Cullowhee (pronounced "CULL-uh-wee"), located on Highway 107 between Sylva and Cashiers, is the home of Western Carolina University. WCU's **Mountain Heritage Center** (in the lobby of the H. F. Robinson Administration Building on WCU campus, 828/227-7327, www.wcu.edu/2389.asp, 8 A.M.–5 P.M. Mon.–Fri. year-round, plus 2–5 P.M. Sun. June–Oct.) is a small museum with a great collection that will fascinate anyone interested in Appalachian history. The permanent exhibit, "Migration of the Scotch-Irish People," is full of artifacts like a 19th-century covered wagon, wonderful photographs, and homemade quilts, linens,

musical instruments, and more. The Mountain Heritage Center also hosts two traveling exhibits at a time in addition to the permanent installation, and the annual **Mountain Heritage Day** festival (in late Sept.). Mountain Heritage Day brings together many of western North Carolina's best and most authentic traditional musicians and artisans, in a free festival that draws up to 25,000 visitors.

Robbinsville and the Valley Towns

Another region at the heart of Cherokee life, both past and present, is found between Robbinsville and the Georgia state line. Near Robbinsville, the area known as Snowbird is one of the most traditional Cherokee communities, where the Cherokee language is still spoken by native speakers, and the old crafts and folkways are alive as well. Here also is the grave of Junaluska, one of the Eastern Band's most prominent ancestors.

The town of Murphy is closely linked with the great tragedy of Cherokee history, the Trail of Tears. About 16,000 Cherokees, including children and the elderly and infirm, were arrested and made to leave their homes and farms in North Carolina, Georgia, and Tennessee. They were brought here to Fort Butler, where they began their forced march to Oklahoma. The names of these people, many of whom died along the way, are inscribed in Cherokee on a memorial at the L&N Depot in Murphy.

In addition to the places of historic significance to Cherokee culture, this farthest southwest corner of North Carolina has other compelling sights and sites. Brasstown, a tiny village on the Georgia line, is the home of the John C. Campbell Folk School, an artists colony nearly a century old, where visitors can stroll among studios and along trails, and stop in to a gallery shop with some of the most beautiful crafts you'll find in the region. Back up towards Robbinsville, the relentlessly scenic Cherohala Skyway crosses 36 miles of the

"See Rock City" signs can still be found in the Smokies.

Cherokee and Nantahala Forests. This road is a major destination for motorcyclists and sports car drivers, as well as day-trippers and vacationers.

ROBBINSVILLE

The whole southwestern corner of North Carolina is rich with Cherokee history and culture, and the Robbinsville area has some of the deepest roots, and sites of greatest significance

JUNALUSKA

Among the most important figures in the history of the Eastern Band of the Cherokee is Junaluska, who was born in 1776 near Dillard, Georgia. During the wars against the Creek Indians (1812–1814), the Cherokee fought alongside the United States forces, and it's said that young Junaluska saved the life of Andrew Jackson at the battle of Horse Shoe Bend in Alabama.

Almost 20 years later, Andrew Jackson, now president, thanked the Cherokee by signing the Indian Removal Act, which ordered that they and four other major Southern tribes be forced off of their lands and marched to the new Indian Territory of Oklahoma. Junaluska traveled all the way to Washington to try to convince Jackson to be merciful to the Cherokee, but his plea fell on deaf ears.

Junaluska was one of about 16,000 members of the Cherokee nation who were made to walk the thousand miles to Oklahoma. In Tennessee he led an attempted escape, but was captured, and made the rest of the march in manacles and leg irons. In 1841, he was finally able to leave Oklahoma, and made the 17-day trip by horseback all the way back to North Carolina. Supposedly Junaluska once said, "If I had known what Andrew Jackson would do to the Cherokees, I would have killed him myself that day at Horse Shoe Bend."

He spent his latter years in Cherokee County, on land that was given to him by the state of North Carolina. He and his third wife, Nicie, are buried at Robbinsville, at what is now the Junaluska Memorial and Museum. A marker was commissioned in 1910 by the Daughters of the American Revolution, and during the dedication ceremony, a eulogy was delivered in the Cherokee language by the Reverend Armstrong Cornsilk. His words were transcribed and translated thus:

Ladies and gentlemen, friends: We have met here at Junaluska's grave. We have met as friends and brothers and sisters.

We are refreshing our memories over Juno's burial.

We appreciate his going to war, and gaining the big victory for Jackson. The Cherokees and whites were fighting the Creeks at that time. And we Cherokees feel that it was through him that we have the privilege of being here today.

I knew Juno at that time. I knew him well. I recollect how he looked. He wore the hair cut off the back of his head, and he would plait the hair on top of his head so as to make it stick up like horns.

He was a good man. He was a good friend. He was a good friend in his home and everywhere. He would ask the hungry man to eat. He would ask the cold one to warm by his fire. He would ask the tired one to rest, and he would give a good place to sleep. Juno's home was a good home for others.

He was a smart man. He made his mind think good. He was very brave. He was not afraid.

Juno at this time has been dead about 50 years. I am glad he is up above [pointing upward]. I am glad we have this beautiful monument. It shows Junaluska did good, and it shows we all appreciate him together –having a pleasant time together.

I hope we shall all meet Junaluska in heaven [pointing upward] and all be happy there together.

to the modern and historical generations of the tribe. In little towns and crossroads a few miles outside Robbinsville, several hundred people known as the Snowbird community keep alive some of the Cherokee tribe's oldest ways. The Cherokee language is spoken here—it is still some residents' first language—and some of the Eastern Band's most admired basket makers, potters, and other artists continue to make and teach their ancient arts.

Sights

Outside Robbinsville in the ancient Stecoah Valley, an imposing old rock schoolhouse, built in 1930 and used as a school until the mid-1990s, has been reborn as the **Stecoah Valley Center** (121 Schoolhouse Rd., Stecoah, 828/479-3364, www.visitsvcenter.com). This is the home of a weaver's guild, a native plants preservation group, a concert series, several festivals, and a great **gallery shop** (828/497-3098, 10 A.M.–5 P.M. Mon.–Fri. year-round, plus every Sat. in Apr.) of local artisans' work. Concerts in the Appalachian Evening summer series, featuring area musicians, are preceded by community suppers of traditional mountain cuisine.

On Robbinsville's Main Street is the **Junaluska Memorial** (Main St., approx. 0.5 miles north of the Graham County Courthouse, 828/479-4727, 9 A.M.–4 P.M. Mon.–Sat.). Here Junaluska and his third wife, Nicie, are buried. The marker was dedicated in 1910 by the Daughters of the American Revolution. The gravesite is maintained by the Friends of Junaluska, who also operate the **Junaluska Museum** (www.junaluska.com) on the same site. At the museum you'll find ancient artifacts from life in Cheoah thousands of years ago. There are also contemporary Cherokee crafts on display, and outside you can walk a path that highlights the medicinal plants used for generations in this area.

Fourteen miles outside Robbinsville, down a winding country road, **Yellow Branch Pottery and Cheese** (136 Yellow Branch Circle, Robbinsville, 828/479-6710, www.yellow branch.com, noon– 5 P.M. Tues.–Sat. or by

appointment) is a beautifully rustic spot for an afternoon's excursion. Bruce DeGroot, Karen Mickler, and their herd of jersey cows produce prize-winning artisan cheeses and graceful, functional pottery. (The cows don't actually help with the pottery.) Visitors are welcome at their farm and shop.

Entertainment and Events

Every year on the Saturday of Memorial Day Weekend, the Snowbird Cherokee host the **Fading Voices Festival** in Robbinsville. The festival features a mound-building ceremony, and all of the usual festival attractions—music, dancing, storytelling, crafts, and lots of food—but in the deeply traditional forms carried on by the Snowbird community. (Contact the Junaluska Museum for more information.)

Sports and Recreation

The **Joyce Kilmer Memorial Forest** (Joyce Kilmer Rd., off of Hwy. 143 west of Robbinsville, 828/479-6431, www.western ncattractions.com/JKMF.htm) is one of the largest remaining tracts of virgin forest in the eastern United States, where 450-year-old tulip polar trees have grown to 100 feet tall and 20 feet around. The two-mile loop (or two one-mile loops) makes for an easy hike through a remarkable forest.

Accommodations

The **Snowbird Mountain Lodge** (4633 Santeetlah Rd., 11 miles west of Robbinsville, 800/941-9290, www.snowbirdlodge.com, from $180) was built in the early 1940s, a rustic chestnut and stone inn atop a 3,000-foot mountain. The view is exquisite, and the lodge is perfectly situated between the Cherohala Skyway, Lake Santeetlah, and the Joyce Kilmer Forest. Guests enjoy a full breakfast, picnic lunch, and four-course supper created from seasonal local specialties. Another pleasant place to stay near Robbinsville is the **Tapoco Lodge Resort** (14981 Tapoco Rd., 15 miles north of Robbinsville, 800/822-5083, www .tapocolodge.com, from $109 en suite, $75 economy rooms with shared bath, open

Apr.–Nov.). Built in 1930, the lodge is on the National Register of Historic Places, and has the feel of an old-time hotel. Rooms in the main lodge and surrounding cabins are simple but comfortable, and the resort overlooks the Cheoah River, a legendary run for rafters at the several times each year when pent-up water is released to form crazy-fast rapids.

HAYESVILLE AND BRASSTOWN

Between Hayesville and Brasstown, you can get a really good sense of the art that has come out of this region over the years. These two small towns run along the Georgia border on U.S. 64.

◖ John C. Campbell Folk School

One of North Carolina's most remarkable cultural institutions, the John C. Campbell Folk School (1 Folk School Rd., Brasstown, 800/365-5724, www.folkschool.org) was born of the unusual honeymoon of unusual newlyweds from up North, who traveled through Appalachia 100 years ago to educate themselves about Southern highland culture. John C. and Olive Dame Campbell, like other notable Northern liberals in their day, directed their humanitarian impulses toward the education and economic betterment of Southern mountaineers. John Campbell died a decade later, but Olive, joining forces with her friend Marguerite Butler, set out to establish a "folk school" in the Southern mountains that she and John had visited. She was inspired by the model of the Danish *folkehojskole*, workshops that preserved and taught traditional arts as a means of fostering economic self-determination and personal pride in rural communities. Brasstown, North Carolina, was chosen as the site for this grand experiment, and in 1925, the John C. Campbell Folk School opened its doors.

Today, thousands of artists travel every year to this uncommonly lovely, remote valley, the site of an ancient Cherokee village. In week-and weekend-long classes, students of all ages and skill levels learn about traditional arts

native to this region (such as pottery, weaving, dyeing, storytelling, and chair-caning) as well as contemporary and exotic crafts (such as photography, kaleidoscope-making, book-making, paper-marbling). By all means, visit the website or order a catalog, and see if any of the hundreds of courses offered every year strike your fancy. But even if you're passing through the area on a shorter visit, the Folk School welcomes you to explore the campus. Visitors are sincerely asked to help preserve the quiet atmosphere of learning and concentration when peering at artists' studios, but you can have an up-close look at some of their marvelous wares in the school's **Craft Shop** (bottom floor of Olive Dame Campbell Dining Hall, 8 A.M.–5 P.M. Mon.–Sat., 1–5 P.M. Sun.), one of the nicest such shops in western North Carolina. Exhibits about the school's history, and historic examples of the work of local artists of past generations, are on display at the **History Center,** next to Keith House. There are several nature trails on campus that thread through this lovely valley. Be sure to visit the quarter-mile **Rivercane Walk,** which features outdoor sculpture by some of the greatest living artists of the Eastern Band of the Cherokee. In the evenings you'll often find concerts by traditional musicians, or community square, contra, and English country dances. A visit to the John C. Campbell Folk School, whether as a student or a tourist, is an exceptional opportunity to immerse yourself in a great creative tradition.

Clay County Historical and Arts Council Museum

Hayesville's Old Clay County Jail, built in 1912, is now home to the Clay County Historical and Arts Council Museum (21 Davis Loop, Hayesville, 828/389-6814, 10 A.M.–4 P.M. June–Aug., call for out-of-season hours). This is a small and extremely interesting museum with varied collections, including the medical instruments of an early country doctor, an original jail cell (with a file hidden by a long-ago prisoner, discovered during renovations), an old moonshine still, a collection of beautiful Cherokee masks, and a remarkable crazy quilt embroidered with strange and charming illustrations.

Food

Across from the courthouse in Hayesville, adjoining cafés (each at 1 Sullivan St., Hayesville, 866/724-2302, www.copperdoorcafes.com) provide some nice dining options. The **Copper Door** (5–10 P.M. Mon.–Thurs., 5–11 P.M. Fri. and Sat., $20) serves seafood, steak, veal, lamb chops, and other hearty meals. Next door, the **Café on the Square** (6 A.M.–10 P.M. Mon.–Thurs., 6 A.M.–11 P.M. Fri.–Sat., under $10) is the Copper Door's more casual sister, a spot to nip in for a good cup of coffee and a pastry as you set off on a mountain adventure.

BACKGROUND

The Land

GEOGRAPHY

Encompassing more than 50,000 square miles of land and water, North Carolina is considered to be comprised of three distinct geographical regions. The most easily identified is the **mountain region,** which forms the western edge of the state. The ridges of the Blue Ridge and Great Smoky Mountains run in a general northeast-to-southwest configuration, from the Virginia line to the farthest southwestern corner where the toe of North Carolina tickles Georgia and Tennessee. Smaller ranges are hemmed in among the peaks of the Blue Ridge and Smokies, including the Black Mountains, the Pisgah Range, and the Unaka Range. Though the Black Mountains have a wingspan of only about 15 miles, confined to Yancey County, they are the loftiest in the state, and six of the 10 highest mountains in the eastern United States are found here, including the very highest, 6,684-foot Mount Mitchell.

Since the mid-19th century, the **Piedmont** has been the primary locus of the state's population and industry. Most of the major cities are in the Piedmont, including the Raleigh-Durham metro area, Charlotte, Winston-Salem, and Greensboro. The textile and furniture industries, which, along with tobacco, generated most of the state's wealth in the late 19th and

© JIMMY MCDONALD

GEOGRAPHICAL VOCABULARY

North Carolina has some unusual landscapes and environments, and some unusual vocabulary to describe them. As you explore the state, you may encounter the following terms.

POCOSIN

Pronounced "puh-CO-sin," the word is said to come from the Algonquin for "swamp on a hill." A pocosin is a moist peat bog of a kind unique to the Southeast and particularly associated with eastern North Carolina. The peat layer is thinnest around the edges, and usually supports communities of pine trees. Moving towards the center of the bog, the ground becomes slightly higher, the peat thicker and more acidic, and less welcoming of plant species. Because the soil is so poor and leached of nutrients, carnivorous plants, who have their meals delivered rather than depending on the soil's bounty, are particularly well suited to life in pocosins.

CAROLINA BAY

The word bay here refers not to an inlet on the coast, but to another kind of upland swamp – sort of like an inside-out pocosin. The bays' origins are mysterious, and their regularity of form and commonness in this region most uncanny. If you look down at eastern North and South Carolina from an airplane, or in a satellite image, the bays are unmistakable. They're oval-shaped depressions, varying in size from Lake Waccamaw to mere puddles, and are always aligned in a northeast-to-southwest configuration. Unlike ponds and regular swamps, Carolina bays are usually unconnected to any groundwater source, but are fed solely by rainwater. Like pocosins, bays attract colonies of carnivorous plants, which love to establish their dens of iniquity in such unwholesome soil.

SANDHILLS

If you're in Wilmington or Southport, or somewhere else along the southeastern coast, take note of what the soil beneath your feet looks like. Now, turn your back to the ocean and head inland. Travel 100 miles west and then look down again. What you'll see is very similar – sandy, light-colored ground, wiry vegetation (and a few carnivorous plants), maybe even some scattered shells. About 20 million years ago, during the Miocene Epoch, the areas of present-day Fayetteville and Southern Pines and Sanford were sand dunes on the shores of an ocean that covered what is now North Carolina's coastal plain. Imagine the landscape millions of years ago, when the Uwharrie Mountains, just west of the Sandhills, towered 20,000 feet over an ocean that swirled at their feet.

HOLLER

Here's a term that's really more of a regional pronunciation than a unique word. A holler is what is on paper termed a "hollow" – a mountain cove – it's just that we in the South aren't much for rounding words that end in "ow." If you don't believe me, just beller out the winda to that feller wallering in yonder meada.

BALD

An ecological mystery, the Appalachian bald is a mountaintop area on which there are no trees, even though surrounding mountaintops of the same elevation may be forested. Typically a bald is either grassy or a heath. Heaths are more easily explicable, caused by soil conditions that don't support forest. Grassy balds, though, occur on land where logically one would expect to find trees. Some theories hold that grassy balds were caused by generations of livestock grazing, but soil studies show that they were grassy meadows before the first mountain farmer turned his cattle or sheep out to pasture. Grazing may still be the answer, though. The balds may originally have been chomped and trampled down by prehistoric megafauna – ancient bison, mastodons, and mammoths. Today, in the absence of mammoths as well as free-ranging cattle, some balds are gradually sealing up in woodland, except where deliberately maintained.

© SARAH BRYAN

ripe cotton at an old homestead near Snow Hill

entire 20th century, was concentrated in the Piedmont, as were a not-insignificant number of tobacco farms. Though now nearly vanished due to the "outsourcing" of their work overseas, the textile mills (factories) were a tremendous cultural as well as economic force in the state's history. The earliest mills were generally water-powered, harnessing the energy of the strong, swift currents of the rocky rivers that charge downhill towards the coast.

The **Coastal Plain** is the third region, and though the basic western delineator of the region is I-95, the Sandhills section of the state is also geologically part of the Coastal Plain. Wedged in between the southern Piedmont and the swampy lowlands of the Cape Fear Valley (the delta stretching from Fayetteville to Wilmington), the Sandhills are actually a range of sand dunes, which millions of years ago marked the Carolina coast. Over millennia the ocean retreated a hundred or so miles to the coastline of our own epoch.

Eastern North Carolina is characterized by its sandy soil, its wide swaths of fresh- and saltwater wetlands, its deep rivers, and the tremendous northern sounds, which separate the mainland from the Outer Banks. Dotting the landscape are pocosins and Carolina bays, two distinct regional forms of wetlands. Pocosins are wet, peaty expanses of moist ground that are slightly elevated in the middle. Carolina bays, ovoid bodies of water that lie on diagonal axes, are an unexplained peculiarity seen especially in the Carolina Low Country.

The **Outer Banks** form a magnificent, sweeping arc from the Virginia line at the north, out to its eastern ultima thule at Cape Hatteras, to the edge of the Croatan Forest and Bogue Banks at the south. South of Bogue Banks, a crazed margin of marshes and barrier islands shelter the coast. An ever-changing sandbar, the Outer Banks shift imperceptibly from day to day as the tides nudge them back and forth, but in a hurricane can be transformed in just a few hours when wind and water join forces to rearrange geography.

CLIMATE

There are not very many generalizations that can be made about the climate in North Carolina. It's not as hot as the equator and it's not as cold as the poles. Within that range of variables, each region of the state has to be characterized separately, because their geography causes such different climatic conditions.

The mountains are much cooler than the Piedmont and coast, and winter lasts much longer there. Asheville and Boone can get snow when the trees down in the Piedmont are already green and leafy, but the average winter temperatures in the mountains stay mostly above freezing. The state's coldest temperature on record, -25°F, was measured in 1966 on top of Grandfather Mountain. In the summer it can be chilly in the mountains, especially in the evening, but plenty of days hit the 80s.

Central North Carolina, on the other hand, can be incredibly hot in the summer, and plenty hot in the spring and fall. East-central towns like Lumberton and Fayetteville can feel like the boilingest places on earth, and it was in fact in Fayetteville that the state's hottest temperature, 110°F, was recorded in 1983. It's often in the 50s on winter afternoons, though there are lots of nights, and some days, when the temperature stays below freezing. The Piedmont sees snow, though not nearly so much as the mountains, and the counties to the east of I-95 are likelier to have rain during winter storms.

Temperatures on the coast of North Carolina are somewhat more moderate than those in the Piedmont. The warm Gulf Stream, so close to the Outer Banks, keeps the air from getting too frigid in the winter, while the circulation of sea breezes makes it ever so slightly less steamy in the summer. The difference is subtle, though, and chances are that on the coldest day in January or the hottest in August, the relief won't be perceptible.

North Carolina is subject to hazardous weather with some regularity. The Outer Banks are terribly vulnerable to **hurricanes,** jutting so far out into the Atlantic, and the coastline to the south of the Banks has suffered plenty of hits too. Hurricane season here lasts from June through November, and it's towards the end of the summer that we really start to be watchful. There is usually plenty of warning before storms hit—by the time they reach us, we've had the Weather Channel on for days, perhaps watching as the Caribbean and Florida take the first hits. Wind and rain, of course, are the first weapons that hurricanes unleash, but the ocean and rivers get in on the act too. Flooding and storm surges can be even more dangerous than the terrifically strong winds. 1999's Hurricane Floyd killed 35 people in North Carolina. It also caused billions of dollars of damage, untold emotional trauma, and permanent alterations to the landscape. The eastern rivers flooded to 500-year levels (and higher in some cases), leaving one-third of Rocky Mount underwater, and causing devastating damage to Tarboro, Kinston, and other important towns in the region. Princeville, the oldest African American town in the United States, was nearly destroyed. A decade later, many eastern North Carolina towns are still badly scarred by the damage Floyd did to their infrastructures and economies.

Tornadoes, though most common in the spring, can whip up trouble any time of year. For example, a rare November twister in 2005 touched down very suddenly in the community of Riegelwood, in Columbus County, killing seven people. Plain old **thunderstorms** can be dangerous too, bringing lightning, flash flooding, and difficult driving conditions. **Snowstorms** with significant accumulation are more likely in the mountains than at lower elevations, though central Carolina sees at least a little bit of snow most winters, and the coast has occasional flurries. In addition to the innate dangers of driving in snowy or icy weather, the fact that many non-mountaineer North Carolinians are woefully inexperienced snow drivers also brings some peril. Luckily, we (talking now only about flatlanders) tend to fly into blind panics when the forecast calls for even the lightest flurries, so after we denude every grocery store of its milk, bread, and tabloids, we seal ourselves up in our homes and dream of camellias and wisteria.

Flora

In the early 1700s, John Lawson, an English explorer who would soon be the first victim of the Tuscarora War, recorded a fanciful tale he'd picked up in the very young colony of North

Strawberries grow large in North Carolina.

Carolina. "I have been informed of a Tulip-Tree," he wrote, "that was ten Foot Diameter; and another, wherein a lusty Man had his Bed and Household Furniture, and liv'd in it, till his Labour got him a more fashionable Mansion. He afterwards became a noted Man, in his Country, for Wealth and Conduct." Whether or not there was ever really a tulip poplar large enough to serve as a furnished bachelor pad, colonial North Carolina's virgin forests must have seemed miraculous to the first Europeans to happen upon them.

FORESTS

Few old-growth forests exist today, after generations of logging and farming throughout the state, but those enclaves of virgin woods, like the Joyce Kilmer Forest in the Smoky Mountains, are a sight to behold and make Lawson's anecdote seem like a fairy tale that might actually be true. Scores of specialized

ecosystems throughout the state support a marvelous diversity of plant and animal life, from the cypress swamps in the east to the longleaf pine forests in the Sandhills to the fragrant balsam forests of the high country.

Because the state is so geographically and climatically varied, there is a greater diversity of tree species here than anywhere else in the eastern United States. We've got quantity going for us too; in the Piedmont and eastern Carolina, more than half of the land remains forested. Coastal forests are dominated by hardwoods—**oaks** of many varieties, and **gum** and **cypress,** species that thrive in wetlands. There are also vast swathes of loblolly **pineywoods** along the coast. In the Piedmont, oak and **hickory** predominate, but share their range with smaller bands of pineywoods. In the mountains too, oak and hickory woods are the rule. **Pine, balsam,** and other conifers put in appearances as well.

North Carolina figures prominently in the history of forestry, as it was here that the science and profession was born. In the 1880s and '90s, George W. Vanderbilt, lord of the manor at Biltmore, engaged Gifford Pinchot and then Carl Shenck to be the stewards of his thousands of acres of wooded land in the Pisgah section near Asheville. The contributions these men made to the nascent field are commemorated at the Cradle of Forestry Museum near Brevard.

Longleaf Pine

Arguably, the most important plant in North Carolina history is the longleaf pine, also called the pitch pine. Though something of a rarity today, the vast stands of longleaf pine that formerly covered our state, particularly in the east, allowed us to build a naval stores industry in the 18th and 19th centuries, producing turpentine, pitch, tar, and lumber. Overuse has something to do with the disappearance of Carolina's once legendary pine barrens, but a more perverse reason is the efficiency of

ONLINE RESOURCES FOR NORTH CAROLINA NATURE

CONSERVATION AND LAND TRUSTS

Carolina Farm Stewardship Association:
www.carolinafarmstewards.org

Carolina Mountain Land Conservancy:
www.carolinamountain.org

Conservation Council of North Carolina:
www.conservationcouncilnc.org

Conservation Fund: www.conservationfund.org/southeast/northcarolina

Conservation Trust for North Carolina:
www.ctnc.org

Friends of the Blue Ridge Parkway:
www.blueridgefriends.org

National Forests in North Carolina:
www.cs.unca.edu/nfsnc/

North Carolina Coastal Federation:
www.nccoast.org/

North Carolina Coastal Land Trust:
www.coastallandtrust.org

North Carolina Department of Environment and Natural Resources:
www.enr.state.nc.us

North Carolina Farm Transitions Network:
www.ncftn.org

North Carolina Museum of Natural Sciences:
www.naturalsciences.org

North Carolina Natural Heritage Program:
www.ncnhp.org

North Carolina Nature Conservancy:
www.nature.org/wherewework/northamerica/states/northcarolina

North Carolina Sierra Club:
http://nc.sierraclub.org

North Carolina Wildlife Resources Commission: www.ncwildlife.org

Sandhills Area Land Trust:
www.sandhillslandtrust.org

Southern Environmental Law Center:
www.southernenvironment.org

Triangle Land Conservancy: www.tlc-nc.org

Western North Carolina Alliance:
www.wnca.org

RIVER CONSERVATION AND CANOEING

Canoe North Carolina: www.canoenc.org

---

modern firefighting. Longleaf pines depend on periodic forest fires that clear out the competition from the surrounding underbrush and produce a nutritious layer of singed ground. In some of North Carolina's longleaf-harboring nature preserves, periodic controlled burns keep the forests vital. Longleaf pineywoods are crucial habitats for several endangered species, including the red cockaded woodpecker and the pine barrens tree frog.

A pretty place to glimpse the ecosystem that once covered so much of the Southeast is Weymouth Woods Sandhills Preserve, near Southern Pines. Some of the longleafs here are estimated to be nearly 500 years old. Many century-old trees bear scars from the days of the naval stores extravaganza, when turpintiners carved deep gashes in their bark and nailed up boxes to collect the resin that they bled.

Cape Fear Paddlers Association:
www.capefearpaddlers.org

Cape Fear River Watch: www.cfrw.us

Carolina Canoe Club:
www.carolinacanoeclub.com

Coastal Carolina Kayakers:
http://groups.yahoo.com/group/
CoastalCarolinaKayakers

Crystal Coast Canoe and Kayak Club:
www.ccckc.org

Eno River Association: www.enoriver.org

Haw River Assembly: www.hawriver.org

National Committee for the New River:
www.ncnr.org

North Carolina Paddle Trails Association:
www.ncpaddletrails.info

Neuse Riverkeeper: www.neuseriver.org
Pamlico-Tar River Foundation: www.ptrf.org

Roanoke River Basin Association:
www.rrba.org

Roanoke River Partners:
www.roanokeriverpartners.org

Stewards of the White Oak River Basin:
www.whiteoakstewards.org

Triad River Runners: www.trronline.org

Twin Rivers Paddle Club (Neuse and Trent
Rivers, New Bern area): www.twinrivers.org

WILDLIFE

Audubon North Carolina:
www.ncaudubon.org

Carolina Bird Club: www.carolinabirdclub.org

Carolina Raptor Center:
www.carolinaraptorcenter.org

North Carolina Birding Trail:
www.ncbirdingtrail.org

North Carolina Hummers
(tracking vagrant hummingbirds):
www.naturalsciences.org/nchummers

North Carolina Partners in Amphibian and
Reptile Conservation: www.ncparc.org

North Carolina Partners in Flight:
http://faculty.ncwc.edu/mbrooks/pif

Piedmont Wildlife Center:
www.piedmontwildlifecenter.org

Wings over Water Festival:
www.northeast-nc.com/wings

Western North Carolina Nature Center:
www.wildwnc.org

FLOWERS

Some Carolina flora put on great annual shows, drawing flocks of admirers—the gaudy **azaleas** of springtime in Wilmington, the **wildflowers** of the first warm weather in the hills, the **rhododendrons** and **mountain laurel** of the Appalachian summer. The Ericaceae family, which includes azaleas, rhododendrons, and laurel—a race of great woody bushes with star-shaped blossoms—is the headliner in North Carolina's floral fashion show. Spring comes earliest to the southeastern corner of the state, and the Wilmington area is explosively beautiful when the azaleas are in bloom. The **Azalea Festival,** held annually for more than 50 years, draws hundreds of thousands of people to the city in early to mid-April, around the time that historic plantations (Orton in particular, at Winnabow) and public gardens and private yards are spangled with azaleas.

The flame azalea makes a late spring appearance on the mountainsides of the Blue Ridge and Great Smokies, joined by its cousins the mountain laurel and Catawba rhododendron in May and June. The ways of the rhododendron are a little mysterious; not every plant will bloom every year, and there's no surefire way of predicting when they'll put on big shows. The area's widely varying elevation also figures into bloom times. If you're interested in timing your trip to coincide with some of these flowering seasons, your best bet is to call ahead and speak with a ranger from the Great Smoky Mountains National Park or the Blue Ridge Parkway, and find out how the season is coming along.

Around the end of April and into May, when spring finally arrives in the mountains but the forest floor is not yet sequestered in leafy shade, a profusion of delicate flowers emerge. **Violets** and **chickweed** emerge early on, as do the quintessentially mountain-y white **trillium** blossoms, and the Wake Robin (also a trillium), which looks something like a small poinsettia. Every year since 1950, around the end of April, the Great Smoky Mountains National Park has hosted the **Spring Wildflower Pilgrimage,** a weeklong festival featuring scores of nature walks (to look not only for wildflowers but salamanders, birds, wild hogs, and all manner of beasts), workshops, art exhibits, and more. Visit www.springwildflowerpilgrimage.org for upcoming events.

One of the best places in North Carolina to view displays of wildflowers is, rather unexpectedly, along the major highways. For more than 20 years, the state Department of Transportation has carried out a highway beautification project that involves planting large banks of wildflowers alongside highways and in wide medians. Not landscaped but rather allowed to grow up in unkempt profusion, and often planted in inspired combinations of wildly contrasting colors, the flowerbeds are a genuinely beautiful addition to the environment. The Department of Transportation website (www.ncdot.org) offers a guide to the locations and seasons of the wildflower beds.

FALL FOLIAGE

Arriving as early as mid-September at the highest elevations, and gradually sliding down the mountains through late October, autumn colors bring a late-season wave of visitors to western North Carolina. Dropping temperatures change trees' sugar production, resulting in one palette of colors, while simple fatigue causes the green to fade in others, exposing underlying hues. Countless climatic factors can alter the onset and progress of leaf season, so the mountains blush at slightly different times every year. The latter weeks of October tend to be the peak, though. During those weeks it can be very difficult to find lodging in the mountains, so be sure to plan ahead. Some of the best places for leaf peeping are along the Blue Ridge Parkway, and in the Great Smoky Mountains National Park.

CARNIVOROUS PLANTS

You've probably seen **Venus flytraps** for sale in nurseries, and maybe you've even bought one and brought it home to stuff with kitchen bugs. Venus flytraps grow in the wild only in one tiny corner of the world, and that happens to be here, in a narrow band of counties between Wilmington, North Carolina, and Myrtle Beach, South Carolina. They and their dozens of carnivorous Tar Heel kin, like pitcher plants, abattoirs of the bug world, and Dr. Seussian sundews, are fondest of living in places with nutrient-starved soil, like pine savannas and pocosins, where they have little competition for space and sunlight and can feed handsomely on meals that come right to them.

We have many species of **pitcher plants** here, a familiar predator of the plant world. Shaped like tubular vases, with a graceful elfin flap shading the mouth, pitcher plants attract insects with an irresistible brew. Unsuspecting bugs pile in, thinking they've found a keg party, but instead find themselves paddling in a sticky mess from which they're unable to escape, pinned down by spiny hairs that line the inside of the pitcher. Enterprising frogs and spiders that are either strong or clever enough to come and go safely from inside the pitcher will often set up shop inside a plant, and help themselves to stragglers.

Another local character is the **sundew,** perhaps the creepiest of the carnivorous plants. Sundews extend their paddle-shaped leaf-hands up into the air, hairy palms baited with a sticky mess that bugs can't resist. When a fly lands among the hairs, the sundew closes on it like a fist, and gorges its nasty self until it's ready for more.

There are several places where you can see wild carnivorous plants in North Carolina. A couple of the best are Carolina Beach State Park, and the Green Swamp Preserve in Brunswick County. There's also a good collection of them on display at Chapel Hill's North Carolina Botanical Garden.

Fauna

Of the wildlife who make their presence known to humans on a regular basis in North Carolina, most will be recognizable to anyone who's spent time in the woods, rural areas, and suburbs of the South and Mid-Atlantic. **White-tailed deer** are ubiquitous out in the country and in the woods, and populate suburban areas in large numbers as well. **Raccoons** and **possums** prowl at night, as happy to scavenge from trash cans as from the forest floor. **Skunks** are around too, particularly in the mountains, and are often smelled rather than seen. They leave an ambience something like a cross between grape soda and Sharpie markers. We even have a fair number of **black bears,** not only in the mountains, but in swamps and deep woods elsewhere across the state.

In woods and yards alike, **grey squirrels** and a host of familiar **songbirds** are daily presences. Different species of **tree frogs** produce beautiful choruses on spring and summer nights, while **fireflies** mount sparkly shows in the trees and grass. Down along the southeast coast, **alligators** sun themselves on many a golf course and creekside back yard. We also have some rather exotic creatures in our woods and streams, and amid the dunes.

The town of Brevard, in the Blue Ridge south of Asheville, is famous for its population of ghostly **white squirrels.** They're regular old gray squirrels, the kind that live in most any backyard in North America, but their fur ranges from speckled gray and white to pure, bone-white. It's not a form of albinism, though there are albino squirrels in the world. Rather, it's thought that Brevard's white squirrels are

© JIMMY MCDONALD

There are two species of pelicans in North Carolina.

cousins of a clan that lives in Florida, and that their ancestors may have found their way to the Blue Ridge in a circus or with a dealer of exotic pets in the early 20th century. It would seem that at least two escaped, because many of them are still spotted at backyard feeders and in parks all around Brevard.

The Carolina woods also harbor colonies of **Southern flying squirrels.** It's very unlikely that you'll see one, unless it's at a nature center

MYSTERY ANIMAL

I have been inform'd by the Indians, that on a Lake of Water towards the Head of Neus River, there haunts a Creature, which frightens them all from Hunting thereabouts. They say, he is the Colour of a Panther, but cannot run up Trees; and that there abides with him a Creature like an Englishman's Dog, which runs faster than he can, and gets his Prey for him. They add, that there is no other of that Kind that ever they met withal; and that they should have no other way to avoid him, but by running up a Tree. The Certainty of this I cannot confirm by my own Knowledge, yet they all agree in this Story. As for Lions, I never saw any in America; neither can I imagine, how they should come here.

John Lawson, *A New Voyage to Carolina*, 1709.

panthers—have been extinct in North Carolina for some time. But ask any mountain outdoorsman, and he'll set you straight; there are still panthers in the Blue Ridge and Smokies, and most everyone up there has seen one or knows someone who has.

WILD PONIES

On a dwindling number of Outer Banks beaches, small herds of wild ponies still roam as they have for at least 400 years. More accurately termed feral horses, the Banker ponies, as they're called locally, are descendants of Spanish horses, a fact recently established by DNA testing. How they arrived here is not fully known. They're believed to have been in the Outer Banks since the 1500s, which makes it likely that they arrived either with the early English colonists (who may have purchased Spanish horses in the Caribbean), or with even earlier Spanish explorers. Oral history holds that they swam ashore from long-ago shipwrecks. The primary herds today are located at Corolla and on Shackleford Banks in the Cape Lookout National Seashore. Since they roam freely in areas that the public can visit, you may find one staring you down from behind a sand dune. Please remember that, despite their resemblance to domestic horses, they really are wild animals. Feeding or approaching the ponies only does them harm in the long run. They pose some danger in return; all it takes for them to show a human who's boss is one swift kick. You can find out more about the horses and their history at www.shackleford-horses.org and www.corollawildhorses.org.

REINTRODUCED SPECIES

In the 1990s and early 2000s, a federal program to reestablish **red wolf** colonies in the Southeast focused its efforts on parkland in North Carolina. Red wolves, thought to have existed in North Carolina in past centuries, were first reintroduced to the Great Smoky Mountains National Park. They did not thrive, though, and so the colony was moved to the Alligator River National Wildlife Refuge on the northeast coast. The packs have fared better

or wildlife rehabilitation clinic, because flying squirrels are both nocturnal and shy. They're also, to put objectivity aside for a moment, almost unspeakably cute. Fully extended, they're about nine inches long snout to tail, weigh about four ounces, and have super-silky fur and pink noses, and like many nocturnal animals have comically long whiskers and huge, wide-set eyes that suggest amphetamine use. When they're flying—gliding, to be more accurate—they spread their limbs to extend the patagium, the membrane that stretches between their front and hind legs, and glide along like little magic carpets.

Also deep in the Smokies are some herds of **wild hogs,** game boar brought to the area about a hundred years ago, and allowed to go feral. The official line among wildlife officials is that **mountain lions**—referred to in this region as in this corner of the state, and now roam several wilderness areas in the sound country.

The Smokies proved a more hospitable place for the reintroduction of **elk.** Now the largest animals in the Great Smoky Mountains National Park, elk, which can grow up to 700 pounds, are most often observed in the Cataloochee section of the park, grazing happily and lounging in the mist in early morning and at twilight.

AMPHIBIANS

Dozens of species of **salamanders** and their close kin (like **mudpuppies, sirens,** and **amphiumas**) call North Carolina home (or would if they could talk), and the Great Smoky Mountains National Park harbors so many of them that it's known as the Salamander Capital of the World. **Frogs** and **toads** are numerous and vociferous, especially the many species of dainty **treefrogs** found across the state. Two species, the gray treefrog and the spring peeper, are found in every part of North Carolina, and beginning in late winter create the impression that the trees are filled with ringing cell phones (with very pleasant ringtones).

Hellbenders are quite possibly the strangest animal in North Carolina. They're enormous salamanders—not the little slickery, pencil-thin, four- and five-inch salamanders easily spotted along creeks, but hulking brutes that grow to more than two feet long and can weigh five pounds. Rare and hermetic, they live in rocky mountain streams, venturing out from under rocks at night to gobble up crayfish and minnows. They're hard to see even if they do emerge in the daytime, because they're lumpy and mud-colored, camouflaged against streambeds. Aggressive with each other, the males often sport battle scars on their stumpy legs. They've been known to bite humans, but as rare as it is to spot a hellbender, it's an exponentially rarer occurrence to be bitten by one.

REPTILES

Turtles and **snakes** are our most common reptiles. **Box turtles,** found everywhere, and **bog turtles,** found in the Smokies, are our

The alligators at Merchants Millpond live at their species' farthest northern range.

only land terrapins. A great many freshwater turtles inhabit the swamps and ponds, and on a sunny day every log or branch sticking out of fresh water will become a sunbathing terrace for as many turtles as it can hold. Common water turtles include **cooters, sliders,** and **painted turtles. Snapping turtles** can be found in fresh water throughout the state, so mind your toes. They grow up to a couple of feet long and can weigh more than 50 pounds. Not only will they bite—hard!—if provoked, but they will actually initiate hostilities, lunging for you if they so much as disapprove of the fashion of your shoes. They're vicious boogers, even the tiny hatchlings, and are best granted a wide berth. Finally, we are visited often by **sea turtles,** a gentle and painfully dwindling race of seafarers. The most frequent visitor is the **loggerhead,** a reddish-tan living coracle that can weigh up to 500 pounds, and nests as far north as Ocracoke. Occasional visitors include the **leatherback** (a 1,500-pound goliath at its largest), **hawksbills,** and **green and Ridley's turtles.**

There are not many kinds of **lizard** native to North Carolina, but those who are present make up for their homogeneity with ubiquity. **Anoles,** tiny, scaly dragons that dart along most any outdoor surface, are found in great numbers in the southeastern part of the state, up the coast, and along the South Carolina line to west of Charlotte. They put on great shows by puffing their ruby-red dewlaps, and by vacillating between drab brown and gray or lime-Slurpee-green, depending on the color of the background they wish to hide on. The ranks of lizard-kind are rounded out by several varieties of **skinks** and **glass lizards** (also called glass snakes, though they're not really snakes), and **fence lizards.**

Of real **snakes** we have aplenty. The vast majority are shy, gentle, and totally harmless to anything larger than a rat. There are a few species of venomous snakes, though—very dangerous ones at that—which are discussed in greater detail in the Safety section of the Essentials chapter. These include three kinds of **rattlesnake** (the huge diamondback, whose diet of rabbits testifies to its size and strength;

the pigmy; and the timber or canebrake rattler); the beautiful, mottled **copperhead;** the **cottonmouth or water moccasin,** famous for flinging its mouth open in hostility and flashing its brilliant white palate; and the **coral snake,** fantastically beautiful and venomous in equal degrees. Luckily, most Carolina snakes are entirely benign neighbors to humans. We have many species, including such old familiars as **black racers** and **king snakes,** and **milk, corn,** and **rat snakes.** One particularly endearing character is the **hognose snake,** which can be found throughout North Carolina but is most common in the east. The hognose snake, colloquially known as a spreading adder, compensates for its total harmlessness with amazing displays of histrionics. If you startle one, it will first flatten and greatly widen its head and neck area, and hiss most passionately. If it sees that you're not frightened by Plan A, it will panic and go straight to Plan Z: playing dead. The hognose snake won't simply lay inert until you go away, though; it goes to the lengths of flipping onto its back, exposing its pitiably vulnerable belly, opening its mouth, throwing its head back limply, and sticking out its tongue as if having just drunk poison. Goodbye, cruel world! Such a devoted method actor is the hognose snake that, should you call its bluff and poke it back onto its belly, it will fling itself energetically back into the mortuary pose, and resume being deceased.

Alligators make most of their reptilian kin look like dust mites. Tar Heel gators are most abundant in the area south of Wilmington, but they've been seen all up and down the state's coast (note how far north the Alligator River is), and even as far north and inland as Merchants Millpond State Park near the Virginia line. The biggest boys can reach 1,000 pounds and measure 10–15 feet long. Smaller gators are more plentiful, but the six- and eight-foot females are only teeny in comparison to the massive bull gators. They have approximately a zillion sharp teeth, and even hatchlings can pack a nasty bite. These amazing, prehistoric-looking amphibious assault machines appear to spend most of their waking hours not awake, splayed out in the sun with their eyes closed, or floating motionless in the water. Don't fall for it, it's their fiendishly clever (or primitively simple—it's hard to tell with gators) ploy to make you come closer. When they take a notion, they can launch themselves at prey as if spring-loaded, and are more than capable of catching and eating a dog or cat, or even a small child. It happens very rarely, but large gators can and will eat a grown man, given the chance. The best course of action, as with most wildlife, is to admire them from a distance.

History

ANCIENT CIVILIZATION

By the time the first colonist thought to call this place Carolina, the land had already sustained some 20,000 years of human history. We know that Paleo people hunted these lands during the last ice age, when there were probably more mammoths and saber-toothed tigers in North Carolina than people. Civilization came around 4,000 BC, when early Carolinians settled down to farm, and to make art and trade goods. By the time the Christian era began on the other side of the globe, Southern Woodland and Mississippian Indians were also living in advanced societies with complex religious belief systems, economic interaction between communities, advanced farming methods, and the creation of art and architecture that are marveled at today.

When Europeans saw North Carolina for the first time, there were more than a dozen major Native American groups within the present state lines. The Cherokees ruled the mountains, while the Catawba, Pee Dees, Tutelo, and Saura, among others, were their neighbors down in the Piedmont. In the east, the Cheraw, Waccamaw, and Tuscarora were some of the larger communities, while many bands occupied land along the Outer Banks and Sounds.

CONQUEST

The first white feet to touch North Carolina's soil were Spanish. Hernando de Soto and his men marched around western North Carolina in 1539, but they were just passing through. In 1566, another band of Spaniards came for a longer visit. A group of explorers led by Juan Pardo were making a circuitous trek in the general direction of Mexico, and along the way Pardo established several forts in what are now the Carolinas and Tennessee. One of these forts, called San Juan, has been identified by archaeologists outside present-day Morganton, in a community called Worry Crossroads. Although the men who were garrisoned for a year and a half at Fort San Juan eventually disappeared into the woods or were killed, it's theorized that they may have had a profound impact on the course of history, possibly spreading European diseases among the native inhabitants and weakening them so much that, a couple of decades later, the tribes would be unable to repel effectively the invasion of English colonists.

The next episode in the white settlement of North Carolina is one of the strangest mysteries in American history, that of the Lost Colonists of Roanoke. After two previous failed attempts to establish an English stronghold on the island of Roanoke, fraught by poor planning and even worse diplomacy, a third group of English colonists tried their luck. Some time between being dropped off in the New World, and one of their leaders returning three years later to resupply them, all of the colonists—including Virginia Dare, the first English person born in the Americas—had vanished into the woods. To this day their fate is unknown, although a host of fascinating theories are still debated, and probably always will be.

Of course, the disappearance of the Roanoke colonists did little to slow the process of the European conquest of North America. In the

RAISED FROM THE DEAD

In 1587, Thomas Hariot, an English man of science, visited Roanoke Island and the surrounding areas. Acting in effect as an early ethnographer, he learned Algonquin during his time in the New World, and recorded social customs of the Native Americans, along with observations of the region's natural resources, in his 1587 *An Account of the Inhabitants and Commodities of Virginia*. From conversing with priests, he learned the following about the religious beliefs of native inhabitants.

They believe also the immortality of the soul, that after this life as soon as the soul is departed from the body, according to the work it has done, it is either carried to heaven the habitat of the gods, there to enjoy perpetual bliss and happiness, or else to a great pit or hole, which they think to be in the furtherest parts of their part of the world toward the sunset, there to burn continually. The place they call Popogusso.

For the confirmation of this opinion, they told me two stories of two men that had been lately dead and revived again, the one happened but a few years before our coming into the country of a wicked man, which having been dead and buried, the next day the earth of the grave being seen to move, was taken up again, who made declaration where his soul had been, that is to say, very near entering into Popogusso, had not one of the gods saved him, and given him leave to return again, and teach his friends what they should do to avoid that terrible place of torment. The other happened in the same year we were there, but in a town that was 60 miles from us, and it was told me for strange news, that one being dead, buried, and taken up again as the first, showed that although his body had lain dead in the grave, yet his soul was alive, and had traveled far in a long broad way, on both sides whereof grew most delicate and pleasant trees, bearing more rare and excellent fruits, than he had seen before, or was able to express, and at length came to most brave and fair houses, near which he met his father that had been dead before, who gave him great charge to go back again, and show his friends what good they were to do to enjoy the pleasures of that place, which when he had done he should after come again.

new century, after the establishment of the Virginia colony, new English settlers began to trickle southward into Carolina, while Barbadians and Europeans from Charles Town (in present-day South Carolina) gradually began to populate the area around present-day Wilmington. The town of Bath was established in 1706, and New Bern was born shortly thereafter. The bloody Tuscarora War followed, and after a crushing defeat near present-day Snow Hill, in which hundreds of Tuscarora were killed, that tribe retreated and opened the land along the Neuse River to white colonization.

COLONIALISM

The European-Indian conflict was not the only world-changing cultural encounter going on in the Southern colonies. By the mid-18th century, there were nearly 100,000 African slaves in North Carolina, and by the end of the century, a few areas, particularly around Wilmington, were majority-African. While North Carolina did not experience slavery on as vast a scale as South Carolina, there were a handful of plantations with hundreds of slaves, and many smaller plantations with smaller populations. Africans and African Americans early became a potent cultural force in North

Carolina, as in the rest of the South, influencing everything from the economy and politics to language, music, architecture, and cuisine.

In the 1730s, the Great Wagon Road was built through the Mid-Atlantic and Southern backcountry, connecting Pennsylvania with Georgia by way of Virginia and North Carolina. Down this road came German and Scotch-Irish settlers. Meanwhile, by way of the port of Wilmington a Gaelic-speaking Scottish community took root in the area around what is now Fayetteville. Shortly before the American Revolution, a group of German-speaking religious pilgrims known as the Moravians constructed beautiful and industrious villages around present-day Winston-Salem. Their pacifist beliefs, German, Swiss, and central European heritage, and artistry set them apart from other colonial North Carolina communities, and they left an indelible signature on the state's history.

The 18th century brought one conflict after another to the colony, from fights over the Vestry Act in the early 1700s, which attempted to establish the Anglican church as the one official faith of the colony, through various regional tribal conflicts, and events that played out at a global level during the French and Indian War. At mid-century, though the population and economic importance of the Piedmont was growing exponentially, colonial representation continued to be focused along the coast. Protesting local corruption and lack of governmental concern for the western region, a group of backcountry farmers organized themselves into an armed posse in resistance to colonial corruption. Calling themselves the Regulators, they eventually numbered more than 6,000. Mounting frustrations led to an attack by the Regulators on the Orange County courthouse in Hillsborough. Finally a colonial militia was dispatched to crush the movement, which it did at the Battle of Alamance in 1771. Six Regulators were captured and hanged at Hillsborough.

REVOLUTION AND STATEHOOD

The War of the Regulation was just one of the manifestations of the tensions between colonists and colonial governments that characterized the era leading up to the American Revolution. When the Intolerable Acts were imposed by the crown, further diminishing colonial rights to self-determination, the ladies of Edenton declared their support of a boycott on British goods, in a genteel protest known as the Edenton Tea Party. Against Royal Governor Josiah Martin's wishes, North Carolina sent delegates to the 1774 Continental Congress, and colonists pulled together a provincial government.

After the battles of Lexington and Concord, Governor Martin removed himself from New Bern, the first colonial governor to buck his post. Mecklenburg County (the Charlotte area) also made history by passing the first colonial declaration in rejection of the crown's authority.

Political opinion in North Carolina was far from unanimous, and significant pockets of loyalist sentiments existed. Among the most noteworthy was the community of highland Scots in the Cape Fear Valley, around present-day Fayetteville. Men from this community were among the fallen at the bloody Battle of Moore's Creek in the late winter of 1776, near Wilmington, in which 30 Scotsmen died. That spring, the Provincial Congress in North Carolina authorized its representatives to advocate for independence from Britain at the upcoming Second Continental Congress. A few months after the adoption of Declaration of Independence, North Carolina drafted and ratified its own state constitution.

North Carolinians fought all over the eastern seaboard during the Revolution, including about 1,000 who were with Washington at Valley Forge. The year 1780 brought fighting back home, particularly in the area around Charlotte which a daunted Cornwallis referred to as the Hornets' Nest. The battle of Kings Mountain, west of Charlotte, was a pivotal moment in the war, and one that was particularly costly to the Loyalist forces. Cornwallis received another blow at the Battle of Guilford Courthouse which, thought technically a British victory, weakened his forces considerably. By the time the war ended, thousands of North Carolinians were dead, and the treasury was far into the red. But North Carolina was now a state, with the business of statehood to attend to. The capital was moved inland to Raleigh, and 20-some miles away at Chapel Hill, ground was broken for the establishment of the University of North Carolina, the first state university in the United States.

THE FEDERAL ERA

The early 19th century in North Carolina was a good deal more peaceful than the previous hundred years had been. The first decade of the 1800s brought a religious awakening in which thousands of North Carolinians became devout Christians. The introduction of the cotton gin and of bright leaf tobacco were economic boons to the state, and particularly to the eastern counties. Railroads and plank roads made trade immeasurably more efficient, bringing new prosperity to the Piedmont.

There was also tragedy in the early 19th century. Andrew Jackson's administration presided over the passage of the Indian Removal Act in 1830, which assigned reservations in the Indian Territory of present-day Oklahoma to the "Five Civilized Tribes" of the southeastern United States—the Cherokee, Choctaw, Creek, Chickasaw, and Seminole. Thousands upon thousands of Cherokees were forced out of western North Carolina, North Georgia, eastern Tennessee, and Alabama, and marched west on the Trail of Tears. About 4,000 died along the way. Another thousand or so people, through hiding, fighting, and negotiation, managed to win the right to stay in North Carolina—an act of resistance that was the birth of the modern Eastern Band of the Cherokee, which is still centered in and around the town of Cherokee on the Qualla Boundary in North Carolina's Great Smoky Mountains.

THE CIVIL WAR

Politically moderate compared to South Carolina and some other Southern states, and less invested economically and politically in slavery, North Carolinians were painfully divided as the War Between the States approached. The state's voters rejected a ballot measure to authorize a secession convention, but North Carolina's

hand was forced when fighting erupted at Fort Sumter in Charleston harbor. Secessionist Governor John Ellis rejected Lincoln's call to federalize state militias, and instead seized control for the state of all federal military installations in North Carolina, as well as the Charlotte mint. North Carolina seceded on May 20, 1861. A few weeks later, the Union blockade of the North Carolina coast began. New Bern fell in the spring of 1862, and became a major locus of strategic operations for the Union military, as well as a thriving political base for free African Americans and escaped slaves. To the south, Fort Fisher on Cape Fear, near Wilmington, was a crucial outlet for blockade runners. It kept the city of Wilmington in Confederate hands until nearly the end of the war, and when it finally did fall to Union forces in late February 1865, it required what would remain the largest amphibious assault in American military history until World War II.

The diversity of opinion felt by Southerners regarding the War Between the States was particularly manifest in North Carolina. At least 5,000 African Americans from North Carolina joined and fought in the Union Army, and there were strong pockets of Unionist sentiments among white Carolinians—particularly in the mountains, but in other parts of the state as well. At least 10,000 white North Carolinians fought for the Union. Zebulon Vance, who won the gubernatorial election in 1862 and served the state through the duration of the war, was a native of Weaverville, near Asheville, and hence felt acutely the state's ambivalence towards the Confederacy. To the consternation of Richmond, Governor Vance was adamant in his refusal to put the interests of the Confederacy over those of his own state. Mountain communities suffered tremendously during the war from acts of terrorism by deserters and rogues from both armies.

The latter years of the Civil War were particularly horrible in North Carolina, as they were throughout the South. Approximately 4,000 North Carolina men died at the Battle of Gettysburg alone. After laying waste to Georgia and South Carolina, General

Sherman's army entered North Carolina in the spring of 1865, destroying civilians' homes and farms. The last major battle of the war was fought in North Carolina, when Sherman and Confederate General Joseph Johnston engaged at Bentonville. Johnston surrendered to Sherman in Durham in April 1865.

By the end of the war, more than 40,000 North Carolina soldiers were dead—a number roughly equivalent to the entire present-day population of the city of Hickory, Goldsboro, or Wilson.

RECONSTRUCTION AND THE NEW SOUTH

The years immediately after the War were painful as well, as a vast population of newly free African Americans tried to make a new life for themselves economically and politically in the face of tremendous opposition, and often violence, from whites. The Ku Klux Klan was born during this era, inaugurating an era of horror for African Americans throughout the South and beyond. Federal occupation and domination of the Southern states' political and legal systems also exacerbated resentment towards the North. The state's ratification of the Fourteenth Amendment on July 4, 1868, brought North Carolina back into the Union.

The late 1800s saw large-scale investment in North Carolina's railroad system, punching the state's ticket for the industrial boom of the New South. Agriculture changed in this era too, as the rise of tenancy created a new form of enslavement for many farmers—black, white, and Native American. R. J. Reynolds, Washington Duke, and other entrepreneurs built a massively lucrative empire of tobacco production, from field to factory. Textile and furniture mills sprouted throughout the Piedmont, creating a new cultural landscape as rural Southerners migrated to mill towns.

THE 20TH CENTURY AND CONTEMPORARY TIMES

The early decades of the 1900s brought an expanded global perspective to North Carolina, not only through the expanded economy and the coming of radio, but as natives of the state scattered across the globe. About 80,000 North Carolinians served in World War I, many of those young men who had never left the state— or perhaps even their home counties—much less gone overseas. Hundreds of thousands of African Americans migrated north during what became known as the Great Migration. The communities created by black North Carolinians in the Mid-Atlantic and Northeast are still closely connected by culture and kinship to their cousins whose ancestors remained here. The invasion of the boll weevil hastened the departure of Southerners of all races who had farmed cotton. The Depression hit hard across all economic sectors of the state, but New Deal employment programs were a boon to North Carolina's infrastructure, bringing about the construction of hydroelectric dams, the Blue Ridge Parkway, and other public works.

North Carolina's modern-day military importance largely dates to the era of World War II. Installations at Fort Bragg, Camp Lejeune, and other still-vital bases were constructed or expanded. About 350,000 North Carolinians fought in World War II—7,000 of them died.

Old-timers in the coastal area of the Carolinas remember World War II especially vividly, because they actually witnessed it. When my father was a child, he saw at least one German U-boat in the waters off Myrtle Beach, and countless others had similar experiences as Nazi subs approached so near the coast as to be visible from the beach. Residents of the Outer Banks often encountered flotsam, corpses, and sometimes live, wounded sailors who washed up on their beaches. More than 10,000 German prisoners were literally farmed out in North Carolina, as were others across the United States, and put to work in private and larger-scale agriculture and other industries. (Some Germans were so happy during their internment that they returned to North Carolina after the war, and married and raised families here.)

In the 1950s and '60s, African Americans in North Carolina, and throughout the United States, struggled against the monolithic system of segregation and racism. The Ku Klux Klan stepped up its efforts in political and physical violence—against Indians as well as blacks, as in the famous 1958 "Battle of Maxton," in which 500 armed Lumbees foiled a Klan rally and sent the Knights running for their lives. Change arrived slowly. The University of North Carolina accepted its first African American graduate student in 1951, and the first black undergraduates four years later. Sit-ins in 1960 at the Woolworth's lunch counter in Greensboro began with four African American men, students at North Carolina A&T. On the second day of their protest, they were joined by 23 other demonstrators, by 300 on the third day, and by about 1,000 on day four. This was a pivotal moment in the national civil rights movement, sparking sit-ins across the country in which an estimated 50,000 people participated. Even as victories were won at the level of the federal courts and Congress, as in *Brown v. the Board of Education* and the 1964 Civil Rights Act, actual change on the ground was inexorably slow and hard-won. North Carolina's contribution to the civil rights movement was—and continues to be—an invaluable gift to the whole nation.

North Carolina continues to adapt and contribute to the global community. It is now a state of great national and ethnic diversity, growing especially in Hispanic heritage. In 2007, an estimated 6.5 percent of North Carolinians were Hispanic, and that number is sure to climb. There are also significant communities of Dega and Hmong people from Southeast Asia, and eastern Europeans—among countless other populations.

Global trade has been a largely destructive force in North Carolina during the past two decades. The textile industry has collapsed, creating an economic vacuum that the state is still struggling to fill. This, combined with the ongoing slow death of tobacco, and the loss of the fishing industry to international commerce as well, is causing the government and people of North Carolina to look towards tourism, the biotech field, and new approaches to agriculture to define our role in a changing world.

Government and Economy

POLITICAL LIFE
Liberal Enclaves

Though historically a reddish state, North Carolina's large populations of college students and artists have created boisterous enclaves of progressive political sentiment. The story may be apocryphal, but supposedly Senator Helms once questioned the need to spend public money on the construction of a state zoo in North Carolina, "when we can just put up a fence around Chapel Hill." The Chapel Hill area is the heart of North Carolina's liberal community, with its little-sister town of Carrboro forming a rumbling epicenter. During the 2004 elections, Dennis Kucinich made a campaign stop here—the first presidential candidate ever to stump in Carrboro—and this leftmost leftist congressmen was serenaded with peace chants and protest songs, while the mayor officially proclaimed a citywide Dennis Kucinich Day. Throughout the Iraq War, protestors have held regular rallies in front of the post office and the organic grocery store. Halfway through the second President Bush's second term, one local organization sold t-shirts, somewhat prematurely, that read "Carrboro: The Cradle of Impeachment."

Although you'll find a mixture of political views in every city in North Carolina, the Triangle is not the only famously liberal community. In Asheville, left-wing politics is part and parcel of the community's devotion to all things organic and DIY. Significant pockets of liberalism also exist in Boone, the cities of the Triad, and Wilmington.

Famous Figures

Several major players in modern American

politics are North Carolinians. The best known politician from this state in recent years is former Senator John Edwards, who has made two runs for the White House, the first leading to the Vice Presidential spot on the Democratic ticket. Edwards was born in South Carolina but grew up in the Sandhills, attended North Carolina State and UNC, and today lives in Chapel Hill. At the other end of the political spectrum, Monroe native Jesse Helms spent 30 years in the U.S. Senate, becoming one of the most prominent and outspoken conservative Republicans of our times. Upon his retirement, Helms was succeeded in the Senate by Salisbury-born Duke graduate Elizabeth Dole, who had previously served in the Reagan and first Bush cabinets, was president of the American Red Cross, and had had a close brush with the White House herself when her husband, Kansas Senator Bob Dole, ran for president in 1996.

MAJOR INDUSTRIES

North Carolina has experienced tremendous shifts in its economy during the last generation, as the industries that were largely responsible for the wealth and development of the state in the preceding centuries have fallen by the wayside in the new world. The **tobacco** industry dominated the state's economy for generations, employing countless Carolinians from field to factory and funding an inestimable portion of the state's fundamental physical and cultural infrastructure. The gradual decline of the worldwide tobacco industry from the 1980s on has changed the state forever, particularly in the rural east. (Other fields of agriculture, particularly **livestock**—chickens and hogs— are still important in the east.) Likewise, the **textile** industry, an industrial giant from the late 19th century until the late 20th century, and the **furniture** businesses of the Piedmont, have fallen off to nearly nothing as manufacturers send their labor opportunities overseas. The once-thriving **fishing** industry too is in steep decline, due to globalization and pollution.

New industries and fields have taken up where the former staples left off. **Pharmaceutical** and **high-tech** corporations are an important draw of labor and revenue to the area around the Triangle. Charlotte is second only to New York City among the United States' largest **banking** centers. **Tourism** is crucial, and the **film** industry has also established itself as a contributor to North Carolina's economy. **Agriculture** continues to be very important, though increasingly specialized, particularly as demand for organic products is allowing a new generation of back-to-the-landers to make their living homesteading in rural Kakalak.

Tourism

North Carolina has always had a fairly robust travel industry, given the state's considerable natural attractions and long tradition of cultural wealth. As the economy's old standbys like textiles and tobacco have faded into history, the tourist sector has become ever more important. The landscapes of the state, particularly its mountains and beaches, sell themselves, and hardly need a push from travel industry think tanks. Increasingly, though, new markets are highlighted, leading to more specialized promotions of niche destinations. Prominent examples include the growth of the **wine industry** in the Yadkin Valley and the boom in **NASCAR** tourism. **Culinary and agricultural tourism** have become popular, as North Carolina continues to be an important proving grounds in the locavore, organic foods, and agricultural diversification movements. **Heritage tourism** is also enormously important, with guidebooks and "trails" (usually driving tours) being developed to promote history, traditional music, folk arts, and literary achievement. The state Department of Commerce estimates that the 45 million people visit North Carolina every year, bringing in more than $16.5 billion, and that nearly 200,000 state residents work in industries directly related to and dependent upon tourism.

DISTRIBUTION OF WEALTH

For the most part, North Carolina is a fairly working-class state. Pockets of significant wealth exist in the urban areas, and, particularly as more and more retirees relocate to

North Carolina, in the mountains and coastal counties (which also receive major financial boosts from tourism). Extensive white-collar job availability makes the Triangle a comparatively prosperous region, with household incomes in the mid-2000s approaching $60,000, much higher than the state's average, which is just over $40,000.

On the other hand, the state also experiences significant **poverty.** The poverty rate has been rising since 2000, a period not only of national economic slowdown, but one that has seen the derailment of many of North Carolina's backbone industries. As recently as 15 years ago, a high school graduate in small-town North Carolina could count on making a living wage in a mill or factory. Nowadays, opportunities have dried up, and the poverty rate in 2005, the most recent year for which data are verified, was nearly 15 percent. Even more distressing, the childhood poverty rate is over 20 percent, with that of children under five climbing towards 25 percent.

The northeastern quadrant of North Carolina is the most critically impoverished, which points to **financial inequality** correlating to race, as this is a region of significant African American population. Broken down by ethnicity, the data are shocking, revealing that while both urban and rural white poverty rest at under 10 percent, Hispanics, African Americans, and Native Americans, both rural and urban, all experience poverty rates of 20–30 percent.

Luckily, the state is blessed with many hardworking organizations and activists who are trying to alleviate the economic hardship found in North Carolina. National organizations like **Habitat for Humanity** (www.habitat.org) and regional groups like the **Southern Coalition for Social Justice** (http://southerncoalition. org), and the **Institute for Southern Studies** (www.southernstudies.org) bring community activism and research to the state. There are also excellent North Carolina–based advocates in such groups as the **North Carolina Rural Economic Development Center** (www.ncrural center.org), the **North Carolina Justice Center** (www.ncjustice.org), the **Black Family Land Trust** (www.bflt.org), and **Student Action with Farmworkers** (http://cds.aas .duke.edu/saf).

People and Culture

DEMOGRAPHICS

The 10th most populous state in the union, North Carolina's nine million residents are slightly more than the population of New Jersey, and slightly fewer than that of Georgia. More than two-thirds of North Carolinians are white, primarily of German and Scotch-Irish descent, and not quite one-third are African American. The state's population is about 6.5 percent Latino, and has the sixth-largest Native American population of any state, behind only California, Arizona, Oklahoma, New Mexico, and Texas.

More than 40 percent of North Carolinians are between the ages of 25 and 59, but the older population is steadily rising, due in large part to the state's popularity with retirees. The majority—about 70 percent—of North Carolinians live in family groups, with married couples constituting about half of those, and married couples with children (not mutually exclusive data sets) making up almost a quarter of households. Of the remaining third of the state's population who live in "nonfamily households"—that is, not with blood kin or a legally recognized spouse—the vast majority are individuals living on their own. Unmarried couples, both straight and gay, have a much lower rate of cohabitation here than in more urban parts of the United States, but such households are very common and accepted in the Triangle, Asheville, Charlotte, and other urban areas.

Native Americans

Many Americans have never heard of the

HOW CAN YOU TELL A TAR HEEL?

What manner of man is a North Carolinian? How can you tell a Tar Heel? What ingredients went into his making? Is he different, and if so, how and why?

There is no slide-rule answer to these questions, but it may be interesting to explore them. The Tar Heel is not a distinct species, but he may have some distinguishing marks.

[We are] independent, courageous, resourceful, democratic, gregarious and individualistic, although we would use plainer words than these Latin terms to describe ourselves.

...There is a progressive strain in this Tar Heel, a realistic and resourceful determination to get ahead with the work for a better way of life for himself and his fellows...There is often a kindness in the voice which covers a lot of humanity in its acceptance of all sorts and conditions of men...

...But there is no pouring Tar Heels into a mold. The point is that we are by preference and habit individualists, or what we call "characters."

So much for our good side. Generally, we are liable to be pretty good folks, but we have a bad side too, and the truth is that we can be, when we take a notion or for no reason at all, as violent, ornery, cantankerous, stubborn, narrow and lazy as any people anywhere on earth, civilized or uncivilized.

We cut and shoot one another at a rate not even equaled in the centers of urban civilization. True, we consider our violence too valuable to waste on outsiders and so confine it to ourselves... Tar Heels hardly ever kill or maim anybody unless he is either an old friend or a close relative.

The North Carolina Guide. Robinson, Blackwell P., ed., UNC Press, 1955.

Lumbee, despite the fact that they are the largest Native American tribe east of the Mississippi. This is in part due to the federal government's refusal to grant the Lumbee official recognition as an Indian tribe. (The state of North Carolina does recognize the tribe officially.) The Lumbee are primarily based in and around Robeson County, in the swampy southeastern corner of the state, where they have lived for centuries. In the Great Smoky Mountains, the town of Cherokee on the Qualla Boundary (Cherokee tribal lands) is the governmental seat of the **Eastern Band of the Cherokee.** The Eastern Band are largely descended from those Cherokees who escaped arrest during the tribe's removal on the Trail of Tears in the 19th century, or who made the forced march to Oklahoma but lived to walk

home to the mountains again. The Lumbee and Cherokee are both enormously important cultural groups in North Carolina. Many other tribes are native to the state as well. The other six recognized by the state are the **Waccamaw-Siouan, Occaneechi Band of the Saponi Nation, Haliwa-Saponi, Coharie, Sappony,** and **Meherrin.**

Latinos

North Carolina has one of the fastest-growing Latino populations in the United States, a community whose ranks swelled since the 1990s, in particular as hundreds of thousands of **Mexican and Central American laborers** came this way to try their fortunes in the agricultural, industrial, and formerly-booming construction trades. Their presence in such large numbers makes for some unexpectedly quirky cultural juxtapositions, as in the small rural towns that are now majority-Latino, or in Charlotte, where, due in a large part to the rise of the Latino population, the most common religion is now Catholicism.

Other Immigrants

Significant numbers of non-Latino immigrants also live in North Carolina. Charlotte is a dizzying hodgepodge of nationalities and ethnicities, where native Southerners live and work alongside **Asians, Africans,** and **Middle Easterners,** where mosques and synagogues and wats welcome worshipers just down the street from Baptist churches and Houses of Prayer. Many **Hmong** and other **Southeast Asian** immigrants have settled in the northern foothills and the Piedmont Triad, and the dense thicket of universities in the Triangle attract scholars from around the world.

RELIGION

As early as the 17th century, North Carolina's religious landscape foreshadowed the diversity we enjoy today. The first Christians in North Carolina were Quakers, and they were soon followed by Anglicans, Presbyterians, and Baptists, and Moravians, Methodists, and Catholics. Native American and African faiths, present in the early colonial days, were never totally quashed by European influence, and Barbadian Sepahardic Jews were on the scene very early as well. All of these faiths remain with us today, while the religious landscape is further enriched by the presence of Muslims, Buddhists, and an amazing mosaic of Christian denominations.

North Carolina claims as its own one of the world's most influential modern religious figures. Billy Graham was raised on a dairy farm outside Charlotte, and experienced his conversion in Charlotte in 1934. After preaching in person to more people around the world than anyone in human history, and playing a part in the administration of every president since Harry Truman, Billy Graham is now at home in his native state, where he divides his time between Charlotte and Montreat, outside of Asheville.

LANGUAGE

Few states can boast of such linguistic diversity as North Carolina. In language, dialect, and accent, North Carolina speech varies widely from region to region and even county to county. These variations have to do with the historical patterns of settlement in a given area—whether Scots-Irish or German ancestry is common, how long tribal languages survived after the arrival of Europeans, the presence or lack of African influence—as well as other historical patterns of trade and communication.

Of our distinct regional accents, the **"Outer Banks brogue"** is probably the best known. Much like the residents of the Chesapeake islands in Maryland and Virginia, "Hoi Toiders," as Outer Bankers are jokingly called because of how they pronounce the phrase "high tide," have a striking accent that sounds much like that of parts of the north of England. "I"s are rounded into "Oi"s, "R"s are often born down on hard, and many distinctive vocabulary words survive from long-ago English and Scots-Irish ancestry. Not dissimilar is the Appalachian accent heard through much of the mountains. Though the effect is a bit more subtle than in the Outer Banks, the "Oi" sound stands for "I" in Appalachian English too, and "R"s are emphasized. A telltale sign of upcountry origins is the pronunciation of the A sound in words like bear and hair, which in the mountains is flattened almost inside-out so that the words are pronounced something like "barr" and "harr."

Piedmont Carolinians, both white and black, have a wide spectrum of linguistic influences. The heart of the state has always been a cultural and commercial crossroads, from the days of the Great Wagon Road, which brought 18th-century white settlers into the Southern backcountry, to the magnetic influence of cigarette factories and textile mills, which drew rural Southerners from all over the region. The product of this linguistic mix-and-match is probably the closest thing that we have in North Carolina to the generic Hollywood version of "the Southern Accent," but Piedmont speech is far from homogenous

UNDERSTANDING LOCAL LINGO

North Carolina speech features all sorts of delightful and sometimes perplexing regional vocabulary and grammar. Following are a selection of some of the common Carolinianisms most likely to stump the traveler or newcomer.

Bless your/his/her heart: A complex declaration with infinitely varied intentions, interpreted depending on context or tone. In its most basic use, "Bless your heart" is a sincere thank-you for a favor or a kindness paid. It's also an exclamation of affection, usually applied to children and the elderly, as in, "You are *not* 92 years old! You are? Well, bless your heart." Frequently, though, hearts are blessed to frame criticism in a charitable light, as in, "Bless his heart, that man from New York don't know not to shout."

buggy: a shopping cart, as at a grocery store.

carry: convey, escort, give a ride to. "I carried my mother up to the mountains for her birthday."

cattywompus: topsy-turvy and mixed up. Used especially in the Piedmont and farther west.

Come back: Often uttered by shopkeepers as a customer leaves, not to signify that something was left behind for which one should return immediately, but simply an invitation to patronize the establishment again some day.

Coke: any soft drink, may be called "pop" in the mountains

dinner: the midday meal

evening: not just the twilight hours, but all the hours between about 3 P.M. and nightfall.

ever-how: however; similarly, "ever-when," "ever-what," and "ever-who."

Fair to middling: so-so, in response to "How you?"

fixing: about to or preparing to do something. "She's fixing to have a baby any day now."

holler: hollow, a mountain cove.

Kakalak: Carolina. (Also Kakalaky, Cakalack)

mash: press, as a button. "I keep mashing the button, but that old elevator just won't come."

mess: discombobulated, in a rut, not living right. "I was a mess until I joined the church."

might could/should/would: could/should/would perhaps. "Looks like it's fixing to rain. You might should go roll up your car windows."

mommocked: see *cattywompus*. Used especially on the Outer Banks and in rural southeastern North Carolina.

piece: a vague measure of distance, as in, "down the road a piece" (a little ways down the road) or "a fair piece" (a long way).

poke: a bag, such as a paper shopping bag. Used especially in the mountains.

reckon: believe, think. Often used in interrogative statements that end with periods, as in, "Reckon what we're having for dinner." (That is, "What do you suppose is for lunch?")

right: quite, very. Variations include "right quick" (soon, hurriedly), "right much" (often), and "a right many" or "a right smart of" (a great quantity).

sorry: worthless, lame, shoddy. "I wanted to play basketball in college, but I was too sorry of an athlete."

speck so: "I expect so," or, "Yes, I guess that's correct."

supper: the evening meal (as opposed to "dinner," i.e., lunch)

sy-goggling: see *cattywompus, mommocked*. Used especially in the mountains.

ugly: mean or unfriendly, spiteful. Sometimes referred to as "acting ugly." "Hateful" is a common synonym. The favorite Southern injunction that "God don't like ugly" does not mean that God wants us to be pretty (except inasmuch as pretty is as pretty does), but rather that we should be nice.

wait on: To wait for. "We've been waiting on the waiter to come wait on us for 20 minutes."

Y'all: Pronoun used to address any group of two or more people.

yonder: over there.

Y'uns: Y'all, used in the mountains.

within the region. For example, native central Carolinians are equally likely to call the Queen City "Charrlitt" as "Shollutt," depending on individual influences.

There are a great many smaller linguistic zones peppered throughout the state. Folks from up around the **Virginia border** in eastern North Carolina may have a distinctively Virginian accent. Listen for the classic telltale word, "house." Southside Virginians and their neighbors just south of the state line will pronounce it "heause," with a sound like the Canadian "about." **Cherokee English,** heard in the Smokies, combines the Appalachian sound with a distinctively Cherokee rhythm, while **Lumbee English,** spoken in and around Robeson County in the southeast, combines an accent somewhat like those of the Outer Banks or deep mountains with a wealth of unusual grammatical structures and vocabulary of mysterious origin. (Oft-cited examples are the Lumbee construction "bees," a present-tense form of "to be," and words like "ellick" for coffee and—not that this comes up much in conversation—"juvember" for slingshot. "Get me some more ellick please if you bees going to the market.") Residents of the **Sandhills** area bounded approximately by the Uwharries to the west, Sanford to the north, and Southern Pines to the southeast, have a highly unusual rhythm to their speech, a rapid, soft, almost filigreed way of talking, delivered in bursts between halting pauses. Down around Wilmington and south to the South Carolina line, African American English, and white English to a lesser extent, have some of the inflections of the **Gullah language** of the

Lowcountry. These are only a few of our dialects, and even these have sub-variations. Old-timers can pinpoint geographical differences within these categories—whether a Lumbee speaker is from Prospect or Drowning Creek, say, or whether a Banker is from Ocracoke or Hatteras.

Of course, English is hardly the only language spoken here. We also have languages that pre- and post-date the emergence of English as the primarily language of the Carolinas. If you visit Cherokee, you'll see that many street and commercial signs bear pretty, twisty symbols that almost look like a cross between Khmer or Sanskrit and Cyrillic. This is, of course, **written Cherokee,** following the syllabary famously devised by Sequoyah in the early 19th century. Cherokee also survives as a spoken language. Native speakers are numbered among the elders in traditional communities such as Snowbird, near Robbinsville, and among younger members of the tribe there is a determination to learn and in turn teach their ancestral tongue.

Spanish is widely spoken throughout the state as the Latino population continues to rise rapidly. Within the Latino communities here are many national and regional accents and dialects. Some Central American immigrants, being speakers of indigenous languages, arrive unable to understand English *or* Spanish. Anyone who doubts that newcomers to this country are dedicated to the task of becoming part of American society need only consider the incredibly difficult task faced by such immigrants, who must first learn Spanish before they can enroll in ESL programs to learn English.

The Arts

As much as we brag about our homegrown athletes—and with good reason—it is in the arts that North Carolina most distinguishes herself. The state's incredibly rich and complex cultural heritage, as well as the unflagging support of the North Carolina Arts Council and a wide network of local and regional arts organizations, have supplied inspiration and sustenance for generation after generation of remarkable musicians, writers, actors, and other artists.

LITERATURE

Storytelling seems to come naturally to Southerners. From the master tellers of Jack Tales in the Blue Ridge to the distinguished journalists we see every night on television, North Carolinians have a singular gift for communication. Thomas Wolfe was an Asheville native, and O. Henry (whose real name was William Sidney Porter) was born and raised in Greensboro. Tom Robbins *(Even Cowgirls Get the Blues)* was born in Blowing Rock. Charles Frazier *(Cold Mountain)* is from Asheville. Sarah Dessen *(Just Listen)* is from Chapel Hill. Kaye Gibbons, Lee Smith, Fred Chappell, Randal Kenan, and Jill McCorkle, leading lights in Southern fiction, are all natives or residents of North Carolina. Also closely associated with the state are Carl Sandburg, David Sedaris, Armistead Maupin, and Betsy Byars, who have all lived here at some point in their lives.

North Carolina has also given the world some of the giants of 20th-century journalism. Edward R. Murrow, Charles Kuralt, David Brinkley, and Howard Cosell were all sons of Carolina, and Charlie Rose carries their torch today.

MUSIC

It's hard to know where to begin in describing the importance of music to North Carolinians. From fiddlers' conventions to renowned symphony orchestras to a thriving gospel music industry, there is no escaping good music here.

From the earliest days of recorded country music, North Carolinians shared their traditional songs and tunes with the world. Charlie Poole and Wade Mainer (who is still playing at over 100 years old) were profoundly influential artists in the 1930s. Come 1945, Shelby banjo player Earl Scruggs was defining what has come to be the quintessential sound of American **bluegrass** music. Ronnie Milsap, Donna Fargo, and Charlie Daniels made big names for themselves in the 1970s, '80s, and '90s **country** music scene, and Randy Travis has been one of the most prominent Nashville artists for more than 20 years.

The history of **jazz** and **funk** would be unimaginably different were it not for a tradition of musical innovators that approaches that of New Orleans. John Coltrane was raised in High Point, and Thelonious Monk was a native of Rocky Mount. Hot on their heels were North Carolinians Nina Simone, Roberta Flack, and George Clinton. Maceo Parker and a startlingly long list of fellow Kinston and eastern North Carolina natives were to a large degree responsible for the invention of the funk sound that emerged from their days in James Brown's band.

Eastern North Carolina is electric with African American **gospel** music, and the Smoky Mountains have produced many of the greats in the largely white tradition of Southern gospel. There are also thriving gospel traditions among the state's Native American tribes.

To the world of **pop** music, North Carolina has contributed James Taylor, Tori Amos, and Clay Aiken, while the Squirrel Nut Zippers and Southern Culture on the Skids have distilled the eccentricities of Chapel Hill into their own genre-defying sounds.

But even more remarkable than the number of North Carolinians who have made music on the world stage is the vitality of the state's home-grown, home-played music. At many hundreds of country stores, barbershops, and oprys throughout the state, old-time Appalachian and bluegrass musicians jam simply for the pleasure of making music with their friends. In countless churches on Sunday mornings and at annual homecomings and "gospel explosions," contemporary and traditional African American gospel music uplifts fans and congregations. Homegrown hip-hop and rap are very strong in both urban and rural areas, and the DIY aesthetic inspires punk and garage bands in the college towns.

THEATER

Drama plays an important role in North Carolina's artistic life. Regional theater companies, like the venerable Flat Rock Playhouse near Hendersonville, make great theater accessible in small towns and rural areas. The North Carolina School for the Arts in Winston-Salem mints great actors and filmmakers, among other artists. The film and television industries have long recognized North Carolina as a hotbed of talent as well as a state full of amazing locations on which to film.

You'll find throughout this book references to **outdoor historical dramas,** a genre that for some reason has long flourished in North Carolina. The most famous such production is North Carolina playwright Paul Green's *Lost Colony,* which has been performed every summer since 1937 on Roanoke Island, except for the war years when German U-boats lurked nearby. The Cherokee and Lumbee tribes each tell of emblematic episodes in their history in outdoor dramas, *Unto these Hills* (in production since 1950) and *Strike at the Wind,* respectively. The community of Boone has presented *Horn in the West* since 1952, and it is joined by Valdese and several other communities in North Carolina in turning to performance tableaux to commemorate their heritage. It's especially important to note that among the characteristics of outdoor drama in North Carolina is the fact that casts, crews, and often producers and playwrights, are typically members of the communities whose stories the plays tell.

ARTS AND CRAFTS

North Carolina rivals any state in the nation in the vitality of its tradition of both folk and "studio" craft. Several communities here are known throughout the world for their local traditions, and countless individual artists and studios and galleries can be found across North Carolina.

Seagrove, a miniscule town that sits almost at dead-center of the state, has been the home of hundreds and hundreds of **potters** since the 18th century. What began as a commercial enterprise to turn out a workhorse product made for trade on the Great Wagon Road became an increasingly artistic form in the early 20th century. Some of the finest potters in the world work in Seagrove today, and many of them are descendants of founding members of the community.

Cherokee craft is another important aesthetic school, encompassing a wide range of techniques and media, from wood- and stone-carving to fiber arts to traditional weaponry to avant-garde sculpture and painting. **Qualla Arts and Crafts Mutual,** located in downtown Cherokee, has a wonderful sales gallery that will absolutely dazzle the lover of fine craft.

Asheville too is an epicenter of the arts, the heart of a vast community of artists that stretches throughout western North Carolina and includes such major folk schools as **John C. Campbell** in Brasstown, near the Georgia line, and **Penland,** close to the Tennessee border in the northeastern mountains. In Asheville you can see and purchase a seemingly infinite variety of crafts, from handmade baskets and quilts to furniture and clothing to jewelry and iron architectural elements. The **Southern Highland Craft Guild,** an old and accomplished organization, deserves a lot of credit for the thriving health of the craft movement in Western North Carolina. Its website (www.southernhighlandguild.org) has a great deal of information about contemporary master crafters and their work.

As humans become more and more accustomed to living in a world where most every object that we see and handle and use was mass-produced far away, we develop an ever deeper appreciation for the depth of skill and aesthetic complexity that went into the production of everyday objects in past generations. North Carolinians have always been great crafters of utilitarian and occupational necessities. As you travel through the state, keep an eye out for objects that one might not immediately recognize as art—things like barns, fishing nets, and woven chair bottoms—but which were made with the skill and artistry of generations-old traditions. In North Carolina, art is everywhere.

Food

You'll probably have heard, and maybe even eaten, your fill of North Carolina's most famous specialties—**barbeque, Brunswick stew,** and **hush puppies.** But are you brave enough to venture deeper into the hinterlands of Carolina cooking?

Few snacks are more viscerally craved by Carolinians, and more revolting to non-Southerners, than **boiled peanuts.** For my part, I'd eat nothing else if my doctor would let me. The recipe is wonderfully simple: Green peanuts are boiled, in their shells and usually a peck or more at a time, in water as salty as the chef can palate. Once they're soft and slimy, the peanuts are dumped into a strainer, and are ready to eat. Since all you need to make them is a big kettle and a heat source, boiled peanuts are often made and sold in small bags at roadside stands, primarily in the Lowcountry and coastal plain, but increasingly up in the mountains as well.

Here's how to eat a boiled peanut: Pick it up by the ends with your thumb and forefinger and lay it lengthwise between your front teeth. Gently crack open the shell—don't bite through!—and detach the halves. Pry off half of the shell, and nip or slurp the peanuts out, as if you're eating an oyster. (Boiled peanuts often show up at Lowcountry oyster roasts.) Toss the shell out the window—chances are you're driving as you eat—and have another. Be sure you have a big soda close at hand, because you'll be real thirsty real soon.

Most cultures have a recipe that makes thrifty use of the leftover meat scraps that are too small or too few or too disgusting to be served alone. For upper Piedmont Carolinians, particularly those of German ancestry and raised in the wavy ribbon of towns between Charlotte and Winston-Salem, that delicacy is **livermush.** If you're from the Mid-Atlantic and familiar with scrapple, you'll have a pretty good idea of what livermush is like. By North Carolina law (really), livermush must contain at least 30 percent hog liver, which is supplemented with sundry scraps from hog heads, sometimes some skin, and cornmeal. At the factory, it's mashed up and cooked in loaves. In the kitchen, it's sliced and fried. You can eat it at breakfast like sausage, or in a sandwich, or even on a stick if you go to Drexel and Shelby's annual livermush festivals.

In the eastern part of the state, a similar aesthetic underlies the creation of **hog hash.** Hog hash is best made directly after an old-time hog killing, when the animal's organs are pulled steaming hot out of the carcass in the frosty fall morning. The liver, lungs, and a variety of other organs and appendages are dumped in a kettle with potatoes, a liquid base (broth or milk, or just water), and some vegetables and seasonings. Unlike livermush, hog hash is served in bowls or tubs as a dark, musky stew.

A great deal more delicate craftsmanship goes into the production of **dandoodle,** also called **tom thumbs.** You have to look pretty hard for dandoodle, and will likely only find it in far northeastern North Carolina and the bordering Virginia counties. At hog-killing time, the stomach is removed, and stuffed with sausage and flavorings. Then it's tied shut and hung up in the smokehouse for a good seasoning with hickory smoke. Like livermush, dandoodle comes out in a sort of a loaf shape, held together by the stomach membrane. Some people toss their tom thumbs in a pot to boil, either by themselves or with greens, while others slice them and lay them out with sliced boiled eggs, just as dainty as you like.

Up in the Great Smoky Mountains, the early spring is the season for **ramps**—super-pungent wild onions that grow along creekbeds in the deep mountains; they're another of those foods passionately defended by those who grew up eating them, but greeted with trepidation by outsiders. The reason they're feared by the uninitiated is their atomically powerful taste, which will radiate from every part of your person for days. Ramps taste like a cross between regular onions, garlic, leeks, shallots…and kryptonite. But they're so good. Folks skillet-cook them, fry them up in grease, boil them with fatback, or just chomp on them raw. For a really special treat, and a gentle introduction to ramps, stop in at the Stecoah Valley Center near Robbinsville and pick up a bag of the Smoky Mountain Native Plants Association's special cornmeal mix with dried ramps, and make yourself a skillet of deliciously tangy cornbread. You can also try them at the local ramps festivals held in Robbinsville and Cherokee in the springtime.

You can read all about these and other acquired tastes at **NCFOOD** (http://ncfolk.word press.com), a food blog, or on the **Southern Foodways Alliance** (www.southernfoodways. com) or **Dixie Dining** (www.dixiedining.com) websites.

Vegetarians and devotees of organic foods, fear not; North Carolina is an unusually progressive state when it comes to healthy and homegrown grub. Nevertheless, if avoiding meat, one needs to be cautious when ordering at a restaurant. Vegetarians know the drill: Make sure the beans are made with vegetable oil rather than lard, ask if the Caesar salad dressing contains anchovies, beware hidden fish and oyster sauce in Asian cooking. To these usual rules of the road, add the caution that much traditional Southern cooking makes liberal use of fatback and other animal products. Greens are quite often boiled with a strip of fatback or a hambone, as are most soups and stews. Even pie crusts are suspect, still made with lard in many old-time cooks' kitchens.

In all of the major cities, you'll find organic grocery stores. Earth Fare and Whole Foods are the most common chains, but there are also plenty of small, independent markets. Farmers markets and roadside stands just about have to fight for space, they're so plentiful. Visit the state Department of Agriculture's **North Carolina Farm Fresh** site (www.ncfarmfresh. com) for directories of farmers markets and pick-your-own farms and orchards.

ESSENTIALS

Getting There

BY AIR

The state where air travel began has over 75 public airports or jetports, almost 300 privately owned airfields, and about 20 "fly-in" communities (where residents share an airstrip and either own or rent their own hangar space). Nine airports have regularly scheduled passenger service, and four are international jetports. The state's Department of Transportation estimates that more than 35 million people fly in and out of North Carolina every year. The main hubs are North Carolina's international airports in Charlotte, Greensboro, and Raleigh-Durham (with Wilmington qualifying as an international airport with more limited service).

The 10th busiest airport in the country and 30th in the world, **Charlotte-Douglas International Airport** (5501 Josh Birmingham Pkwy., Charlotte, 800/359-2342, www.charmeck .org/departments/airport) has more than 600 daily departures and is served by dozens of airlines. There are direct, non-stop flights to over 100 domestic destinations, as well as international flights between Charlotte and many cities in Latin America and the Caribbean, as well as London, Frankfurt, Munich, and Toronto. Parking is abundant and inexpensive, with parking shuttles from 5 A.M. on.

Raleigh-Durham International Airport (2600 W. Terminal Blvd., Morrisville,

NO FISHING FROM FERRY

919/840-2123, www.rdu.com), located in Wake County about midway between Raleigh and Durham, offers service to most major domestic air hubs, as well as London, Toronto, and Cancun. Hourly and daily parking is available for reasonable rates within walking distance of the terminals, and in satellite lots linked by shuttles.

Piedmont Triad Airport (6415 Bryan Blvd., Greensboro, 336/665-5600, www.flyfrompti.com) serves the Greensboro and Winston-Salem area, with flights to and from many domestic destinations, particularly in the South, Midwest, and Mid-Atlantic. There are several smaller airports around the state, including **Wilmington International Airport** (1740 Airport Blvd., Wilmington, 910/341-4125, www.flyilm.com), **Asheville Regional Airport** (61 Terminal Dr., Fletcher, 828/684-2226, www.flyavl.com), and **Fayetteville Regional Airport** (400 Airport Rd., Fayetteville, 910/433-1160, http://flyfay.ci.fayetteville.nc.us).

In addition to the Wilmington airport (served by Delta, US Airways, and Allegiant), five regional airports offer regularly scheduled passenger service: Asheville, Fayetteville, Greenville, New Bern, and Jacksonville/Richland. You can fly Delta to any of them. In addition, Continental, US Airways, and Northwest will take you to Asheville, and US Airways also serves Fayetteville, Greenville, New Bern, and Jacksonville/Richland, while United offers air service to Greenville.

If you pilot your own plane or engage a charter flight via small prop craft, you can fly into any of over 75 regional, county, and municipal air strips, from Cullowhee's Jackson County Airport in the west to the Ocracoke Island Airport and First Flight Airport (Kill Devil Hills) on the Outer Banks. Visit www.ncairports.org for the full list, where you'll also find phone numbers, website links, navigational information, airstrip specifications, and aerial photos. (Historically, there are more municipal airports in the central and western parts of the state, because when the North Carolina legislature started handing out grants for small

public airstrips in the 1950s there were already many surplus military airfields in the eastern part, the legacy of World War II.)

BY CAR

Several major interstates spider across North Carolina, so if you're driving here and would prefer that your trip be efficient rather than scenic, you've got several convenient choices. If you're coming from most anywhere along the eastern seaboard, you'll likely be on I-95 for much of the trip. I-95 slices through the eastern third of the state, making for easy access to the beaches (most are 1–2 hours east of I-95) and to the Triangle area (just under an hour west via U.S. 64, U.S. 70, or I-40). If you're coming to the Triangle from the north, you might also choose to veer southwest at Richmond, Virginia, on I-85; this is a particularly efficient route to Durham and Chapel Hill, as well as to the Triad and Charlotte regions.

I-40 starts near Los Angeles, and runs east all the way to Wilmington, paring the state in half horizontally much as it does the continent. It's a fast road all the way through North Carolina, though weather (ice in the fall, winter, and spring, and fog any time of year) might slow you down considerably between Knoxville, Tennessee, and Asheville.

U.S. 64 and I-77 connect North Carolina to the Midwest. I-77 cuts through the toe of Virginia, in the mountains, for a straight shot to Charlotte, while U.S. 64 meanders east through the Triangle and all the way to Roanoke Island and the Outer Banks. If you're coming from the Deep South or Texas, your best bet is probably to catch Highway 20 to Atlanta, and from there pick up I-85 to Charlotte (or U.S. 19 or 23 if you're going to the mountains).

There are no checkpoints at the state line to inspect vehicles for produce or animals, but sobriety checkpoints are established and manned at holidays and other times throughout the year. Some rules to remember while driving in North Carolina: buckling up your seat belt is the law; child safety seats are mandatory for anyone under the age of eight or weighing less than 80 pounds; and if it's raining hard enough for you to need windshield wipers, you must also turn your headlights on.

Write *HP (*47) on a sticky note and affix it to your dashboard. That's the direct, free cell phone hotline to the North Carolina Highway Patrol, which will send help if you're danger, or send out law enforcement if you spot someone driving dangerously. Please don't hesitate to report aggressive, reckless, or drunk motorists to the highway patrol. You may save someone's life. And don't forget that you might be reported by another driver if you're tailgating, speeding, weaving, or driving aggressively. What passes for normal driving in the Northeast, Florida, and many other parts of the United States is regarded as aggressive driving in the South. We're not being unfriendly by turning others in, we just don't want to be endangered by someone else's impatience. Thank you in advance for driving carefully.

BY BUS

Travel to and through North Carolina can be accomplished easily and cheaply by bus. **Greyhound** (800/229-9424, www.greyhound.com) offers daily service to a long list of towns and cities. Greyhound runs to Ahoskie, Asheville, Burlington, Camp Lejeune, Charlotte, Concord, Durham, Edenton, Elizabeth City, Fayetteville, Gastonia, Goldsboro, Greensboro, Greenville, Henderson, High Point, Jacksonville, Kinston, New Bern, Raleigh, Rocky Mount, Salisbury, Smithfield, Wallace, Washington, Waynesville, Williamston, Wilmington, Wilson, and Winston-Salem. There is currently no Greyhound service to the Outer Banks, or to mountain locations in North Carolina other than Asheville and Waynesville, but you can sneak around the back way by coming through one of the Tennessee cities close to the state line, like Knoxville or Johnson City.

Before you make a bus reservation by phone or in person, be sure to check out special discounts on the Greyhound website. There are often regional promotions going on, as well as special "Go Anywhere" fares (for as low as $29 each way with 14-day advance booking), for example, as well as regular discounts for students and seniors.

These days, the large motor coaches used by Greyhound and its local subsidiaries are clean and comfortable, and if you make a reservation ahead of time you can choose your seat (some travelers like to sit close to the driver). One word of caution, however: Some bus stations are located in the seedier parts of town, so it's smart to make sure that adequate taxi service is available at your destination station after dark.

BY TRAIN

Although it does not currently serve the mountains or the coast, **Amtrak** (800/872-7245, www.amtrak.com) is a great way to get to and around central North Carolina. The three main New York–to–Florida routes—the Auto Train, the Silver Meteor, and the Silver Star—pass through North Carolina. The first two follow roughly the I-95 corridor, while the Silver Star makes a dogleg west to Raleigh before continuing south. The New York–to–New Orleans route, the Crescent, goes through both Raleigh and Charlotte. Two interstate routes serve the Carolinas as their primary destinations; the Carolinian runs from New York to Charlotte, by way of Raleigh, and the Palmetto goes from New York to Savannah, crossing the eastern third of both Carolinas.

Getting Around

BY CAR

North Carolina's highway system, with the largest network of state-maintained roads in the country and a good grid of interstates, is quite efficient in giving access to the whole state. I-95 crosses north–south, demarcating the eastern third of the state, and I-85 makes a sweeping northeast-to-southwest crescent from north of the Triangle area through Charlotte. I-40 is the primary east–west route, from Wilmington in the east through the Smoky Mountains to Knoxville, Tennessee.

The highest speed limit here, which applies (only in some places) to rural interstates and four-lanes, is 70 miles per hour. Highways, even interstates, in developed areas have much lower speed limits, and in residential areas it's a good idea to keep it under 25 miles per hour.

You can take your pick of rental car agencies at the major North Carolina airports at Charlotte, Winston Salem, and Raleigh-Durham, with a more limited menu of choices at the smaller regional airports, and pick-up and drop-off offices within many towns. For full information and for reserving in advance, it's best to call or email the company of your choice direct. Rental car companies serving North Carolina include Alamo (800/462-5266, www.alamo.com), Avis (800/331-1212, www.avis.com), Budget (800/527-0700, www.budget.com), Dollar Rent-a-Car (800/800-3665, www.dollar.com), Enterprise (800/261-7331, www.enterprise.com), Hertz (800/654-3131, www.hertz.com), National (800/227-7368, www.nationalcar.com), Thrifty (800/847-4389, www.thrifty.com), and Triangle Rent-A-Car (800/643-7368, www.trianglerentacar.com).

To rent a car you'll need to be at least 25 years of age and have both a valid driver's license and valid credit card (though some companies will accept a cash security deposit—a significant one—in lieu of credit card; better call or email ahead to make sure).

Driving to and through the Outer Banks can be a bit complicated, depending on which island you're aiming for. Bridges are few and far between. The northern banks are linked to the mainland by bridges between Point Harbor and Kitty Hawk, and from Manns Harbor over Roanoke Island to just south of Nags Head. There are no bridges to Hatteras, and in fact none until you get all the way to the southern end of the banks, where bridges link Morehead City and Cedar Point to the towns along Bogue Banks. Making up the difference is the state's excellent ferry system, which is an awfully fun way to travel. Detailed information is available at the North Carolina Department of Transportation's website (www.ncdot.org/transit /ferry). Several ferries link mainland points to each other across sounds and rivers, while ferries from Currituck to Knotts Island, and from both Swan Quarter and Cedar Island to Ocracoke, will carry you to the Outer Banks.

At the far opposite end of the state, the Great Smoky Mountains and Blue Ridge pose some driving difficulties as well. For the most part these are encountered in times of bad weather—fog, snow, and ice particularly, all of which like to hang around in the mountains. In terms of driving time, the major interstates that cross the mountains are quite efficient, and if you're traveling from one major town to another, highways like U.S. 19, 74, and 421 will get you where you need to go in pretty short order. On any smaller highways, though, you should count on much slower traveling. The Blue Ridge Parkway, while scenic and geographically direct, is very slow. The maximum speed is 45 miles per hour, but there are few stretches of the Parkway where it's safe to drive even that fast. The numbered roads are often the same way, with surprise hairpin turns or narrow cliffside shoulders. Allow yourself plenty of time to get from point to point. On some roads it'll take you an hour to cover 20 miles.

Take it slow and easy, and be alert to twists and turns, weather and wildlife. People who grow up in the mountains and learn to drive up

DRIVING TRAILS

The state of North Carolina and a variety of regional organizations have created a wonderful network of "trails" – thematic itineraries in different parts of the state, showcasing North Carolina's treasures. Check out the destinations on this sampling of trails.

Blue Ridge Music Trails:
www.blueridgemusic.org

Cherokee Heritage Trails:
www.cherokeeheritagetrails.org

Cherokee Heritage Itinerary: www.ncfolk.org

Civil War Traveler:
www.civilwartraveler.com/east/nc

Core Sound Itinerary: www.ncfolk.org

Dare to Dream (African American historical tour of the Winston-Salem area):
www.culturalcorridors.com/daretodream.html

Discover Craft North Carolina:
www.discovercraftnc.org

Fingerprint Friendly (kids' tour of the Winston-Salem area):
www.culturalcorridors.com/fingerprint.html

Great Wagon Road to Wachovia
(Moravian history tour):
www.culturalcorridors.com/wagonroad.html

Historic Albemarle Tour (Northeast coast):
www.historicalbemarletour.com

Homegrown Handmade Art Roads and Farm Trails:
www.homegrownhandmade.com

North Carolina Scenic Byways:
www.ncdot.org/doh/operations/
dp_chief_eng/roadside/scenic

Pottery Itinerary for the Seagrove Area:
www.ncfolk.org

Reynolda Mile (Reynolds family's cultural impact in Winston-Salem area):
www.culturalcorridors.com/reynoldamile
.html

Trail of Tears National Historic Trail,
North Carolina Chapter:
www.arch.dcr.state.nc.us/tears

Wine Trails of the Yadkin Valley:
www.culturalcorridors.com/winetrails.html

---

there will often zip along the roads as if they're racing in Monaco. Sometimes they'll tailgate slower drivers. This kind of tailgating is different from the aggressive driving one sees on major highways—tailgaters up here are more likely to be people who are genuinely in a hurry on their way to work or home, and are baffled as to why anyone would need to drive so slowly on these roads they've known all their lives. We slow drivers probably are inconveniencing the surer mountain motorists, but this is one of those cases in which safety must always trump manners. Keep driving as slowly as you feel is safe, and when you get to a good pull-off spot, pull over and allow the faster drivers to pass. As

a native flatlander, I know that my tenderfoot way of driving in the mountains is frustrating to the highcountry folks who share the roads with me, but I encourage all of my fellow nervous drivers to join me in resisting the pressure of tailgating.

HIGHWAY SAFETY
The North Carolina Highway Patrol is always a free cell phone call away. If you need help, if you spot someone else who needs help, or if you see someone driving dangerously, call *HP (*47) on your cell phone and you'll be connected to a dispatcher.

The state Department of Crime Control and

Public Safety has many good safe-driving tips on its website (www.nccrimecontrol.org). Pull well off the road and turn on your hazard lights if you have an accident. If you can't safely pull your vehicle out of traffic, at least get yourself far from the roadway. A distressing number of disabled motorists as well as pedestrians are struck and killed every year. State law requires that whenever we need to use our windshield wipers, we also turn on the headlights.

Weather Considerations

If you're driving in the mountains in the morning or at night (or at most any other time), you may run into heavy **fog**. Because the clouds perch on and around mountaintops, you may find yourself in clear weather one moment and, only seconds later, in a fog with little to no visibility. It can be dangerous and frightening, but if this happens, slow way down, keep a sharp eye out for the lines on the road (in extreme cases, these may be totally invisible) and for other cars, and put on your low beams. As in any kind of bad weather, it's always best to find a safe place to pull over and wait for the weather to improve. Fogs can dissipate as quickly as they appear.

In the winter you might encounter icy roads in any part of the state, and up in the mountains you might hit **ice and snow** three seasons of the year. Like many Southerners, we in the Piedmont and flatlands tend to panic when snow is forecast. (Folks in the mountains keep their wits about them no matter the weather.) In anticipation of a half-inch dusting of snow, schools and businesses may close, fleets of sand and salt trucks hit the highway, and residents mob the grocery stores as if they've just heard that every dairy and bakery in the country has been destroyed by meteors. On the one hand, our overreaction to snow makes the roads a little safer, because we're likelier to be at home regarding the precipitation in abject terror, in bed under a pile of quilts, than to be in our cars on the highways. On the other hand, those of us who do go out driving in winter weather are less likely to know how to drive on ice than the average Yankee or Midwesterner. That can

make the roads hazardous for all of us, so even if you yourself are an experienced snow driver, stay alert, and gangway. We'll try not to run into you, but can't make any promises.

While North Carolinians from the mountains are a lot more experienced at driving in snowy or icy weather, the roads themselves can be very dangerous. The safest plan is simply to avoid driving in the mountains in bad weather. But if you must go, keep in mind that mountain roads, even highways, may close—especially those maintained by the National Park Service, like the Blue Ridge Parkway and roads in the Great Smoky Mountains National Park. The National Park Service offers the following advice: "When driving downhill on slippery mountain roads, shift to a lower gear (2, 1, or L on automatic transmissions) to avoid using brakes more than necessary. Leave extra room between you and the vehicle in front of you. Be aware that icy sections persist on mountain roads even when the weather is warm in the lowlands."

Wildlife on the Road

A final note about highway travel: Please be conscious of wildlife. Deer, rabbits, turtles, foxes, coyotes, raccoons, and possums litter our highways. Head-on collisions with deer can be fatal to the parties of both species, and we lose many smaller animals because drivers are simply going too fast to avoid running over them. If you see an injured animal and are able to help it without putting yourself in danger, you'll find a phalanx of wildlife rehabilitators standing by throughout the state to give it the care it needs.

We have many deer in North Carolina, in urban and suburban areas as well as out in the country, and they are, unfortunately, the cause as well as the victims of many highway accidents. In clear weather when there's not much oncoming traffic, you may wish to use your high beams so that you'll see deer from farther off. (Remember to turn the brights off when another car is approaching you.) If you see one deer cross the road in front of you, the coast isn't necessarily clear. Deer usually travel in groups, and there may be several more waiting to jump out in front of you.

Road Etiquette

Certain rules of etiquette apply to traffic in North Carolina. These aren't written rules, but rather customs of conduct that make our time spent on the road a less stressful part of the day than it might otherwise be. North Carolina drivers are very willing to let others drivers get in front of them, whether merging onto the highway or leaving a parking lot to return to a street. Please remember to wave thanks when someone lets you in; positive reinforcement helps keep these habits alive. Folks will often wave at drivers in oncoming traffic on country roads, usually on two-lanes, and there is an expectation of a quick wave between car occupants and pedestrians as well. In all of these cases, the waves aren't big productions, festive swooping gestures or Queen Mum waves, but simply a lifting of two or three fingers of the driver's right hand off the steering wheel. A general rule of thumb is that if you're able to discern the facial features of someone outside your car, a wave is appropriate.

It goes without saying that we're expected to get out of the way or pull over to let emergency vehicles pass. In fact, it's the law. There's also an old tradition of pulling over to allow funeral processions to pass. Very few drivers here are willing to merge into or cross a train of cars headed for a funeral, but in rural areas you will still see (and perhaps wish to join) drivers in pulling all the way off the road and waiting for a procession to pass before resuming driving. It's meant as a gesture of respect to both the deceased and the mourners. Having been among the coterie of mourners in many a Carolina funeral, I can attest first-hand to how moving and deeply appreciated this gesture is.

In all of these situations, safety should be the top priority. No need to wave at or make eye contact with someone you feel is threatening, and don't pull off the road if there's no safe place to do so. But if you show courtesy to other drivers when you're able, you'll find that the traffic karma will work its way back around to you when it's most needed.

BY BUS

For local, regularly scheduled bus services within the Carolinas, check out **Carolina Trailways** (919/833-3601; since it's now operating as a division of Greyhound Lines, its website, www.carolinatrailways.com, will redirect you to Greyhound for schedule information and reservations).

In addition to local municipal bus service in the larger towns and Carolina Trailways service between many towns, some of the more popular tourist areas offer comfortable, affordable tour bus service. In Asheville, for example, **Riverfront Bus Tours** (828/252-8474 or visit www.riverlink.org) offers historical tours along the French Broad and Swannanoa Rivers, and **Hatteras Tours** (www.hattarastours.com, 252/986-2995) offers narrated tours of the islands of the Outer Banks, with a focus on the region's colorful history. There are ghost tours, Christian tours, farm tours, home and garden tours, Civil War history tours, ecology tours, and many other specialized tours, as well as historic site tours within many cities and towns: Check out www.visitnc.com to search for bus tours by town, region, or keyword.

BY BIKE

Before the Wright brothers made transportation history as the first flyers, they were bicycle men. With its temperate climates, abundance of scenic roads, and full spectrum of terrain—from mountainous to hilly to dinner-plate flat—North Carolina is bicycling heaven. There are hundreds of organized bicycling events every year, many of them in support of charities, and they welcome participants from all over. Some of the most popular bike events are held several times during the spring, summer, and fall, including a six-day Ocracoke Vacation Tour from New Bern to the tip of the Outer Banks, regular scenic rides through wine country, and rides along the Blue Ridge (including a five-day bicycling vacation starting in Blowing Rock). But that's just the beginning. Each month of the year except December sees as many as a dozen cycling events open to the public, including January's New Year's Day Breakfast Ride in Jacksonville, February's Frostbite Tour in Raleigh, and March's Uwharrie National Forest Mountain Bike Race (starting in Southern Pines); in April there's the annual "Circle the Bald" Bike Ride starting in Hayesville, and in May there's Mount Airy's Tour de Mayberry; June has bicycling events as part of the North Carolina Blueberry Festival (Burgaw), July has North Wilkesboro's Hurt, Pain and Agony Century Race, and August sees a Beginner Skills Bicycling Camp (Asheville); in late September comes the state-spanning Annual Cycle North Carolina Fall Ride from the mountains to the coast and even, by ferry, to the islands of the Outer Banks, in which approximately 1,000 cyclists take part; in October there's Rutherfordton's Tour de Pumpkin, and in November Wilson's Whirligig Festival Bike Ride. This list gives just a hint of the dozens of races, vacations, and rides for charity in this cyclist-friendly state. For a full roster see the official **Calendar of Bicycling Events** at www.ncdot.org/transit/nicycle/events/events_calendar.html.

Baggage cars on Amtrak's Piedmont line are equipped with bicycle racks, and welcome cyclists who'd like to make part of their journey by train. Call 800/872-7245 to reserve bike space on a train (you pay a $5 extra fee upon boarding). Towns where you and your bike can get aboard are Raleigh, Durham, Greensboro, Charlotte, Burlington, High Point, Salisbury, Kannapolis, and Cary. And you can take your bicycle on any of North Carolina's seven ferries: call 800/293-3779 or go to www.ncdot.org/transit/ferry for schedules and other information.

BY TRAIN

North Carolina enjoys an unusually comprehensive rail system between the major cities in the central part of the state. **Amtrak** (800/872-7245, www.amtrak.com) serves North Carolina with its Auto Train, Carolinian, Crescent, Palmetto, Piedmont (between Raleigh and Charlotte), Silver Meteor, and Silver Star. Cities on the lines include Raleigh and Durham, Rocky Mount, High Point, Winston-Salem, Gastonia, Kannapolis, and Charlotte, with smaller stops in between.

BY FERRY

For hundreds of years, ferries were a crucial link of transportation and commerce between points on North Carolina's water-logged coast, and they still provide an essential service today. The North Carolina Department of Transportation's Ferry Division (877/368-4968, www.ncdot.org/transit/ferry) operates seven primary ferry routes in the eastern part of the state. All ferries have restrooms, and some can accommodate cars and allow pets. Commercial ferries also operate throughout the coastal region. Information about specific routes is found in the coastal chapters of this book.

Conduct and Customs

GREETINGS

Values of common courtesy like saying "please" and "thank you," being deferential to the elderly, and demonstrating concern for others, are hardly proprietary customs exclusive to the South. No matter where you're from, chances are your parents raised you to "act like folks," as we call it here. The difference is that in North Carolina and elsewhere in the South, manners are a somewhat more ritualized performance, a currency that we constantly exchange and without which we feel terribly lost.

If you're unfamiliar with Southern ways, the thing you may find most strange is the friendliness of strangers. When passing a stranger on the sidewalk or in a corridor, riding together in an elevator, or even washing hands in the restroom, eye contact and a quick greeting are usually in order. (I must admit that, being a female, I'm not sure what the customs are regarding greetings in men's rooms.) Most common greetings are "Hey," "How you doing," and "How you." "How you," spoken more as a statement than as an interrogative—that is, "How you." rather than "How you?"—is shortened to a very speedy "I-U" (or, when "Hey" is added, "A-I-U"). The reply is usually equally casual, "Doing good, how about you" (which is a four-syllable sentence, "Doin' good, 'bout you"), and again spoken like a statement rather than a question. Often that's the end of the conversation, though passengers on elevators in particular sometimes wish each other a good day when one gets out. In these encounters, eye contact needn't be lingering, there's no expectation that one will be saccharine, and there is certainly no obligation to engage someone who makes you uncomfortable.

It's standard courtesy in most any retail or similarly casual transaction to inquire as to the well-being of the person serving you. It really adds very little time to tack on the friendly preamble, especially when delivered in the spoken shorthand most of us use. For instance, a cashier at McDonalds in another part of the country might greet you with "What would you like?" or simply wait for your order and not speak until asking for your money. The transaction here would more likely start with the "How you"/"Doin' good, 'bout you" exchange. With that two- or three-second dialogue, a bit of human warmth and mutual respect is shared.

It's expected that we will hold doors open for each other, and thank each other for doing so.

In addressing someone elderly whom you don't know well, the standard courtesy is to use a title, Mr. or Ms. Last Name, or, in friendlier situations, Mr. or Ms. First Name. The South was way ahead of the curve in adopting the "Ms." designation. We've always pronounced both "Mrs." and "Miss" as "Miz," so we got a free pass on having to learn that one. North Carolinians will likely address you as ma'am or sir, regardless of your age. Don't worry, this doesn't mean they think you're old.

TIPPING

Please remember to tip not only restaurant servers, but also motel and hotel housekeeping staff, bartenders, cab drivers, bellhops, redcaps, valet parking staff, and other service workers. Standard tipping rates are 20 percent for meals, 15 percent for a taxi ride, and $1 per piece of luggage for a redcap or porter, though tipping extra for good service is always a gracious and appropriate gesture.

Tips for Travelers

LGBT TRAVELERS

North Carolina law offers precious little protection against discrimination based on sexual orientation or gender identity. The state's anti-sodomy law, which applied to couples of any orientation, was struck down in 2003. However, there has not been a great deal of progress since. Same-sex couples are not protected by the law here in matters of custody, hospital visitation, workplace discrimination, or marriage. Hate crime statutes do not address violence targeting victims because of their sexual orientation or gender identity. While keeping in mind the above facts, please don't close the book on North Carolina. Rest assured that, while our laws may be retrogressive in this respect, our people are not. Much of North Carolina is very gay-friendly.

Despite being a red state, North Carolina has a strong purple streak. North Carolina's metropolitan areas have active, open queer communities, offering numerous organizations and social groups, publications, human rights advocacy services, and community centers. Like anywhere in the United States, smaller and more rural communities are less likely to be gay-friendly, though there are exceptions and pleasant surprises. As a general rule, though, a same-sex couple will attract little attention holding hands on Durham's Ninth Street, Asheville's Patton Avenue, or Weaver Street in Carrboro, whereas they may not be received warmly at the Dew Drop Inn Diner in Lizard Holler Falls (not a real place, but you get the idea).

Gay, lesbian, bisexual, and transgender travelers planning to visit North Carolina can learn a great deal online about community resources and activities. Check out **QNotes** (www.q-notes.com), **Carolina Purple Pages** (www.carolinapurplepages.com, serving Charlotte, Asheville, and the Triangle), **Gay Triad** (http://gaytriadnc.homestead.com), the **Out Wilmington Community Center** (www.outwilmington.com), and **Out in Asheville** (http://outinasheville.com).

SENIOR TRAVELERS

North Carolina has attracted a tremendous number of retirees in recent years—new residents of the mountains and coast especially, as well as central Carolina communities. It's also an increasingly popular destination for older travelers. For those who wish to visit the state through organized programs, **Elderhostel** (www.elderhostel.org) is a great choice. Tours and classes are available throughout the state, and the offerings in the mountains are particularly rich, with a great variety of courses and hands-on workshops about Appalachian culture and crafts.

The North Carolina chapter of the **AARP** (919/755-9757, www.aarp.org/statepages/nc.html) is a good resource for senior issues and information. **VisitNC** (800/VISIT-NC, www.visitnc.com) can also answer many of your questions about activities and accessibility.

WOMEN TRAVELERS

Women from other parts of the country might find male strangers' friendliness a little disconcerting, but please keep in mind that, while someone may, of course, be flirting with you, it's just as likely (no offense) that he's simply being courteous. When a Southern man holds a door open for you, offers to help you carry something, or even calls you "honey" or "darlin'" or "dear heart," usually he has no ulterior or sinister motives, nor does he intend any paternalistic condescension, but is probably just showing that he was raised up right. Again, though, manners should never preclude safety, so if some sketchy character is coming on to you in a way that gives you the creeps, trust your instincts.

TRAVELERS WITH DISABILITIES

An excellent, up-to-date guide on the comparative accessibility (or lack thereof) of hundreds of cultural, recreational, historical, environmental, and commercial sites of interest is a goldmine of travel-planning information. Call 919/855-3500 or TTY 919/855-3579 and ask for the current edition of *Access North Carolina,* published by the state Department of Health and Human Services. (For downloadable versions in either text or PDF formats, go to http://dvr.dhhs.state.nc.us.) The guide is divided into Mountains, Foothills, Piedmont, Coastal Plain, and Coast divisions, and broken down by counties within each division. All sites are described, with addresses, phone numbers, websites, hours of operation, admissions costs, and other types of information, and then rated in terms of accessibility.

Health and Safety

CRIME

As safe and as nice a place as North Carolina is to live or visit, we're not immune to crime. Common sense about safety applies, particularly for women, but for everyone else too. Lock your doors immediately upon getting in the car, park in well-lit areas as close as possible to your destination, and don't hesitate to ask a security guard or other trustworthy type to see you to your car. Don't carry too much money with you. Pepper spray is a good idea for men as well as women. It can save your life if you're attacked, whether by a human or a bear.

Note that 911 service is available throughout the state, but cell phone signals are not dependable everywhere.

SPECIAL WEATHER CONCERNS
Hurricanes

Hurricanes are a perennial danger, but luckily we tend to have plenty of warning when one is approaching. Evacuation orders should always be heeded, even if they are voluntary. It's also a good idea to leave sooner rather than later, so as to avoid being trapped in traffic when the storm hits. The Department of Crime Control and Public Safety (www.nccrimecontrol.org) posts a map online every year showing evacuation routes. You'll also see evacuation routes marked along the highways.

Tornadoes

Tornadoes can happen in any season, and have killed North Carolinians in recent years. Pay close attention to tornado watches and warnings, and don't take chances: Find a safe place to shelter until the danger is over.

Rip Currents

More than 100 people die every year on American beaches because of rip currents. Also called riptides, these dangerous currents can occur on any beach and can be very difficult to identify by sight. In rip current conditions, channels of water flow swiftly out towards deep water, and even if you are standing in relatively shallow water, you can in a matter of moments be swept under and out into deep water. Rip current safety tips are available on the National Weather Service's NOAA website at www.ripcurrents.noaa.gov. Among NOAA's advice are the following: "Don't fight the current. Swim out of the current, and then to shore. If you can't escape, float or tread water. If you need help, call or wave for assistance." Heed riptide warnings, and try to swim within sight of a lifeguard. Even good swimmers can drown in a rip current, so if you have any doubts about your swimming abilities or beach conditions, play it safe and stay close to shore.

ANIMAL THREATS

We have a handful of dangerous creatures across the state, ranging in size from microscopic to monstrous, which can pose risks to health and safety. Be on the lookout for our home guard of mean bugs. **Ticks** can carry Lyme disease and Rocky Mountain spotted fever, both serious and lingering conditions. Most likely to climb on you if you are walking through brush or bushes, but liable to be lurking about anywhere, ticks come in many sizes and shapes, from barely visible pin-prick-sized boogers to that thing that looks like a grape hanging off your dog's neck. Wear insect repellant if you're going to be tramping around outside, and check yourself and your travel companions thoroughly—your clothing as well as your skin—for stowaways. They'll attach themselves to any soft surface on your body, but they particularly like people's heads, often latching on to the scalp an inch or so behind the ears. If you find a tick on yourself or a human or canine companion, don't remove it roughly, no matter how freaked out you are. Yanking can leave the tick's snout in your skin, increasing the risk of infection. Grasp the tick in a pinching motion, and pull slowly but firmly. You may have to hang on for several moments, but eventually it will decide to let go. Dab the bite with antiseptic, and over the next several weeks be alert for a bull's-eye-shaped irritation around the bite, and for flu-like symptoms such as fever, aching, malaise, and fatigue. If you have any of these signs, visit your doctor for a blood test.

Mosquitoes can carry West Nile virus, La Crosse encephalitis, and Eastern equine encephalitis. Wearing insect repellant and clothes that cover your arms and legs are the best ways to avoid bites. Though not disease vectors, **fire ants** are among our most feared insects. It's easy to stumble onto one of their nests, and before you realize what you've stepped in, they can be swarming up your legs and biting the living daylights out of you. Certainly this is a painful and frightening experience, but it's also potentially dangerous. There have been documented cases in recent years of adult humans being swarmed and killed by fire ants. Watch where you step, and keep an eye out for areas of disturbed ground and turned-up soil. Sometimes their nests look like conventional anthills, sometimes like messy piles of dirt, and other times just soft spots on the ground.

Another reason to mind where you tread: snakes. The vast majority of snakes in North Carolina are utterly harmless and shy, but we do have a few pit vipers. **Copperheads** are quite common in every part of the state and in most any kind of wooded or semi-wooded terrain—even in back yards, where they can lurk in bushes and leaf piles, under porches and in storage sheds, and even in the walls of a house. (Are you squirming yet?) They have a gorgeous pattern of light and dark brown splotches, which makes them incredibly difficult to spot against the ground in autumn. Copperheads are usually less than three feet long, though they sometimes approach four feet. Their bite is very poisonous, though usually not fatal.

Found in the eastern half of the state and up into the Sandhills, **cottonmouths**—also referred to as water moccasins—are very dangerous. They range in color from reddish brown to black, can grow up to five and a half feet long, and are easily mistaken for harmless water snakes (and vice-versa). Though they will

alligator warning sign, Pollocksville

sometimes venture into the woods and fields, cottonmouths are most commonly seen on or near water. Be especially careful walking along creek beds or in riverside brush. When threatened, they display the inside of their mouths, a startling and really quite beautiful cottony white. Their bite is potentially lethal.

Coral snakes are endangered in North Carolina, but if you're going to be in the woods in the southeastern quarter of the state, keep an eye out nevertheless. These jewel-toned snakes are generally small and slim, rarely more than a couple of feet long. Like the harmless scarlet kingsnake and scarlet snake, coral snakes have alternating bands of red, yellow, and black. The way to tell coral snakes from their harmless kinfolk is to note the order of colors. On coral snakes, the yellow bands separate the black and the red, whereas on their imitators, red and black touch. An adage advises, "Red and black, friend of Jack; red and yellow, kill a fellow." Coral snakes can also be told by their sinister black snouts, making them look like cartoon burglars, whereas scarlet snakes and scarlet kingsnakes have red clown noses. This is all a lot to remember in that instant of panic when you notice a coil of red and yellow and black stripes at your feet regarding you testily. Rather than stopping to figure out if the snake is friend or foe, better just to step away fast. Coral snakes' venom works on its prey's respiratory system, and can kill humans. They're not-too-distant cousins of cobras. Corals are some of the most beautiful snakes we have in these parts, but having grown up in an area to which they're endemic, I can attest that many natives fear them even more intensely than they do the huge, lumpy-headed, tusky-fanged vipers that appear outwardly to be more threatening.

As if the previous three characters weren't trouble enough, we have three more poisonous native snakes, all of them rattlers. The **Eastern diamondback rattlesnake** is the largest rattlesnake in the world, and here they can grow to nearly six feet long, and as fat around as an adult human's arm. They are extremely dangerous—powerful enough to catch and eat rabbits, and willing, if sufficiently provoked, to kill a person. Eastern diamondbacks are rare, but can be found in the southeastern sandy swamp counties. Also large are **canebrake rattlers,** more formally known as timber rattlers. They are found throughout most of the state, including the mountains. Their bite can be fatal to humans. To make them even scarier, they too can grow to nearly six feet in length, and in cold weather like to congregate in large numbers to hibernate. **Pygmy rattlesnakes** are found along most of the state's coastline, up into the sandhills, and around Crowder's Mountain. Generally up to about a foot and a half long, pygmies are venomous too.

At this point in our discussion of dangerous wildlife, I ought to recuse myself and turn the narration over to a more objective source, because the next animal is one of which I'm passionately fond. **Alligators** are incredible creatures, scaly battleships that can exceed 15 feet snout-to-tail (females generally mature at around 10 feet) and can weigh 1,000 pounds, with a steel-trap maw of 75–80 fangs. They are found sporadically through much of eastern North Carolina, even as far north as Merchants

Millpond State Park, near the Virginia border, but are most common from Wilmington into South Carolina and beyond. You don't have to trek into the depths of a swamp to see gators; they like to sun themselves on golf courses, next to roadside drainage ditches, even in yards that back up to freshwater. Their behavior is deceptive, because though they seem to spend 90 percent of their time in a motionless stupor, they can awaken and whirl around to grab you before you have time to back away. They also spend much of their time submerged, sometimes entirely underwater, and more often drifting just below the surface, with only their nostrils and brow ridges visible. Be aware too of floating logs, as they may have teeth attached. Alligators will gladly eat dogs that venture too close, so it goes without saying that small children should never be allowed to wander alone near potential alligator habitats. An adult alligator can kill a grown man, and even the cute little ones will be only too happy to help themselves to your foot, so beware, and don't tempt fate for the sake of a photo or a closer look. If you're determined to get a close-up picture, visit one of the state's aquariums.

Bear attacks are rare and usually defensive, but considering that the creatures can weigh up to 800 pounds (though most Carolina bears don't get that large), caution would seem to be indicated. They are present in woods in various parts of the state, especially up in the mountains and in the deep swamps and pocosins along the coast. They're quite shy, apt to gallop into the brush if they see a human coming. They will investigate potential meals, though, so securing your food when camping is crucial. If your car is nearby, lock up the food; otherwise, hoist it into a tree with a rope, too high to reach from the ground and out of reach from the tree trunk. The National Park Service recommends the following course of action if a bear approaches you. First, try backing away slowly. If the bear follows, stand your ground. If he continues to menace you, try to scare him: Make yourself look bigger and more threatening by standing on a rock or next to whomever is with you. Try waving sticks and throwing rocks. In the extremely unlikely

© CHRIS SNYDER

black bear pilfering from birdfeeder

event that you actually find yourself in hand-to-hand combat with a bear, remember the Park Service's advice to "fight back aggressively with any available object." Your chances of seeing a bear in North Carolina, much less being threatened by one, are pretty slim, so rest easy.

DISEASES AND NATURAL THREATS

Among the invisible villains here is **giardia,** a single-celled bacterium that can be contracted by drinking untreated water, among other risk factors. Hikers and campers should avoid drinking from streams unless they first boil the water vigorously for at least one minute. Filtering (with a filter of 0.1–1 micrometer absolute pore size) and chemically treating (iodine or, if iodine is not available, chlorine) water is less reliable than thorough boiling.

There's a fairly high incidence of **rabies** in North Carolina's raccoons, bats, foxes, groundhogs, and skunks. If you're bringing a pet into the state, be sure that its vaccinations, including

rabies, are up to date. If you plan to go hiking with your dog, it may even be wise to bring a copy of its rabies vaccination certificate, in case of a situation in which you'd have to prove the pet's immunity. If you yourself are bitten by a wild animal, seek medical help immediately, even if you're out in the woods. Rabies is deadly to humans too, and it's of the utmost importance that you start booster shots immediately.

HEALTH PRECAUTIONS
Emergencies

As is the case throughout the United States, calling 911 in North Carolina will summon medical help, police, and/or firemen. On the highways, blue road signs marked with an "H" point the way to hospitals, but if you're experiencing a potentially critical emergency, it's sometimes best to call 911 and let the ambulance come to you. There are plenty of rural places in the state where cell phone coverage is spotty to nonexistent, so if you have a medical condition from which an emergency could arise, keep this in mind.

Summer Weather

Heat, humidity, and air pollution often combine in the summer (and sometimes in the spring and fall) to create very dangerous conditions for children, the elderly, and people with heart and lung conditions. Even if you're young and hale, don't take chances in the heat. Carry drinking water with you, avoid exertion and being outside at the hottest part of the day, and stay in the shade. Even young, healthy people can die from the heat. Remember too, please, that even if it doesn't feel very warm outside, children and pets are in grave danger when left in cars. Temperatures can rise to fatal levels very quickly inside closed vehicles.

Information and Services

MONEY

For international travelers, currency exchange services can be found in the big cities, at some of the major banks as well as currency exchange business. Numerous money transfer services, from old familiars like Western Union to a multitude of overseas companies, are easily accessible throughout the state. The easiest place to wire or receive money is at a grocery store—most have Western Union or a proprietary wiring service—or at a bank. Banking hours vary by location and chain, but most are closed on Sundays and federal holidays. ATMs are located at most bank branches, and in many grocery stores and convenience stores.

COMMUNICATIONS AND MEDIA
Newspapers and Radio

North Carolina has several major newspapers, the largest of which is the Pulitzer Prize–winning *Charlotte Observer* (www.charlotte.com). In addition to the print edition, the *Charlotte Observer* has extensive online-only content for travelers and new residents. The Raleigh *News & Observer* (www.newsobserver.com) serves the Triangle area and much of central Carolina. Other prominent newspapers include the Wilmington *Star-News* (www.starnewsonline.com) and the Asheville *Citizen-Times* (www.citizen-times.com). Alternative papers like the *Mountain Xpress* (www.mountainx.com) and the Triangle-area *Independent* (www.indyweek.com), available in print and online, cover the state's independent and counter-culture. Among the many local and regional radio stations here is a good grid of NPR affiliates. There are few parts of the state where you won't be able to tune into a clear NPR signal.

Internet Access

Internet access is plentiful. Coffee shops are always a good place to find Wi-Fi, usually free but sometimes for a fee. Some small towns have free municipal wireless access, though as of yet this is still rather unusual. Most chain motels and major hotels offer free wireless, and smaller hotels and bed-and-breakfasts often have wireless access, though they're more likely to carry a surcharge. This holds true for remote areas as well. While you're not going to be able to pirate a stray unsecured wireless signal when you're 100 miles from the nearest office building, you'll probably be able to get online at your place of lodging or the coffee shop in town.

Cell Phones

Cell phone coverage is not consistent across North Carolina. You'll have a signal in all of the cities, and most of the areas in between. You may hit drop-out spots in central North Carolina, but there are fairly few. On the other hand, service is dodgy in the eastern and western thirds. Up in the mountains, you may have a good signal on one side of a ridge and none on the other. Driving along the Blue Ridge Parkway, you'll find that signals come and go. This is also true on the coast and in rural eastern North Carolina. Along the sounds, and certainly on the Outer Banks, there are plenty of areas where you could drive 50 miles before finding a blip of reception. Besides the concerns of practicality and convenience, spotty cell phone coverage is a safety issue as well. If you're treed by a bear or run out of gas on a backwoods coquina track, 911 may be unreachable.

MAPS AND TOURIST INFORMATION

Among the best sources for travel information in North Carolina is the state's tourism website: **VisitNC** (www.visitnc.com) keeps an up-to-date list of festivals and events, tours and trails, and most anything else you might want to know. Also excellent is the magazine **Our State,** which is available at grocery stores, drugstores, and bookshops. Their website (www.ourstate.com) monitors upcoming events in the state as well.

North Carolina Welcome Centers, located at several major highways' entry points to the state, are sources for more free brochures and maps than one person could carry. They are located on the Virginia line at I-77 near Mount Airy, on I-85 in Warren County, and on I-95 in Northampton County; on the Tennessee line on I-26 in Madison County and I-40 in Haywood County; and along the South Carolina line on I-26 in Polk County, I-85 in Cleveland County, I-77 just outside Charlotte, and I-95 in Robeson County.

For basic planning, the maps at www.visit nc.com will give you a good sense of the layout of the state and its major destinations. Many areas of the state are expanding rapidly, particularly around Charlotte and the Triangle, so if your map is only a few months out of date you may not know about the newest bypass or subdivision. For features that don't change, like mountains, rivers, back roads, and small towns, atlas-style books of state maps are indispensable. My own favorite is DeLorme's *North Carolina Atlas & Gazetteer.* As of yet, the newest edition is from 2006, but you'll be in good shape if you carry both DeLorme's and the most recent convenience store map of the state that you can find.

RESOURCES

Suggested Reading

TRAVEL

Duncan, Barbara and Brett Riggs. *Cherokee Heritage Trails.* UNC Press, 2003 (online companion at www.cherokeeheritage.org). A fascinating guide to both the historic and present-day home of the Eastern Band of the Cherokee in North Carolina, Tennessee, and Georgia, from ancient mounds and petroglyphs to modern-day arts co-ops and sporting events.

Eubanks, Georgann. *Literary Trails of the North Carolina Mountains: A Guidebook.* UNC Press, 2007. The first in what will be a series of such guides to introduce fans of Southern literature—of which North Carolina is a prodigiously fertile field—to the places that produced and inspired our scribes, and the best bookstores and book events across the state where you can get your print fix.

Fields, Jay, and Betty Hurst. *Craft Heritage Trails of Western North Carolina.* HandMade in America, 2003. A look at yet another dazzlingly rich aspect of western North Carolina's culture, that of its craft tradition. HandMade's website (www.handmadeinamerica.org) gives great travel suggestions for central and eastern North Carolina as well.

Fussell, Fred, with photographs by Cedric N. Chatterley. *Blue Ridge Music Trails: Finding a Place in the Circle.* UNC Press, 2003 (http://uncpress.unc.edu or www.ncfolk.org, online companion at www.blueridgemusic.org).

A guide to destinations—festivals, restaurants, oprys, church singings—in the North Carolina and Virginia mountains where great, authentic bluegrass, old-time, and sacred music can be experienced by visitors. The exceptional photography in both this book and *Cherokee Heritage Trails*—reproduced in full color and great profusion—and the depth of context conveyed, make these two guides in particular well worth buying even if you're not touring the region.

Love, Jan, and Elizabeth Hunter, Mary Lynn White, and L. M. Sawyer. *Farms, Gardens, and Countryside Trails of Western North Carolina.* HandMade in America, 2002. This will show you the way to farmers markets, botanical gardens, cut-your-own Christmas tree farms, and locavore restaurants.

North Carolina Atlas and Gazetteer. DeLorme, 2006. I have always been partial to DeLorme's state atlases, including this excellent one. This series represents in great detail the topography and other natural features of an area, giving far more useful and comprehensive information than the standard highway map.

Our State. www.ourstate.com. For a lively and informative look at North Carolina destinations and the cultural quirks and treasures you may find in your travels, *Our State* magazine is one of the best resources around. The magazine is easy to find, sold at most bookstores and even on grocery store and drugstore magazine racks. Back issues are coveted collectibles. It covers arts, nature, folklore, history, scenery, sports, and food (lots of food), all from a traveler's perspective.

HISTORY AND CULTURE

Cecelski, David. *A Historian's Coast: Adventures into the Tidewater Past.* UNC Press, 2000. A collection of absorbing short essays about life on the coast, long ago and today.

Cecelski, David. *The Waterman's Song: Slavery and Freedom in Maritime North Carolina.* UNC Press, 2000. A marvelous treatment of the African American heritage of resistance in eastern North Carolina, and how the region's rivers and sounds were passages to freedom for many slaves.

Powell, William S. *North Carolina: A History.* UNC Press, 1988. A readable, concise account of our fascinatingly varied past.

Powell, William S., and Jay Mazzocchi, editors. *Encyclopedia of North Carolina.* UNC Press, 2006. A fantastic compendium of all sorts of North Carolina history, letters, politics, and more. If you can lift this mammoth book, you'll learn about everything from Carolina basketball to presidential elections to ghosts.

SPORTS

Blythe, Will. *To Hate Like This is to Be Happy Forever: A Thoroughly Obsessive, Intermittently Uplifting, and Occasionally Unbiased Account of the Duke–North Carolina Basketball Rivalry.* Harper-Collins, 2006. A highly entertaining book about the hatred that exists between partisans of UNC and Duke, and how our famous basketball rivalry brings out the best and worst in us.

Thompson, Neal. *Driving with the Devil: Southern Moonshine, Detroit Wheels, and the Birth of NASCAR.* Three Rivers Press, 2007. The creation story of another of our great sports, the rise of stock car racing from moonshiners' getaway wheels to a multibillion-dollar industry.

Internet Resources

NEWSPAPERS

North Carolina newspapers have unusually rich online content, and are great resources for travel planning.

Charlotte Observer
www.charlotte.com

This website is packed with information about the arts, food, newcomer issues, and more.

Raleigh News & Observer
www.newsobserver.com
Raleigh's paper of record.

Asheville Citizen-Times
www.citizen-times.com
A good online edition for this Ashville-based paper.

Mountain Xpress
www.mountainx.com

Also covering the Asheville area, with a politically progressive and artistically countercultural bent—much like Asheville itself.

Independent Weekly
www.indyweek.com

A great source for the Triangle on the local music scene, politics, food, and more.

ARTS AND CULTURE

North Carolina's arts and history have an ever-growing online dimension, telling the story of our state in ways that paper and ink simply can't.

North Carolina Folklife Institute
www.ncfolk.org

The website of the North Carolina Folklife

Institute will fill you in on the many organizations across the state that promote traditional music, crafts, and folkways. You'll also find a calendar of folklife-related events in North Carolina, and travel itineraries for weekends exploring Core Sound, the Seagrove potteries, and Cherokee heritage in the Smokies.

NCFOOD
http://ncfolk.wordpress.com

This wonderful food blog, maintained by the Folklife Institute, features articles by historian and foodie David Cecelski about the culinary back roads of the state.

North Carolina Arts Council
www.ncarts.org

The Arts Council will hook you up with information about performing arts, literature, cultural trails, galleries, and fun happenings.

North Carolina ECHO
(Exploring Cultural Heritage Online)
www.ncecho.org

This great site does exactly what its title describes, with links to hundreds of online exhibits and brick-and-mortar museums.

Carolina Music Ways
www.carolinamusicways.org

A lively guide to the extremely varied musical traditions of the North Carolina Piedmont.

Blue Ridge Heritage Area
www.blueridgeheritage.com

A resource that not only has a huge amount of mountain-area travel information, but an ever-growing directory of traditional artists of all kinds in the Carolina mountains.

Southern Highland Craft Guild
www.southernhighlandguild.org

An Asheville-based regional arts giant, with an extensive online guide to craftspeople throughout the region.

OUTDOORS

Great online resources exist for folks planning outdoor adventures in North Carolina, a state where even our volcanically rich arts and blockbuster sports are matched, if not overshadowed, by our natural resources.

North Carolina chapter of
the Sierra Club
http://northcarolina.sierraclub.org

Here you'll find information about upcoming hikes and excursions, as well as good overall information about the state's natural areas and the environmental issues that we confront.

North Carolina Birding Trail
www.ncbirdingtrail.org

This trail will eventually cover the whole state, but for now it's got its hands full with the eastern third of the state, which is a world-famous bird-watching mecca. Here you can read about dozens of pristine locations and active flyways up and down the coast.

Carolina Canoe Club
www.carolinacanoeclub.com

A clearinghouse of statewide canoeing resources.

CanoeNC
www.canoenc.org

This is a nice starting point for planning a flat-water paddling trip in eastern North Carolina.

North Carolina Outdoors
www.northcarolinaoutdoors.com

This privately operated site is full of excellent information and cross-referenced sources for state and national parkland and wilderness throughout the state.

Index

Map Index

Acknowledgments

Thanks to my family—my husband Peter Honig, mother Cristina Bryan, brother Will Bryan, and grandmother, Magda Freeman—for their essential help with this project and their patience with my busy schedule. A big thank you to Naomi Adler Dancis, whose wisdom and hard work improved this book immeasurably, and who has been a most amiable guide. Thanks to the many friends and relatives who shared recommendations about their favorite places in North Carolina, and were so understanding of my antisocial behavior during the last year and a half. I'm especially grateful to David Cecelski, Cedric Chatterley, Rayna Gellert, Gail Gillespie, Liz Lindsey, and Beverly Patterson. I also greatly appreciate the generosity of the wonderful photographers who were willing to share their work for this project. Many people have contributed to this book, and I'm grateful to all of them. Hark the sound of Tar Heel voices!

Acknowledgements

www.moon.com

For helpful advice on planning a trip, visit www.moon.com for the **TRAVEL PLANNER** and get access to useful travel strategies and valuable information about great places to visit. When you travel with Moon, expect an experience that is uncommon and truly unique.

HANDBOOKS | METRO | OUTDOORS | LIVING ABROAD

MAP SYMBOLS

▭▭▭	Expressway	◖	Highlight	✗	Airfield	♟	Golf Course
────	Primary Road	○	City/Town	✗	Airport	🅿	Parking Area
····	Secondary Road	◉	State Capital	▲	Mountain	▱	Archaeological Site
─ ─ ─	Unpaved Road	⊛	National Capital	✛	Unique Natural Feature	⛪	Church
- - -	Trail	★	Point of Interest			⛽	Gas Station
········	Ferry	•	Accommodation	⌇	Waterfall		
×─×─×	Railroad	▼	Restaurant/Bar	▲	Park	◠	Glacier
▭▭▭	Pedestrian Walkway	▪	Other Location	▣	Trailhead	▨	Mangrove
▥▥▥	Stairs	△	Campground	⛷	Skiing Area	▦	Reef
						▦	Swamp

CONVERSION TABLES

°C = (°F - 32) / 1.8
°F = (°C x 1.8) + 32
1 inch = 2.54 centimeters (cm)
1 foot = 0.304 meters (m)
1 yard = 0.914 meters
1 mile = 1.6093 kilometers (km)
1 km = 0.6214 miles
1 fathom = 1.8288 m
1 chain = 20.1168 m
1 furlong = 201.168 m
1 acre = 0.4047 hectares
1 sq km = 100 hectares
1 sq mile = 2.59 square km
1 ounce = 28.35 grams
1 pound = 0.4536 kilograms
1 short ton = 0.90718 metric ton
1 short ton = 2,000 pounds
1 long ton = 1.016 metric tons
1 long ton = 2,240 pounds
1 metric ton = 1,000 kilograms
1 quart = 0.94635 liters
1 US gallon = 3.7854 liters
1 Imperial gallon = 4.5459 liters
1 nautical mile = 1.852 km

°FAHRENHEIT / °CELSIUS thermometer:

°FAHRENHEIT	°CELSIUS	
230	110	
220		
210	100	WATER BOILS
200		
190	90	
180	80	
170		
160	70	
150		
140	60	
130	50	
120		
110	40	
100		
90	30	
80		
70	20	
60		
50	10	
40		
30	0	WATER FREEZES
20		
10	-10	
0		
-10	-20	
-20	-30	
-30		
-40	-40	

Clock face showing 24-hour markings: 12/24, 13/1, 14/2, 15/3, 16/4, 17/5, 18/6, 19/7, 20/8, 21/9, 22/10, 23/11

INCH ruler: 0 1 2 3 4

CM ruler: 0 1 2 3 4 5 6 7 8 9 10

MOON NORTH CAROLINA
Avalon Travel
A member of the Perseus Books Group
1700 Fourth Street
Berkeley, CA 94710, USA
www.moon.com

Editor: Naomi Adler Dancis
Series Manager: Kathryn Ettinger
Copy Editor: Ellie Behrstock
Graphics Coordinator: Stefano Boni
Production Coordinator: Tabitha Lahr
Cover Designer: Stefano Boni
Cartography Director: Mike Morgenfeld
Map Editor: Brice Ticen
Cartographers: Kat Bennett, Chris Markiewicz
Indexer: Rachel Kuhn

ISBN-10: 1-56691-598-8
ISBN-13: 978-1-56691-598-4
ISSN: 1540-3831

Printing History
1st Edition – 1999
3rd Edition – November 2008
5 4 3 2 1

Some photos and illustrations are used by permission and are the property of the original copyright owners.

Front cover photo: © Darlene Bordwell.com/DRR.net

Title page photo: © Bob Sowa

Pg. 4, © Sarah Bryan; pg. 5, © Warren Reed; pg. 6, © Sarah Bryan; pg. 6/7, © Richard McGee; pg. 7, (top) © John Richburg, (bottom) © Wendy Moody; pg. 8, © Keith M. Morgan; pgs. 9-10, © Sarah Bryan; pg. 11, © Joe Miller, Oneonta, AL; pgs. 13-14, © Sarah Bryan; pg. 17, © Chris Lawrence; pgs. 19-20, Courtesy of Oncle Bernard on Flickr.com.

Printed in the United States by RR Donnelley

KEEPING CURRENT

If you have a favorite gem you'd like to see included in the next edition, or see anything that needs updating, clarification, or correction, please drop us a line. Send your comments via email to feedback@moon.com, or use the address above.